Argument-Driven Inquiry in BIOLOGY

LAB INVESTIGATIONS for GRADES 9–12

Argument-Driven Inquiry in BIOLOGY

LAB INVESTIGATIONS for GRADES 9–12

Victor Sampson, Patrick Enderle, Leeanne Gleim, Jonathon Grooms, Melanie Hester, Sherry Southerland, and Kristin Wilson

NSTA press
National Science Teachers Association
Arlington, Virginia

NSTA press®
National Science Teachers Association

Claire Reinburg, Director
Wendy Rubin, Managing Editor
Andrew Cooke, Senior Editor
Amanda O'Brien, Associate Editor
Amy America, Book Acquisitions Coordinator

Art and Design
Will Thomas Jr., Director

Printing and Production
Catherine Lorrain, Director

National Science Teachers Association
David L. Evans, Executive Director
David Beacom, Publisher

1840 Wilson Blvd., Arlington, VA 22201
www.nsta.org/store
For customer service inquiries, please call 800-277-5300.

17 16 15 14 5 4 3 2

NSTA is committed to publishing material that promotes the best in inquiry-based science education. However, conditions of actual use may vary, and the safety procedures and practices described in this book are intended to serve only as a guide. Additional precautionary measures may be required. NSTA and the authors do not warrant or represent that the procedures and practices in this book meet any safety code or standard of federal, state, or local regulations. NSTA and the authors disclaim any liability for personal injury or damage to property arising out of or relating to the use of this book, including any of the recommendations, instructions, or materials contained therein.

Library of Congress Cataloging-in-Publication Data
Argument-driven inquiry in biology : lab investigations for grades 9-12 / Victor Sampson [and six others].
1 online resource.
Includes bibliographical references.
Description based on print version record and CIP data provided by publisher; resource not viewed.
ISBN 978-1-938946-20-2 -- ISBN 978-1-938946-66-0 (e-book) 1. Biology--Study and teaching (Secondary)--Handbooks, manuals, etc. I. Sampson, Victor, 1974- II. National Science Teachers Association.
QH315
570.71'2--dc23
2014001437

Cataloging-in-Publication Data for the e-book are also available from the Library of Congress.

SECTION 3—Life Sciences Core Idea 2
Ecosystems: Interactions, Energy, and Dynamics

INTRODUCTION LABS

APPLICATION LABS

SECTION 4—Life Sciences Core Idea 3

Heredity: Inheritance and Variation of Traits

INTRODUCTION LABS

APPLICATION LABS

SECTION 6—Appendixes

PREFACE

The *Next Generation Science Standards* (NGSS Lead States 2013) outline a new set of expectations for what students should know and be able to do in science. The overarching goal of the *NGSS,* as defined by the National Research Council (NRC) in *A Framework for K–12 Science Education* (NRC 2012), is

> to ensure that by the end of 12th grade, *all* students have some appreciation of the beauty and wonder of science; possess sufficient knowledge of science and engineering to engage in public discussions on related issues; are careful consumers of scientific and technological information related to their everyday lives; are able to continue to learn about science outside school; and have the skills to enter careers of their choice, including (but not limited to) careers in science, engineering, and technology. (p. 1)

To accomplish this goal, teachers will need to help students become proficient in science by the time they graduate from high school. The NRC suggests that students need to understand four core ideas in the life sciences, be aware of seven crosscutting concepts that span the various disciplines of science, and learn how to participate in eight fundamental scientific practices in order to be considered proficient in science (NRC 2012). The three dimensions of the *Framework,* which form the basis for the *NGSS,* are summarized in Figure 1.

FIGURE 1

The three dimensions of the framework for the *NGSS*

Life Sciences Core Ideas	
From molecules to organisms: Structures and processes Ecosystems: Interactions, energy, and dynamics Heredity: Inheritance and variation of traits Biological evolution: Unity and diversity	
Crosscutting Concepts	**Scientific Practices**
• Patterns • Cause and effect: Mechanism and explanation • Scale, proportion, and quantity • Systems and system models • Energy and matter: Flows, cycles, and conservation • Structure and function • Stability and change	• Asking questions • Developing and using models • Planning and carrying out investigations • Analyzing and interpreting data • Using mathematics and computational thinking • Constructing explanations • Engaging in argument from evidence • Obtaining, evaluating, and communicating information

The NRC also calls for teachers to use new instructional approaches that are designed to foster the development of science proficiency. This book will help teachers accomplish this task by providing a set of 27 lab investigations that were designed using an innovative approach to laboratory instruction called argument-driven inquiry (ADI). The lab investigations are aligned with the content, crosscutting concepts, and scientific practices outlined in the NRC *Framework*. These lab investigations allow students to develop the disciplinary-based literacy skills outlined in the *Common Core State Standards*, for English language arts (NGAC and CCSSO 2010), because the ADI instructional model calls for students to give presentations to their peers; respond to questions; and then write, evaluate, and revise reports as part of each lab. Thus, this book can help teachers make lab instruction more meaningful for students and enable students to learn more inside the school science laboratory.

References

National Governors Association Center for Best Practices and Council of Chief State School Officers (NGAC and CCSSO). 2010. *Common core state standards*. Washington, DC: NGAC and CCSSO.

National Research Council (NRC). 2012. *A framework for K–12 science education: Practices, crosscutting concepts, and core ideas*. Washington, DC: National Academies Press.

NGSS Lead States. 2013. *Next Generation Science Standards: For states, by states*. Washington, DC: National Academies Press. *www.nextgenscience.org/next-generation-science-standards*.

ACKNOWLEDGMENTS

The development of this book was supported by the Institute of Education Sciences, U.S. Department of Education, through grant R305A100909 to Florida State University. The opinions expressed are those of the authors and do not represent the views of the institute or the U.S. Department of Education.

ABOUT THE AUTHORS

Victor Sampson is an associate professor of science education and the director of the Center for Education Research in Mathematics, Engineering, and Science (CERMES) at Florida State University (FSU). He received a BA in zoology from the University of Washington, an MIT from Seattle University, and a PhD in curriculum and instruction with a specialization in science education from Arizona State University. Victor taught high school biology and chemistry for nine years before taking his current position at FSU. He specializes in argumentation in science education, teacher learning, and assessment. To learn more about his work in science education, go to *www.vicsampson.com.*

Patrick Enderle is a research faculty member in CERMES at FSU. He received his BS and MS in molecular biology from East Carolina University. Patrick then spent some time as a high school biology teacher and several years as a visiting professor in the Department of Biology at East Carolina University. He then attended FSU, where he graduated with a PhD in science education. His research interests include argumentation in the science classroom, science teacher professional development, and enhancing undergraduate science education.

Leeanne Gleim received a BA in elementary education from the University of Southern Indiana and a MS in science education from FSU. While at FSU, she worked as a research assistant for Dr. Sampson. After graduating, she taught biology and honors biology at FSU Schools, where she participated in the development of the argument-driven inquiry (ADI) model. Leeanne was also responsible for writing and piloting many of the lab investigations included in this book.

Jonathon Grooms received a BS in secondary science and mathematics teaching with a focus in chemistry and physics from FSU. Upon graduation, Jonathon joined FSU's Office of Science Teaching, where he directed the physical science outreach program Science on the Move. He entered graduate school at FSU and earned a PhD in science education. He now serves as a research scientist in CERMES at FSU.

Melanie Hester has a BS in biological sciences with minors in chemistry and classical civilizations from Florida State University and an MS in secondary science education from FSU. She has been teaching for more than 20 years, with the last 13 at the FSU School in Tallahassee. Melanie was a Lockheed Martin Fellow and a Woodrow Wilson fellow and received a Teacher of the Year award in 2007. She frequently gives presentations about innovative approaches to teaching at conferences and works with preservice teachers. Melanie was also responsible for writing and piloting many of the lab investigations included in this book.

Sherry Southerland is a professor at Florida State University and the co-director of FSU-Teach. FSU-Teach is a collaborative math and science teacher preparation program between the College of Arts and Sciences and the College of Education.

She received her BS and MS in biology from Auburn University and her PhD in curriculum and instruction from Louisiana State University, with a specialization in science education and evolutionary biology. Sherry has worked as a teacher educator, biology instructor, high school science teacher, field biologist, and forensic chemist. Her research interests include understanding the influence of culture and emotions on learning—specifically evolution education and teacher education—and understanding how to better support teachers in shaping the way they approach science teaching and learning.

Kristin Wilson attended Florida State University and earned a BS in secondary science teaching with an emphasis in biology and Earth-space science. Kristin teaches biology at FSU School. She helped develop the ADI instructional model and was responsible for writing and piloting many of the lab investigations found in this book.

INTRODUCTION

The Importance of Helping Students Become Proficient in Science

The new aim of science education in the United States is for all students to become proficient in science by the time they finish high school. *Science proficiency,* as defined by Duschl, Schweingruber, and Shouse (2007), consists of four interrelated aspects. First, it requires individuals to know important scientific explanations about the natural world, to be able to use these explanations to solve problems, and to be able to understand new explanations when they are introduced. Second, it requires individuals to be able to generate and evaluate scientific explanations and scientific arguments. Third, it requires that individuals understand the nature of scientific knowledge and how scientific knowledge develops over time. Finally, and perhaps most important, it requires that individuals be able to participate in scientific practices (such as designing and carrying out investigations, constructing explanations, and arguing from evidence) and communicate in a scientific manner. Science proficiency, in other words, involves more than an understanding of important concepts; it also involves being able to do science.

In the past decade, however, the importance of learning how to participate in scientific practices has not been acknowledged in state standards. In addition, many states have attempted to make their science standards "more rigorous" by adding more content to them rather than designing them so they emphasize the core ideas and crosscutting concepts described by the National Research Council (NRC) in *A Framework for K–12 Science Education* (NRC 2012). The increasing number of science standards, along with the pressure to "cover" them that results from the use of high-stakes tests targeting facts and definition, has unfortunately forced teachers "to alter their methods of instruction to conform to the assessment" (Owens 2009, p. 50). Teachers, as a result, tend to focus on content and neglect the practices of science inside the classroom. Teachers also tend to move through the science curriculum quickly to ensure that they cover all the standards before the students are required to take the high-stakes assessment.

The current focus on covering all the standards, however, does not seem to be working. For example, *The Nation's Report Card: Science 2009* (National Center for Education Statistics 2011) indicates that only 21% of all 12th-grade students who took the National Assessment of Educational Progress in science scored at the proficient level. The performance of U.S. students on international assessments is even bleaker, as indicated by their scores on the science portion of the Programme for International Student Assessment (PISA). PISA is an international study that was launched by the Organisation for Economic Co-operation and Development (OECD) in 1997, with the goal of assessing education systems worldwide; more than 70 countries have participated in the study. The test is designed to assess reading, math, and science achievement and is given every three years. The mean score for students in the United States on the science portion of the PISA in 2012 is below the international mean, and there has been no significant change in the U.S. mean score since 2000 (OECD 2012; see Table 1). Students in countries such as China, Korea, Japan, and Finland score significantly higher than student in the United States. These results suggest that U.S. students are not learning what they need to learn to become proficient in science, even though teachers are covering a great deal of material.

TABLE 1

PISA scientific literacy performance for U.S. students

Year	U.S. mean score*	U.S. rank/Number of OECD countries assessed	Top three performers
2000	499	14/27	Korea (552) Japan (550) Finland (538)
2003	491	22/41	Finland (548) Japan (548) Hong Kong-China (539)
2006	489	29/57	Finland (563) Hong Kong-China (542) Canada (534)
2009	499	15/43	Japan (552) Korea (550) Hong Kong-China (541)
2012	497	36/65	Shanghai-China (580) Hong Kong-China (555) Singapore (551)

*The mean score of the PISA is 500 across all years.
Source: OECD 2012

In addition to the poor performance of U.S. students on national and international assessments, empirical research in science education indicates that a curriculum that emphasizes breadth over depth and neglects the practices of science can actually hinder the development of science proficiency (Duschl, Schweingruber, and Shouse 2007; NRC 2005, 2008). As noted in the *Framework* (NRC 2012),

> K–12 science education in the United States fails to [promote the development of science proficiency], in part because it is not organized systematically across multiple years of school, emphasizes discrete facts with a focus on breadth over depth, and does not provide students with engaging opportunities to experience how science is actually done." (p. 1)

The NRC goes on to recommend that science teachers spend more time focusing on key ideas to help students develop a more enduring understanding of biology content. They also call for science teachers to start using instructional strategies that give students more opportunities to learn how to participate in the practices of science. Without this knowledge and these abilities, students will not be able to engage in public discussions about scientific issues related to their everyday lives, to be consumers of scientific information, or to have the skills needed to enter a science or science-related career. We think the school science laboratory is the perfect place to focus on key ideas and engage students in the practices of science and thus to help them develop the knowledge and abilities needed to be proficient in science.

How School Science Laboratories Can Help Foster the Development of Science Proficiency

Laboratory activities look rather similar in most high school classrooms (we define a school science laboratory activity as "an opportunity for students to interact directly with the material world using the tools, data collection techniques, models, and theories of science" [NRC 2005, p. 3]) (Hofstein and Lunetta 2004; NRC 2005). The teacher usually begins a laboratory activity by first introducing his or her students to a concept through a lecture or some other form of direct instruction. The teacher then gives the students a hands-on task to complete. To support students as they complete the task, teachers often provide students with a worksheet that includes a procedure explaining how to collect data, a data table to fill out, and a set of analysis questions. The hope is that the experience gained through completion of the hands-on task and worksheet will illustrate, confirm, or otherwise verify the concept that was introduced to the students at the beginning of the activity. This type of approach, however, is an ineffective way to help students understand the content under investigation, learn how to engage in important scientific practices, improve communication skills, or develop scientific habits of mind (Duschl, Schweingruber, and Shouse 2007; NRC 2005). Most laboratory activities therefore do little to promote the development of science proficiency.

One way to address this problem is to change the focus of laboratory instruction. A change in focus will require teachers to place more emphasis on "how we know" (i.e., how new knowledge is generated and validated) in addition to "what we know" about life on Earth (i.e., the theories, laws, and unifying concepts). Science teachers will also need to focus more on the abilities and habits of mind that students need to have in order to construct and support scientific knowledge claims through argument and to evaluate the claims or arguments made by others (NRC 2012). As explained in the *Framework* (NRC 2012), argumentation (i.e., the process of proposing, supporting, and evaluating claims) is essential practice in science:

> Scientists and engineers use evidence-based argumentation to make the case for their ideas, whether involving new theories or designs, novel ways of collecting data, or interpretations of evidence. They and their peers then attempt to identify weaknesses and limitations in the argument, with the ultimate goal of refining and improving the explanation or design (p. 46).

The NRC therefore calls for argumentation to play a more central role in the teaching and learning of science.

In addition to changing the focus of instruction, teachers will need to change the nature of laboratory instruction to promote and support the development of science proficiency. To change the nature of instruction, teachers need to make laboratory activities more authentic by giving students an opportunity to engage in scientific practices instead of giving them a worksheet with a procedure to follow and a data table to fill out. These activities, however, also need to be educative for students in order to help students develop the knowledge and abilities associated with science proficiency; students need to receive feedback about how to improve, and teachers need to help students learn from their mistakes.

The argument-driven inquiry (ADI) instructional model (Sampson and Gleim 2009; Sampson, Grooms, and Walker 2009, 2011) was designed as a way to make lab activities more authentic and educative for students and thus help teachers promote and support the development of science proficiency inside the classroom. This instructional model reflects research about how people learn science (NRC 1999) and is also based on what is known about how to engage students in argumentation and other important scientific practices (Berland and Reiser 2009; Erduran and Jimenez-Aleixandre 2008; McNeill and Krajcik 2008; Osborne, Erduran, and Simon 2004; Sampson and Clark 2008).

Organization of This Book

The remainder of this book is divided into two parts. Part I begins with two text chapters describing the ADI instructional model and the development and components of the ADI lab investigations. Part II contains the lab investigations, including notes for the teacher, student handouts, additional information for students, and checkout questions. Four appendixes contain standards alignment matrices, timeline and proposal options for the investigations, and a form for assessing the investigation reports.

References

Berland, L., and B. Reiser. 2009. Making sense of argumentation and explanation. *Science Education* 93 (1): 26–55.

Duschl, R. A., H. A. Schweingruber, and A. W. Shouse, eds. 2007. *Taking science to school: Learning and teaching science in grades K–8*. Washington, DC: National Academies Press.

Erduran, S., and M. Jimenez-Aleixandre, eds. 2008. *Argumentation in science education: Perspectives from classroom-based research*. Dordrecht, the Netherlands: Springer.

Hofstein, A., and V. Lunetta. 2004. The laboratory in science education: Foundations for the twenty-first century. *Science Education* 88: 28–54.

McNeill, K., and J. Krajcik. 2008. Assessing middle school students' content knowledge and reasoning through written scientific explanations. In *Assessing science learning: Perspectives from research and practice,* ed. J. Coffey, R. Douglas, and C. Stearns, 101–116. Arlington, VA: NSTA Press.

National Center for Education Statistics. 2011. *The nation's report card: Science 2009.* Washington, DC: U.S. Department of Education.

National Research Council (NRC). 1999. *How people learn: Brain, mind, experience, and school.* Washington, DC: National Academies Press.

National Research Council (NRC). 2005. *America's lab report: Investigations in high school science*. Washington, DC: National Academies Press.

National Research Council (NRC). 2008. *Ready, set, science: Putting research to work in K–8 science classrooms*. Washington, DC: National Academies Press.

National Research Council (NRC). 2012. *A framework for K–12 science education: Practices, crosscutting concepts, and core ideas*. Washington, DC: National Academies Press.

Organisation for Economic Co-operation and Development (OECD). 2012. OECD Programme for International Student Assessment. *www.oecd.org/pisa.*

Osborne, J., S. Erduran, and S. Simon. 2004. Enhancing the quality of argumentation in science classrooms. *Journal of Research in Science Teaching* 41 (10): 994–1020.

Owens, T. 2009. Improving science acheivment through changes in education policy. *Science Educator* 18 (2): 49–55.

Sampson, V., and D. Clark. 2008. Assessment of the ways students generate arguments in science education: Current perspectives and recommendations for future directions. *Science Education* 92 (3): 447–472.

Sampson, V., and L. Gleim. 2009. Argument-driven inquiry to promote the understanding of important concepts and practices in biology. *American Biology Teacher* 71 (8): 471–477.

Sampson, V., J. Grooms, and J. Walker. 2009. Argument-driven inquiry: A way to promote learning during laboratory activities. *The Science Teacher* 76 (7): 42–47.

Sampson, V., J. Grooms, and J. Walker. 2011. Argument-driven inquiry as a way to help students learn how to participate in scientific argumentation and craft written arguments: An exploratory study. *Science Education* 95 (2): 217–257.

SECTION 1

Using Argument-Driven Inquiry

CHAPTER 1
Argument-Driven Inquiry

Stages of Argument-Driven Inquiry

The argument-driven inquiry (ADI) instructional model consists of eight stages, as shown in Figure 2). These stages are designed to ensure that students have an opportunity to engage in the practices of science during a laboratory investigation and receive the feedback and explicit guidance that they need in order to improve on each aspect of science proficiency over the course of a school year.

Stage 1: Identification of the Task and the Guiding Question; "Tool Talk"

The teacher initiates the laboratory activity by identifying a phenomenon to investigate and a guiding question for the students to answer. The goal of the teacher at this stage of the model is to capture the students' interest and provide them with a reason to design and carry out an investigation. To do this, the teacher should make a photocopy of the student handout that is included with each lab investigation and distribute one to each student in the class. The handout includes a brief introduction that describes a puzzling phenomenon or a problem to solve and provides a guiding question for the investigation. This handout also includes information about the medium they will use to present their argument (e.g., a whiteboard), a list of materials that can be used, helpful tips on how to get started, and some criteria to judge argument quality (e.g., the sufficiency of the explanation and the quality of the evidence). The teacher should have a different student read each section of the handout aloud and then pause after each section so the teacher can clarify expectations, answer questions, and provide additional information as needed.

It is also important for the teacher to hold a "tool talk" during this stage, taking a few minutes to explain how to use specific lab equipment, how to use specific indicators, how to use a computer simulation, or even how to use software to analyze data. Teachers need to hold a tool talk because students are often unfamiliar with lab equipment; even if they are familiar with the equipment, they will often use it incorrectly or in an unsafe manner. A tool talk can also be productive during this stage because students often find it difficult to design a method to collect the data needed to answer the guiding question (the task of stage 2) when they do not understand how to use the available materials. Once all the students understand the goal of the activity and how to use the available materials, the teacher should divide the students into small groups (we recommend three students per group) and move on to the second stage of the model.

FIGURE 2

Stages of the argument-driven inquiry instructional model

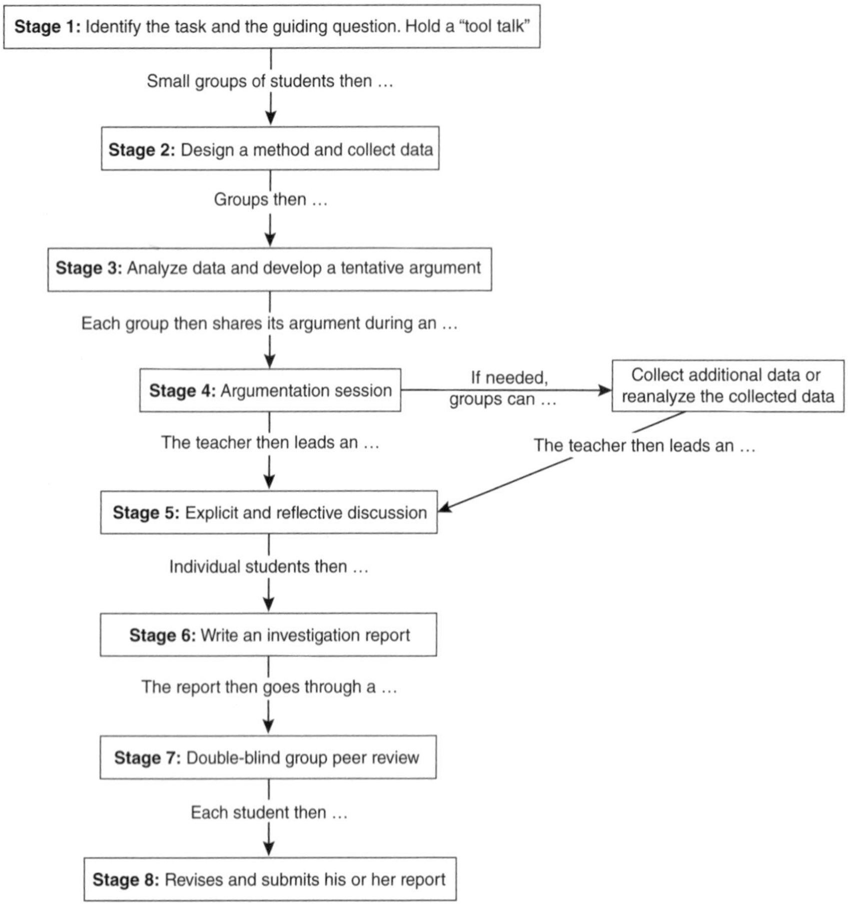

Stage 2: Designing a Method and Collecting Data

In this stage of the ADI model, small groups of students work together to (1) develop a method that they can use to gather the data needed to answer the guiding question and then (2) carry out the method. How students complete this stage depends on the nature of the investigation. Some investigations call for groups to answer the guiding question by designing a controlled experiment, whereas others require students to analyze an existing data set. To assist students with the process of designing their method, the teacher can have students complete an investigation proposal. These proposals guide students through the process of developing a method by encouraging them to think about what type of data they will need to collect, how to collect it, and how to analyze it. We have included three different investigation proposals in Appendix 3 (p. 399): Investigation proposal A or investigation proposal B can be used when students need to design a controlled experiment to test alternative explanations or claims; investigation proposal C can be used when students need to design and conduct a systematic observation of some natural phenomenon in order to develop an explanation or claim (rather than testing alternative explanations) during their investigation.

The overall intent of stage 2 of the ADI model is to provide students with an opportunity to interact directly with the natural world (or in some cases with data drawn from the natural world) using appropriate tools and data collection techniques and to learn how to deal with the ambiguities of empirical work. This stage also gives students a chance to learn why some methods work better than others and how the method used during a scientific investigation is based on the nature of the question and the phenomenon under investigation. At the end of this stage, students should have collected all the data they need to answer the guiding question.

Stage 3: Data Analysis and Development of a Tentative Argument

The third stage of the instructional model calls for students to develop a tentative argument in response to the guiding question. To do this, each group needs to be encouraged to first "make sense" of the measurements (size, temperature, and so on) they collected and/or the observations (appearance, location, behavior, and so on) they made during stage 2. Once the groups have analyzed and interpreted their data, they can create their arguments. Each argument consists of a claim, the evidence they are using to support their claim, and a justification of their evidence (Figure 2). The *claim* is their answer to the guiding question. The *evidence* consists of the data (measurements or observations) they collected, an analysis of the data, and an interpretation of the analysis. The *justification of the evidence* is a statement that defends their choice of evidence by explaining why it is important and relevant by making the concepts or assumption underlying the analysis and interpretation explicit.

The following example illustrates each of the three structural components of an argument. This argument was made in response to the guiding question, "Are dolphins more closely related to fish or dogs?"

> *Claim:* Dolphins are more closely related to dogs than fish.
>
> *Evidence:* Dolphins and dogs are warm-blooded, get oxygen from the air, and produce milk. Fish are cold-blooded, get the oxygen they need from water, and do not produce milk. Therefore, dolphins and dogs have more traits in common than dolphins and fish.
>
> *Justification of the evidence:* We examined similarities in traits because evolution, or descent with modification, indicates that organisms that share a common ancestor will have more traits in common. Organisms that share a common

ancestor in the more recent past are more closely related than organisms that share a common ancestor in the distant past.

The claim in this argument provides an answer to the guiding question. The evidence used to support the claim includes an analysis of the data collected by the students/authors (by highlighting similarities and differences between the groups of organisms) and an interpretation of their analysis (by explaining what can be inferred from the observed similarities and differences). Finally, the justification of the evidence makes explicit the underlying concepts and assumptions guiding the analysis and interpretation of the data (Figure 3).

FIGURE 3

Framework for the components of a scientific argument and some criteria that can be used to evaluate the merits of the argument

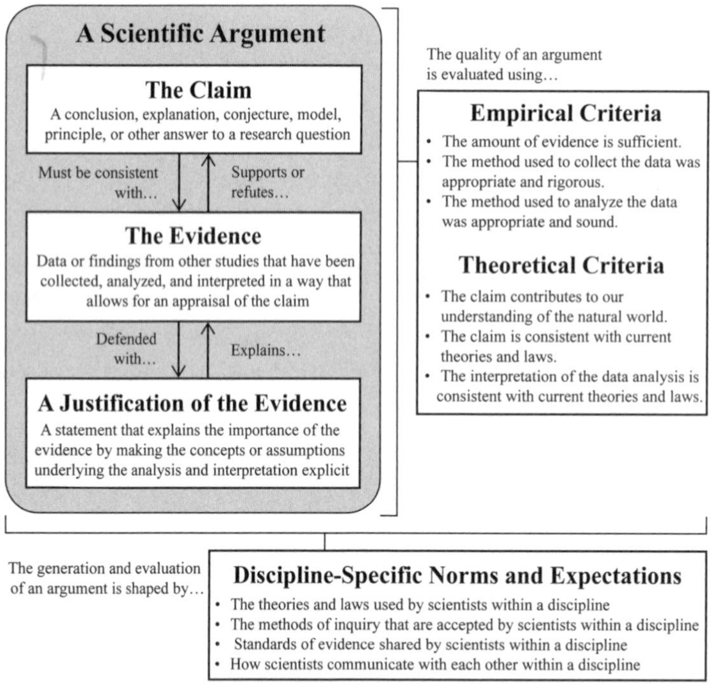

It is also important for students to understand that some arguments are better than others in science. An important aspect of scientific argumentation involves the evaluation of the various components of the arguments put forward by others. The framework provided in Figure 3 highlights several types of criteria that students can and should use to evaluate an argument in science. Empirical criteria include

- how well the claim fits with all available evidence,

- the sufficiency of the evidence,
- the relevance of the evidence,
- the appropriateness of the method used to collect the data, and
- the appropriateness of the method used to analyze the data.

Theoretical criteria refer to standards that are important in science but are not empirical in nature, including

- the sufficiency of the claim (i.e., it includes everything it needs to);
- the usefulness of the claim (e.g., it allows us to engage in new inquiries or understand a phenomenon);
- how consistent the claim is with other accepted theories, laws, or models; and
- the appropriateness of the interpretation of the data analysis.

What counts as quality within these different categories of criteria, however, varies from discipline to discipline (e.g., biology, physics, geology) and within the specific fields of each discipline (e.g., cell biology, evolutionary biology, genetics). The variation is due to differences in the types of phenomena investigated, what counts as an accepted mode of inquiry (e.g., experimentation vs. fieldwork), and the theory-laden nature of scientific inquiry. It is therefore important to keep in mind that "what counts" as a quality argument in science is discipline and field dependent.

Each group of students should create their tentative argument in a medium that can easily be viewed by the other groups. We recommend using a 2′ × 3′ whiteboard or a large piece of butcher paper. Students should devote a section of the board or paper to each component of the argument (Figure 4). Students can also create their tentative arguments using presentation software such as Microsoft's PowerPoint or Apple's Keynote and devote one slide to each component of an argument.

FIGURE 4

Suggested layout of the components of an argument on a whiteboard

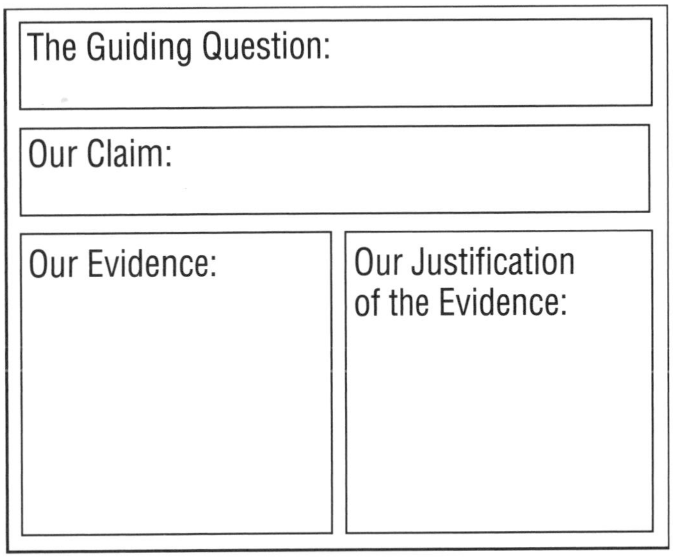

The choice of medium is not important as long as students are able to easily modify the content of their argument as they work.

The intention of this stage of the model is to provide students with an opportunity to make sense of what they are seeing or doing during the investigation. As students work together to create a tentative argument, they must talk with each other and determine how to analyze the data and how to best interpret the trends, differences, or relationships that they identify (Figure 5). They must also decide if the evidence (data that has been analyzed and interpreted) that they chose to include in their argument is relevant, sufficient, and convincing enough to support their claim. This, in turn, enables the groups of students to evaluate competing ideas and weed out any claim that is inaccurate, does not fit with all the available data, or contains contradictions.

FIGURE 5

An example of an argument created by students

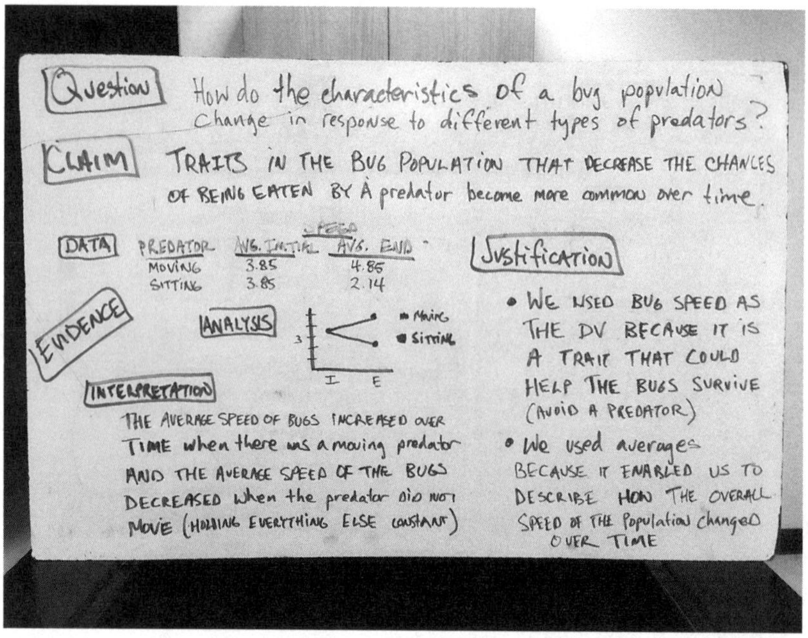

This stage of the model, however, can be challenging for students because they are rarely asked to make sense of a phenomenon based on raw data. We therefore recommend that the teacher circulate from group to group to act as a resource person for the students. It is the goal of the teacher at this stage of the model to ensure that students think about what they are doing and why. For example, the teacher should ask students probing questions to help them remember the goal of the activity (e.g., "What are you trying to figure out?"), to encourage them to think about whether or not the data are relevant (e.g., "Why is that characteristic important?"), or to help them remember to use rigorous criteria to evaluate the merits of a tentative idea (e.g., "Does that fit with all the data or what we know about natural selection?"). It is also important to remember that students will struggle to develop arguments at the beginning of the year and will often rely on inappropriate criteria such as plausibility (e.g., "That sounds good to me.") or how they fit with personal experience (e.g., "That's what I saw on TV once.") as they attempt to make sense of their data. However, over time and with enough practice students will improve their skills. This is an important principle underlying the ADI instructional model.

Stage 4: Argumentation Session

In this stage, each group is given an opportunity to share, evaluate, and revise their tentative arguments with the other groups. The argumentation session (Figure 6) is included in the model because scientific argumentation (i.e., arguing from evidence) is an important practice in science and critique leads to better outcomes. In addition, research indicates that students learn more about the content and develop better critical-thinking skills when they are exposed to the alternative ideas, respond to the questions and challenges of other students, and evaluate the merits of competing ideas (Duschl, Schweingruber, and Shouse 2007). Argumentation also provides an opportunity for students to learn how to distinguish between ideas using rigorous scientific criteria and to develop more scientific habits of mind (such as treating ideas with initial skepticism, insisting that the reasoning and assumptions be made explicit, and insisting that claims be supported by valid evidence).

FIGURE 6

A high school student presents her group's argument to another group during the argumentation session.

It is important to note, however, that supporting and promoting this type of interaction between students inside the classroom is often difficult because this type of discussion is foreign to most students. This is one reason why students are required to generate their arguments in a medium that can be seen by others, to help students focus their attention on evaluating evidence rather than attacking the source of the ideas. We also recommend that teachers use a round-robin format rather than a whole-class presentation format. In the round-robin format, one member of the group stays at his or her workstation to share the group's ideas while the other group members go to different groups one at a time to listen to and critique the explanations developed by their classmates. This type of format ensures that all ideas are heard and more students are actively involved in the process.

It is also important for the teacher to be involved in the discussion during the argumentation session. The teacher should move from group to group to not only keep students on task but also model good scientific argumentation. The teacher can ask the presenter questions such as "How did you analyze the available data?" or "Were there any data that did not fit with your claim?" to encourage students to use empirical criteria to evaluate the quality of the arguments. The teacher can also ask presenters to explain how the claims they are presenting fit with the theories, laws, or models of science or why the evidence they used is important. In addition, the teacher can also ask the students who are listening to the presentation questions such as "Do you think their analysis is accurate?" or "Do you think their interpretation is sound?" or even "Do you think their claim fits with what we know about X?"; the purpose of the teacher's questions is to remind the students to use empirical and theoretical criteria to evaluate an argument during the discussions. Overall, it is the goal of the teacher at this stage of the lesson to encourage students to think about how they know what they know and why some claims are more valid or acceptable in science. This stage of the model, however, is not the time to tell students that they are right or wrong.

After the students have finished sharing and critiquing the various arguments, the original groups should be given an opportunity to reconvene and discuss what they learned by interacting with individuals from the other groups. The teacher should encourage the students to modify their tentative argument, by modifying the content of the claim or by reinterpreting their analysis of the data as needed, during this time. Teachers can also encourage students to collect new data or conduct a new analysis of the original data if there was substantial disagreement between the various groups or students realized that there was a major flaw in the way they collected data during the second stage of the model.

Stage 5: Explicit and Reflective Discussion

The teacher leads a whole-class discussion during this stage of the model. The teacher should begin the discussion by giving students an opportunity to share what they learned about the phenomenon under investigation. The teacher should remind students of any important theories, models, laws, or principles that students can use to provide a justification for their evidence. The teacher can also use this time to help clarify any student misconceptions about the content and to highlight and discuss the crosscutting concepts at the heart of the investigation.

The teacher should encourage students to reflect on the strengths and weaknesses of the investigations they designed and carried out during the whole-class discussion. For example, the teacher might ask students to discuss what made the investigation more or less scientific and why. The teacher can then ask students to consider ways to make their investigation more scientific. This is an excellent time to discuss ways to improve data collection methods, reduce bias and measurement error, and eliminate potential confounding factors. The teacher should also offer tips, hints, and suggestions for improving the nature of their investigations. This stage of the model provides an opportunity for the teacher to help students see how to use what they have learned about investigation design in the future.

Next, the teacher should discuss one or two crosscutting concepts from the *Framework* (NRC 2012) that are well aligned with the investigation. For example, a teacher might decide to discuss the concept of Patterns and the concept of Cause and Effect: Mechanism and Explanation. After explaining these concepts, the teacher should encourage students to think about how these concepts played a role in the investigation that was just completed. It is important to discuss these crosscutting concepts during this stage of the model to help students make connections between what they did and these overarching ideas, so students can begin to see why they are so important in science.

Last, and perhaps most important, the teacher should discuss one or two concepts of the nature of science or the nature of scientific inquiry, using what the students did during their investigations to illustrate these important concepts. For example, a teacher might decide to talk about what does and does not count as an experiment in science, the variety of methods that scientists can use to collect data, or the role creativity and imagination play during an investigation. Other possible topics include the differences between observations and inferences, data and evidence, qualitative data and quantitative data, or theories and laws. This stage of the model, in other words, provides a context for teachers to explain the nature of scientific knowledge and how this knowledge develops over time. Current research suggests that students only develop an appropriate understanding of the nature of science and scientific inquiry when teachers discuss these concepts in an explicit fashion (Abd-El-Khalick and Lederman 2000; Akerson, Abd-El-Khalick, and Lederman 2000; Lederman and Lederman 2004; Lederman et al. 2014; Schwartz, Lederman, and Crawford 2004).

Stage 6: Writing the Investigation Report

In this stage of the ADI model, each student is required to write an investigation report using his or her group's argument that was developed and then evaluated by his or her classmates during the argumentation session. The report can be written during class or assigned as homework. The report is centered on three fundamental questions:

1. What question were you trying to answer and why?
2. What did you do and why?
3. What is your argument?

An important component of this process is to encourage students to use tables or graphs to help organize the data they gathered and require them to reference the tables or graphs in the body of the report. This method allows them to learn how to construct an explanation, argue from evidence, and communicate information. It also enables students to master the disciplinary-based writing skills outlined in the *Common Core State Standards,* in English language arts (*CCSS ELA;* National Governors Association Center for Best Practices and Council of Chief State School Officers 2010).

The format of the report is designed to emphasize the persuasive nature of science writing and to help students learn how to communicate in multiple modes (words, figures, tables, and equations). The three-question format is well aligned with the components of a traditional laboratory report (i.e., introduction, procedure, results, and discussion) but allows students to see the important role argument plays in science. We recommend that teachers limit the length of the investigation report to two double-spaced pages or one single-spaced page, which is less intimidating to students than a lengthier report requirement. This limitation also encourages students to write in a clear and concise manner, since there is little room for extraneous information.

This stage is included in the instructional model because writing is an important part of doing science. Scientists must be able to read and understand the writing of others as well as evaluate its worth. They also must be able to share the results of their own research through writing. In addition, writing helps students learn how to articulate their thinking in a clear and concise manner, encourages metacognition, and improves student understanding of the content (Wallace, Hand, and Prain 2004). Finally, and perhaps most important, writing makes each student's thinking visible to the teacher, which facilitates assessment, and enables the teacher to provide students with the educative feedback they need in order to improve.

We recommend that teachers provide students with time to write this report in class when first starting to use the ADI model. This type of writing will be, in all likelihood, challenging for students. The teacher therefore needs to scaffold the writing process. There are a number of ways to scaffold students as they write their report. One way is to show the students a good example and a bad example of the report before they begin, so they have a better understanding of what is expected of them. Students can read each section of the sample reports and then discuss what makes one better than the other and why, using the criteria outlined in the peer-review guide. Another way to scaffold the approach is to have students write one section of the report at a time. After writing each section, students can share what they wrote and the teacher can offer feedback. The teacher can also give the students some advice (e.g., what should be included in the next section, how to organize data into a table, or how to make a figure in a specific word processing application) before they move on to the next section. This type of approach helps break the process of writing a three-section investigation report into manageable chunks. Once students are comfortable with scientific writing and understand what is expected of them, the teacher can assign this stage of the model as homework. It is important to keep in mind that not all students will have access to computers or have time to do homework, so it is important to make accommodations for these students.

Stage 7: Double-Blind Group Peer Review

In this stage, each student is required to submit to the teacher three typed copies of his or her investigation report. Students should not place their names on the report; instead, they should use only an identification number to maintain anonymity. The students are then placed back in their original groups and each group receives three sets of reports (i.e., the reports written by three different authors) and one peer-review guide for each author's report (see peer-review guide and instructor scoring rubric in Appendix 4; p. 403). The peer-review guide lists specific criteria that are to be used to evaluate the quality of each section of the investigation report as well as the mechanics of the writing. There is also space for the reviewers to provide the author with feedback about how to improve the report.

Reviewing each report as a group is an important component of the peer-review process because it provides students with a forum to discuss "what counts" as high quality or acceptable and in doing so forces them to reach a consensus during the process. This method also helps prevent students from checking off "Yes" for each criterion on the peer-review guide without thorough consideration of the merits of the paper. It is also important for students to provide constructive and specific feedback to the author when areas of the paper are found to not meet the standards established by the peer-review guide. An additional benefit of the peer-review process is providing students with an opportunity to read good and bad examples of the reports. This helps the students learn new ways to organize and present information, which in turn will help them write better on subsequent reports.

This stage of the model also gives students more opportunities to develop the reading skills that are needed to be successful in science. Students, for example, must be able to determine the central ideas or conclusions of a text and determine the meaning of symbols, key terms, and other domain-specific words. In addition, students must be able to assess the author's line of reasoning and the evidence that an author includes in a text to support his or her claim. Students should also be able to compare or contrast findings presented in a scientific text to those from other sources. Students can develop all these skills, as well as the other discipline-based reading standards found in the *CCSS ELA*, when they are required to read and review reports written by their classmates.

Stage 8: Revision and Submission of the Investigation Report

Once the peer-review process is complete, the final stage in the ADI instructional model is to revise the report based on the suggestions given during the peer review. If the paper met all the criteria, the student may simply submit the paper to the teacher with the original peer-reviewed "rough draft" and the peer-review guide attached; before submission, the student should replace the identification number with his or her name. Students whose reports are found by the peer-review group to be acceptable also have the option to revise the reports if so desired after reviewing the work of other students. If the paper was found to not be acceptable by the group during peer review, however, the author is required to rewrite his or her report using the reviewers' comments and suggestions as a guideline. Once the report is revised, it is turned in to the teacher for evaluation with the original rough draft and the peer-review guide attached.

The author response section of the peer-review guide requires the student/author to explain what he or she did to improve each section of the report in response to the reviewers' suggestions (or explain why the student decided to ignore the reviewers' suggestions). The teacher can then provide scores in the instructor score column of the peer-review guide and use these scores to assign an overall grade. This approach provides students with a chance to improve their writing mechanics and develop their reasoning and understanding of the content. It also offers students the benefit of reducing academic pressure by providing support in obtaining the highest possible grade for their final product.

The Role of the Teacher

The role of the teacher during a laboratory investigation designed using the ADI instructional model is different than a more traditional lab activity. The teacher, first and foremost, needs to act as a resource for the students as they work through each stage of the activity. The teacher also needs to encourage students to think about what they are doing and why they decided to do it throughout the process. Teachers, in other words, should ask students probing questions (e.g., "Why do you want to set up your equipment that way?" or "What type of data will you need to collect to be able to answer that question?") rather the telling or showing students how to do it. Teachers must also take on the responsibility of maintaining high standards for a scientific investigation by requiring students to use rigorous standards for "what counts" as a good method or a strong argument in the context of science. Finally, and perhaps most important, teachers must be willing to let students try and fail and then help them learn from their mistakes during an ADI lab investigation. Therefore, teachers should not try to make the investigations included in this book "student-proof" by providing additional directions to ensure that student do everything right the first time. We have found that students often learn more from an ADI lab investigation when they design a poor method to collect data or analyze their results in an inappropriate manner because their classmates quickly point out these mistakes during the argumentation session and it leads to more teachable moments.

Table 2 describes teacher behaviors that are consistent and inconsistent with each stage of the instructional model. We created this table to help teachers see how the role of the teacher during an ADI activity differs from more traditional forms of lab instruction. This table can also serve as a guide for teachers when first attempting to implement the lab investigations found in the book.

TABLE 2

Teacher behaviors during the stages of the ADI instructional model

Stage	Teacher behaviors: Consistent with ADI model	Teacher behaviors: Inconsistent with ADI model
1: Identification of the task and the guiding question; "tool talk"	• Sparks students' curiosity • "Creates a need" for students to design and carry out an investigation • Organizes students into collaborative groups • Supplies students with the materials they will need • Holds a "tool talk" to show students how to use equipment and/or to illustrate proper techniques • Provides students with hints	• Does not have students read the lab handout • Tells students that there is one correct answer • Tells students what they "should expect to see" or what results "they should get"
2: Designing a method and collecting data	• Encourages students to ask questions as they design their investigations • Asks groups questions about their method (e.g., "Why do you want to do it this way?") and the type of data they expect from that design • Reminds students of the importance of specificity when completing their investigation proposal	• Gives students a procedure to follow • Does not question students about their method or the type of data they expect to collect • Approves vague or incomplete investigation proposals

Table 2 *(continued)*

Stage	Teacher behaviors: Consistent with ADI model	Teacher behaviors: Inconsistent with ADI model
3: Data analysis and development of a tentative argument	• Reminds students of the research question and the components of a scientific argument • Requires students to generate an argument that provides and supports a claim with genuine evidence (data + an analysis of the data + an interpretation of the analysis) • Asks students what opposing ideas or rebuttals they might anticipate • Encourages students to justify their evidence with scientific concepts	• Requires only one student to be prepared to discuss the argument • Moves to groups to check on progress without asking students questions about why they are doing what they are doing • Does not interact with students (uses the time to catch up on other responsibilities) • Tells students that their claim is right
4: Argumentation session	• Reminds students of appropriate behaviors during discussions • Reminds students to critique ideas, not people • Encourages students to ask peers questions • Keeps the discussion focused on the elements of the argument • Encourages students to use appropriate criteria for determining what does and does not count	• Allows students to criticize or tease each other • Asks questions about students' claims before other students can ask • Allows students to use inappropriate criteria for determining what does and does not count
5: Explicit and reflective discussion	• Discusses the content at the heart of the investigation and important theories, laws, or principles that students can use to justify their evidence when writing their investigation reports • Explains one or two crosscutting concepts using what happened during the lab investigation as an example • Highlights one or two aspects of the nature of science and/or scientific inquiry using what happened during the lab investigation as examples • Encourages students to identify strengths and limitations of their investigations • Discusses ways that students could improve future investigations	• Provides a lecture on the content • Skips over the discussion about the nature of science and the nature of scientific inquiry in order to save time • Tell students "what they should have learned" or "this is what you all should have figured out"

Table 2 *(continued)*

Stage	Teacher behaviors: Consistent with ADI model	Teacher behaviors: Inconsistent with ADI model
6: Writing the investigation report	• Reminds students about the audience, topic, and purpose of the report • Provides the peer-review guide in advance • Provide examples of a high-quality report and an unacceptable report • Takes time to write the report in class in order to scaffold the process of writing each section of the report	• Has students write only a portion of the report • Allows students to write the report as a group • Does not require students to write the report, in order to save time
7: Double-blind peer group review	• Reminds students of appropriate behaviors for the peer-review process • Ensures that all groups are giving a quality and fair peer review to the best of their ability • Encourages students to remember that while grammar and punctuation are important, the main goal is an acceptable scientific claim with supporting evidence and a justification of the evidence • Ensures that students provide genuine feedback to the author when they identify a weakness or an omission. • Holds the reviewers accountable	• Allows students to make critical comments about the author (e.g., "This person is stupid") rather than their work (e.g., "This claim needs to be supported by evidence") • Allows students to just check off "Yes" on each item without providing a critical evaluation of the report
8: Revision and submission of the investigation report	• Requires students to edit their reports based on the reviewers' comments • Requires students to respond to the reviewers' ratings and comments • Has students complete the checkout questions after they have turned in their report	• Allows students to turn in a report without a completed peer-review guide • Allows students to turn in a report without revising it first

References

Abd-El-Khalick, F., and N. G. Lederman. 2000. Improving science teachers' conceptions of nature of science: A critical review of the literature. *International Journal of Science Education* 22: 665–701.

Akerson, V., F. Abd-El-Khalick, and N. Lederman. 2000. Influence of a reflective explicit activity-based approach on elementary teachers' conception of nature of science. *Journal of Research in Science Teaching* 37 (4): 295–317.

Duschl, R. A., H. A. Schweingruber, and A. W. Shouse, eds. 2007. *Taking science to school: Learning and teaching science in grades K–8*. Washington, DC: National Academies Press.

Lederman, N. G., and J. S. Lederman. 2004. Revising instruction to teach the nature of science. *The Science Teacher* 71 (9): 36–39.

Lederman, J., N. Lederman, S. Bartos, S. Bartels, A. Meyer, and R. Schwartz. 2014. Meaningful assessment of learners' understanding about scientific inquiry: The Views About Scientific Inquiry (VASI) questionnaire. *Journal of Research in Science Teaching* 51 (1): 65–83.

National Governors Association Center for Best Practices and Council of Chief State School Officers (NGAC and CCSSO). 2010. *Common core state standards*. Washington, DC: NGAC and CCSSO.

National Research Council (NRC). 2012. *A framework for K–12 science education: Practices, crosscutting concepts, and core ideas*. Washington, DC: National Academies Press.

Schwartz, R. S., N. Lederman, and B. Crawford. 2004. Developing views of nature of science in an authentic context: An explicit approach to bridging the gap between nature of science and scientific inquiry. *Science Education* 88: 610–645.

Wallace, C., B. Hand, and V. Prain, eds. 2004. *Writing and learning in the science classroom*. Boston: Kluwer Academic Publishers.

CHAPTER 2
Lab Investigations

This book includes 27 laboratory investigations that were designed using the argument-driven inquiry (ADI) instructional model. The investigations are not meant to replace an existing curriculum but rather to transform the laboratory component of a biology course. A teacher can use these investigations as a way to introduce students to new content ("introduction labs") or as a way to give students an opportunity to apply a theory, law, or unifying concept introduced in class in a novel situation ("application labs"). To facilitate curriculum and lesson planning, the lab investigations have been aligned with *A Framework for K–12 Science Education* (National Research Council [NRC] 2012); the *Common Core State Standards*, in English language arts (CCSS ELA) and mathematics (CCSS Mathematics); and various aspects of the nature of science (NOS) and the nature of scientific inquiry (NOSI; Abd-El-Khalick and Lederman 2000; Lederman et al. 2002, 2014). The matrices in Appendix 1 (p. 386) illustrate these alignments.

Many of the ideas for the investigations in this book came from existing resources; however, we transformed the activities from those resources so they were consistent with the focus and nature of the ADI instructional model. For example, many teachers have their students create models of cells using dialysis tubing to teach them about osmosis or have their students measure changes in oxygen levels of plants in closed containers to explore the process of photosynthesis. What makes the lab investigations in this book novel and innovative is how they are designed and how these investigations give students an opportunity to participate in the practices of science throughout the school year. The ADI instructional model provides teachers with a way to transform classic or traditional laboratory activities into authentic and educative investigations that enable students to become more proficient in science.

Once we created the ADI laboratory investigations, they were reviewed for content accuracy by several practicing biologists. The investigations were then piloted in all sections of a high school biology course (including general and honors sections). After the pilot year, each lab investigation and all related instructional materials (such as the investigation proposals and peer-review guides) were modified based on teacher feedback and student learning gains to make them more effective. The modified labs were then piloted and modified for a second time. The final iteration of each lab investigation is included in this book.

These lab investigations were created as part of a three-year research project funded by the Institute of Education Sciences through grant R305A100909. The goal of this project, which took place at Florida State University and Florida State University Schools (a K–12 laboratory school), was to refine the ADI instructional model, develop a set of ADI lab activities for biology, and examine what students learn when they complete a series of ADI labs over the course of a school year. Our research indicates that students have much better inquiry and writing skills after participating in at least eight ADI lab investigations and make substantial gains in their understanding of important content and concepts related to NOS and NOSI (Grooms, Sampson, and Carafano 2012; Sampson et al. 2012, 2013; Sampson, Grooms, and Enderle 2012). To learn more about the research associated with the ADI instructional model and how to use it in the classroom, visit *www.argumentdriveninquiry.com.*

Teacher Notes

Science teachers must determine when to implement specific lab investigations and how to use a lab to best promote and support student learning. To help teachers make instructional decisions about when and how to use the lab activities included in this book, we have included Teacher Notes for each investigation. These notes include information about the purpose of the lab, the content, the time needed to implement each stage of the model for that lab, the materials needed, and hints for implementation. The Teacher Notes also include a topic connections section that shows how each ADI lab investigation is aligned with the NRC *Framework*, the *CCSS ELA* and/or the *CCSS Mathematics*, and NOS or NOSI concepts. In the following subsections, we will describe the information provided in each section of the Teacher Notes.

Purpose

This section of the Teacher Notes describes the main idea of the lab and indicates whether the activity is an introduction lab or an application lab. In either case, the teacher does not need to be overly concerned with making sure the students "get the vocabulary" or "know their stuff" before the lab investigation begins. With the combination of the information provided in the student handout, students' evolving understanding of the actual practice of science, and the various resources available to the students (i.e., the science textbook, the internet, and, of course, the teacher), students will develop a better understanding of the content as they work through the activity. This section also highlights the NOS or NOSI concepts that should be discussed during the explicit and reflective discussion stage.

The Content

This section of the Teacher Notes provides an overview of the concept that is being introduced to the students during the investigation or the concept that students will need to apply during the investigation. It also provides an answer to the guiding question of the investigation.

Timeline

ADI lab investigations typically take three to five instructional days to complete. However, it will often take longer to complete an investigation when teachers first implement this approach because students need to learn what is expected of them during each stage of the model. The amount of time needed to implement an ADI lab also depends on the school context and how many of the stages are assigned as homework. This section of the Teacher Notes therefore includes two options for implementing the lab.

It is important to note that although the days are listed chronologically in the timeline options (see Appendix 2, p. 391), they do not necessarily have to fall on consecutive days. In some cases, such as when students need to write an investigation report, teachers can allow students to have more than one night to complete their work, especially when they are getting used to what is expected of them. Finally, some of the lab stages do not take an entire class period to complete, especially once students learn how to better participate in the practices of science throughout the academic year.

Materials and Preparation

This section of the Teacher Notes describes the lab supplies and instructional materials (i.e., lab sheets, investigation proposals, and peer-review guide) needed to implement the lab activity. The lab supplies listed are designed for one group; however, multiple groups can share if resources are scarce. We have also included specific suggestions for some lab supplies that were found to work best during the pilot tests. However, if needed, substitutions can be made. All supplies should be tested before conducting the lab investigation with the students. We also explain in this section how to prepare the materials needed for the investigation. Some labs require preparation 24 hours or more before the investigation is scheduled to begin, so teachers should read this section two days before conducting the investigation in the classroom.

For labs that involve online databases or simulations, you will need computers with internet access. Any of the typical internet browsers (e.g., Chrome, Firefox, Explorer, or Safari) will work.

Topics for the Explicit and Reflective Discussion

This section advises teachers about which theories, laws, or principles they should discuss to help students provide an adequate justification for their evidence. This section also provides advice about how to encourage students to reflect on the strengths and limitations of their investigations and ways to improve the way they design their investigations in the future. Finally, and perhaps most important, this section provides an overview of the crosscutting concepts from the *Framework* and the concepts related to NOS and NOSI that the teacher needs to discuss during stage 5 of the lab activity.

Hints for Implementing the Lab

The "hints" section of the Teacher Notes has suggestions for all stages of the ADI process. These suggestions address some of the issues that can arise during the investigation (e.g., students struggling to make sense of the data they collect, problems with equipment, investigations taking too long to complete) and should make the investigation run smoothly.

Topic Connections

This section of the Teacher Notes includes a table that highlights which scientific practices, crosscutting concepts, and core ideas from the NRC *Framework* are aligned with the lab activity. This table also outlines specific concepts, which we describe as supporting ideas, that are addressed during the activity. In addition, the table lists the *CCSS ELA* and the *CCSS Mathematics* that are a focus of the lab investigation. Finally, the table provides a list of the aspects of NOS/NOSI that teachers can highlight during the explicit and reflective discussion. This information is included in the Teacher Notes to facilitate curriculum and lesson planning.

Instructional Materials

The instructional materials included in this book are reproducible copy masters that are designed to support students as they participate in an ADI lab investigation. The materials include lab handouts, additional information sheets (not in all labs), investigation proposals, the peer-review guide and instructor rubric, and checkout questions. For those wishing to use less paper, condensed-format versions of the lab handouts are available at *www.nsta.org/publications/press/extras/argument.aspx*. In the following subsections, we will provide an overview of these important materials.

Lab Handout

At the beginning of each lab investigation, each student should be given a copy of the lab handout. This handout provides information about the phenomenon that the students will investigate and a guiding question for the students to answer. The handout also provides (1) hints for students to help them design their investigation in the Getting Started section, (2) information about what to include in their tentative argument, and (3) the requirements for the investigation report.

Safety Precautions

The "doing" of science activities through hands-on, process, and inquiry-based activities/experiments helps to foster the learning and understanding of science for students. However, for a safer experience, appropriate safety compliance procedures based on professional best practices and legal standards must be followed. Throughout this book, there are a series of "safety precautions," which help to make science a safer learning experience for students and their teachers.

Prior to starting any laboratory activities, teachers need to review and model general safety procedures with students. In addition, a safety acknowledgment form needs to be reviewed and signed by both the student and parents or guardians. Before each activity, applicable safety procedures must be reviewed with students. Note that in most cases, eye protection is required. Safety glasses and/or safety goggles noted must meet the ANSI Z87.1 safety standard.

For additional safety information, check out the NSTA "Safety in the Science Classroom" (*www.nsta.org/pdfs/SafetyInTheScienceClassroom.pdf*) and also at the NSTA Safety Portal (*www.nsta.org/portals/safety.aspx*).

Additional Information

Some lab investigations include additional information that students will need to use as part of their investigation. The additional information provides data that students will need during the investigation or supplemental information about the theory, model, law, or important concept at the heart of the investigation. We recommend that teachers make a class set of the additional information or provide one copy to each lab group.

Investigation Proposal

To help students design better investigations, we have developed and included three different types of investigation proposals in this book (see Appendix 3, p. 399). These investigation proposals are optional, but we have found that students design and carry out much better investigations when they are required to fill out a proposal and then get teacher feedback about their method before they begin. We provide recommendations in the Teacher Notes about which investigation proposal (A, B, or C) to use for a particular lab. If a teacher decides to use an investigation proposal as part of a lab, we recommend providing one copy for each group. The lab handout for students also has a heading "Investigation Proposal Required?" that is followed by boxes to check "yes" or "no." Teachers should be sure to have students check the appropriate box on the lab handout when introducing the lab activity.

Peer-Review Guide and Instructor Scoring Rubric

The peer-review guide and instructor scoring rubric (see Appendix 4, p. 403) is designed to make the criteria used to judge the quality of an investigation report explicit. We recommend that teachers make one copy for each student and then provide it to the students before they begin writing their investigation reports. This will ensure that students understand how they will be evaluated. During stage 7 of the model, each group should fill out the peer-review guide portion of the peer-review guide and instructor scoring rubric as they review the reports of their classmates (each group will need to review three or four different reports). The reviewers should rate the report on each criterion and provide advice to the author about ways to improve. Once the review is complete, the author needs to revise the report and respond to the reviewers' ratings and comments in the appropriate sections of the peer-review guide and instructor scoring rubric. The completed peer-review guide should be submitted to the teacher along with the final and first draft of the report for a final evaluation. To score the report, the teacher can simply fill out the instructor score column of the rubric and then total the scores.

Checkout Questions

To facilitate classroom assessment, we have included a set of checkout questions for each lab investigation. The questions target the key ideas, the crosscutting concepts, and the NOS/NOSI concepts addressed in the lab. Students should complete the checkout questions on the same day they turn in their final reports. One handout is needed for each student. The students should complete these questions on their own. Teacher can use the students' responses, along with the report, to determine if the students learned what they needed to during the lab, and then reteach as needed.

References

Abd-El-Khalick, F., and N. G. Lederman. 2000. Improving science teachers' conceptions of nature of science: A critical review of the literature. *International Journal of Science Education* 22: 665–701.

Grooms, J., V. Sampson, and P. Carafano. 2012. The impact of a new instructional model on high school science writing. Paper presented at the annual international conference of the American Educational Research Association.

Lederman, N. G., F. Abd-El-Khalick, R. L. Bell, and R. S. Schwartz. 2002. Views of nature of science questionnaire: Toward a valid and meaningful assessment of learners' conceptions of nature of science. *Journal of Research in Science Teaching* 39 (6): 497–521.

Lederman, J., N. Lederman, S. Bartos, S. Bartels, A. Meyer, and R. Schwartz. 2014. Meaningful assessment of learners' understanding about scientific inquiry: The Views About Scientific Inquiry (VASI) questionnaire. *Journal of Research in Science Teaching* 51 (1): 65–83.

National Governors Association Center for Best Practices and Council of Chief State School Officers (NGAC and CCSSO). 2010. *Common core state standards.* Washington, DC: NGAC and CCSSO.

National Research Council (NRC). 2012. *A framework for K–12 science education: Practices, crosscutting concepts, and core ideas.* Washington, DC: National Academies Press.

Sampson, V., P. Enderle, M. Hester, and J. Grooms. 2012. The development of science proficiency through argument focused lab instruction in high school biology. Paper presented at the annual international conference of the American Educational Research Association.

Sampson, V., P. Enderle, J. Grooms, and S. Witte. 2013. Writing to learn and learning to write during the school science laboratory: Helping middle and high school students develop argumentative writing skills as they learn core ideas. *Science Education* 97 (5): 643–670.

Sampson, V., J. Grooms, and P. Enderle. 2012. Using laboratory activities that emphasize argumentation and argument to help high school students learn how to engage in scientific inquiry and understand the nature of scientific inquiry. Paper presented at the annual international conference of the National Association for Research in Science Teaching.

SECTION 2

Life Sciences Core Idea 1:

From Molecules to Organisms: Structures and Processes

Introduction Lab

Lab 1. Osmosis and Diffusion: Why Do Red Blood Cells Appear Bigger After Being Exposed to Distilled Water?

Teacher Notes

Purpose

The purpose of this lab investigation is to *introduce* the concept of osmosis and help students understand why red blood cells placed in distilled water swell. This lab investigation will also help students learn how to design a controlled experiment to test alternative hypotheses. Students will also learn about the nature of experimentation in science and the difference between data and evidence.

The Content

The red blood cells appear bigger when placed in distilled water because the cells fill with additional molecules of water. The water molecules move into the cells because the relative concentration of water molecules is higher outside the cells than it is inside the cells. Water can pass through the dialysis tubing but the molecules of starch cannot. As a result, there is a net movement of water into the cells until an equilibrium point is reached. The net movement of water from an area of higher concentration to an area of lower concentration is called osmosis.

Timeline

The instructional time needed to implement this lab investigation is 180–250 minutes. Appendix 2 (p. 391) provides options for implementing this lab investigation over several class periods. Option A (250 minutes) should be used if students are unfamiliar with scientific writing because this option provides extra instructional time for scaffolding the writing process. You can scaffold the writing process by modeling, providing examples, and providing hints as students write each section of the report. Option B (180 minutes) should be used if students are familiar with scientific writing and have the skills needed to write an investigation report on their own. In option B, students complete stage 6 (writing the investigation report) and stage 8 (revising the report) as homework.

Materials and Preparation

The materials needed to implement this investigation are listed in the Table 1.1. The dialysis tubing should be soaked at least 30 minutes prior to use. It is helpful to have a piece of dialysis tubing soaking, to show students how to make a model of a cell during the tool talk. If supplies are sufficient, each group can be allowed to cut their own pieces of tubing; if supplies are limited, each group can be given a section of dialysis tubing. You should prepare a starch solution for students to use. To make the solution, simply add water-soluble starch to warm water. The solution should be fairly concentrated, but a specific concentration is not necessary.

TABLE 1.1
Materials list

Item	Quantity
Starch solution	1 L per class
Distilled water	1 L per class
Beaker, 250 ml	4 per group
Graduated cylinder, 25 ml	1 per group
Balance (electronic or triple beam)	1 per group
Dialysis tubing, 22 mm diameter	40 cm per group
Student handout	1 per student
Investigation proposal A*	1 per group
Whiteboard, 2' × 3'†	1 per group
Peer-review guide and instructor scoring rubric	1 per student
Safety goggles and apron	1 per student

* It is recommended but not required that students fill out an investigation proposal for this lab; it is not necessary to do so if students already know how to design a controlled experiment.

† As an alternative, students can use computer and presentation software such as Microsoft PowerPoint or Apple Keynote to create their arguments.

Topics for the Explicit and Reflective Discussion

Concepts That Can Be Used to Justify the Evidence

To provide an adequate justification of their evidence, students must explain why they included the evidence in their arguments and make the assumptions underlying their analysis and interpretation of the data explicit. In this investigation, students can use the following concepts to help justify their evidence:

- Matter has mass.
- Matter is composed of atoms that are in constantly in motion.

- Atoms (or molecules) tend to diffuse from areas of high concentration to areas of low concentration.

We recommend that you review these concepts during the explicit and reflective discussion to help students make this connection.

How to Design Better Investigations

It is important for students to reflect on the strengths and weaknesses of the investigations they designed during the explicit and reflective discussion. Students should therefore be encouraged to discuss ways to eliminate potential flaws, measurement errors, or sources of bias in their investigations. To help students be more reflective about the design of their investigations, you can ask the following questions:

- What were some of the strengths of your investigation? What made it scientific?
- What were some of the weaknesses of your investigation? What made it less scientific?
- If you were to do this investigation again, what would you do to address the weaknesses in your investigation? What could you do to make it more scientific?

Crosscutting Concepts

This investigation is well aligned with three crosscutting concepts found in *A Framework for K–12 Science Education,* and you should review these concepts during the explicit and reflective discussion.

- *Cause and Effect: Mechanism and Explanation:* Natural phenomena have causes, and uncovering causal relationships (e.g., how changes in environmental conditions influence the size of cells) is a major activity of science.
- *Systems and System Models:* Students need to understand that defining a system under study and making a model of it are tools for developing a better understanding of natural phenomena in science.
- *Energy and Matter: Flows, Cycles, and Conservation:* Students should realize that in science it is important to track how energy and matter move into, out of, and within systems.

The Nature of Science and the Nature of Scientific Inquiry

It is important for students to understand the *nature and role of experiments in science.* Scientists use experiments to test the validity of a hypothesis (i.e., a tentative explanation) for an observed phenomenon. Experiments include a test and the formulation of predictions (expected results) if the test is conducted and the hypothesis is valid. The experiment is then carried out and the predictions are compared with the observed results of the experiment. If the predictions match the observed results, then the hypothesis is supported. If the observed results do not match the prediction, then the hypothesis is not supported. A signature feature of an experiment is the control of variables to help eliminate alternative explanations for observed results.

It is also important for students to understand the *difference between data and evidence in science.* Data are measurements, observations, and findings from other studies that are collected as part of an investigation. Evidence, in contrast, is analyzed data and an interpretation of the analysis.

You should review and provide examples of these two important concepts of the nature of science (NOS) and the nature of scientific inquiry (NOSI) during the explicit and reflective discussion.

Hints for Implementing the Lab

- During the experimental design phase, students should be encouraged to think about the number of cells they are using, the size of the cells they are using, and the amount of solution they are going to use. The number of cells for each treatment and the size of cells should be consistent. Have them measure their pieces of dialysis tubing. The amount of solutions should be consistent, particularly those that are added to the dialysis tubing.
- Dialysis tubing clips are available that would eliminate the need for tying the tubes.
- For best results, students should let the cells soak for at least 30 minutes. The cells can also be left to soak overnight.
- Some cells may lose mass because of poor design issues (e.g., not a tight seal when tying or clipping). This is a great teachable moment during the argumentation session. Students whose cells lose mass will struggle to understand their findings, and when viewing other groups' presentations, they will see their group's results as an outlier and may not understand why. It is important to ensure that your classroom is a respectful scientific community and that students understand that design flaws are a part of science; this is an opportunity to emphasize the importance of conducting multiple trials and sharing findings, to help catch flaws in investigations.
- Some students will still try to argue the validity of the first explanation on the student handout (i.e., that molecules such as proteins and starch inside the cell push on the cell membranes and make the cells appear larger) even when their cells increase in mass. This is an excellent context with which to address confirmation bias in science.

Topic Connections

Table 1.2 provides an overview of the scientific practices, crosscutting concepts, disciplinary core ideas, and supporting ideas at the heart of this lab investigation. In addition, it lists NOS and NOSI concepts for the explicit and reflective discussion. Finally, it lists literacy and mathematics skills (*CCSS ELA* and *CCSS Mathematics*) that are addressed during the investigation.

TABLE 1.2

Lab 1 alignment with standards

Scientific practices	• Asking questions • Developing and using models • Planning and carrying out investigations • Analyzing and interpreting data • Using mathematics and computational thinking • Constructing explanations • Engaging in argument from evidence • Obtaining, evaluating, and communicating information
Crosscutting concepts	• Cause and effect: Mechanism and explanation • Systems and system models • Energy and matter: Flows, cycles, and conservation
Core idea	• LS1: From molecules to organisms: Structures and processes
Supporting ideas	• Osmosis • Diffusion • Cell membranes • Molecular-kinetic theory of matter
NOS and NOSI concepts	• Nature and role of experiments • Difference between data and evidence
Literacy connections *(CCSS ELA)*	• *Reading*: Key ideas and details, craft and structure, integration of knowledge and ideas • *Writing*: Text types and purposes, production and distribution of writing, research to build and present knowledge, range of writing • *Speaking and listening*: Comprehension and collaboration, presentation of knowledge and ideas
Mathematics connection *(CCSS Mathematics)*	• Reason quantitatively and use units to solve problems

Lab 1. Osmosis and Diffusion: Why Do Red Blood Cells Appear Bigger After Being Exposed to Distilled Water?

Lab Handout

Introduction

All living things are made of cells. Some organisms, such as bacteria, are *unicellular,* which means they consist of a single cell. Other organisms, such as humans, fish, and plants, are *multicellular,* which means they consist of many cells. All cells have some parts in common. One part found in all cells is the *cell membrane.* The cell membrane surrounds the cell, holds the other parts of the cell in place, and protects the cell. Molecules such as oxygen, water, and carbon dioxide can pass in and out of the cell membrane. All cells also contain *cytoplasm.* The cytoplasm is a jelly-like substance inside the cell where most of the cell's activities take place. It's made out of water and other chemicals.

Some cells found in multicellular organisms are highly specialized and carry out very specific functions. An example of a specialized cell found in vertebrates is the erythrocyte, or red blood cell (RBC). RBCs are by far the most abundant cells in the blood. The primary function of RBCs is to transport oxygen from the lungs to the cells of the body. In the capillaries, the oxygen is released so other cells can use it. Ninety-seven percent of the oxygen that is carried by the blood from the lungs is carried by hemoglobin; the other 3% is dissolved in the plasma. Hemoglobin allows the blood to transport 30–100 times more oxygen than could be dissolved in the plasma alone.

As you can see in the figure to the right, RBCs look like little discs when they are viewed under a microscope. They have no nucleus (the nucleus is extruded from the cell as it matures to make room for more hemoglobin). A unique feature of RBCs is that they can change shape; this ability allows them to squeeze through capillaries without breaking. RBCs will also change shape in response to changes in the environment. For example, if you add a few drops of distilled water to blood on a microscope slide, the cells will look bigger after a few seconds (see the figure's right panel).

Red blood cells before and after distilled water is added

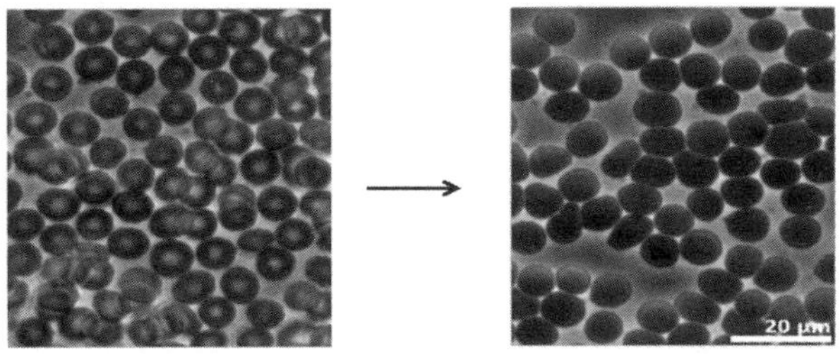

Red blood cells ***before*** adding distilled water

Red blood cells ***after*** adding distilled water

Scientists often develop and test explanations for natural phenomena. In this investigation you will have an opportunity to design and carry out an experiment to test two different explanations for why RBCs appear bigger after they are exposed to distilled water. These are the two explanations that you will test:

1. Molecules such as protein and polysaccharides are more concentrated inside the cell than outside the cell when the cell is in distilled water. These molecules therefore begin to move out of the cell because of the process of diffusion but are blocked by the cell membrane. As a result, these molecules push on the cell membrane and make the cell appear bigger.
2. Water molecules move into the cell because the concentration of water is greater outside the cell than it is inside the cell. As a result, water fills the cell and makes it appear bigger.

Your Task

Design and carry out an experiment to determine which of the two explanations about the appearance of RBCs after exposure to distilled water is the most valid or acceptable from a scientific perspective.

The guiding question of this investigation is, **Why do the red blood cells appear bigger after being exposed to distilled water?**

Materials

You may use any of the following materials during your investigation:

- Starch solution (starch is a polysaccharide)
- Distilled water
- Beakers
- Graduated cylinder
- Balance (electronic or triple beam)
- Dialysis tubing (assume that it behaves just like the membranes of RBCs)
- Safety goggles
- Aprons

Safety Precautions

1. Indirectly vented chemical-splash goggles and aprons are required for this activity.
2. Wash hands with soap and water after completing this lab.
3. Follow all normal lab safety rules.

Getting Started

You will use models of cells rather than real cells during your experiment. You will use cell models for two reasons: (1) a model of a cell is much larger than a real cell, which makes the process of data collection much easier; and (2) you can create your cell models in any way you see fit, which makes it easier to control for a wide range of variables during your experiment. The cell models will therefore allow you to design a more informative test of the two alternative explanations outlined above.

Tying the dialysis tubing

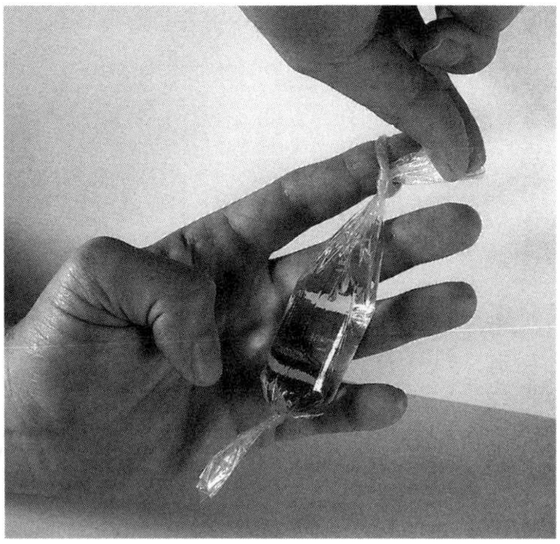

You can construct a model cell by using the dialysis tubing. Dialysis tubing behaves much like a cell membrane. To create a model of a cell, place the dialysis tubing in water until it is thoroughly soaked. Remove the soaked tubing from the water and tightly twist one end several times and either tie with string or tie a knot in the tubing. You can then fill the model cell with either a starch solution (starch is a common polysaccharide) or distilled water. Once filled, twist the open end several times and tie it tightly as shown in the figure. You can then dry the bag and place it into any type of solution you need.

In designing your experiment, you must determine what type of data you will need to collect, how you will collect it, and how you will analyze it. To determine *what type of data you will need to collect,* think about the following questions:

- What will serve as your dependent variable (e.g., mass of the cell or size of the cell)?
- What type of measurements will you need to make during your investigation?

To determine *how you will collect your data,* think about the following questions:

- What will serve as a control (or comparison) condition?
- What types of treatment conditions will you need to set up and how will you do it?
- How many "cells" will you need to use in each condition?
- How often will you collect data and when will you do it?
- How will you make sure that your data are of high quality (i.e., how will you reduce error)?
- How will you keep track of the data you collect and how will you organize the data?

To determine *how you will analyze your data,* think about the following questions:

- How will you determine if there is a difference between the treatment conditions and the control condition?
- What type of calculations will you need to make?
- What type of graph could you create to help make sense of your data?

Investigation Proposal Required? ☐ Yes ☐ No

Connections to Crosscutting Concepts and to the Nature of Science and the Nature of Scientific Inquiry

As you work through your investigation, be sure to think about

- the importance of identifying the underlying cause for observations,
- how models are used to study natural phenomena,
- how matter moves within or through a system,
- the difference between data and evidence in science, and
- the nature and role of experiments in science.

Argumentation Session

Once your group has finished collecting and analyzing your data, prepare a whiteboard that you can use to share your initial argument. Your whiteboard should include all the information shown in the figure below.

Argument presentation on a whiteboard

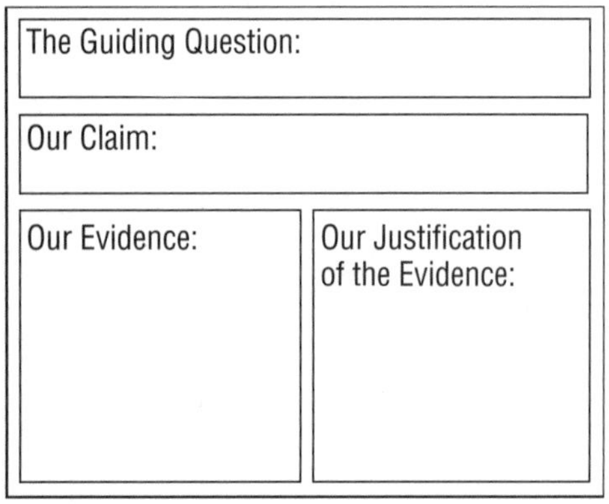

To share your argument with others, we will be using a round-robin format. This means that one member of your group will stay at your lab station to share your group's argument while the other members of your group go to the other lab stations one at a time to listen to and critique the arguments developed by your classmates.

The goal of the argumentation session is not to convince others that your argument is the best one; rather, the goal is to identify errors or instances of faulty reasoning in the arguments so these mistakes can be fixed. You will therefore need to evaluate the content of the claim, the quality of the evidence used to support the claim, and the strength of the justification of the evidence included in each argument that you see. In order to critique an argument, you will need more information than what is included on the whiteboard. You might, therefore, need to ask the presenter one or more follow-up questions, such as:

- How did you collect your data? Why did you use that method? Why did you collect those data?
- What did you do to make sure the data you collected are reliable? What did you do to decrease measurement error?
- What did you do to analyze your data? Why did you decide to do it that way? Did you check your calculations?
- Is that the only way to interpret the results of your analysis? How do you know that your interpretation of your analysis is appropriate?
- Why did your group decide to present your evidence in that manner?
- What other claims did your group discuss before you decided on that one? Why did your group abandon those alternative ideas?
- How confident are you that your claim is valid? What could you do to increase your confidence?

Once the argumentation session is complete, you will have a chance to meet with your group and revise your original argument. Your group might need to gather more data or design a way to test one or more alternative claims as part of this process. Remember, your goal at this stage of the investigation is to develop the most valid or acceptable answer to the research question!

Report

Once you have completed your research, you will need to prepare an ***investigation report*** that consists of three sections that provide answers to the following questions:

1. What question were you trying to answer and why?
2. What did you do during your investigation and why did you conduct your investigation in this way?
3. What is your argument?

Your report should answer these questions in two pages or less. This report must be typed, and any diagrams, figures, or tables should be embedded into the document. Be sure to write in a persuasive style; you are trying to convince others that your claim is acceptable or valid!

Lab 1. Osmosis and Diffusion: Why Do Red Blood Cells Appear Bigger After Being Exposed to Distilled Water?

Checkout Questions

1. A model cell that contains a concentrated starch solution is placed in a beaker of distilled water. Below, complete the illustration of how this will affect the **size** of the model cell. Be sure to explain how this will affect the **mass** of the model cell.

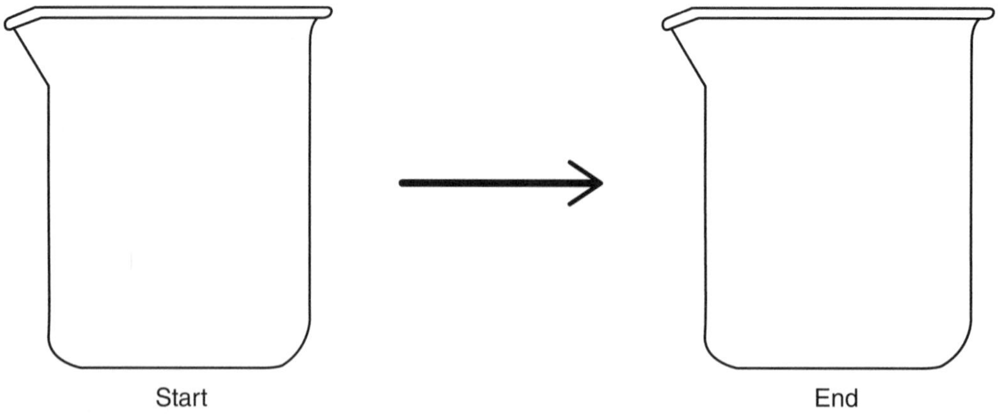

2. Observations are an example of data.

   a. I agree with this statement.
   b. I disagree with this statement.

   Explain your answer.

3. The investigation that you just completed is an example of an experiment.

   a. I agree with this statement.
   b. I disagree with this statement.

   Explain your answer, using information from your investigation about osmosis and diffusion.

4. Scientists often try to explain the underlying cause for their observations. Explain why this is important, using an example from your investigation about osmosis and diffusion.

5. Scientists often use models to help them understand natural phenomena. Explain what a model is and why models are important, using an example from your investigation about osmosis and diffusion.

6. Scientists often track how matter moves within or through a system they are studying. Explain why, using an example from your investigation about osmosis and diffusion.

Application Labs

Lab 2. Cell Structure: How Should the Unknown Microscopic Organism Be Classified?

Teacher Notes

Purpose

The purpose of this lab investigation is for students to *apply* what they know about the characteristics of plant and animal cells to classify an unknown single-celled organism (from the genus *Euglena*). This investigation can also be used to ***introduce*** students to different single-celled organisms, the traits these organisms share, how these organisms are classified, or challenges related to biological classification. Students will also learn about the various types of investigations that can be designed and carried out in science and about the important role that creativity and imagination play in science.

The Content

Euglena is a genus of single-celled eukaryotic organisms. These organisms are not classified as members of the animal kingdom because they have chloroplasts and are autotrophic; neither are they classified as members of the plant kingdom because they can absorb food from their environment, which makes them heterotrophic as well as autotrophic. Organisms that are members of the genus *Euglena* also lack a rigid cell wall, which is a characteristic of plant cells. Because these organisms have features of both animals and plants, early taxonomists found them difficult to classify using the original Linnaean two-kingdom biological classification system. In the late 19th century Ernst Haeckel added a third kingdom (Protista) to the original Linnaean system to help classify these organisms. Today, this kingdom Protista has been split even further to reflect the unique characteristics of eukaryotic organisms that are either unicellular or multicellular but lack specialized tissues.

Timeline

The instructional time needed to implement this lab investigation is 180–250 minutes. Appendix 2 (p. 391) provides options for implementing this lab investigation over several class periods. Option A (250 minutes) should be used if students are unfamiliar with scientific writing because this option provides extra instructional time for scaffolding the writing process. You can scaffold the writing process by modeling, providing examples, and providing hints as students write each section of the report. Option B (180 minutes) should be used if students are familiar with scientific writing and have the skills needed to write an investigation report on their own. In option B, students complete stage 6 (writing the investigation report) and stage 8 (revising the investigation report) as homework.

Materials and Preparation

The materials needed to implement this investigation are listed in Table 2.1. Each group will need a set of the known slides and the unknown slide. Label slides clearly; masking tape works well for this. If supplies are sufficient, each group can be given a slide set; if supplies are limited, the known slides can be shared. If using live specimens, slides can be prepared before the lab to save time. There are also special types of slides that are specifically made for looking at live specimens under a light microscope. If available, microscope cameras add another dimension to data collection. Students can take pictures of their slides as opposed to just drawing their observations.

TABLE 2.1

Materials list

Item	Quantity
Known slide A (plant cells)	1 per group
Known slide B (plant cells)	1 per group
Known slide C (animal cells)	1 per group
Known slide D (animal cells)	1 per group
Slide with an unknown organism (Euglena)	1 per group
Microscope	1–2 per group
Digital microscope camera (optional)	1 per class
Student handout	1 per student
Investigation proposal C*	1 per group
Whiteboard, 2' × 3'†	1 per group
Peer-review guide and instructor scoring rubric	1 per student

* It is recommended, but not required, that students fill out an investigation proposal for this lab; it is not necessary to do so if students already know how to design a controlled experiment.

† As an alternative, students can use computer and presentation software such as Microsoft PowerPoint or Apple Keynote to create their arguments.

Topics for the Explicit and Reflective Discussion

Concepts That Can Be Used to Justify the Evidence

To provide an adequate justification of their evidence, students must explain why they included the evidence in their arguments and make the assumptions underlying their analysis and interpretation of the data explicit. In this investigation, students will need to know the characteristics of plant and animal cells and how differences in structure can be used to classify an organism. We recommend that you review these concepts during the explicit and reflective discussion to help students make this connection.

How to Design Better Investigations

It is important for students to reflect on the strengths and weaknesses of the investigation they designed during the explicit and reflective discussion. Students should therefore be encouraged to discuss ways to eliminate potential flaws, measurement errors, or sources of bias in their investigations. To help students be more reflective about the design of their investigation, you can ask the following questions:

- What were some of the strengths of your investigation? What made it scientific?
- What were some of the weaknesses of your investigation? What made it less scientific?
- If you were to do this investigation again, what would you do to address the weaknesses in your investigation? What could you do to make it more scientific?

Crosscutting Concepts

This investigation is aligned with two crosscutting concepts found in *A Framework for K–12 Science Education,* and you should review these concepts during the explicit and reflective discussion.

- *Patterns:* Observed patterns in nature (e.g., all living things are composed of at least one cell) guide organization and classification systems in biology.
- *Structure and Function:* In nature, the way a living thing is structured or shaped determines how it functions and places limits on what it can and cannot do.

The Nature of Science and the Nature of Scientific Inquiry

It is important for students to understand that *scientists use different methods to answer different types of questions*. Examples of methods include experiments, systematic observations of a phenomenon, literature reviews, and analysis of existing data sets; the choice of method depends on the objectives of the research. There is no universal step-by-step scientific method that all scientists follow; rather, different scientific disciplines (e.g., biology vs. physics) and fields within a discipline (e.g., ecology vs. molecular biology) use different types of methods, use different core theories, and rely on different standards to develop scientific knowledge.

It is also important for students to understand that *science requires imagination and creativity.* Students should learn that developing explanations for or models of natural phenomena and then figuring out how they can be put to the test of reality is as creative as writing poetry, composing music, or designing skyscrapers. Scientists must also use their imagination and creativity to figure out new ways to test ideas and collect or analyze data.

You should review and provide examples of these two important concepts of the nature of science (NOS) and the nature of scientific inquiry (NOSI) during the explicit and reflective discussion.

Hints for Implementing the Lab

- Make sure that the known animal and plant slides are very clear and defined as to their cell type. The following cells are recommended:
  - Plant cells: onion root tip cell, lettuce leaves, elodea
  - Animal cells: human cheek cell, human kidney, fish egg development
- Students should know how to use a microscope before beginning their investigations.
- You should circulate frequently as students are making observations with the microscopes to ensure that they are looking at actual specimens rather than air bubbles or dust.

Topic Connections

Table 2.2 provides an overview of the scientific practices, crosscutting concepts, disciplinary core ideas, and supporting ideas at the heart of this lab investigation. In addition, it lists NOS and NOSI concepts for the explicit and reflective discussion. Finally, it lists literacy skills (*CCSS ELA*) that are addressed during the investigation.

TABLE 2.2

Lab 2 alignment with standards

Scientific practices	• Asking questions • Developing and using models • Planning and carrying out investigations • Analyzing and interpreting data • Constructing explanations • Engaging in argument from evidence • Obtaining, evaluating, and communicating information
Crosscutting concepts	• Patterns • Structure and function
Core idea	• LS1: From molecules to organisms: Structures and processes
Supporting ideas	• Animal cell • Plant cell • Organelles • Biological classification
NOS and NOSI concepts	• Methods used in scientific investigations • Imagination and creativity in science
Literacy connections *(CCSS ELA)*	• *Reading*: Key ideas and details, craft and structure, integration of knowledge and ideas • *Writing*: Text types and purposes, production and distribution of writing, research to build and present knowledge, range of writing • *Speaking and listening*: Comprehension and collaboration, presentation of knowledge and ideas

Lab 2. Cell Structure: How Should the Unknown Microscopic Organism Be Classified?

Lab Handout

Introduction

Plant and animal cells have many organelles in common, including the nucleus, nucleolus, nuclear envelope, rough and smooth endoplasmic reticulum, Golgi apparatus, ribosomes, cell membrane, and mitochondria. Some organelles found in plant cells, however, are not found in animal cells and vice versa. For example, animal cells have centrioles (which help organize cell division in animal cells), but plant cells do not. These differences can be used to distinguish between cells that come from a plant and cells that come from an animal. The figure to the right shows animal cells from the inside of a human cheek.

Human cheek cells

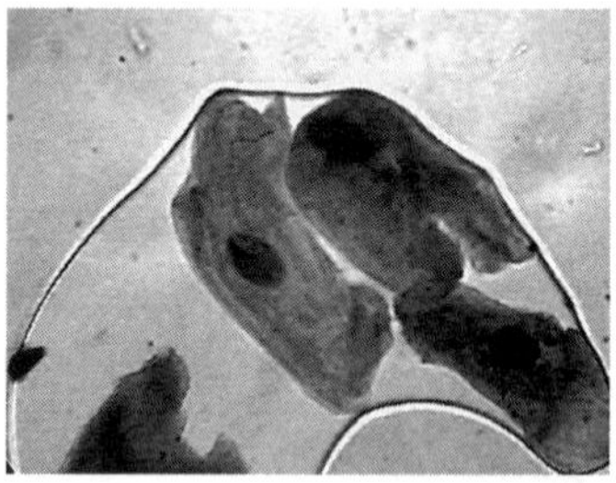

Your Task

Document the traits of an unknown microscopic organism. Then classify it based on what you know about the characteristics of plant and animal cells.

The guiding question of this investigation is, **How should the unknown microscopic organism be classified?**

Materials

You may use any of the following materials during your investigation:

- Known slide A (plant cells)
- Known slide B (plant cells)
- Known slide C (animal cells)
- Known slide D (animal cells)
- Slide with an unknown organism
- Microscope

Safety Precautions

1. Glass slides can have sharp edges—handle with care to prevent cutting of skin.

2. Use caution when working with electrical equipment. Keep away from water sources in that they can cause shorts, fires, and shock hazards. Use only GFI-protected circuits.
3. Wash hands with soap and water after completing this lab.
4. Follow all normal lab safety rules.

Getting Started

To answer the guiding question, you will need to conduct a systematic observation of the cell samples provided. To accomplish this task, you must first determine what type of data you will need to collect, how you will collect it, and how you will analyze it. To determine *what type of data you will need to collect,* think about the following questions:

- What type of measurements or observations will you need to make during your investigation?
- How will you quantify any differences or similarities you observe in the different cells?

To determine *how you will collect your data,* think about the following questions:

- How will you make sure that your data are of high quality (i.e., how will you reduce error)?
- How will you keep track of the data you collect and how will you organize the data?

To determine *how you will analyze your data,* think about the following questions:

- How will you define the different categories of cells (e.g., what makes a plant cell a plant cell, what makes an animal cell an animal cell)?
- What type of calculations will you need to make?
- What type of graph could you create to help make sense of your data?

Investigation Proposal Required? ☐ Yes ☐ No

Connections to Crosscutting Concepts and to the Nature of Science and the Nature of Scientific Inquiry

As you work through your investigation, be sure to think about

- the importance of looking for patterns during an investigation,
- how structure is related to function in organisms,
- the different type of methods that are used to answer research questions in science, and

- the importance of imagination and creativity in science.

Argumentation Session

Once your group has finished collecting and analyzing your data, prepare a whiteboard that you can use to share your initial argument. Your whiteboard should include all the information shown in the figure below.

Argument presentation on a whiteboard

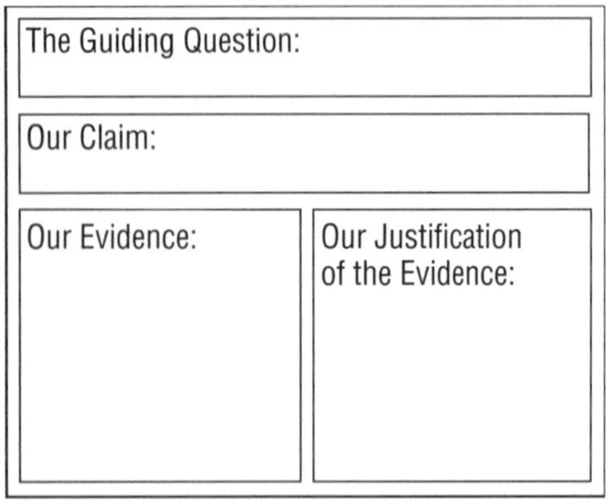

To share your argument with others, we will be using a round-robin format. This means that one member of your group will stay at your lab station to share your group's argument while the other members of your group go to the other lab stations one at a time to listen to and critique the arguments developed by your classmates.

The goal of the argumentation session is not to convince others that your argument is the best one; rather, the goal is to identify errors or instances of faulty reasoning in the arguments so these mistakes can be fixed. You will therefore need to evaluate the content of the claim, the quality of the evidence used to support the claim, and the strength of the justification of the evidence included in each argument that you see. In order to critique an argument, you will need more information than what is included on the whiteboard. You might, therefore, need to ask the presenter one or more follow-up questions, such as How did you collect your data? Why did you use that method? Why did you collect those data?

- What did you do to make sure the data you collected are reliable? What did you do to decrease measurement error?
- What did you do to analyze your data? Why did you decide to do it that way?
- Is that the only way to interpret the results of your analysis? How do you know that your interpretation of your analysis is appropriate?
- Why did your group decide to present your evidence in that manner?
- What other claims did your group discuss before you decided on that one? Why did your group abandon those alternative ideas?
- How confident are you that your claim is valid? What could you do to increase your confidence?

Once the argumentation session is complete, you will have a chance to meet with your group and revise your original argument. Your group might need to gather more data or design a way to test one or more alternative claims as part of this process. Remember, your

goal at this stage of the investigation is to develop the most valid or acceptable answer to the research question!

Report

Once you have completed your research, you will need to prepare an ***investigation report*** that consists of three sections that provide answers to the following questions:

1. What question were you trying to answer and why?
2. What did you do during your investigation and why did you conduct your investigation in this way?
3. What is your argument?

Your report should answer these questions in two pages or less. This report must be typed, and any diagrams, figures, or tables should be embedded into the document. Be sure to write in a persuasive style; you are trying to convince others that your claim is acceptable or valid!

Lab 2. Cell Structure: How Should the Unknown Microscopic Organism Be Classified?

Checkout Questions

1. As a biologist working for NASA you are given the task of looking for microscopic life forms on rocks brought back from Mars. Upon further investigation with a microscope, you find what you think are cells. These objects have a round shape with a defined outer boundary, a small dark-colored object in the center, and a long tail-like structure on the outside. How would you classify this object?

    a. It is an animal cell.
    b. It is a plant cell.
    c. There is not enough information to classify it.

    Why?

2. All scientists follow the same step-by-step method during an investigation.

    a. I agree with this statement.
    b. I disagree with this statement.

    Explain your answer, using information from your investigation about cell structure.

3. There is no room for imagination or creativity in science.

   a. I agree with this statement.
   b. I disagree with this statement.

   Explain your answer, using information from your investigation about cell structure.

4. Scientists often look for patterns in nature. Explain why this is important, using an example from your investigation about cell structure.

5. Scientists can learn a great deal about how an organism lives by looking at its structure. Explain why, using an example from your investigation about cell structure.

Lab 3. Cell Cycle: Do Plant and Animal Cells Spend the Same Proportion of Time in Each Stage of the Cell Cycle?

Teacher Notes

Purpose

The purpose of this lab investigation is for students to *apply* what they know about the process of cell division to determine the proportion of time animal and plant cells spend in each phase of the cell cycle. Students will also learn about the difference between an observation and an inference and about the tentative but durable nature of scientific knowledge.

The Content

There is no significant difference between animal cells and plant cells in terms of the proportion of time spent in each stage of the cell cycle. The amount of time a cell spends in the various stages of cell division, however, is highly dependent on the function of the cell, the location of the cell, or the developmental stage of the organism. Both onion root tips and whitefish blastulae are areas of rapid cell division in that these are actively growing segments of each organism. Thus, it is expected that numerous cells will be undergoing the process of cell division. However, regardless of the type of tissue, the highest proportion of time is still spent in the interphase stage.

Timeline

The instructional time needed to implement this lab investigation is 130–200 minutes. Appendix 2 (p. 391) provides options for implementing this lab investigation over several class periods. Option C (200 minutes) should be used if students are unfamiliar with scientific writing because this option provides extra instructional time for scaffolding the writing process. You can scaffold the writing process by modeling, providing examples, and providing hints as students write each section of the report. Option D (130 minutes) should be used if students are familiar with scientific writing and have the skills needed to write an investigation report on their own. In option D, students complete stage 6 (writing the investigation report) and stage 8 (revising the investigation report) as homework.

Materials and Preparation

The materials needed to implement this investigation are listed in Table 3.1. Each group will need a set of slides, but the slides can be shared if supplies are limited. A microscope for every two students is preferred. Students should be familiar with how to use a microscope before the lab. If they are not familiar with it, be sure to teach students the skills they need as part of the investigation or as a stand-alone lesson before the lab.

If available, microscope cameras add another dimension to data collection. Students can take pictures of their slides; this will reduce the size of their field of view and actually make counting cells easier.

TABLE 3.1

Materials list

Item	Quantity
Prepared slide from an onion root tip	1 per group
Prepared slide from a whitefish blastula	1 per group
Microscope	1–2 per group
Student handout	1 per student
Whiteboard, 2' × 3'*	1 per group
Peer-review guide and instructor scoring rubric	1 per student

* As an alternative, students can use computer and presentation software such as Microsoft PowerPoint or Apple Keynote to create their arguments.

Topics for the Explicit and Reflective Discussion

Concepts That Can Be Used to Justify the Evidence

To provide an adequate justification of their evidence, students must explain why they included the evidence in their arguments and make the assumptions underlying their analysis and interpretation of the data explicit. In this investigation, students can use the following concepts to help justify their evidence:

- Eukaryotic cells go through the same phases during the process of mitosis.
- The portion of cells in each phase of mitosis should correspond closely with the amount of time spent by each cell in each phase.
- A sample of cells can be used to infer the characteristics of the whole organism.

We recommend that you review these concepts during the explicit and reflective discussion to help students make this connection.

How to Design Better Investigations

It is important for students to reflect on the strengths and weaknesses of the investigation they designed during the explicit and reflective discussion. Students should therefore be encouraged to discuss ways to eliminate potential flaws, measurement errors, or sources of bias in their investigations. To help students be more reflective about the design of their investigation, you can ask the following questions:

- What were some of the strengths of your investigation? What made it scientific?
- What were some of the weaknesses of your investigation? What made it less scientific?
- If you were to do this investigation again, what would you do to address the weaknesses in your investigation? What could you do to make it more scientific?

Crosscutting Concepts

This investigation is aligned with three crosscutting concepts found in *A Framework for K–12 Science Education,* and you should review these concepts during the explicit and reflective discussion.

- *Patterns:* Observed patterns in nature, such as how all eukaryotic cells go through the same stages of cell division, guide the way scientists organize and classify life on Earth. Scientists also explore the relationships between and the underlying causes of the patterns they observe in nature.
- *Scale, Proportion, and Quantity:* Students need to understand that it is critical for scientists to be able to recognize what is relevant at different sizes, time frames, and scales. Scientists must also be able to recognize proportional relationships between categories or quantities.
- *Stability and Change:* In nature, many living things go through a period of stability followed by a period of rapid change. The cell cycle is an example of this phenomenon.

The Nature of Science and the Nature of Scientific Inquiry

It is important for students to understand the *difference between observations and inferences in science.* An observation is a descriptive statement about a natural phenomenon, whereas an inference is an interpretation of an observation. Students should also understand that current scientific knowledge and the perspectives of individual scientists guide both observations and inferences. Thus, different scientists can have different but equally valid interpretations of the same observations due to differences in their perspectives and background knowledge.

It is also important for students to understand that *scientific knowledge can change over time.* A person can have confidence in the validity of scientific knowledge but must also accept that scientific knowledge may be abandoned or modified in light of new evidence or because existing evidence has been reconceptualized by scientists. There are many examples in the history of science of both evolutionary changes (i.e., the slow or gradual refinement of ideas) and revolutionary changes (i.e., the rapid abandonment of a well-established idea) in scientific knowledge.

You should review and provide examples of these two important concepts of the nature of science (NOS) and the nature of scientific inquiry (NOSI) during the explicit and reflective discussion.

Hints for Implementing the Lab

- You should circulate among the groups as students are making observations to ensure they are looking at actual cells and not air bubbles or dust.

- Encourage students to use a higher magnification when they are collecting data; it reduces the field of view, making counting cells easier.
- You can have students use a chi-square test to determine if observed differences in frequency counts are statistically significant.

Topic Connections

Table 3.2 provides an overview of the scientific practices, crosscutting concepts, disciplinary core ideas, and supporting ideas at the heart of this lab investigation. In addition, it lists NOS and NOSI concepts for the explicit and reflective discussion. Finally, it lists literacy and mathematics skills (*CCSS ELA* and *CCSS Mathematics*) that are addressed during the investigation.

TABLE 3.2

Lab 3 alignment with standards

Scientific practices	• Asking questions • Planning and carrying out investigations • Analyzing and interpreting data • Using mathematics and computational thinking • Constructing explanations • Engaging in argument from evidence • Obtaining, evaluating, and communicating information
Crosscutting concepts	• Patterns • Scale, proportion, and quantity • Stability and change
Core idea	• LS1: From molecules to organisms: Structures and processes
Supporting ideas	• Cell division • Cell types
NOS and NOSI concepts	• Observations and inferences • Science as a body of knowledge
Literacy connections *(CCSS ELA)*	• *Reading*: Key ideas and details, craft and structure, integration of knowledge and ideas • *Writing*: Text types and purposes, production and distribution of writing, research to build and present knowledge, range of writing • *Speaking and listening*: Comprehension and collaboration, presentation of knowledge and ideas
Mathematics connections *(CCSS Mathematics)*	• Create equations that describe numbers or relationships • Solve equations and inequalitities in one variable • Reason quantitatively and use units to solve problems

Lab 3. Cell Cycle: Do Plant and Animal Cells Spend the Same Proportion of Time in Each Stage of the Cell Cycle?

Lab Handout

Introduction

The cell cycle is an important process, and we need to understand it to appreciate how animals and plants are able to grow, heal, and reproduce. The figure below provides pictures of plant and animal cells in various stages of the cell cycle.

The cell cycle of (a) plant cells and (b) animal cells

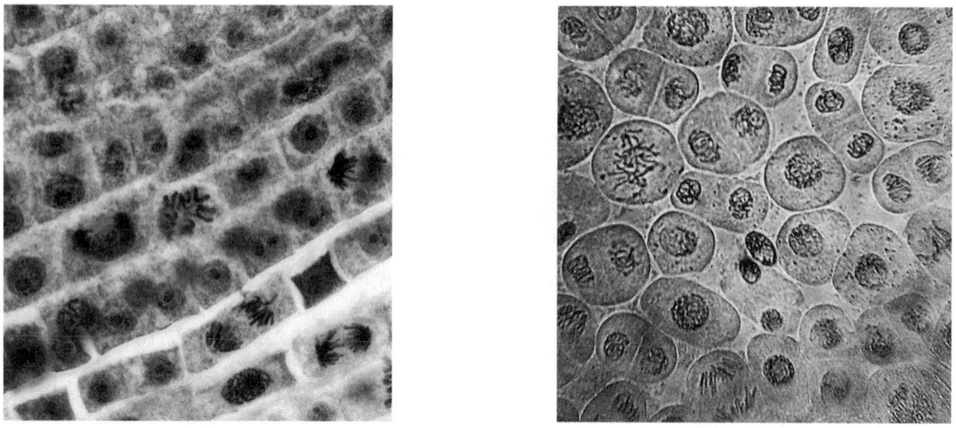

(a) (b)

The picture of the plant cells was taken from the cells in the tip of an onion root. The roots of plants are good for studying the cell cycle because they are constantly growing and, as a result, many of the cells in the tip of the root are in the process of dividing. To create the picture in the figure (a) above, a very thin slice of onion root was placed onto a microscope slide. The root was then stained with a dye that made the chromosomes visible. These photos provide us with a clear view of the various stages of the cell cycle, yet this information tells us little about how long a cell spends in each stage and if the amount of time in each stage is different for plants and animals.

To figure out how long cells spend in each stage of the cell cycle, we need to look at the proportion of cells in a given area that are in each phase. From this information you can then determine the relative amount of time a cell spends in each stage. The portion of cells in each phase should correspond closely with the amount of time spent by each cell in each phase.

Your Task

Determine the proportion of time animal and plant cells spend in each phase of the cell cycle.

The guiding question of this investigation is, **Do plant and animal cells spend the same proportion of time in each stage of the cell cycle?**

Materials

You may use any of the following materials during your investigation:

- A prepared slide from an onion root tip
- A prepared slide from a whitefish blastula
- Microscope

Safety Precautions

1. Glass slides can have sharp edges—handle with care to prevent cutting of skin.
2. Use caution when working with electrical equipment. Keep away from water sources in that they can cause shorts, fires, and shock hazards. Use only GFI-protected circuits.
3. Wash hands with soap and water after completing this lab.
4. Follow all normal lab safety rules.

Getting Started

To answer the guiding question, you will need to design and conduct an investigation. You will be presented with slides that you can use to see the cells in the tip of an onion root and in a whitefish blastula. Both slides will have cells in various stages of the cell cycle. To accomplish this task, you must determine what type of data you will need to collect, how you will collect it, and how you will analyze it. To determine *what type of data you will need to collect*, think about the following questions:

- What type of measurements or observations will you need to record during your investigation?
- How will you quantify any differences or similarities you observe in the different cells?

To determine *how you will collect your data*, think about the following questions:

- How will you determine how many cells are in each stage on each slide (i.e., how many cells are in interphase, how many cells are in metaphase, and so on)?

- How will you make sure that your data are of high quality (i.e., how will you reduce error)?
- How will you keep track of the data you collect and how will you organize the data?

To determine how you will analyze your data, think about the following questions:

- What type of calculations will you need to make? (Hint: You will need to determine the number of cells in each stage and the total number of cells you counted and use those numbers to predict how much time a dividing cell spends in each phase.)
- What type of graph could you create to help make sense of your data?

Investigation Proposal Required? ☐ Yes ☐ No

Connections to Crosscutting Concepts and to the Nature of Science and the Nature of Scientific Inquiry

As you work through your investigation, be sure to think about

- the importance of identifying and explaining patterns,
- why it is important to look for proportional relationships,
- how living things move through stages of stability and change,
- the difference between observations and inferences in science, and
- how scientific knowledge can change over time.

Argumentation Session

Argument presentation on a whiteboard

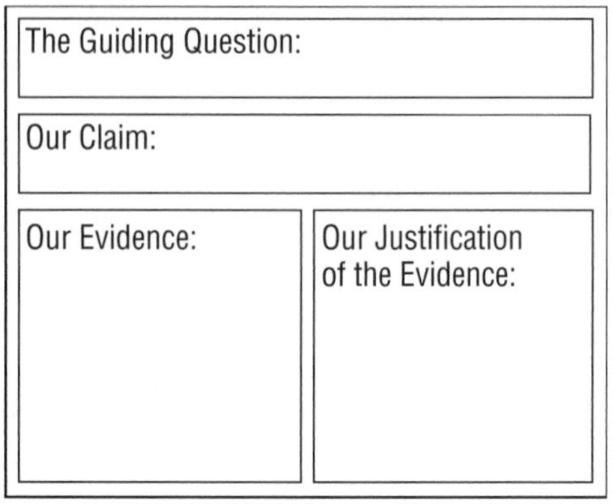

Once your group has finished collecting and analyzing your data, prepare a whiteboard that you can use to share your initial argument. Your whiteboard should include all the information shown in the figure to the left.

To share your argument with others, we will be using a round-robin format. This means that one member of your group will stay at your lab station to share your group's argument while the other members of your group go to the other lab stations one at a time to listen to and critique the arguments developed by your classmates.

The goal of the argumentation session is not to convince others that your argument is the best one; rather, the goal is to identify errors or instances of faulty reasoning in the arguments so these mistakes can be fixed. You will therefore need to evaluate the content of the claim, the quality of the evidence used to support the claim, and the strength of the justification of the evidence included in each argument that you see. In order to critique an argument, you will need more information than what is included on the whiteboard. You might, therefore, need to ask the presenter one or more follow-up questions, such as:

- How did you collect your data? Why did you use that method? Why did you collect those data?
- What did you do to make sure the data you collected are reliable? What did you do to decrease measurement error?
- What did you do to analyze your data? Why did you decide to do it that way? Did you check your calculations?
- Is that the only way to interpret the results of your analysis? How do you know that your interpretation of your analysis is appropriate?
- Why did your group decide to present your evidence in that manner?
- What other claims did your group discuss before you decided on that one? Why did your group abandon those alternative ideas?
- How confident are you that your claim is valid? What could you do to increase your confidence?

Once the argumentation session is complete, you will have a chance to meet with your group and revise your original argument. Your group might need to gather more data or design a way to test one or more alternative claims as part of this process. Remember, your goal at this stage of the investigation is to develop the most valid or acceptable answer to the research question!

Report

Once you have completed your research, you will need to prepare an investigation report that consists of three sections that provide answers to the following questions:

1. What question were you trying to answer and why?
2. What did you do during your investigation and why did you conduct your investigation in this way?
3. What is your argument?

Your report should answer these questions in two pages or less. This report must be typed, and any diagrams, figures, or tables should be embedded into the document. Be sure to write in a persuasive style; you are trying to convince others that your claim is acceptable or valid!

Lab 3. Cell Cycle: Do Plant and Animal Cells Spend the Same Proportion of Time in Each Stage of the Cell Cycle?

Checkout Questions

1. Describe the process of cell division.

2. Scientific knowledge never changes.

   a. I agree with this statement.
   b. I disagree with this statement.

   Explain your answer, using information from your investigation about the cell cycle.

3. All scientists, regardless of their background or training, will make the same observation about an event.
   a. I agree with this statement.
   b. I disagree with this statement.

   Explain your answer, using examples from your investigation about the cell cycle in plants and animals.

4. Scientists often look for patterns in nature. Explain why this is important, using an example from your investigation about the cell cycle.

5. Scientists often look for proportional relationships during an investigation. Explain why this is important, using an example from your investigation about the cell cycle.

Lab 4. Normal and Abnormal Cell Division: Which of These Patients Could Have Cancer?

Teacher Notes

Purpose

The purpose of this lab is for students to *apply* their understanding of cell division to solve a problem that requires them to examine the cellular structure of tissues and diagnose a disease. Students also have an opportunity to learn about the relationship between abnormal cell division and cancer. In addition, students will learn about observations and inferences in science as well as how scientific knowledge develops over time.

The Content

Cancer is the result of cells that grow and divide uncontrollably and do not die. Normal cells in the body follow an orderly path of growth, division, and death. The genetic material of a cell that promotes and regulates normal cell growth and division, however, can be damaged or changed, which alters the function of these genes. When this happens, cells do not die when they should and new cells are produced when the body does not need them. Programmed cell death is called *apoptosis*, and when this process breaks down it leads to a mass of abnormal cells that grows out of control. The mass of abnormal cells is called a tumor.

Tumors can be *benign* or *malignant*. Benign tumors are not cancerous. They can often be removed, and, in most cases, they do not come back. Cells in benign tumors do not spread to other parts of the body. Malignant tumors are cancerous, and cells in these tumors can invade nearby tissues and spread to other parts of the body. The spread of cancer from one part of the body to another is called *metastasis*.

Cancer types can be grouped into four main categories:

- Carcinoma, which is found in the skin or in tissues that line or cover internal organs
- Sarcoma, which is found in bone, cartilage, or other connective or supportive tissue
- Leukemia, which is found in blood-forming tissue such as the bone marrow and causes large numbers of abnormal blood cells to be produced and enter the blood
- Lymphoma and myeloma, which are found in the cells of the immune system

Pathologists can identify tumors by examining the cells of a tissue. Cancerous cells tend to be large and irregularly shaped, have more than one nucleus, or have a nucleus with multiple, large nucleoli (see Figure 4.1). In addition to the abnormal appearance of cancerous cells, these cells also divide at a much quicker rate than they should. As a result, there are fewer cells in interphase (and more cells in the other stages of mitosis) than there should be in a given tissue. Abnormal cell structure and frequent cell division in a tissue (especially if frequent cell division is uncommon in a particular tissue) are therefore indicators of cancer.

FIGURE 4.1

Normal and cancer cells side by side, with normal and cancerous characteristics identified

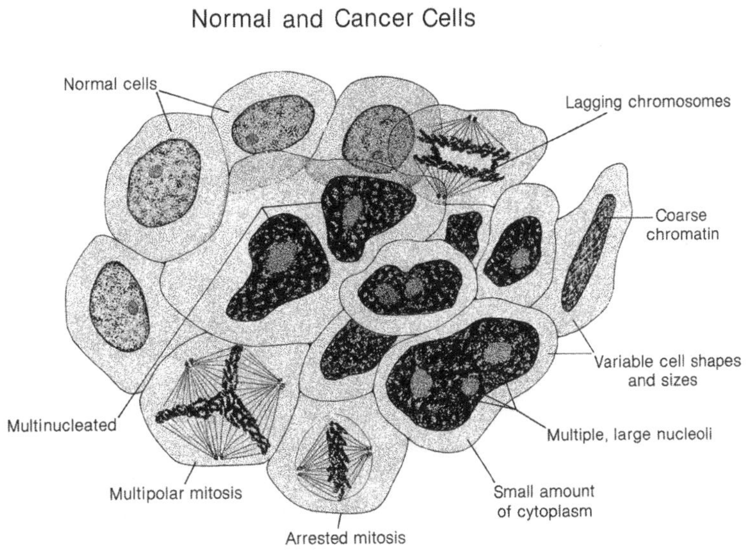

In this investigation, students examine slides from four fictitious patients (the slides are available at *www.nsta.org/publications/press/extras/argument.aspx*). The slides from patients 2 and 3 do not indicate the presence of cancer. The slides from patients 1 and 4, however, do indicate cancer. Patient 1 has an adenocarcinoma of the stomach (see upper-left-hand corner of the photo in the student handout). Patient 4 has an adenocarcinoma of the pancreas (see center of the photo in the student handout).

Timeline

The instructional time needed to implement this lab investigation is 130–200 minutes. Appendix 2 (p. 391) provides options for implementing this lab investigation over several class periods. Option C (200 minutes) should be used if students are unfamiliar with scientific writing because this option provides extra instructional time for scaffolding the writing process. You can scaffold the writing process by modeling, providing examples, and providing hints as students write each section of the report. Option D (130 minutes) should be used if students are familiar with scientific writing and have the skills needed to write an investigation report on their own. In option D, students complete stage 6 (writing the investigation report) and stage 8 (revising the investigation report) as homework.

Materials and Preparation

The materials needed to implement this investigation are listed in Table 4.1. Each group should have access to a set of histological slides (available from biological supply companies such as Carolina, Flinn Scientific, and Ward's Science), but several groups can share the slides if supplies are limited. If histological slides are not available, other animal mitosis slides (e.g., whitefish blastula) can be used in their place. Each group will need the pictures for all four patients.

A microscope for every two students is preferred. Students should be familiar with how to use a microscope before the lab. If they are not familiar with how to use it, be sure to teach students the skills they need as part of the investigation or as a stand-alone lesson before the lab. If available, microscope cameras add another dimension to data collection. Students can take pictures of their slides; this will reduce the size of their field of view and actually make counting cells easier.

TABLE 4.1

Materials list

Item	Quantity
Prepared histological slide from stomach—thin section, H&E	1 per group
Prepared histological slide from pancreas—thin section, H&E	1 per group
Image of histological slide from patient 1	1 per group
Image of histological slide from patient 2	1 per group
Image of histological slide from patient 3	1 per group
Image of histological slide from patient 4	1 per group
Microscope	1–2 per group
Student handout	1 per student
Whiteboard, 2' × 3'*	1 per group
Peer-review guide and instructor scoring rubric	1 per student

* As an alternative, students can use computer and presentation software such as Microsoft PowerPoint or Apple Keynote to create their arguments.

Topics for the Explicit and Reflective Discussion

Concepts That Can Be Used to Justify the Evidence

To provide an adequate justification of their evidence, students must explain why they included the evidence in their arguments and make the assumptions underlying their analysis and interpretation of the data explicit. In this investigation, students can use the following concepts to help justify their evidence:

- All eukaryotic cells share specific features.
- All cells that go through the process of mitosis do so in a predictable way.
- Cells from the same tissue should have the same basic structure.
- Abnormal cell structure and frequent cell division in a tissue are indicators of cancer.
- A sample of cells can be used to infer the characteristics of the whole organism.

We recommend that you review these concepts during the explicit and reflective discussion to help students make this connection.

How to Design Better Investigations

It is important for students to reflect on the strengths and weaknesses of the investigation they designed during the explicit and reflective discussion. Students should therefore be encouraged to discuss ways to eliminate potential flaws, measurement errors, or sources of bias in their investigations. To help students be more reflective about the design of their investigation, you can ask the following questions:

- What were some of the strengths of your investigation? What made it scientific?
- What were some of the weaknesses of your investigation? What made it less scientific?
- If you were to do this investigation again, what would you do to address the weaknesses in your investigation? What could you do to make it more scientific?

Crosscutting Concepts

This investigation is well aligned with three crosscutting concepts found in *A Framework for K–12 Science Education,* and you should review these concepts during the explicit and reflective discussion.

- *Patterns:* Observed patterns in nature (e.g., all eukaryotic cells go through the same stages of cell division; cells that make up a tissue have the same appearance) guide the way scientists organize and classify life on Earth. Scientists also explore the relationships between and the underlying causes of the patterns they observe in nature.
- *Scale, Proportion, and Quantity:* Students need to understand that it is critical for scientists to be able to recognize what is relevant at different sizes, times, and scales. Scientists must also be able to recognize proportional relationships between categories, groups, or quantities.
- *Structure and Function:* In nature, the way a living thing is structured determines how it functions and places limits on what it can and cannot do.

The Nature of Science and the Nature of Scientific Inquiry

It is important for students to understand the *difference between observations and inferences in science.* An observation is a descriptive statement about a natural phenomenon, whereas an inference is an interpretation of an observation. Students should also understand that current scientific knowledge and the perspectives of an individual scientist guide both observations and inferences. Thus, different scientists can have different but equally valid interpretations of the same observations due to differences in their perspectives and background knowledge.

It is also important for students to understand that *scientific knowledge can change over time.* A person can have confidence in the validity of scientific knowledge but must also accept that scientific knowledge may be abandoned or modified in light of new evidence or because existing evidence has been reconceptualized by scientists. There are many examples in the history of science of both evolutionary changes (i.e., the slow or gradual refinement of ideas) and revolutionary changes (i.e., the rapid abandonment of a well-established idea) in scientific knowledge.

You should review and provide examples of these two important concepts of the nature of science (NOS) and the nature of scientific inquiry (NOSI) during the explicit and reflective discussion.

Hints for Implementing the Lab

- You should circulate among the groups as students are making observations to ensure they are looking at actual cells instead of air bubbles or particles of dust.
- Encourage students to use a higher magnification when they are collecting data; it reduces the field of view, making counting cells easier.
- You can have students use a chi-square test to determine if observed differences in frequency counts are statistically significant.

Topic Connections

Table 4.2 (p. 66) provides an overview of the scientific practices, crosscutting concepts, disciplinary core ideas, and supporting ideas at the heart of this lab investigation. In addition, it lists NOS and NOSI concepts for the explicit and reflective discussion. Finally, it lists literacy and mathematics skills (*CCSS ELA* and *CCSS Mathematics*) that are addressed during the investigation.

TABLE 4.2

Lab 4 alignment with standards

Scientific practices	• Asking questions • Planning and carrying out investigations • Analyzing and interpreting data • Using mathematics and computational thinking • Constructing explanations • Engaging in argument from evidence • Obtaining, evaluating, and communicating information
Crosscutting concepts	• Patterns • Scale, proportion, and quantity • Structure and function
Core idea	• LS1: From molecules to organisms: Structures and processes
Supporting ideas	• Tissues • Cell cycle • Control of cell growth
NOS and NOSI concepts	• Observations and inferences • Science as a body of knowledge
Literacy connections *(CCSS ELA)*	• *Reading*: Key ideas and details, craft and structure, integration of knowledge and ideas • *Writing*: Text types and purposes, production and distribution of writing, research to build and present knowledge, range of writing • *Speaking and listening*: Comprehension and collaboration, presentation of knowledge and ideas
Mathematics connections *(CCSS Mathematics)*	• Create equations that describe numbers or relationships • Solve equations and inequalitities in one variable • Reason quantitatively and use units to solve problems

Lab 4. Normal and Abnormal Cell Division: Which of These Patients Could Have Cancer?

Lab Handout

Introduction

Hundreds of genes control the process of cell division in normal cells. Normal cell growth requires a balance between the activity of those genes that promote cell division and those that suppress it. It also relies on the activities of genes that signal when damaged cells should undergo apoptosis (programmed cell death). Cells become cancerous after mutations accumulate in the various genes that control cell division. Some mutations occur in genes that stimulate cell division, which triggers these cells to start dividing. Other cancer-related mutations inactivate the genes that suppress cell division or those that signal the need for apoptosis. Gene mutations accumulate over time as a result of independent events.

The figure below provides an illustration of normal and cancerous cells. A normal cell often has a great deal of cytoplasm and one nucleus, and it is about the same size and shape as the cells that it borders. A cancerous cell, in contrast, often has a small amount of cytoplasm, more than one nucleus, and an abnormal shape. Cancerous cells also divide

Normal and cancer cells side by side, with normal and cancerous characteristics identified

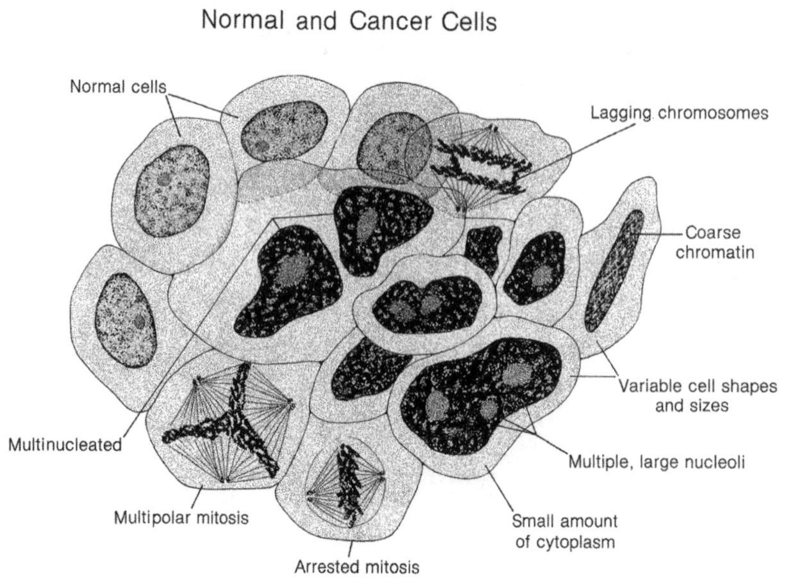

faster than normal cells do, so there is a greater chance that these cells will be in one of the stages of mitosis. The stages of mitosis in a cancerous cell, however, will often look different than they do in a normal cell. For example, the chromosomes may be pulled toward three or more centrioles (instead of two), and some chromosomes may lag behind others during anaphase. These types of abnormalities are often present because the genes in the cells that trigger apoptosis are no longer functional.

As a mass of cancerous cells grows, it develops into a tumor. Tumors often remain confined within the normal boundaries of a tissue during the early stages of cancer. As time passes, however, tumors will often break through the boundaries of a tissue and invade adjoining tissues. These tumors are described as malignant. Sometimes individual cancer cells will break off from a malignant tumor and travel to other parts of the body, leading to the formation of new tumors at those sites. This process is called metastasis, and it occurs during the terminal stages of cancer. Tumors that are not capable of invading adjoining tissue are described as benign.

A medical doctor will often order a procedure called a biopsy if he or she suspects that a patient has a tumor. As part of a biopsy, the doctor or other medical professional will remove a piece of tissue or a sample of cells from a patient's body so that it can be examined in a laboratory by a pathologist. The pathologist will prepare several histological slides of the tissue and use a microscope to look for the presence of cancerous cells. The pathologist will then prepare a pathology report for the medical doctor. The pathology report describes the results of the analysis and the opinion of the pathologist.

Your Task

You will be provided with images of histological slides from four different individuals. Examine these images and use what you know about the appearance of cells and what proportion of time cells tend to spend in each stage of mitosis to determine if any of the individuals have cancer.

The guiding question of this investigation is, **Which of these patients could have cancer?**

Materials

You may use any of the following materials during your investigation:

- Histological slide from stomach (thin section, H&E)
- Histological slide from pancreas (thin section, H&E)
- Images of histological slides from patients 1, 2, 3, and 4
- Microscope

Safety Precautions

1. Glass slides can have sharp edges—handle with care to prevent cutting of skin.
2. Use caution when working with electrical equipment. Keep away from water sources in that they can cause shorts, fires, and shock hazards. Use only GFI-protected circuits.
3. Wash hands with soap and water after completing this lab.
4. Follow all normal lab safety rules.

Getting Started

To answer the guiding question, you will need to design and conduct an investigation to examine the characteristics of typical cells found within the stomach and pancreas. You will then compare these cells with the cells taken from four fictitious patients. To accomplish this task, you must determine what type of data you will need to collect, how you will collect it, and how you will analyze it. To determine *what type of data you will need to collect,* think about the following questions:

- What type of measurements or observations will you need to record during your investigation? (Hint: What are the characteristics of cancerous cells?).
- Will you collect one type of data (appearance of cells only) or multiple types of data (appearance of cells and proportion of time spent in various stages of the cell cycle)?

To determine *how you will collect your data,* think about the following questions:

- What will serve as a control (or comparison) condition?
- How will you collect data? (Hint: Higher magnifications make counting cells and comparing easier.)
- How will you make sure that your data are of high quality (i.e., how will you reduce error)?
- How will you keep track of the data you collect and how will you organize the data?

To determine *how you will analyze your data,* think about the following questions:

- What type of calculations will you need to make?
- What type of graph could you create to help make sense of your data?

Investigation Proposal Required? ☐ Yes ☐ No

Connections to Crosscutting Concepts and to the Nature of Science and the Nature of Scientific Inquiry

As you work through your investigation, be sure to think about

- the importance of identifying patterns,
- what is and is not important at different scales or time periods,
- how structure is related to function in living things,
- the difference between observations and inferences in science, and
- the nature of scientific knowledge.

Argumentation Session

Once your group has finished collecting and analyzing your data, prepare a whiteboard that you can use to share your initial argument. Your whiteboard should include all the information shown in the figure to the right.

Argument presentation on a whiteboard

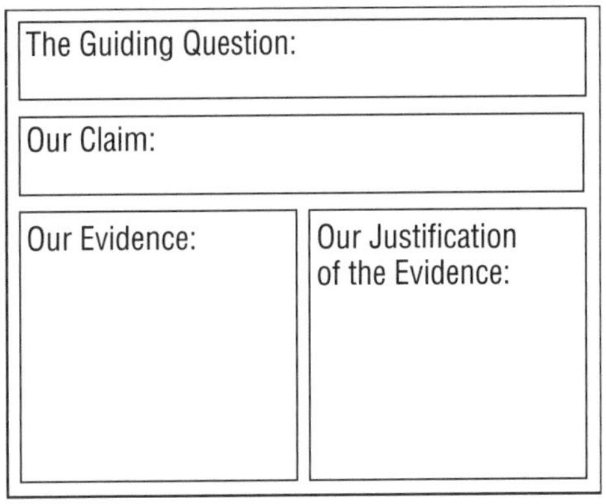

To share your argument with others, we will be using a round-robin format. This means that one member of your group will stay at your lab station to share your group's argument while the other members of your group go to the other lab stations one at a time to listen to and critique the arguments developed by your classmates.

The goal of the argumentation session is not to convince others that your argument is the best one; rather, the goal is to identify errors or instances of faulty reasoning in the arguments so these mistakes can be fixed. You will therefore need to evaluate the content of the claim, the quality of the evidence used to support the claim, and the strength of the justification of the evidence included in each argument that you see. In order to critique an argument, you will need more information than what is included on the whiteboard. You might, therefore, need to ask the presenter one or more follow-up questions, such as:

- Why did you decide to focus on those data?
- What did you do to analyze your data? Why did you decide to do it that way? Did you check your calculations?
- Is that the only way to interpret the results of your analysis? How do you know that your interpretation of your analysis is appropriate?
- Why did your group decide to present your evidence in that manner?

- What other claims did your group discuss before you decided on that one? Why did your group abandon those alternative ideas?
- How confident are you that your claim is valid? What could you do to increase your confidence?

Once the argumentation session is complete, you will have a chance to meet with your group and revise your original argument. Your group might need to gather more data or design a way to test one or more alternative claims as part of this process. Remember, your goal at this stage of the investigation is to develop the most valid or acceptable answer to the research question!

Report

Once you have completed your research, you will need to prepare an investigation report that consists of three sections that provide answers to the following questions:

1. What question were you trying to answer and why?
2. What did you do during your investigation and why did you conduct your investigation in this way?
3. What is your argument?

Your report should answer these questions in two pages or less. This report must be typed, and any diagrams, figures, or tables should be embedded into the document. Be sure to write in a persuasive style; you are trying to convince others that your claim is acceptable or valid!

Lab 4. Normal and Abnormal Cell Division: Which of These Patients Could Have Cancer?

Checkout Questions

1. Describe cancer in terms of the cell cycle.

2. Scientists often make different inferences based on the same observations.

   a. I agree with this statement.
   b. I disagree with this statement.

   Explain your answer, using examples from your investigation about normal and abnormal cell division.

3. All scientific knowledge, including the concepts found in science textbooks, can be discarded or changed when new evidence justifies it.

   a. I agree with this statement.
   b. I disagree with this statement.

   Explain your answer, using information from your investigation about normal and abnormal cell division.

4. Scientists often look for patterns during an investigation. Explain why this is important, using an example from your investigation about normal and abnormal cell division.

5. Scientists often need to determine what is and what is not important at different scales or time periods. Explain why this is important, using an example from your investigation about normal and abnormal cell division.

6. Scientists can often tell a lot about cells by looking at their structure. Explain why, using an example from your investigation about normal and abnormal cell divisions.

Lab 5. Photosynthesis: Why Do Temperature and Light Intensity Affect the Rate of Photosynthesis in Plants?

Teacher Notes

Purpose

The purpose of this lab is for students to *apply* their understanding of the process of photosynthesis to determine how different environmental factors, such as temperature and light intensity, influence the rate of photosynthesis. This lab also gives students an opportunity to learn about observation and inference in science and the nature and role of experiments in science.

The Content

Environmental factors such as temperature and light intensity affect the rate of photosynthesis in plants. Cold temperatures result in molecules moving more slowly, thus slowing down the rate of chemical reactions. Because photosynthesis is a series of chemical reactions, slowing down the individual reactions slows down the rate of the whole process. Although heat typically speeds up chemical reactions because it speeds up the movement of molecules involved in the reaction, it only works to a point. High temperatures will result in the breakdown of the enzymes involved in the reaction. Thus, photosynthesis will cease at extremely high temperatures. The energy necessary for photosynthesis to take place is provided by light. As light intensity increases, so does the amount of available energy. More energy results in a greater rate of reaction. There is a point, however, at which higher light intensity does not increase the rate of photosynthesis, because other factors involved in the photosynthesis reaction will act as a limiting factor.

Timeline

The instructional time needed to implement this lab investigation is 180–250 minutes. Appendix 2 (p. 391) provides options for implementing this lab investigation over several class periods. Option A (250 minutes) should be used if students are unfamiliar with scientific writing because this option provides extra instructional time for scaffolding the writing process. You can scaffold the writing process by modeling, providing examples, and providing hints as students write each section of the report. Option B (180 minutes) should be used if students are familiar with scientific writing and have the skills needed to write an investigation report on their own. In option B, students complete stage 6 (writing the investigation report) and stage 8 (revising the report) as homework.

Materials and Preparation

The materials needed to implement this investigation are listed in Table 5.1, p. 76. Each group is responsible for investigating only one factor, so the equipment needed will vary by group. Figure 5.1 shows how the equipment can be set up. Five or six spinach leaves can be placed in a 250 ml Erlenmeyer flask. A carbon dioxide (CO_2) gas sensor or an oxygen (O_2) gas sensor (available from Vernier or Pasco) can then be placed on the flask (be sure to create an airtight seal), and the flask can be placed in a large beaker (600 ml or larger). Tap water can then be added to beaker so that it creates a heat shield. Students can monitor the temperature of the flask using a thermometer. Students can then measure changes in CO_2 or O_2 levels inside the flask over time to examine differences in the rate of photosynthesis under different environmental conditions.

FIGURE 5.1

Equipment setup for measuring changes in CO_2 or O_2

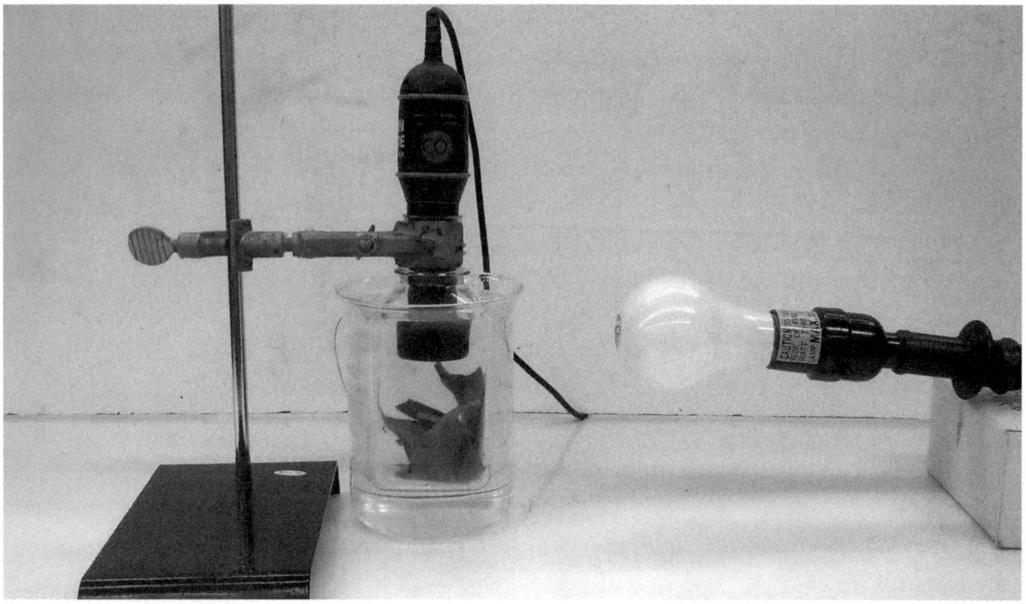

Students can add crushed ice to the water bath or place the water bath on a hot plate to vary the temperature inside the flask. Students can use different-wattage lightbulbs (40 W, 60 W, 100 W) to vary the intensity of light. Students should make sure that the leaves are going through the process of photosynthesis before they start collecting their data. This should take about five minutes. If the leaves are not going through photosynthesis, have students adjust the sensor or use different leaves.

Be sure to use fresh spinach leaves (available from a grocery store). Soak the leaves in cold water for at least 30 minutes before the lab. Keep the leaves in cold water and covered when students are not using them (thermal lunch bags or small plastic coolers work well for this). Students need to use whole leaves with no brown spots or damage, and they need to be careful when putting the leaves into the flask so as not to break or rip them. Make sure the students DO NOT pack more than five or six leaves in the flask.

TABLE 5.1

Materials list

Item	Quantity
Fresh spinach leaves	60 per group
Erlenmeyer flask, 250 ml	3 per group
CO_2 or O_2 gas sensor	1 per group
Sensor interface (compatible with sensor)	1 per group
Beaker, 600 ml (or larger)	1 per group
Thermometer (or temperature probe)	1 per group
Hot plate	1 per group
Ring stand	1 per group
Ring stand clamps	2 per group
Floodlight	1 per group
Crushed ice	1 L per class
Cooler (for ice)	1 per class
Bulb, 40 W	1 per group
Bulb, 60 W	1 per group
Bulb, 100 W	1 per group
Student handout	1 per student
Investigation proposal A*	1 per group
Whiteboard, 2' × 3'†	1 per group
Peer-review guide and instructor scoring rubric	1 per student
Safety goggles and aprons	1 per student

* It is recommended but not required that students fill out an investigation proposal for this lab; it is not necessary to do so if students already know how to design a controlled experiment.

† As an alternative, students can use computer and presentation software such as Microsoft PowerPoint or Apple Keynote to create their arguments.

Topics for the Explicit and Reflective Discussion

Concepts That Can Be Used to Justify the Evidence

To provide an adequate justification of their evidence, students must explain why they included the evidence in their arguments and make the assumptions underlying their analysis and interpretation of the data explicit. In this investigation, students can use the following concepts to help justify their evidence:

- Modification of basic building block compounds to make new and different compounds through specific chemical reactions
- The inputs (CO_2 and water) and the outputs (O_2 and sugar) of photosynthesis
- The role of light in the process of photosynthesis

We recommend that you review these concepts during the explicit and reflective discussion to help students make this connection.

How to Design Better Investigations

It is important for students to reflect on the strengths and weaknesses of the investigation they designed during the explicit and reflective discussion. Students should therefore be encouraged to discuss ways to eliminate potential flaws, measurement errors, or sources of bias in their investigations. To help students be more reflective about the design of their investigation, you can ask the following questions:

- What were some of the strengths of your investigation? What made it scientific?
- What were some of the weaknesses of your investigation? What made it less scientific?
- If you were to do this investigation again, what would you do to address the weaknesses in your investigation? What could you do to make it more scientific?

Crosscutting Concepts

This investigation is well aligned with three crosscutting concepts found in *A Framework for K–12 Science Education,* and you should review these concepts during the explicit and reflective discussion.

- *Cause and Effect: Mechanism and Explanation:* One of the main objectives of science is to identify and establish relationships between a cause and effect. It is also important to understand the mechanisms by which these causal relationships are mediated.

- *Systems and System Models:* Students need to understand that it is critical for scientists to be able to define the system under study and then make a model of it to understand it.
- *Energy and Matter: Flows, Cycles, and Conservation:* Scientists often strive to learn more about how energy and matter flow into, out of, and within an organism to develop a better understanding of how that organism functions.

The Nature of Science and the Nature of Scientific Inquiry

It is important for students to understand the *difference between observations and inferences in science.* An observation is a descriptive statement about a natural phenomenon, whereas an inference is an interpretation of an observation. Students should also understand that current scientific knowledge and the perspectives of individual scientists guide both observations and inferences. Thus, different scientists can have different but equally valid interpretations of same observations due to differences in their perspectives and background knowledge.

It is also important for students to understand the *nature and role of experiments in science.* Scientists use experiments to test the validity of a hypothesis (i.e., a tentative explanation) for an observed phenomenon. Experiments include a test and the formulation of predictions (expected results) if the test is conducted and the hypothesis is valid. The experiment is then carried out and the predictions are compared with the observed results of the experiment. If the predictions match the observed results, then the hypothesis is supported. If the observed results do not match the prediction, then the hypothesis is not supported. A signature feature of an experiment is the control of variables to help eliminate alternative explanations for observed results.

You should review and provide examples of these two important concepts of the nature of science (NOS) and the nature of scientific inquiry (NOSI) during the explicit and reflective discussion.

Hints for Implementing the Lab

- Carefully check group investigation proposals before starting the lab, but be sure to allow groups to design their own methods for collecting data.
- If equipment is available, groups can test both O_2 and CO_2 at the same time. They should be able to directly observe the inverse relationship between the two gases.
- Depending on equipment type and availability, data collection can take more than one day.
- After each aspect of the parameter is tested, groups should remove the old spinach leaves and flood their flask with water. This will remove any excess gas that has collected there during the photosynthesis process. Empty out the flask, and dry and replace the leaves with new ones.

- Be sure all group members keep track of the data that is collected by their group; this will help when they are writing their investigation reports.

Topic Connections

Table 5.2 provides an overview of the scientific practices, crosscutting concepts, disciplinary core ideas, and supporting ideas at the heart of this lab investigation. In addition, it lists NOS and NOSI concepts for the explicit and reflective discussion. Finally, it lists literacy and mathematics skills (*CCSS ELA* and *CCSS Mathematics*) that are addressed during the investigation.

TABLE 5.2

Lab 5 alignment with standards

Scientific practices	• Asking questions • Developing and using models • Planning and carrying out investigations • Analyzing and interpreting data • Using mathematics and computational thinking • Constructing explanations • Engaging in argument from evidence • Obtaining, evaluating, and communicating information
Crosscutting concepts	• Cause and effect: Mechanism and explanation • Systems and system models • Energy and matter: Flows, cycles, and conservation
Core ideas	• LS1: From molecules to organisms: Structures and processes • LS2: Ecosystems: Interactions, energy, and dynamics
Supporting ideas	• Photosynthesis • Enzymes • Energy
NOS and NOSI concepts	• Observations and inferences • Nature and role of experiments
Literacy connections *(CCSS ELA)*	• *Reading*: Key ideas and details, craft and structure, integration of knowledge and ideas • *Writing*: Text types and purposes, production and distribution of writing, research to build and present knowledge, range of writing • *Speaking and listening*: Comprehension and collaboration, presentation of knowledge and ideas
Mathematics connections *(CCSS Mathematics)*	• Create equations that describe numbers or relationships • Solve equations and inequalities in one variable • Reason quantitatively and use units to solve problems

Lab 5. Photosynthesis: Why Do Temperature and Light Intensity Affect the Rate of Photosynthesis in Plants?

Lab Handout

Introduction

You have learned that green plants have the ability to produce their own supply of sugar through the process of photosynthesis. Photosynthesis is a complex chemical process in which green plants produce sugar and oxygen for themselves. The equation for photosynthesis is as follows:

$$\text{Carbon dioxide } (CO_2) + \text{water } (H_2O) \rightarrow \text{sugar } (C_6H_{12}O_6) + \text{oxygen } (O_2) + \text{water } (H_2O)$$

The plant uses the sugar it produces through photosynthesis to grow and produce more leaves, stems, and roots—the biomass of the plant. Plants therefore get their mass from air. The process of photosynthesis, however, does not happen all the time, and when it happens depends on a number of environmental factors. For example, plants need a supply of water, carbon dioxide, and light energy for photosynthesis to work. Plants must get these resources from the surrounding environment. The process of photosynthesis can also slow down or speed up depending on environmental conditions. In this lab investigation, you will explore how two different environmental conditions affect how quickly photosynthesis takes place within a plant. You will then develop a conceptual model that explains why.

Your Task

Design a series of experiments to determine how temperature and light intensity affect the rate of photosynthesis in spinach. Then develop a conceptual model that explains why these environmental factors affect the rate of photosynthesis in the way that they do.

The guiding question of this investigation is, **Why do temperature and light intensity affect the rate of photosynthesis in plants?**

Materials

You may use any of the following materials during your investigation:

- Spinach leaves
- Erlenmeyer flask (250 ml)
- CO_2 or O_2 gas sensor
- Sensor interface
- Beaker (600 ml or larger)

- Thermometer or temperature probe
- Hot plate
- Ring stand and clamps
- Floodlight
- Ice
- 40-W bulb
- 60-W bulb
- 100-W bulb
- Goggles and aprons

Safety Precautions

1. Safety goggles and aprons are required for this activity.
2. Use caution when working with electrical equipment. Keep away from water sources in that they can cause shorts, fires, and shock hazards. Use only GFI-protected circuits.
3. Lightbulbs and hot plates can become hot and burn skin. Handle with care!
4. Wash hands with soap and water after completing this lab.
5. Follow all normal lab safety rules.

Getting Started

The first step in developing your model is to design and carry out a series of experiments to determine how temperature and light intensity affect the rate of photosynthesis. You will therefore need a way to calculate a rate of photosynthesis. A photosynthesis rate can be calculated by measuring how much CO_2 a plant consumes or how much O_2 a plant produces over time using the following equation:

$$\text{Photosynthesis rate} = \frac{\text{change in } CO_2 \text{ or } O_2 \text{ level}}{\text{time}}$$

To measure how much CO_2 spinach consumes (or O_2 it produces) over time, simply put five spinach leaves inside a 250 ml flask and seal the flask with a CO_2 gas sensor or O_2 gas sensor. Next, fill a 600 ml (or larger) beaker with water to create a water bath in order to keep the spinach leaves at a constant temperature. You can place the flask in the water bath (see the "Equipment setup" figure on the next page) or place the water bath between the flask and the light source.

Equipment setup

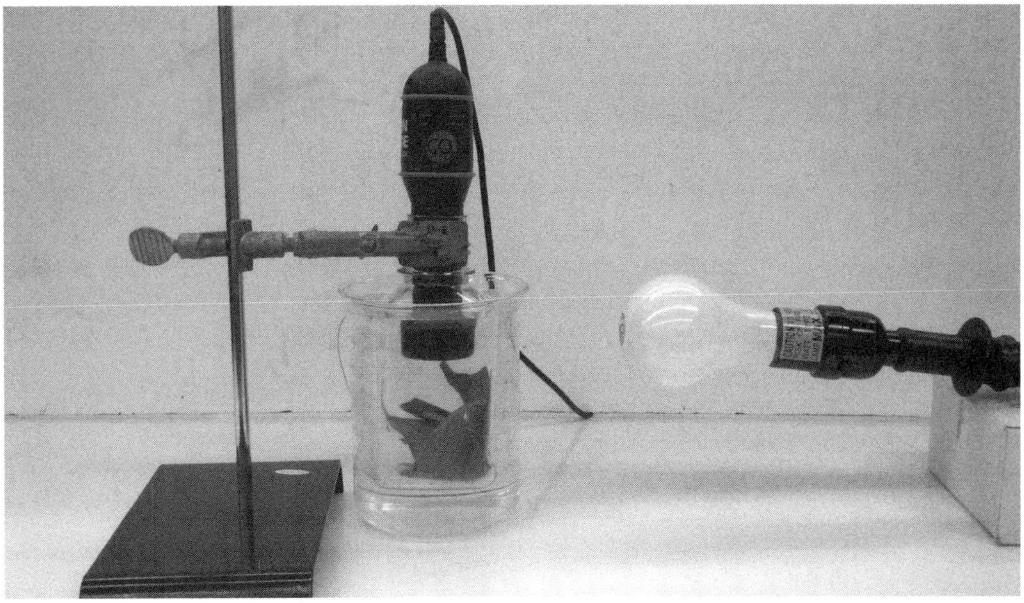

The next step is to think about how you will collect the data and how you will analyze it. To determine *how you will collect your data*, think about the following questions:

- What will serve as a control (or comparison) condition?
- What will serve as the treatment condition(s)? (Hint: To investigate the effect of temperature on photosynthesis rate, you will need to determine how to vary the temperature inside the flask. To investigate the effect of light intensity on photosynthesis rate, you can use lightbulbs with different wattages.)
- How will you make sure that your data are of high quality (i.e., how will you reduce error)?
- How will you keep track of the data you collect and how will you organize the data?

To determine *how you will analyze your data*, think about the following questions:

- How will you determine if there is a difference between the treatment and the control conditions?
- What type of calculations will you need to make?
- What type of graph could you create to help make sense of your data?

Once you have carried out your series of experiments, your group will need to develop a conceptual model. Your model needs to explain why these two environmental factors affect the rate of photosynthesis in the way that they do. The model should also explain what is happening at the submicroscopic level during the process of photosynthesis.

Investigation Proposal Required? ☐ Yes ☐ No

Connections to Crosscutting Concepts and to the Nature of Science and the Nature of Scientific Inquiry

As you work through your investigation, be sure to think about

- the importance of identifying the underlying cause for observations,
- how models are used to study natural phenomena,
- how energy and matter move within or through a system,
- the difference between observations and inferences in science, and
- the nature and role of experiments in science.

Argumentation Session

Once your group has finished collecting and analyzing your data, prepare a whiteboard that you can use to share your initial argument. Your whiteboard should include all the information shown in the figure below.

Argument presentation on a whiteboard

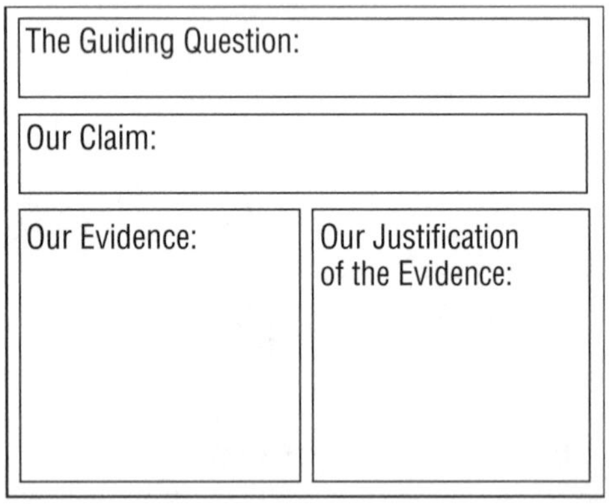

To share your argument with others, we will be using a round-robin format. This means that one member of your group will stay at your lab station to share your group's argument while the other members of your group go to the other lab stations one at a time to listen to and critique the arguments developed by your classmates.

The goal of the argumentation session is not to convince others that your argument is the best one; rather, the goal is to identify errors or instances of faulty reasoning in the arguments so these mistakes can be fixed. You will therefore need to evaluate the content of the claim, the quality of the evidence used to support the claim, and the strength of the justification of the evidence included in each argument that you see. In order to critique an argument, you will need more information than what is included on the whiteboard. You might, therefore, need to ask the presenter one or more follow-up questions, such as:

- How did you collect your data? Why did you use that method? Why did you collect those data?

- What did you do to make sure the data you collected are reliable? What did you do to decrease measurement error?
- What did you do to analyze your data? Why did you decide to do it that way? Did you check your calculations?
- Is that the only way to interpret the results of your analysis? How do you know that your interpretation of your analysis is appropriate?
- Why did your group decide to present your evidence in that manner?
- What other claims did your group discuss before you decided on that one? Why did your group abandon those alternative ideas?
- How confident are you that your claim is valid? What could you do to increase your confidence?

Once the argumentation session is complete, you will have a chance to meet with your group and revise your original argument. Your group might need to gather more data or design a way to test one or more alternative claims as part of this process. Remember, your goal at this stage of the investigation is to develop the most valid or acceptable answer to the research question!

Report

Once you have completed your research, you will need to prepare an investigation report that consists of three sections that provide answers to the following questions:

1. What question were you trying to answer and why?
2. What did you do during your investigation and why did you conduct your investigation in this way?
3. What is your argument?

Your report should answer these questions in two pages or less. This report must be typed, and any diagrams, figures, or tables should be embedded into the document. Be sure to write in a persuasive style; you are trying to convince others that your claim is acceptable or valid!

Lab 5. Photosynthesis: Why Do Temperature and Light Intensity Affect the Rate of Photosynthesis in Plants?

Checkout Questions

1. Plant A and plant B are of the same species and are located in an environment with hot conditions. However, plant A is located in an open field and plant B is situated under a tree, receiving little sunlight. Which plant would go through the process of photosynthesis more quickly?

   a. Plant A
   b. Plant B

   Why?

2. Inferences are based on observations.

   a. I agree with this statement.
   b. I disagree with this statement.

   Explain your answer, using examples from your investigation about photosynthesis.

3. This investigation was an example of an experiment.

   a. I agree with this statement.
   b. I disagree with this statement.

   Explain your answer, using information from your investigation about photosynthesis.

4. An important goal in science is to explain the underlying cause for observations. Explain why this is important, using an example from your investigation about photosynthesis.

5. Scientists often use models to study or explain natural phenomenon. Explain what a model is and why models are important, using an example from your investigation about photosynthesis.

6. Scientists often need to track how matter moves in, out, and through a system during an investigation. Explain why this is important, using an example from your investigation about photosynthesis.

Lab 6. Cellular Respiration: How Does the Type of Food Source Affect the Rate of Cellular Respiration in Yeast?

Teacher Notes

Purpose

The purpose of this lab is for students to *apply* their understanding of the processes of cellular respiration to determine if the nature of a food source influences the rate of cellular respiration. This lab also gives students an opportunity to learn how to design a controlled experiment to answer the investigation question. Students will learn about differences between theories and laws from a scientific standpoint as well as the role of imagination and creativity in science.

The Content

All living things, including multicellular and unicellular organisms, need energy for a wide range of cellular activities. *Adenosine triphosphate* (ATP) is a special molecule that provides energy in a form that cells can use to build or break down molecules and to create various cell components. *Cellular respiration* is the name given to the chemical process that cells use to transfer the energy found in sugar into ATP. The following equation summarizes the chemical changes that occur during cellular respiration.

Sugar + oxygen (O_2) → water + carbon dioxide (CO_2) + ATP (a usable form of energy)

Organisms can use a wide range of molecules as a source of sugar for cellular respiration because they can convert molecules into different ones. Organisms, for example, can break down complex carbohydrates such as polysaccharides and disaccharides into a simple sugar that can then be used for cellular respiration. This conversion process, however, requires a specific enzyme for each type of molecule. In addition to being able to break down polysaccharides and disaccharides, organisms can also break down other molecules such as lipids and proteins. There are, however, many more steps involved in the process of breaking down a lipid or protein molecule into its various subcomponents and then converting the subcomponents into new molecules that can be used to make ATP through the process of cellular respiration. The entire conversion process therefore takes much longer than it does to simply break down carbohydrates. The conversion process also requires more than one enzyme to complete.

In this investigation, students explore how the nature of a food source influences the rate of cellular respiration in yeast. Yeast, like many other organisms, can use a wide range of food sources. For example, yeast can convert the disaccharide sucrose into a simple sugar that it can use for cellular respiration because it produces the enzyme sucrase. It can also break down the polysaccharide starch and the disaccharide maltose into simple sugars because it produces the enzymes amylase and maltase. Yeast can therefore use many different types of complex sugars as a source of energy. There is one complex sugar, however, that yeast cannot break down into a simple sugar. That sugar is the disaccharide lactose. Yeast cannot break down lactose into simple sugars because it does not produce the enzyme lactase. Yeast can also use proteins and lipids as a food source. However, it takes yeast longer to convert these molecules into a form that can be used in the process of cellular respiration.

Thus, the nature of the food source affects the rate of cellular respiration in yeast. The rate of cellular respiration in yeast will be higher when the food source is a carbohydrate and lower when the food source is a lipid or a protein. The one exception to this general rule is the disaccharide lactose. The rate of cellular respiration in yeast will be low when lactose is the food source because it cannot break down this complex carbohydrate into a simple sugar.

Timeline

The instructional time needed to implement this lab investigation is 180–250 minutes. Appendix 2 (p. 391) provides options for implementing this lab investigation over several class periods. Option A (250 minutes) should be used if students are unfamiliar with scientific writing because this option provides extra instructional time for scaffolding the writing process. You can scaffold the writing process by modeling, providing examples, and providing hints as students write each section of the report. Option B (180 minutes) should be used if students are familiar with scientific writing and have the skills needed to write an investigation report on their own. In option B, students complete stage 6 (writing the investigation report) and stage 8 (revising the report) as homework.

Materials and Preparation

The materials needed to implement this investigation are listed in Table 6.1. Prepare a yeast solution at least 30 minutes before starting the investigation. Brewer's yeast is preferred, but baker's yeast will work as well. Prepare 1-liter stock solutions of the food sources in advance. Corn starch or potato starch works well as the polysaccharide; table sugar is sufficient for the sucrose. Albumin or unflavored gelatin works best for the protein. Vegetable oil, corn oil, or olive oil is an appropriate choice for the lipid. Carbon dioxide (CO_2) sensors and oxygen (O_2) sensors can be purchased from companies such as Vernier and Pasco. Each group should have access to either a CO_2 sensor or an O_2 sensor; if both sensors are available, students can test both CO_2 and O_2. Figure 6.1 shows how the equipment can be set up.

LAB 6

TABLE 6.1

Materials list

Item	Quantity
Yeast solution	1 L per class
Corn or potato starch solution (polysaccharide)	1 L per class
Sucrose solution (disaccharide)	I L per class
Lactose solution (disaccharide)	1 L per class
Glucose solution (monosaccharide)	1 L per class
Albumin or gelatin solution (protein)	1 L per class
Vegetable oil (lipid)	1 L per class
CO_2 or O_2 gas sensor	1 per group
Sensor interface (compatible with sensor)	1 per group
Erlenmeyer flask, 250 ml	2 per group
Test tubes	7 per group
Test tube rack	1 per group
Beaker, 600 ml	1 per group
Ring stand	1 per group
Ring stand clamps	2 per group
Student handout	1 per student
Investigation proposal B*	1 per group
Whiteboard, 2' × 3'†	1 per group
Peer-review guide and instructor scoring rubric	1 per student
Safety goggles and aprons	1 per student

* It is recommended but not required that students fill out an investigation proposal for this lab; it is not necessary to do so if students already know how to design a controlled experiment.

† As an alternative, students can use computer and presentation software such as Microsoft PowerPoint or Apple Keynote to create their arguments.

FIGURE 6.1

A CO_2 or an O_2 gas sensor can be used to measure changes in gas concentration.

Topics for the Explicit and Reflective Discussion

Concepts That Can Be Used to Justify the Evidence

To provide an adequate justification of their evidence, students must explain why they included the evidence in their arguments and make the assumptions underlying their analysis and interpretation of the data explicit. In this investigation, students can use the following concepts to help justify their evidence:

- The ability of cells to convert molecules into other molecules
- The use of cellular respiration to produce a usable form of energy called ATP
- The inputs (O_2 and sugar) and the outputs (CO_2 and water) of cellular respiration
- Why calculating a rate of change (change over a period of time) in concentration is more useful than measuring the concentration at a single point in time

We recommend that you review these concepts during the explicit and reflective discussion to help students make this connection.

How to Design Better Investigations

It is important for students to reflect on the strengths and weaknesses of the investigation they designed during the explicit and reflective discussion. Students should therefore be encouraged to discuss ways to eliminate potential flaws, measurement errors, or sources of bias in their investigations. To help students be more reflective about the design of their investigation, you can ask the following questions:

- What were some of the strengths of your investigation? What made it scientific?
- What were some of the weaknesses of your investigation? What made it less scientific?
- If you were to do this investigation again, what would you do to address the weaknesses in your investigation? What could you do to make it more scientific?

Crosscutting Concepts

This investigation is well aligned with three crosscutting concepts found in *A Framework for K–12 Science Education,* and you should review these concepts during the explicit and reflective discussion.

- *Cause and Effect: Mechanism and Explanation:* One of the main objectives of science is to identify and establish relationships between a cause and effect. It is also important to understand the mechanisms by which these causal relationships are mediated.

- *Energy and Matter: Flows, Cycles, and Conservation:* Scientists often strive to learn more about how energy and matter flow into, out of, and within an organism to develop a better understanding of how that organism functions.
- *Structure and Function:* The way an object (e.g., a carbohydrate, protein, or lipid molecule) is shaped or structured determines many of its properties and if it can or cannot be used by an organism.

The Nature of Science and the Nature of Scientific Inquiry

It is important for students to understand the *difference between laws and theories in science.* A scientific law describes the behavior of a natural phenomenon or a generalized relationship under certain conditions; a scientific theory is a well-substantiated explanation of some aspect of the natural world. Theories do not become laws even with additional evidence; they explain laws. However, not all scientific laws have an accompanying explanatory theory. It is also important for students to understand that scientists do not discover laws or theories; the scientific community develops them over time.

It is also important for students to understand that science requires imagination and creativity. Students should learn that developing explanations for or models of natural phenomena and then figuring out how they can be put to the test of reality is as creative as writing poetry, composing music, or designing skyscrapers. Scientists must also use their imagination and creativity to figure out new ways to test ideas and collect or analyze data.

You should review and provide examples of these two important concepts of the nature of science (NOS) and the nature of scientific inquiry (NOSI) during the explicit and reflective discussion.

Hints for Implementing the Lab

- For best results use the food sources recommended in the "Materials and Preparation" section. DO NOT use protein powders as protein sources, because they often have other ingredients that interfere with the results.
- The yeast suspension should be placed in the flask before adding the food source. Allow the sensors to equilibrate in between adding the yeast suspension and the food source; this equilibration period should take about five minutes. Then groups can begin data collection.
- Yeast lacks the enzymes necessary to break down lactose, so students should not see much respiration occurring with this sugar as compared with the other sugar types.
- After each food source is tested, groups should pour out their yeast solutions and flood their flask with water. This will remove any excess gas that has collected there during the respiration process. Empty out the flask, dry and replace the yeast, and then add a new food source.

- Depending on equipment type and availability, data collection can take more than one day.
- It is important to approve each group's investigation proposal before starting the investigation.
- Be sure all groups record data for each food source individually for use when writing the investigation report.

Topic Connections

Table 6.2 provides an overview of the scientific practices, crosscutting concepts, disciplinary core ideas, and supporting ideas at the heart of this lab investigation. In addition, it lists NOS and NOSI concepts for the explicit and reflective discussion. Finally, it lists literacy and mathematics skills (*CCSS ELA* and *CCSS Mathematics*) that are addressed during the investigation.

TABLE 6.2

Lab 6 alignment with standards

Scientific practices	• Asking questions • Developing and using models • Planning and carrying out investigations • Analyzing and interpreting data • Using mathematics and computational thinking • Constructing explanations • Engaging in argument from evidence • Obtaining, evaluating, and communicating information
Crosscutting concepts	• Cause and effect: Mechanism and explanation • Energy and matter: Flows, cycles, and conservation • Structure and function
Core ideas	• LS1: From molecules to organisms: Structures and processes • LS2: Ecosystems: Interactions, energy, and dynamics
Supporting ideas	• Cellular respiration • Biomolecules
NOS and NOSI concepts	• Scientific theories and laws • Imagination and creativity in science
Literacy connections *(CCSS ELA)*	• *Reading:* Key ideas and details, craft and structure, integration of knowledge and ideas • *Writing:* Text types and purposes, production and distribution of writing, research to build and present knowledge, range of writing • *Speaking and listening:* Comprehension and collaboration, presentation of knowledge and ideas
Mathematics connections *(CCSS Mathematics)*	• Create equations that describe numbers or relationships • Reason quantitatively and use units to solve problems

Lab 6. Cellular Respiration: How Does the Type of Food Source Affect the Rate of Cellular Respiration in Yeast?

Lab Handout

Introduction

One characteristic of living things is they must take in nutrients and give off waste in order to survive. This is because all living tissues (which are composed of cells) are constantly using energy. In plants, animals, and fungi this energy comes from a reaction called cellular respiration. Cellular respiration refers to a process that occurs inside cells. During this process oxygen is used to convert the chemical energy found within a molecule of sugar into a form that is usable by the organism. The following equation describes this process:

Sugar + oxygen (O_2) → water + carbon dioxide (CO_2) + adenosine triphosphate (ATP), a usable form of energy

Sugar is a generic term used to describe molecules that contain the elements carbon, hydrogen, and oxygen with the general chemical formula of $(CH_2O)n$, where n is 3 or more. Biologists also call sugars carbohydrates or saccharides. There are many different types of sugar (see the figure below). Simple sugars are called monosaccharides; examples include glucose and fructose. Complex sugars include disaccharides and polysaccharides. Examples of disaccharides include lactose, maltose, and sucrose. Examples of polysaccharides include starch, glycogen, and cellulose.

Examples of three different types of sugar

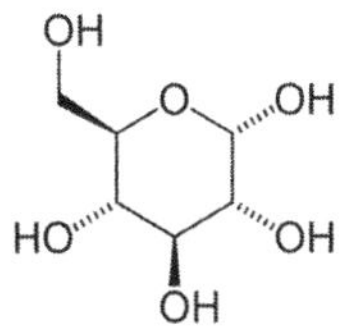

Glucose—a monosaccharide

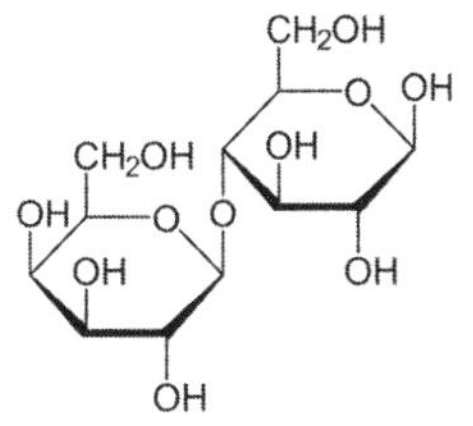

Lactose—a disaccharide

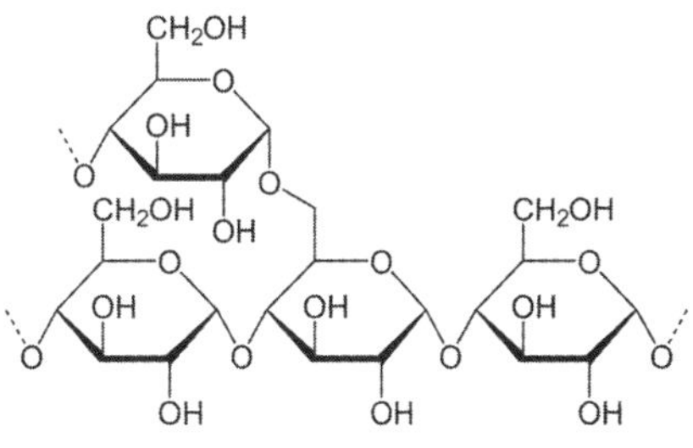

Starch—a polysaccharide

In addition to carbohydrates there are other type of molecules found in plants and animals that could serve as potential energy sources because they also contain the elements carbon, hydrogen, and oxygen. These molecules include lipids and proteins, as shown in the figure below. Lipids do not share a common molecular structure like carbohydrates. The most commonly occurring class of lipids, however, is triglycerides (fats and oils), which have a glycerol backbone bonded to three fatty acids. Proteins contain other atoms such as nitrogen and sulfur, in addition to carbon, hydrogen, and oxygen.

Examples of (a) a lipid and (b) an amino acid found in proteins

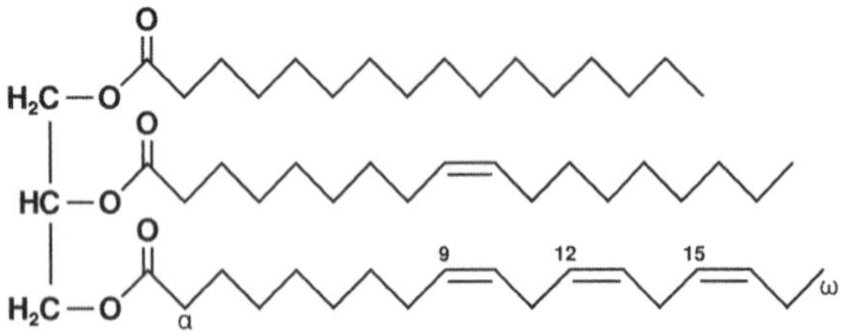

(a) Triglyceride—a lipid

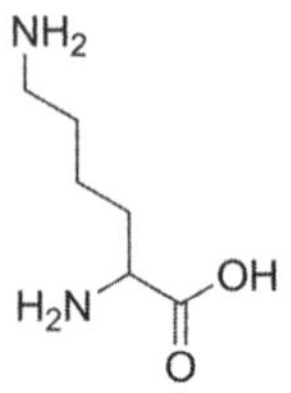

(b) Lysine—an amino acid found in proteins

Yeast, like most types of fungi, produce the energy they need to survive through cellular respiration. In this investigation, you will determine if yeast can use a wide range of nutrients (e.g., proteins, fats, and different types of carbohydrates) to fuel the process of cellular respiration.

Your Task

Design a controlled experiment to determine how the type of food source available affects the rate of cellular respiration in yeast. To do this, you will need to use a CO_2 or O_2 gas sensor as shown in the figure on the next page to determine if yeast produces CO_2 (or uses O_2) at different rates in response to a change in a food source.

The guiding question of this investigation is, **How does the type of food source affect the rate of cellular respiration in yeast?**

Materials

You may use any of the following materials during your investigation:

- Yeast suspension
- Food source 1: starch (polysaccharide)
- Food source 2: sucrose (disaccharide)
- Food source 3: lactose (disaccharide)
- Food source 4: glucose (monosaccharide)
- Food source 5: protein
- Food source 6: lipid

- CO_2 or O_2 gas sensor
- Sensor interface
- 2 Erlenmeyer flasks (each 250 ml)
- Ring stand and clamps
- Beaker (600 ml)
- 7 Test tubes
- Test tube rack
- Safety goggles and aprons

Safety Precautions

1. Safety goggles and aprons are required for this activity.
2. Use caution when working with electrical equipment. Keep away from water sources in that they can cause shorts, fires, and shock hazards. Use only GFI-protected circuits.
3. Wash hands with soap and water after completing this lab.
4. Follow all normal lab safety rules.

Getting Started

To answer the guiding question, you will need to design and conduct a controlled experiment. To accomplish this task, you must determine what type of data you will need to collect, how you will collect it, and how you will analyze it. To determine *what type of data you need to collect,* think about the following question:

- What type of information will you need to collect during the experiment to determine the respiration rate of yeast? (Hint: The figure to the right shows a sensor being used to measure changes in CO_2 or O_2 levels in a 250 ml flask.)

A CO_2 or an O_2 gas sensor can be used to measure changes in gas concentration.

To determine *how you will collect your data,* think about the following questions:

- What will serve as the dependent variable during the experiment?
- What will serve as the independent variable?
- What other factors will you need to keep constant?
- What will serve as a control condition?

- How will you make sure that your data are of high quality (i.e., how will you reduce measurement error)?
- How will you keep track of the data you collect and how will you organize the data?

To determine *how you will analyze your data*, think about the following questions:

- What type of calculations will you need to make?
- What type of graph could you create to help make sense of your data?

Investigation Proposal Required? ☐ Yes ☐ No

Connections to Crosscutting Concepts and to the Nature of Science and the Nature of Scientific Inquiry

As you work through your investigation, be sure to think about

- the importance of identifying the underlying cause for observations,
- how energy and matter move within or through a system,
- how structure determines function in living things,
- the difference between theories and laws in science, and
- the importance of imagination and creativity in science.

Argumentation Session

Once your group has finished collecting and analyzing your data, prepare a whiteboard that you can use to share your initial argument. Your whiteboard should include all the information shown in the figure below.

Argument presentation on a whiteboard

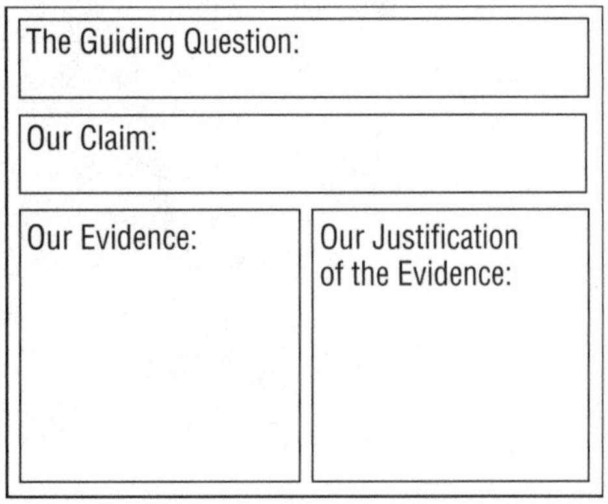

To share your argument with others, we will be using a round-robin format. This means that one member of your group will stay at your lab station to share your group's argument while the other members of your group go to the other lab stations one at a time to listen to and critique the arguments developed by your classmates.

The goal of the argumentation session is not to convince others that your argument is the best one; rather, the goal is to identify errors or instances of faulty reasoning in the arguments so these mistakes can be fixed. You will therefore need to evaluate the content of the claim, the quality of the evidence used to support the claim, and the strength of the justification of the evidence included in each argument that you see. In order to critique an argument, you will need more information than what is included on the whiteboard. You might, therefore, need to ask the presenter one or more follow-up questions, such as:

- How did you collect your data? Why did you use that method? Why did you collect those data?
- What did you do to make sure the data you collected are reliable? What did you do to decrease measurement error?
- What did you do to analyze your data? Why did you decide to do it that way? Did you check your calculations?
- Is that the only way to interpret the results of your analysis? How do you know that your interpretation of your analysis is appropriate?
- Why did your group decide to present your evidence in that manner?
- What other claims did your group discuss before you decided on that one? Why did your group abandon those alternative ideas?
- How confident are you that your claim is valid? What could you do to increase your confidence?

Once the argumentation session is complete, you will have a chance to meet with your group and revise your original argument. Your group might need to gather more data or design a way to test one or more alternative claims as part of this process. Remember, your goal at this stage of the investigation is to develop the most valid or acceptable answer to the research question!

Report

Once you have completed your research, you will need to prepare an investigation report that consists of three sections that provide answers to the following questions:

1. What question were you trying to answer and why?
2. What did you do during your investigation and why did you conduct your investigation in this way?
3. What is your argument?

Your report should answer these questions in two pages or less. This report must be typed, and any diagrams, figures, or tables should be embedded into the document. Be sure to write in a persuasive style; you are trying to convince others that your claim is acceptable or valid!

Lab 6. Cellular Respiration: How Does the Type of Food Source Affect the Rate of Cellular Respiration in Yeast?

Checkout Questions

1. Describe the reactants and products of cellular respiration.

2. Scientific laws are theories that have been proven true.

   a. I agree with this statement.

   b. I disagree with this statement.

   Explain your answer, using information from your investigation about cellular respiration.

3. Scientists use their imagination and creativity when they analyze and interpret data.

   a. I agree with this statement.

   b. I disagree with this statement.

   Explain your answer, using examples from your investigation about cellular respiration.

4. An important goal in science is to explain the underlying cause for observations. Explain why this is important, using an example from your investigation about cellular respiration.

5. Scientists often need to track how matter moves in, out, and through a system during an investigation. Explain why this is important, using an example from your investigation about cellular respiration.

6. Structure and function are related in living things. Explain why they are related, using an example from your investigation about cellular respiration.

Lab 7. Transpiration: How Does Leaf Surface Area Affect the Movement of Water Through a Plant?

Teacher Notes

Purpose

The purpose of this lab is for students to *apply* their understanding of transpiration in plants to determine how the structure of leaves can influence the rate of transpiration. This lab also gives students an opportunity to design and carry out a controlled experiment. Students will also learn about the nature of scientific investigation and the difference between observation and inference.

The Content

Plants have pores, or *stoma,* on the underside of leaves. The stomata allow carbon dioxide (CO_2) to enter the plant. Plants need CO_2 for photosynthesis and to prevent desiccation. However, plants also lose a great deal of water through the stomata due to evaporation. The evaporation of water from the plant drives transpiration, but too much water loss can dry out the plant and kill it (especially when there is very little water available in the soil). Although this may seem like a huge problem for the plant, the stomata will open and close in relationship to the turgor pressure of the guard cells around it to help control water loss. Plants have also adapted various structural characteristics to prevent water loss, including thick waxy cuticles, change in leaf shape (decreasing the surface area of leaves decreases water loss), and change in leaf size (having lots of small leaves actually reduces overall surface area).

Timeline

The instructional time needed to implement this lab investigation is 180–250 minutes. Appendix 2 (p. 391) provides options for implementing this lab investigation over several class periods. Option E (250 minutes) should be used if students are unfamiliar with scientific writing because this option provides extra instructional time for scaffolding the writing process. You can scaffold the writing process by modeling, providing examples, and providing hints as students write each section of the report. Option F (180 minutes) should be used if students are familiar with scientific writing and have the skills needed to write an investigation report on their own. In option F, students complete stage 6 (writing the investigation report) and stage 8 (revising the report) as homework.

Materials and Preparation

The materials needed to implement this investigation are listed in Table 7.1. The bean plants should be germinated and growing approximately *3 weeks prior* to the start of the investigation. A minimum of three seedlings with leaves is needed for each group (nine is ideal, six is recommended). Plants need to be seedlings. Bean plants work the best and germinate easily, but other plants can be used. Plants with fibrous root systems work best.

TABLE 7.1
Materials list

Item	Quantity
Test tubes, 150 mm × 15 mm	6 per group
Test tube rack	1 per group
Graduated cylinder, 25 ml	1 per group
Beaker, 600 ml	1 per group
Bean plants (3 weeks old)	6 per group
Graph paper	6 sheets per group
Ruler	1 per group
Electronic balance	3 per class
Floodlight or plant stand with light	1 per group
Glass stirring rod	1 per group
Student handout	1 per student
Investigation proposal A*	1 per group
Whiteboard, 2' × 3'†	1 per group
Peer-review guide and instructor scoring rubric	1 per student
Safety goggles and aprons	1 per student

* It is recommended but not required that students fill out an investigation proposal for this lab; it is not necessary to do so if students already know how to design a controlled experiment.

† As an alternative, students can use computer and presentation software such as Microsoft PowerPoint or Apple Keynote to create their arguments.

Topics for the Explicit and Reflective Discussion

Concepts That Can Be Used to Justify the Evidence

To provide an adequate justification of their evidence, students must explain why they included the evidence in their arguments and make the assumptions underlying their

analysis and interpretation of the data explicit. In this investigation, students can use the following concepts to help justify their evidence:

- The process of evaporation
- The process of transpiration
- The role that water and CO_2 play in the process of photosynthesis
- Why calculating a rate (change over a period of time) of water loss is useful for making comparisons

We recommend that you review these concepts during the explicit and reflective discussion to help students make this connection.

How to Design Better Investigations

It is important for students to reflect on the strengths and weaknesses of the investigation they designed during the explicit and reflective discussion. Students should therefore be encouraged to discuss ways to eliminate potential flaws, measurement errors, or sources of bias in their investigations. To help students be more reflective about the design of their investigation, you can ask the following questions:

- What were some of the strengths of your investigation? What made it scientific?
- What were some of the weaknesses of your investigation? What made it less scientific?
- If you were to do this investigation again, what would you do to address the weaknesses in your investigation? What could you do to make it more scientific?

Crosscutting Concepts

This investigation is well aligned with four crosscutting concepts found in *A Framework for K–12 Science Education,* and you should review these concepts in the explicit and reflective discussion.

- *Cause and Effect: Mechanism and Explanation:* One of the main objectives of science is to identify and establish relationships between a cause and effect. It is also important to understand the mechanisms by which these causal relationships are mediated.
- *Scale, Proportion, and Quantity:* Students need to understand that it is critical for scientists to be able to identify what is meaningful or relevant at different scales or time periods.
- *Energy and Matter: Flows, Cycles and Conservation:* Scientists often strive to learn more about how energy and matter move into, out of, and within an organism to develop a better understanding of how that organism functions.

- *Structure and Function:* Students need to understand that the way an object is shaped or an organism is structured will influence what the object or organism is able to do or how it responds to changes. Scientists can examine the structure of a living thing and make inferences about how it functions.

The Nature of Science and the Nature of Scientific Inquiry

It is important for students to understand the difference between observations and inferences in science. An observation is a descriptive statement about a natural phenomenon, whereas an inference is an interpretation of an observation. Students should also understand that current scientific knowledge and the perspectives of individual scientists guide both observations and inferences. Thus, different scientists can have different but equally valid interpretations of the same observations due to differences in their perspectives and background knowledge.

It is also important for students to understand that *scientists use different methods to answer different types of questions*. Examples of methods include experiments, systematic observations of a phenomenon, literature reviews, and analysis of existing data sets; the choice of method depends on the objectives of the research. There is no universal step-by-biology vs. physics) and fields within a discipline (e.g., ecology vs. molecular biology) use different types of methods, use different core theories, and rely on different standards to develop scientific knowledge.

You should discuss and provide examples of these two important concepts of the nature of science (NOS) and the nature of scientific inquiry (NOSI) during the explicit and reflective discussion.

Hints for Implementing the Lab

- Review structures of a plant before starting the investigation.
- Review the definition and calculation of surface area before starting the investigation.
- Students need to be very careful with the seedlings so as not to harm the root system when putting them in the test tubes. Larger test tubes are preferred.
- It is important for future calculations that students carefully record the total amount of water they place in each test tube.
- Remind students to measure the total water left in the tube using a graduated cylinder.
- Encourage students to think of different ways to test total surface area, such as small leaves versus large leaves, number of leaves on the seedlings (none, one, two, or three), and one-size leaves versus mixed-size leaves.

- As an alternative to tracing leaves on graph paper, groups can use mass to determine leaf surface area. This method requires an electronic balance. Use the following procedure:
    1. Cut all the leaves (not stems) off the plant and determine their mass using a balance.
    2. Estimate the total leaf surface area in square centimeters for the plant by cutting out a section of leaf 5 cm × 5 cm.
    3. Determine the mass for this leaf section and divide by 25 cm^2 to find the mass of 1 cm^2 of leaf.
    4. Divide the total mass of the leaves by the mass of 1 cm^2 to find the total leaf surface area.
- When groups measure surface area using graph paper, make sure they remove all the leaves. Partial boxes will require them to estimate; be sure to have students think about ways to reduce measurement error due to estimation. One way is to have multiple students in the group make an estimate and then take an average.

Topic Connections

Table 7.2 provides an overview of the scientific practices, crosscutting concepts, disciplinary core ideas, and supporting ideas at the heart of this lab investigation. In addition, it lists NOS and NOSI concepts for the explicit and reflective discussion. Finally, it lists literacy and mathematics skills (*CCSS ELA* and *CCSS Mathematics*) that are addressed during the investigation.

TABLE 7.2

Lab 7 alignment with standards

Scientific practices	• Asking questions • Developing and using models • Planning and carrying out investigations • Analyzing and interpreting data • Using mathematics and computational thinking • Constructing explanations • Engaging in argument from evidence • Obtaining, evaluating, and communicating information
Crosscutting concepts	• Cause and effect: Mechanism and explanation • Scale, proportion, and quantity • Energy and matter: Flows, cycles, and conservation • Structure and function
Core ideas	• LS1: From molecules to organisms: Structures and processes • LS2: Ecosystems: Interactions, energy, and dynamics
Supporting ideas	• Transpiration • Water concentration • Surface area • Xylem • Phloem • Evaporation
NOS and NOSI concepts	• Observations and inferences • Methods used in scientific investigations
Literacy connections *(CCSS ELA)*	• *Reading*: Key ideas and details, craft and structure, integration of knowledge and ideas • *Writing*: Text types and purposes, production and distribution of writing, research to build and present knowledge, range of writing • *Speaking and listening*: Comprehension and collaboration, presentation of knowledge and ideas
Mathematics connections *(CCSS Mathematics)*	• Create equations that describe numbers or relationships • Solve equations and inequalities in one variable • Reason quantitatively and use units to solve problems

Lab 7. Transpiration: How Does Leaf Surface Area Affect the Movement of Water Through a Plant?

Lab Handout

Introduction

Plants, just like other organisms, must be able to transport materials from one part to another. Plant transport systems consist of two large tubes made of vascular tissue that run from the roots through the shoots and to the tips of the plant. Sugars produced through the process of photosynthesis are transported through plants from leaves to roots via the vascular tissue known as the phloem. Cells use these sugars to produce the energy needed for the rest of the plant's functions. Sugars move through the plant because they are in highest concentration in the leaves, where photosynthesis takes place, and in lowest concentration in the roots. Many plants will store excess sugars in specialized root structures called tubers.

Water is transported in plants from the roots to the leaves through the vascular tissue known as the xylem. The water then enters the leaf and is used in the process of photosynthesis. In a tree such as the giant redwood of California, water must ascend over 300 ft. to reach the highest leaves. The water moves through the plant because the concentration of water is highest in the roots of a plant and lowest in the leaves. Transpiration, or loss of water from the leaves due to evaporation, helps to create a lower concentration of water (or lower osmotic potential) in the leaf. The differences in water concentration are also responsible for the movement of water from the xylem to the mesophyll layer of the leaves and subsequently out to the atmosphere (see the figure on the next page).

The transpiration rate of a plant (or how quickly water is lost from the leaves due to evaporation) is influenced by a number of environmental factors. One of the most important factors is air temperature; evaporation rates increase as the temperature goes up. Plants that live in hot locations, therefore, can lose large amounts of water from their leaves because of transpiration. When there is plenty of water in the soil, like after a heavy rain, replacing the water that is lost from the leaves because of transpiration is not a problem. However, when water is scarce and the temperature is high, plants can quickly dry out and die. Some plants, therefore, have specific adaptations that enable them to help control water loss. One such adaption could be the number or size of leaves found on a plant.

Your Task

Determine if there is a relationship between leaf surface area (i.e., the total number of leaves or the size of the leaves found on a plant) and transpiration rate.

The guiding question of this investigation is, **How does leaf surface area affect the movement of water through a plant?**

The structure of a leaf featuring the major tissues: the upper and lower epidermis, the palisade and spongy mesophyll, and the guard cells of the stoma.

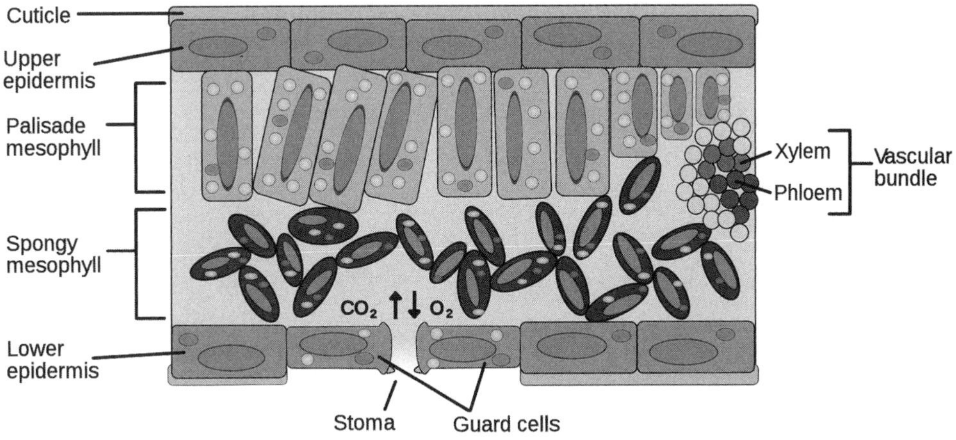

Vascular tissue (veins), made up of xylem and phloem are also shown. The light green circles within cells represent chloroplasts and indicate which tissues undergo photosynthesis.

Materials

You may use any of the following materials during your investigation:

- 6 Test tubes (150 mm × 15 mm)
- Test tube rack
- Graduated cylinder (25 ml)
- 6 Bean plants (about 3 weeks old)
- Graph paper
- Ruler
- Beaker (600 ml)
- Electronic balance
- Floodlight or plant stand with light
- Glass stirring rod
- Safety goggles and aprons

Safety Precautions

1. Safety goggles and aprons are required for this activity.
2. Use caution when working with electrical equipment. Keep away from water sources in that they can cause shorts, fires, and shock hazards. Use only GFI-protected circuits.

3. Lightbulbs can get hot and burn skin. Use caution and handle with care!
4. Wash hands with soap and water after completing this lab.
5. Follow all normal lab safety rules.

Plant setup

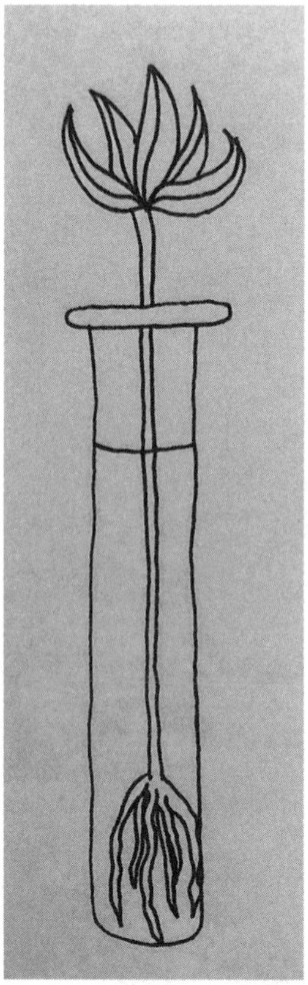

Getting Started

To answer the guiding question, you will need to design and conduct an experiment. To accomplish this task, you must be able to measure the transpiration rate of a plant. You can use the following procedure to measure a transpiration rate (see the figure to the left):

1. Pour 15 ml of tap water into a test tube.
2. Place one plant without soil on the roots into the test tube of water (be careful not to damage the roots).
3. Gently push the roots to the bottom of the tube. (The eraser end of a pencil works well for this, as does a glass stirring rod.)
4. Place this tube into a test tube rack in a warm and lighted place in the room for at least 24 hours (48 hours is better).
5. Remove the plant from the tube.
6. Remove leaves and trace on graph paper to determine total surface area.
7. Measure the amount of water left in the test tube.
8. Calculate the transpiration rate using the following equation:

$$\text{Transpiration rate} = \frac{\text{original amount of water} - \text{amount of water left}}{\text{minutes}}$$

This procedure will allow you to measure the rate at which water moves through the plant. Now you must determine what type of data you will need to collect, how you will collect it, and how will you analyze it for your actual investigation. To determine *what type of data you will need to collect,* think about the following question:

- What type of measurements will you need to record during your investigation?

To determine *how you will collect your data,* think about the following questions:

- What will serve as a control (or comparison) condition?
- What types of treatment conditions will you need to set up and how will you do it?
- How many trials will you need to do?
- How often will you collect data and when will you do it?

- How will you keep track of the data you collect and how will you organize the data?

To determine *how you will analyze your data,* think about the following questions:

- How will you determine if there is a difference between the treatment conditions and the control condition?
- What type of calculations will you need to make?
- What type of graph could you create to help make sense of your data?

Investigation Proposal Required? ☐ Yes ☐ No

Connections to Crosscutting Concepts and to the Nature of Science and the Nature of Scientific Inquiry

As you work through your investigation, be sure to think about

- the importance of identifying the underlying cause for observations,
- what is and what is not relevant at different scales or time frames,
- how matter moves within or through a system,
- how structure determines function in living things,
- the difference between observations and inferences in science, and
- the different methods scientists can use to answer a research question in science.

Argumentation Session

Once your group has finished collecting and analyzing your data, prepare a whiteboard that you can use to share your initial argument. Your whiteboard should include all the information shown in the figure to the right.

Argument presentation on a whiteboard

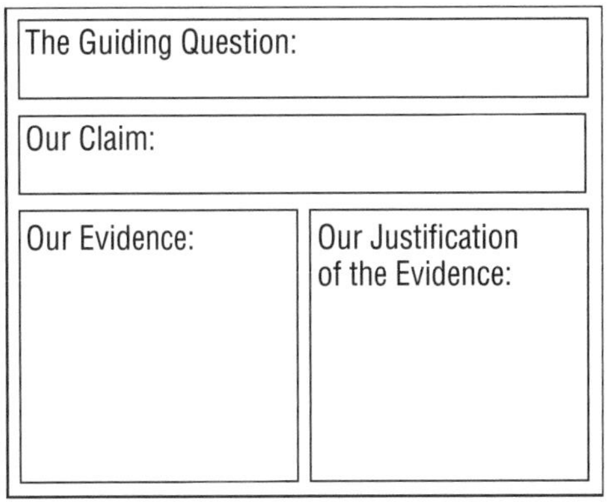

To share your argument with others, we will be using a round-robin format. This means that one member of your group will stay at your lab station to share your group's argument while the other members of your group go to the other lab stations one at a time to listen to and critique the arguments developed by your classmates.

The goal of the argumentation session is not to convince others that your argument is the best one; rather, the goal is to identify errors or instances of faulty reasoning in the arguments so these mistakes can be fixed. You will therefore need to evaluate the content of the claim, the quality of the evidence used to support the claim, and the strength of the justification of the evidence included in each argument that you see. In order to critique an argument, you will need more information than what is included on the whiteboard. You might, therefore, need to ask the presenter one or more follow-up questions, such as:

- How did you collect your data? Why did you use that method? Why did you collect those data?
- What did you do to make sure the data you collected are reliable? What did you do to decrease measurement error?
- What did you do to analyze your data? Why did you decide to do it that way? Did you check your calculations?
- Is that the only way to interpret the results of your analysis? How do you know that your interpretation of your analysis is appropriate?
- Why did you decide to present your evidence in that manner?
- What other claims did your group discuss before you decided on that one? Why did your group abandon those alternative ideas?
- How confident are you that your claim is valid? What could you do to increase your confidence?

Once the argumentation session is complete, you will have a chance to meet with your group and revise your original argument. Your group might need to gather more data or design a way to test one or more alternative claims as part of this process. Remember, your goal at this stage of the investigation is to develop the most valid or acceptable answer to the research question!

Report

Once you have completed your research, you will need to prepare an investigation report that consists of three sections that provide answers to the following questions:

1. What question were you trying to answer and why?
2. What did you do during your investigation and why did you conduct your investigation in this way?
3. What is your argument?

Your report should answer these questions in two pages or less. This report must be typed, and any diagrams, figures, or tables should be embedded into the document. Be sure to write in a persuasive style; you are trying to convince others that your claim is acceptable or valid!

Lab 7. Transpiration: How Does Leaf Surface Area Affect the Movement of Water Through a Plant?

Checkout Questions

1. Plant A and plant B both have the same number of leaves; however, plant B leaves are overall larger in size. If both plants were placed in a hot environment, which plant would undergo transpiration at greater rate?

   a. Plant A
   b. Plant B

   Why?

2. Observations and inferences are the same.

   a. I agree with this statement.
   b. I disagree with this statement.

   Explain your answer, using examples from your investigation about transpiration.

3. The investigation that you conducted is an example of a controlled experiment.

   a. I agree with this statement.
   b. I disagree with this statement.

   Explain your answer, using information from your investigation about transpiration.

4. An important goal in science is to explain the underlying cause for observations. Explain why this is important, using an example from your investigation about transpiration.

5. Scientists often need to be aware of the issue of time when designing an investigation. Explain why time frames can influence the outcomes of an investigation, using an example from your investigation about transpiration.

6. Scientists often need to track how matter moves in, out, and through a system during an investigation. Explain why this is important, using an example from your investigation about transpiration.

7. Structure is related to function in living things. Explain why, using an example from your investigation about transpiration.

Lab 8. Enzymes: How Do Changes in Temperature and pH Levels Affect Enzyme Activity?

Teacher Notes

Purpose

The purpose of this lab is for students to *apply* what they know about the function of enzymes to determine how environmental factors affect an enzyme's function. This lab also gives students an opportunity to design and carry out a controlled experiment to investigate the effects of temperature or pH on the action of enzymes. Students will also learn about the nature and role of experiments in science and how science, as a body of knowledge, changes over time.

The Content

Enzymes are proteins. The shape of a protein dictates the function of that protein. Proteins, when exposed to high heat, begin to unravel or denature. When the shape of a protein changes, it is no longer able to complete its original function. Therefore, exposing an enzyme to high temperatures will cause it to lose its shape and stop functioning. Decreases in temperature will also slow down enzyme action. Decreasing the temperature causes the molecules involved to move more slowly. As the molecules slow down, their chances of collision with other molecules decreases, which in turn slows the rate of a chemical reaction. Changes in the pH level can also cause an enzyme to stop functioning because basic and acidic conditions can cause the enzyme to change shape (or denature). Most enzymes, as a result, can only function within a narrow range of pH levels.

Timeline

The instructional time needed to implement this lab investigation is 180–250 minutes. Appendix 2 (p. 391) provides options for implementing this lab investigation over several class periods. Option A (250 minutes) should be used if students are unfamiliar with scientific writing because this option provides extra instructional time for scaffolding the writing process. You can scaffold the writing process by modeling, providing examples, and providing hints as students write each section of the report. Option B (180 minutes) should be used if students are familiar with scientific writing and have the skills needed to write an investigation report on their own. In option B, students complete stage 6 (writing the investigation report) and stage 8 (revising the report) as homework.

TABLE 8.1

Materials list

Item	Quantity
Catalase solution	50 ml per group
3% H_2O_2 solution	250 ml per group
0.1 M HCl solution in a dropper bottle	1 per group
0.1 M NaOH solution in a dropper bottle	1 per group
25 ml graduated cylinder	1 per group
Erlenmeyer flask, 250 ml	2 per group
Beaker, 600 ml	2 per group
Hot plate	1 per group
Ice	250 ml per group
O_2 gas sensor	1 per group
Temperature probe or thermometer	1 per group
pH paper or pH probe	1 per group
Sensor interface	1 per group
Ring stand	1 per class
Ring stand clamps	1 per group
Student handout	1 per student
Investigation proposal B*	1 per group
Whiteboard, 2' × 3'†	1 per group
Peer-review guide and instructor scoring rubric	1 per student
Safety goggles, vinyl gloves, and aprons	1 per student

* It is recommended but not required that students fill out an investigation proposal for this lab; it is not necessary to do so if students already know how to design a controlled experiment.

† As an alternative, students can use computer and presentation software such as Microsoft PowerPoint or Apple Keynote to create their arguments.

Materials and Preparation

The materials needed to implement this investigation are listed in Table 8.1. Purchase or prepare catalase solution prior to the investigation. Catalase can be purchased from a science supply company (such as Carolina, Flinn Scientific, or Ward's Science), or if funds are limited, it can be extracted from liver. To extract catalase from liver, place raw liver and distilled water in a blender and blend until well homogenized. Strain the homogenized liver through several layers of cheesecloth. The resulting solution will contain catalase. Immediately refrigerate the solution or put it on ice, and keep it cold to prevent breakdown. A 3% hydrogen peroxide (H_2O_2) solution can be used directly from the bottle, or if supplies are limited, the concentration can be reduced to 1.5%. If hydrochloride (HCl) and sodium hydroxide (NaOH) are not available, you may substitute vinegar and baking soda or any other acid and base (students need to be able to see a definitive pH change). Students will need to create water baths to alter temperature of the solutions of catalase and H_2O_2.

Topics for the Explicit and Reflective Discussion

Concepts That Can Be Used to Justify the Evidence

To provide an adequate justification of their evidence, students must explain why they included the evidence in their arguments and make the assumptions underlying their analysis and interpretation of the data explicit. In this investigation, students can use the following concepts to help justify their evidence:

- The rearrangement of atoms in chemical reactions
- The difference between products and reactants in a chemical reaction
- The difference between chemical and physical change
- Why calculating a rate (change over a period of time) of oxygen production is useful for making comparisons

We recommend that you review these concepts during the explicit and reflective discussion to help students make this connection.

How to Design Better Investigations

It is important for students to reflect on the strengths and weaknesses of the investigation they designed during the explicit and reflective discussion. Students should therefore be encouraged to discuss ways to eliminate potential flaws, measurement errors, or sources of bias in their investigations. To help students be more reflective about the design of their investigation, you can ask the following questions:

- What were some of the strengths of your investigation? What made it scientific?
- What were some of the weaknesses of your investigation? What made it less scientific?
- If you were to do this investigation again, what would you do to address the weaknesses in your investigation? What could you do to make it more scientific?

Crosscutting Concepts

This investigation is well aligned with three crosscutting concepts found in *A Framework for K–12 Science Education,* and you should review these concepts during the explicit and reflective discussion.

- *Cause and Effect: Mechanism and Explanation:* One of the main objectives of science is to identify and establish relationships between a cause and effect. It is also important to understand the mechanisms by which these causal relationships are mediated.

- *Energy and Matter: Flows, Cycles, and Conservation:* Scientists often strive to learn more about how energy and matter flow into, out of, and within an organism to develop a better understanding of how that organism functions.
- *Structure and Function.* Students need to understand that the way an object is shaped or a molecule is structured (e.g., the shape of an enzyme) will determine how the object or the molecule functions (e.g., the ability to act as a catalyst in a chemical pathway).

The Nature of Science and the Nature of Scientific Inquiry

It is important for students to understand the *nature and role of experiments in science.* Scientists use experiments to test the validity of a hypothesis (i.e., a tentative explanation) for an observed phenomenon. Experiments include a test and the formulation of predictions (expected results) if the test is conducted and the hypothesis is valid. The experiment is then carried out and the predictions are compared with the observed results of the experiment. If the predictions match the observed results, then the hypothesis is supported. If the observed results do not match the prediction, then the hypothesis is not supported. A signature feature of an experiment is the control of variables to help eliminate alternative explanations for observed results.

It is also important for students to understand that *science as a body of knowledge develops over time.* A person can have confidence in the validity of scientific knowledge but must also accept that scientific knowledge may be abandoned or modified in light of new evidence or because existing evidence has been reconceptualized by scientists. There are many examples in the history of science of both evolutionary changes (i.e., the slow or gradual refinement of ideas) and revolutionary changes (i.e., the rapid abandonment of a well-established idea) in scientific knowledge.

You should review and provide examples of these two important concepts of the nature of science (NOS) and the nature of scientific inquiry (NOSI) during the explicit and reflective discussion.

Hints for Implementing the Lab

- It is important to keep the fresh catalase cold during the investigation.
- Remind students during the investigation proposal stage that the environmental conditions need to be applied to the enzyme solution, not the H_2O_2.
- H_2O_2 can be purchased from a local grocery store or drugstore. It lasts longer if kept cold and in the dark.

Topic Connections

Table 8.2 (p. 118) provides an overview of the scientific practices, crosscutting concepts, disciplinary core ideas, and supporting ideas at the heart of this lab investigation. In addition, it lists NOS and NOSI concepts for the explicit and reflective discussion. Finally, it lists literacy and mathematics skills (*CCSS ELA* and *CCSS Mathematics*) that are addressed during the investigation.

TABLE 8.2

Lab 8 alignment with standards

Scientific practices	• Asking questions • Planning and carrying out investigations • Analyzing and interpreting data • Using mathematics and computational thinking • Constructing explanations • Engaging in argument from evidence • Obtaining, evaluating, and communicating information
Crosscutting concepts	• Cause and effect: Mechanism and explanation • Energy and matter: Flows, cycles, and conservation • Structure and function
Core idea	• LS1: From molecules to organisms: Structures and processes
Supporting ideas	• Enzyme structure and function • Biological molecules
NOS and NOSI concepts	• Nature and role of experiments • Science as a body of knowledge
Literacy connections (*CCSS ELA*)	• *Reading*: Key ideas and details, craft and structure, integration of knowledge and ideas • *Writing*: Text types and purposes, production and distribution of writing, research to build and present knowledge, range of writing • *Speaking and listening*: Comprehension and collaboration, presentation of knowledge and ideas
Mathematics connection (*CCSS Mathematics*)	• Reason quantitatively and use units to solve problems

Lab 8. Enzymes: How Do Changes in Temperature and pH Levels Affect Enzyme Activity?

Lab Handout

Introduction

Enzyme effect on chemical reactions

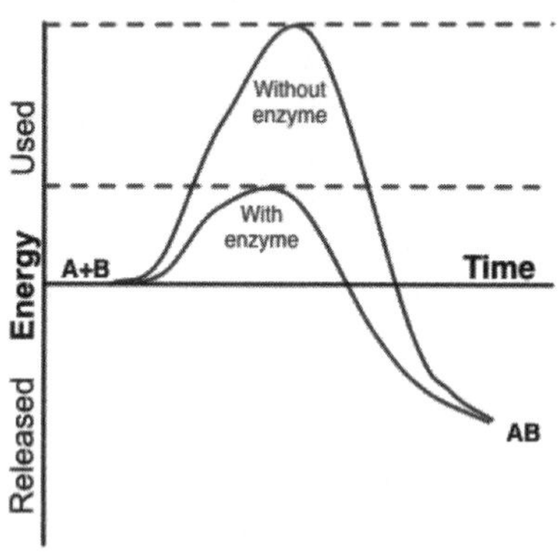

Sugars are vital to all living organisms and are used to produce the energy (in the form of adenosine triphosphate, or ATP) an organism needs for survival. All sugars are carbohydrates, which are molecules that contain the elements carbon, hydrogen, and oxygen with the general chemical formula of $(CH_2O)n$, where n is 3 or more. Living organisms use carbohydrates as sources of energy. Different types of sugars are found in different kinds of foods, but not all of these sugars can be used as energy sources by every type of organism. In order for an organism to make use of a sugar as an energy source, it must be capable of transporting the sugar into its cells and it must have the proper enzymes to break down the chemical bonds of the sugar to release the energy stored inside the molecule.

Enzymes are proteins that are involved in almost every chemical reaction that take place within an organism. They act as catalysts, substances that speed up chemical reactions without being destroyed or altered during the process. The figure above illustrates how an enzyme lowers the amount of energy needed for a reaction to take place, and the figure on the next page illustrates how an enzyme interacts with a substrate. Although most reactions can occur without enzymes, the rate of the reaction would be far too slow to be useful.

An example of an important enzyme in animals is catalase, which is produced in the liver and is used to catalyze the breakdown of hydrogen peroxide (H_2O_2). H_2O_2 is a toxic chemical that is produced as a natural by-product of many reactions that take place within your cells. Because it is toxic, it must be destroyed before it can do too much damage. To destroy H_2O_2, cells convert it into oxygen gas and water based on the following reaction:

$$H_2O_2 \text{ (liquid)} \xrightarrow{\text{catalase}} H_2O \text{ (liquid)} + O_2 \text{ (gas)}$$

Environmental conditions, such as temperature or pH level, can affect the function of enzymes. In this investigation, you will explore how these two environmental conditions affect enzyme activity by measuring the rate at which O_2 is produced when H_2O_2 is exposed to catalase at different pH levels and temperatures.

How an enzyme interacts with a substrate

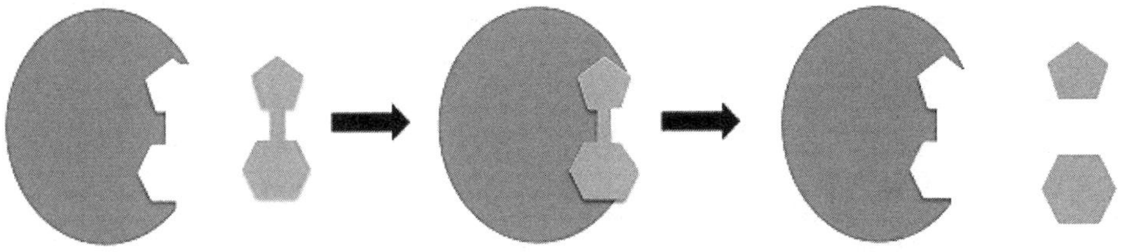

Your Task

Design two controlled experiments to determine how changes in temperature and pH levels affect the activity of the enzyme catalase.

The guiding question of this investigation is, **How do changes in temperature and pH levels affect enzyme activity?**

Materials

You may use any of the following materials during your investigation:

- Catalase solution
- 3% H_2O_2 solution
- 0.1 M hydrochloride (HCl) solution
- 0.1 M sodium hydroxide (NaOH) solution
- Graduated cylinder (25 ml)
- 2 Erlenmeyer flasks (each 250 ml)
- 2 Beakers (each 600 ml)
- Hot plate
- Ice
- O_2 gas sensor
- Sensor interface
- Temperature probe or thermometer
- pH probe or pH paper
- Ring stand and clamps
- Safety goggles, vinyl gloves, and aprons

Safety Precautions

1. Safety goggles, vinyl gloves, and aprons are required for this activity.
2. Use caution when working with electrical equipment. Keep away from water sources in that they can cause shorts, fires, and shock hazards. Use only GFI-protected circuits.
3. Hot plates can get hot and burn skin. Use caution and handle with care!
4. Wash hands with soap and water upon completing this lab.
5. Follow all normal lab safety rules.

Getting Started

To answer the guiding question, you will need to design and conduct two experiments. For each experiment, you must determine what type of data you will need to collect, how you will collect it, and how you will analyze it. To determine *what type of data you will need to collect,* think about the following questions:

- What will serve as your independent variable during each of your experiments?
- What will serve as your dependent variable during each of your experiments?
- What type of measurements or observations will you need to record during each of your experiments? (Hint: What information will you need to calculate a rate?)

To determine *how you will collect your data,* think about the following questions:

- What will serve as a control condition?
- What types of treatment conditions will you need to set up and how will you do it?
- How many trials will you need to conduct?
- How often will you collect data and when will you do it?
- How will you make sure that your data are of high quality (i.e., how will you reduce measurement error)?
- How will you keep track of the data you collect and how will you organize the data?

To determine *how you will analyze your data,* think about the following questions:

- How will you determine if there is a difference between the treatment conditions and the control condition?
- What type of calculations will you need to make?
- What type of graph could you create to help make sense of your data?

Investigation Proposal Required? ☐ Yes ☐ No

Connections to Crosscutting Concepts and to the Nature of Science and the Nature of Scientific Inquiry.

As you work through your investigation, be sure to think about

- the importance of identifying the underlying cause for observations;
- how energy and matter move within or through a system;
- how structure is related to function in living things;
- the nature and role of experiments in science; and
- how science, as a body of knowledge, develops over time.

Argumentation Session

Once your group has finished collecting and analyzing your data, prepare a whiteboard that you can use to share your initial argument. Your whiteboard should include all the information shown in the figure to the right.

Argument presentation on a whiteboard

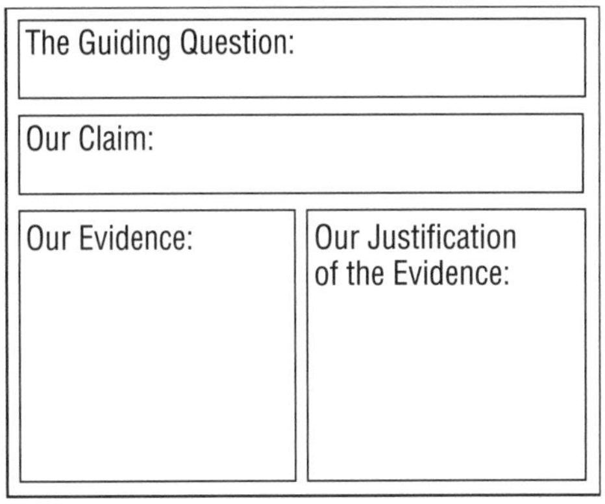

To share your argument with others, we will be using a round-robin format. This means that one member of your group will stay at your lab station to share your group's argument while the other members of your group go to the other lab stations one at a time to listen to and critique the arguments developed by your classmates.

The goal of the argumentation session is not to convince others that your argument is the best one; rather, the goal is to identify errors or instances of faulty reasoning in the arguments so these mistakes can be fixed. You will therefore need to evaluate the content of the claim, the quality of the evidence used to support the claim, and the strength of the justification of the evidence included in each argument that you see. In order to critique an argument, you will need more information than what is included on the whiteboard. You might, therefore, need to ask the presenter one or more follow-up questions, such as:

- How did you collect your data? Why did you use that method? Why did you collect those data?
- What did you do to make sure the data you collected are reliable? What did you do to decrease measurement error?
- What did you do to analyze your data? Why did you decide to do it that way? Did you check your calculations?

- Is that the only way to interpret the results of your analysis? How do you know that your interpretation of your analysis is appropriate?
- Why did you decide to present your evidence in that manner?
- What other claims did your group discuss before you decided on that one? Why did your group abandon those alternative ideas?
- How confident are you that your claim is valid? What could you do to increase your confidence?

Once the argumentation session is complete, you will have a chance to meet with your group and revise your original argument. Your group might need to gather more data or design a way to test one or more alternative claims as part of this process. Remember, your goal at this stage of the investigation is to develop the most valid or acceptable answer to the research question!

Report

Once you have completed your research, you will need to prepare an investigation report that consists of three sections that provide answers to the following questions:

1. What question were you trying to answer and why?
2. What did you do during your investigation and why did you conduct your investigation in this way?
3. What is your argument?

Your report should answer these questions in two pages or less. This report must be typed, and any diagrams, figures, or tables should be embedded into the document. Be sure to write in a persuasive style; you are trying to convince others that your claim is acceptable or valid!

Lab 8. Enzymes: How Do Changes in Temperature and pH Levels Affect Enzyme Activity?

Checkout Questions

1. How do environmental factors, such as temperature and pH, affect enzyme function?

2. All investigations are experiments.

   a. I agree with this statement.
   b. I disagree with this statement.

   Explain your answer, using information from your investigation about enzymes.

3. Scientific knowledge that is based on a well-designed experiment will not change.

   a. I agree with this statement.
   b. I disagree with this statement.

   Explain your answer, using examples from your investigation about enzymes.

4. An important goal in science is to explain the underlying cause for observations. Explain why this is important, using an example from your investigation about enzymes.

5. Scientists often need to track how matter moves in, out, and through a system during an investigation. Explain why this is important, using an example from your investigation about enzymes.

6. Structure and function are related in living things. Explain why, using an example from your investigation about enzymes.

SECTION 3
Life Sciences Core Idea 2:

Ecosystems: Interactions, Energy, and Dynamics

Introduction Labs

Lab 9. Population Growth: How Do Changes in the Amount and Nature of the Plant Life Available in an Ecosystem Influence Herbivore Population Growth Over Time?

Teacher Notes

Purpose

The purpose of this lab is to *introduce* students to how population size changes over time and some of the factors that can affect the size of a population. This lab also gives students an opportunity to design and carry out an investigation using an online simulation. The simulation, called *Rabbits Grass Weeds* (Wilensky 2001), was created using NetLogo, a multiagent programmable modeling environment developed at the Center for Connected Learning and Computer-Based Modeling at Northwestern University (Wilensky 1999). The simulation allows students to explore a simple model ecosystem that consists of rabbits, grass, and weeds. In the simulation, the rabbits wander around randomly. When a rabbit bumps into a plant (grass or weed), it eats it and gains energy. If the rabbit gains enough energy, it reproduces. If it doesn't gain enough energy, it dies. The grass and weeds can be adjusted to grow at different rates and give the rabbits differing amounts of energy. Thus, the simulation can be used to explore how the abundance and nature of plants in an ecosystem influence the size of a herbivore population over time. Students will also learn about the wide range of methods used by scientists and the difference between data and evidence in science.

The Content

A *population* is a group of individuals that belong to the same species and live in the same region at the same time. A population that has access to an abundance of resources (e.g., food, water, space) will grow at an exponential rate because the birth rate will be much higher than the death rate. As the population grows in size, however, individuals within that population will begin to struggle to obtain the resources needed to survive and reproduce. Thus, there is a limit to the number of individuals that can occupy a habitat. Ecologists define the *carrying capacity* of a habitat as the maximum population size that a particular habitat can support without any degradation to the habitat. The carrying capacity of a habitat, however, is not fixed; it varies over time as the amount and kinds of resources available within that habitat change. Population size and the amount or type of resources available within a habitat have a profound effect on the birth and death rates of a population.

Timeline

The instructional time needed to implement this lab investigation is 130–200 minutes. Appendix 2 (p. 391) provides options for implementing this lab investigation over several class periods. Option C (200 minutes) should be used if students are unfamiliar with scientific writing because this option provides extra instructional time for scaffolding the writing process. You can scaffold the writing process by modeling, providing examples, and providing hints as students write each section of the report. Option D (130 minutes) should be used if students are familiar with scientific writing and have the skills needed to write an investigation report on their own. In option D, students complete stage 6 (writing the investigation report) and stage 8 (revising the investigation report) as homework.

Materials and Preparation

The materials needed to implement this investigation are listed in Table 9.1. Wilensky's *Rabbits Grass Weeds* simulation, available at *http://ccl.northwestern.edu/netlogo/models/RabbitsGrassWeeds,* is free to use and can be run online using an internet browser. You should access the simulation and learn how it works before beginning the lab investigation. In addition, it is important to check if students can access and use the simulation from a school computer because some schools have set up firewalls and other restrictions on web browsing.

TABLE 9.1

Materials list

Item	Quantity
Computer with internet access	1 per group
Student handout	1 per student
Investigation proposal B (optional)	1 per group
Whiteboard, 2' × 3'*	1 per group
Peer-review guide and instructor scoring rubric	1 per student

* As an alternative, students can use computer and presentation software such as Microsoft PowerPoint or Apple Keynote to create their arguments.

Topics for the Explicit and Reflective Discussion

Concepts That Can Be Used to Justify the Evidence

To provide an adequate justification of their evidence, students must explain why they included the evidence in their arguments and make the assumptions underlying their analysis and interpretation of the data explicit. In this investigation, students can use the following concepts to help justify their evidence:

- How different types of organisms obtain the energy they need to survive
- How habitats provide the resources organisms need to survive
- The characteristics of a population that influence population growth
- The difference between a birth rate and a death rate

We recommend that you review these concepts during the explicit and reflective discussion to help students make this connection.

How to Design Better Investigations

It is important for students to reflect on the strengths and weaknesses of the investigation they designed during the explicit and reflective discussion. Students should therefore be encouraged to discuss ways to eliminate potential flaws, measurement errors, or sources of bias in their investigations. To help students be more reflective about the design of their investigation, you can ask the following questions:

- What were some of the strengths of your investigation? What made it scientific?
- What were some of the weaknesses of your investigation? What made it less scientific?
- If you were to do this investigation again, what would you do to address the weaknesses in your investigation? What could you do to make it more scientific?

Crosscutting Concepts

This investigation is well aligned with three crosscutting concepts found in *A Framework for K–12 Science Education,* and you should review these concepts during the explicit and reflective discussion.

- *Patterns:* Patterns are often used to guide the organization and classification of life on Earth in biology. In addition, a major objective in biology is to identify the underlying cause of observed patterns, such as how many populations go through cycles of growth and decline over time.
- *Systems and System Models:* It is critical for scientists to be able to define the system under study (e.g., the components of a habitat) and then make a model of it to understand it. Models can be physical, conceptual, or mathematical.
- *Stability and Change:* It is critical to understand what makes a system stable or unstable and what controls rates of change in a system.

The Nature of Science and the Nature of Scientific Inquiry

It is important for students to understand that *scientists use different methods to answer different types of questions*. Examples of methods include experiments, systematic observations of a phenomenon, literature reviews, and analysis of existing data sets; the choice of method depends on the objectives of the research. There is no universal step-by-step scientific method that all scientists follow; rather, different scientific disciplines (e.g., biology vs. physics) and fields within a discipline (e.g., ecology vs. molecular biology) use different types of methods, use different core theories, and rely on different standards to develop scientific knowledge. For example, in this investigation the students use a computer simulation instead of collecting observations in the field. Many scientists use computer simulations to test ideas to explore new phenomena in a wide range of disciplines.

It is also important for students to understand the *difference between data and evidence in science.* Data are measurements, observations, and findings from other studies that are collected as part of an investigation. Evidence, in contrast, is analyzed data and an interpretation of the analysis.

You should review and provide examples of these two important concepts of the nature of science (NOS) and the nature of scientific inquiry (NOSI) during the explicit and reflective discussion.

Hints for Implementing the Lab

- Learn how to use the simulation before the lab begins. It is important for you to know how to use it so you can help students when they get stuck or confused.
- A group of three students per computer tends to work well.
- Allow the students to play with the simulation as part of the tool talk before they begin to design their investigation. This gives students a chance to see what they can and cannot do with the simulation.
- Be sure that students record actual values (e.g., number of rabbits at a point in time) when they run a simulation, rather than just attempting to hand draw the graph that they see on the computer screen.

Topic Connections

Table 9.2 (p. 130) provides an overview of the scientific practices, crosscutting concepts, disciplinary core ideas, and supporting ideas at the heart of this lab investigation. In addition, it lists NOS and NOSI concepts for the explicit and reflective discussion. Finally, it lists literacy and mathematics skills (*CCSS ELA* and *CCSS Mathematics*) that are addressed during the investigation.

TABLE 9.2

Lab 9 alignment with standards

Scientific practices	• Asking questions • Developing and using models • Planning and carrying out investigations • Analyzing and interpreting data • Using mathematics and computational thinking • Constructing explanations • Engaging in argument from evidence • Obtaining, evaluating, and communicating information
Crosscutting concepts	• Patterns • Systems and system models • Stability and change
Core idea	• LS2: Ecosystems: Interactions, energy, and dynamics
Supporting ideas	• Populations • Population growth • Carrying capacity • Herbivores • Producers
NOS and NOSI concepts	• Methods used in scientific investigations • Difference between data and evidence
Literacy connections *(CCSS ELA)*	• *Reading*: Key ideas and details, craft and structure, integration of knowledge and ideas • *Writing*: Text types and purposes, production and distribution of writing, research to build and present knowledge, range of writing • *Speaking and listening*: Comprehension and collaboration, presentation of knowledge and ideas
Mathematics connection *(CCSS Mathematics)*	• Reason quantitatively and use units to solve problems

References

Wilensky, U. 1999. Center for Connected Learning and Computer-Based Modeling, Northwestern Institute on Complex Systems, Northwestern University. Evanston, IL: NetLogo. *http://ccl.northwestern.edu/netlogo.*

Wilensky, U. 2001. NetLogo Rabbits Grass Weeds model. Evanston, IL: Center for Connected Learning and Computer-Based Modeling, Northwestern Institute on Complex Systems, Northwestern University. *http://ccl.northwestern.edu/netlogo/models/RabbitsGrassWeeds.*

Lab 9. Population Growth: How Do Changes in the Amount and Nature of the Plant Life Available in an Ecosystem Influence Herbivore Population Growth Over Time?

Lab Handout

Introduction

A population is a group of individuals that belong to the same species and live in the same region at the same time (the figure to the right shows an example of a rabbit population). Populations have unique attributes such as growth rate, age structure, sex ratio, birth rate, and death rate. The growth rate of population describes how the size of the population changes over a set time period. The age structure refers to the distribution of individuals based on age. The sex ratio is the proportion of males and females in the population. The birth rate is the frequency of births within a population over a set time period. The death rate is the frequency of deaths over a set time period. The characteristics of a population can change over time because of births, deaths, and the dispersal of individuals from one population to another.

The population of rabbits at the Myxomatosis Trial Enclosure on Wardang Island, Australia

Populations of animals interact with each other and their environment in a variety of ways. One of the primary ways a population interacts with the environment and with other populations is through feeding. Animals can eat plants, other animals, or both. Animals that feed on plants are called herbivores. The plants that herbivores eat, however, are not all the same. Some plants grow quickly and are plentiful, which makes them easy to find, whereas others grow slowly and are sparse. Some plants are drought resistant, whereas others do not grow well unless there is plenty of water available. Finally, and perhaps most important, some plants are loaded with nutrients (vitamins and minerals) but low in calories, some are high in calories but have fewer nutrients, and some are high in both calories and nutrients.

There are a number of factors that might influence the size of a herbivore population in an ecosystem. These factors include, but are not limited to, the amount of food available to eat, the type of plants available to eat, and the nutritional value of these plants. In this investigation, you will explore how the size of a herbivore population changes over time in response to changes in the nature and type of plants available for it to eat.

LAB 9

Your Task

Explain how the size of a population of rabbits (herbivores) changes over time in response to changes in the amounts and characteristics of the plants available in an ecosystem.

The guiding question of this investigation is, **How do changes in the amount and nature of the plant life available in an ecosystem influence herbivore population growth over time?**

Materials

You will use an online simulation called *Rabbits Grass Weeds* to conduct your investigation. You can access the simulation by going to the following website: *http://ccl.northwestern.edu/netlogo/models/RabbitsGrassWeeds*.

Safety Precautions

1. Use caution when working with electrical equipment. Keep away from water sources in that they can cause shorts, fires, and shock hazards. Use only GFI-protected circuits.
2. Wash hands with soap and water after completing this lab.
3. Follow all normal lab safety rules.

Getting Started

The *Rabbits Grass Weeds* simulation allows you to explore a simple ecosystem made up of rabbits, grass, and weeds (see the figure on the next page). The rabbits wander around randomly, and the grass and weeds grow randomly. When a rabbit bumps into some grass or weeds, it eats the grass and gains energy. If the rabbit gains enough energy, it reproduces. If it doesn't gain enough energy, it dies. The grass and weeds can be adjusted to grow at different rates and give the rabbits differing amounts of energy.

This simulation is easy to use. Click the SETUP button to set up the ecosystem with rabbits and grass, then click the GO button to start the simulation. It is also easy to adjust the characteristics of the simulated ecosystem. The NUMBER slider controls the initial number of rabbits (0–500). The BIRTH-THRESHOLD slider sets the energy level at which the rabbits reproduce (0–20). Rabbits can reproduce at any time when the threshold is set at zero. When the threshold is set at 20, a rabbit must eat enough food to have an energy level of 20 before it can reproduce. The GRASS-GROWTH-RATE slider controls the rate at which the grass grows (0–20). When the grass growth rate is set to 0, no grass will grow in the simulated ecosystem. The WEEDS-GROWTH-RATE slider controls the rate at which the weeds grow (0–20). The GRASS-ENERGY slider and the WEED-ENERGY slider allow you to set the amount of energy a rabbit can get from a plant when it is eaten (0–10).

A screen shot from the *Rabbits Grass Weeds* simulation

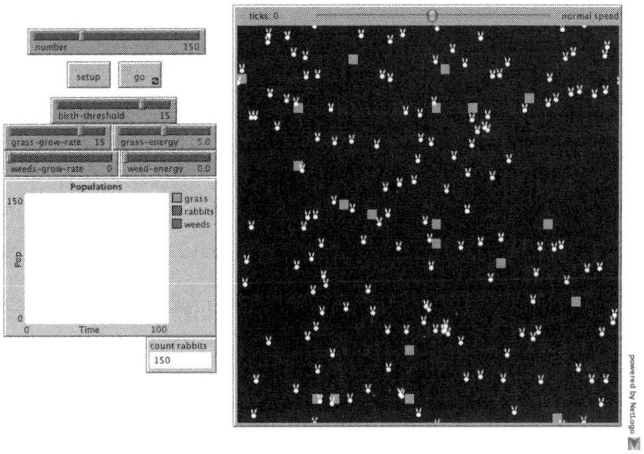

To answer the guiding question, you must determine what type of data you will need to collect, how you will collect it, and how you will analyze it. To determine *what type of data you will need to collect,* think about the following questions:

- What will serve as your independent variables (presence of grass, presence of weeds, grass growth rate, amount of energy obtained from grass, weed growth rate, and so on)?
- What will serve as your dependent variable (population size of rabbits, population size of weeds, population size of grass, and so on)?
- What type of measurements or observations will you need to record during your investigation?

To determine *how you will collect your data,* think about the following questions:

- What will serve as a control (or comparison) condition?
- What types of treatment conditions will you need to set up and how will you do it?
- How long will you need to run each simulation?
- How often will you collect data and when will you do it?
- How will you make sure that your data are of high quality (i.e., how will you reduce measurement error)?
- How will you keep track of the data you collect and how will you organize the data?

To determine *how you will analyze your data,* think about the following questions:

- How will you determine if there is a difference between the treatment conditions and the control condition?
- What type of calculations will you need to make?
- What type of graph could you create to help make sense of your data?

Investigation Proposal Required? ☐ Yes ☐ No

Connections to Crosscutting Concepts and to the Nature of Science and the Nature of Scientific Inquiry

As you work through your investigation, be sure to think about

- the importance of identifying patterns,
- how models are used to study natural phenomena,
- how living things or systems go through periods of stability and change,
- the different types of investigations that can be designed and carried out by scientists, and
- the difference between data and evidence in science.

Argumentation Session

Once your group has finished collecting and analyzing your data, prepare a whiteboard that you can use to share your initial argument. Your whiteboard should include all the information shown in the figure below.

Argument presentation on a whiteboard

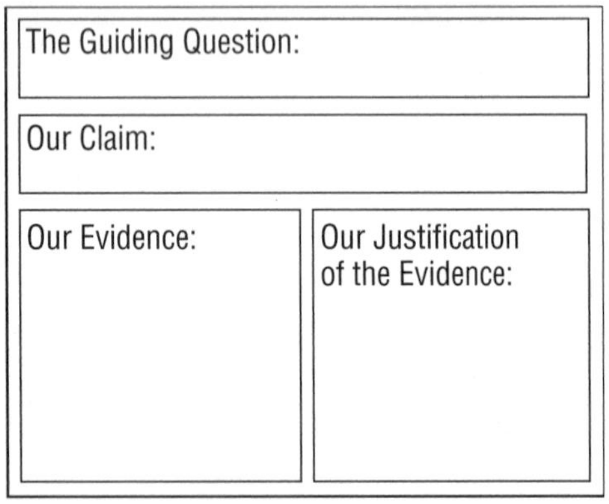

To share your argument with others, we will be using a round-robin format. This means that one member of your group will stay at your lab station to share your group's argument while the other members of your group go to the other lab stations one at a time to listen to and critique the arguments developed by your classmates.

The goal of the argumentation session is not to convince others that your argument is the best one; rather, the goal is to identify errors or instances of faulty reasoning in the arguments so these mistakes can be fixed. You will therefore need to evaluate the content of the claim, the quality of the evidence used to support the claim, and the strength of the justification of the evidence included in each argument that you see. In order to critique an argument, you will need more information than what is included on the whiteboard. You might, therefore, need to ask the presenter one or more follow-up questions, such as:

- How did you use the simulation to collect your data?
- What did you do to analyze your data? Why did you decide to do it that way? Did you check your calculations?

- Is that the only way to interpret the results of your analysis? How do you know that your interpretation of your analysis is appropriate?
- Why did you decide to present your evidence in that manner?
- What other claims did your group discuss before you decided on that one? Why did your group abandon those alternative ideas?
- How confident are you that your claim is valid? What could you do to increase your confidence?

Once the argumentation session is complete, you will have a chance to meet with your group and revise your original argument. Your group might need to gather more data or design a way to test one or more alternative claims as part of this process. Remember, your goal at this stage of the investigation is to develop the most valid or acceptable answer to the research question!

Report

Once you have completed your research, you will need to prepare an investigation report that consists of three sections that provide answers to the following questions:

1. What question were you trying to answer and why?
2. What did you do during your investigation and why did you conduct your investigation in this way?
3. What is your argument?

Your report should answer these questions in two pages or less. This report must be typed, and any diagrams, figures, or tables should be embedded into the document. Be sure to write in a persuasive style; you are trying to convince others that your claim is acceptable or valid!

Lab 9. Population Growth: How Do Changes in the Amount and Nature of the Plant Life Available in an Ecosystem Influence Herbivore Population Growth Over Time?

Checkout Questions

1. In the space below, draw two graphs: the one on the left should show how the size of a population would change over time with unlimited natural resources (food, water, space), and the one on the right should show how the size of a population would grow over time with a limited amount of natural resources.

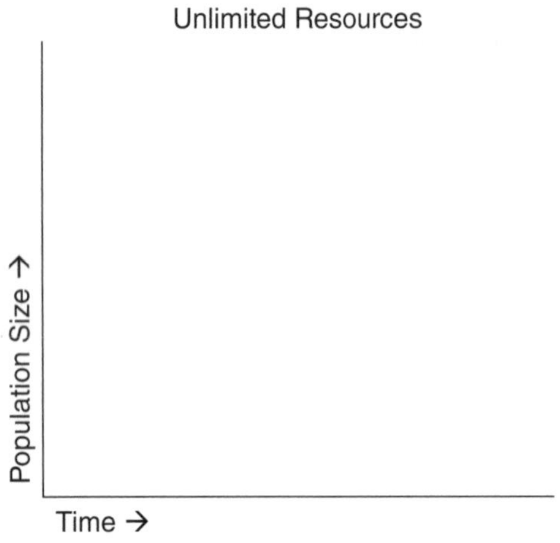

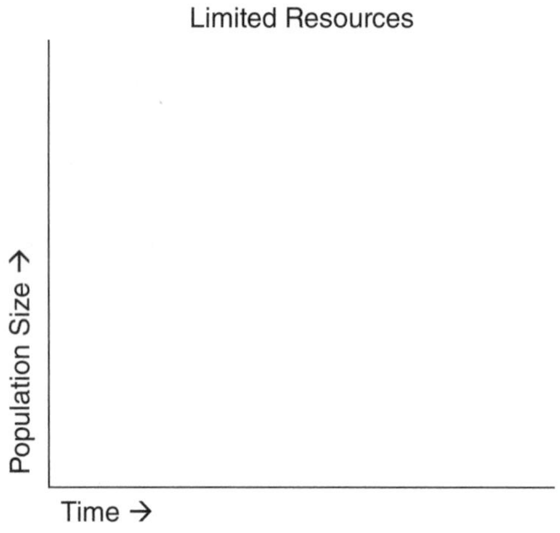

Explain your reasoning. Why did you draw your graphs in the way you did?

2. The method used by a scientist during an investigation depends on what is being studied and the nature of the research question he or she is trying to answer.

   a. I agree with this statement.
   b. I disagree with this statement.

   Explain your answer, using examples from your investigation about population growth.

3. The term *data* and the term *evidence* have the same meaning in science.

   a. I agree with this statement.
   b. I disagree with this statement.

   Explain your answer, using information from your investigation about population growth.

4. Scientists often look for patterns in nature. Explain why this is important, using an example from your investigation about population growth.

5. Scientists often use models to study complex natural phenomenon. Explain what a model is and why models are valuable in science, using an example from your investigation about population growth.

6. Biological systems, such as ecosystems, often go through periods of stability and change. Explain what this means, using an example from your investigation about population growth.

Lab 10. Predator-Prey Population Size Relationships: Which Factors Affect the Stability of a Predator-Prey Population Size Relationship?

Teacher Notes

Purpose

The purpose of this lab is to *introduce* students to the concept of a predator-prey population size relationship and some of the factors that can affect these relationships. This lab also gives students an opportunity to design and carry out an investigation using an online simulation. The simulation, called *Wolf Sheep Predation* (Wilensky 1997), was created using NetLogo, a multiagent programmable modeling environment developed at the Center for Connected Learning and Computer-Based Modeling at Northwestern University (Wilensky 1999). The simulation allows students to explore a simple model ecosystem that consists of wolves, sheep, and grass. In the simulation, the wolves wander around randomly. When a wolf bumps into a sheep, it eats it and gains energy. If a wolf does not gain enough energy, it dies. The sheep must also eat grass to maintain their energy. If a sheep does not gain enough energy, it will also die. The user can adjust the following factors in the simulation:

- The initial population size of the wolves
- The initial population size of the sheep
- How much energy a wolf gains from eating a sheep
- How much energy a sheep gains from eating grass
- How often the wolves reproduce
- How often sheep reproduce

The *Wolf Sheep Predation* simulation can be used to explore how these six factors influence the stability of a predator-prey population size relationship.

Students will also learn about the different methods used in scientific investigations and how social and cultural factors influence the work of scientists.

The Content

Predation is an interaction between two species in which one species, the predator, eats the other, the prey. When predators are scarce, the numbers of prey tend to increase because the death rate of the prey population decreases. Predators, as a result, have plenty of food to eat. The surplus of food available decreases the death rate and increases the birth rate in in the predator population. As the predator population increases, however, more individuals in the prey population are killed. The death rate of the prey population therefore increases and the size of the prey population shrinks. Many of the predators then die due to lack of food; thus, numbers of predators and prey oscillate between two extremes. This oscillation in the size of the two populations is called a predator-prey population size relationship.

This description of a predator-prey population size relationship, however, is far too simplistic to provide an adequate description of what happens in nature. This is because predator numbers are not solely dependent on the number of prey available. Furthermore, there must be an opportunity for some prey to avoid attack; otherwise, extinction of both species may result. Predation will have no effect on numbers of prey if the individuals caught are beyond reproductive age. A final factor is that more than one type of predator often feeds the same population of prey.

Nevertheless, predation is important for maintaining biodiversity in an ecosystem. For example, some prey species can drive other prey species in an ecosystem to extinction through competition for resources (space, water, and so on) when there are no predators around to keep the size of various prey populations small. Predation also drives the evolution of traits in prey populations, such as chemical and physical defenses, and the evolution of traits that make finding and capturing prey less difficult in predator populations. Thus, this relationship between predators and prey is vital to the existence of life as we know it.

Timeline

The instructional time needed to implement this lab investigation is 130–200 minutes. Appendix 2 (p. 391) provides options for implementing this lab investigation over several class periods. Option C (200 minutes) should be used if students are unfamiliar with scientific writing because this option provides extra instructional time for scaffolding the writing process. You can scaffold the writing process by modeling, providing examples, and providing hints as students write each section of the report. Option D (130 minutes) should be used if students are familiar with scientific writing and have the skills needed to write an investigation report on their own. In option D, students complete stage 6 (writing the investigation report) and stage 8 (revising the investigation report) as homework.

Materials and Preparation

The materials needed to implement this investigation are listed in Table 10.1. Wilensky's *Wolf Sheep Predation* simulation, available at *http://ccl.northwestern.edu/netlogo/models/WolfSheepPredation,* is free to use and can be run online using an internet browser. You should access the simulation and learn how it works before beginning the lab investigation. In addition, it is important to check if students can access and use the simulation from a school computer because some schools have set up firewalls and other restrictions on web browsing.

TABLE 10.1
Materials list

Item	Quantity
Computer with internet access	1 per group
Student handout	1 per student
Investigation proposal B (optional)	1 per group
Whiteboard, 2' × 3'*	1 per group
Peer-review guide and instructor scoring rubric	1 per student

* As an alternative, students can use computer and presentation software such as Microsoft PowerPoint or Apple Keynote to create their arguments.

Topics for the Explicit and Reflective Discussion

Concepts That Can Be Used to Justify the Evidence

To provide an adequate justification of their evidence, students must explain why they included the evidence in their arguments and make the assumptions underlying their analysis and interpretation of the data explicit. In this investigation, students can use the following concepts to help justify their evidence:

- How different types of organisms (producers, herbivores, and carnivores) obtain the energy they need to survive
- How habitats provide the resources organisms need
- The characteristics of a population that influence population growth
- How populations tend to grow over time
- How access to resources places limits on the size of a population

We recommend that you review these concepts during the explicit and reflective discussion to help students make this connection.

How to Design Better Investigations

It is important for students to reflect on the strengths and weaknesses of the investigation they designed during the explicit and reflective discussion. Students should therefore be encouraged to discuss ways to eliminate potential flaws, measurement errors, or sources of bias in their investigations. To help students be more reflective about the design of their investigation, you can ask the following questions:

- What were some of the strengths of your investigation? What made it scientific?

- What were some of the weaknesses of your investigation? What made it less scientific?
- If you were to do this investigation again, what would you do to address the weaknesses in your investigation? What could you do to make it more scientific?

Crosscutting Concepts

This investigation is well aligned with four crosscutting concepts found in *A Framework for K–12 Science Education,* and you should review these concepts during the explicit and reflective discussion.

- *Patterns:* Patterns are often used to guide the organization and classification of life on Earth in biology. In addition, a major objective in biology is to identify the underlying cause of observed patterns, such as how many populations go through cycles of growth and decline over time.
- *Cause and Effect: Mechanism and Explanation:* One of the main objectives of science is to identify and establish relationships between a cause and an effect. It is also important to understand the mechanisms by which these causal relationships are mediated.
- *Systems and System Models:* Students need to understand that it is critical for scientists to be able to define the system under study (e.g., the components of a habitat) and then make a model of it to understand it. Models can be physical, conceptual, or mathematical.
- *Stability and Change:* It is critical to understand what makes a system stable or unstable and what controls rates of change in system.

The Nature of Science and the Nature of Scientific Inquiry

It is important for students to understand that *scientists use different methods to answer different types of questions*. Examples of methods include experiments, systematic observations of a phenomenon, literature reviews, and analysis of existing data sets; the choice of method depends on the objectives of the research. There is no universal step-by-step scientific method that all scientists follow; rather, different scientific disciplines (e.g., biology vs. physics) and fields within a discipline (e.g., ecology vs. molecular biology) use different types of methods, use different core theories, and rely on different standards to develop scientific knowledge. For example, in this investigation the students use a computer simulation instead of collecting observations in the field to explore how various factors influence the stability of a predator-prey population size relationship. Scientists often use simulations to model complex phenomena or systems and to explore how different factors influence the behavior of a phenomenon or system.

It is also important for students to understand that *science is influenced by the society and culture in which it is practiced* because science is a human endeavor. Cultural values and expectations determine what scientists choose to investigate, how investigations are conducted, how research findings are interpreted, and what people see as implications. People also view some research as being more important than others because of cultural values and current events. This investigation provides a good context to discuss how funding decisions are made and how value judgments are made about different fields of inquiry, such as ecology or conservation biology, and the types of investigations that are done in these various fields.

You should review and provide examples of these two important concepts of the nature of science (NOS) and the nature of scientific inquiry (NOSI) during the explicit and reflective discussion.

Hints for Implementing the Lab

- Learn how to use the simulation before the lab begins. It is important for you to know how to use the simulation so you can help students when they get stuck or confused.
- A group of three students per computer tends to work well.
- Allow the students to play with the simulation as part of the tool talk before they begin to design their investigation or fill out an investigation proposal. This gives students a chance to see what they can and cannot do with the simulation.
- Be sure that students record actual values (e.g., number of wolves and sheep at a specific point in time) when they run a simulation, rather than just attempting to hand draw the graph that they see on the computer screen.

Topic Connections

Table 10.2 (p. 144) provides an overview of the scientific practices, crosscutting concepts, disciplinary core ideas, and supporting ideas at the heart of this lab investigation. In addition, it lists NOS and NOSI concepts for the explicit and reflective discussion. Finally, it lists literacy and mathematics skills (*CCSS ELA* and *CCSS Mathematics*) that are addressed during the investigation.

TABLE 10.2

Lab 10 alignment with standards

Scientific practices	• Asking questions • Developing and using models • Planning and carrying out investigations • Analyzing and interpreting data • Using mathematics and computational thinking • Constructing explanations • Engaging in argument from evidence • Obtaining, evaluating, and communicating information
Crosscutting concepts	• Patterns • Cause and effect: Mechanism and explanation • Systems and system models • Stability and change
Core idea	• LS2: Ecosystems: Interactions, energy, and dynamics
Supporting ideas	• Predator-prey population size relationships • Populations • Population growth • Predators • Herbivores • Producers
NOS and NOSI concepts	• Methods used in scientific investigations • Social and cultural influences
Literacy connections *(CCSS ELA)*	• *Reading*: Key ideas and details, craft and structure, integration of knowledge and ideas • *Writing*: Text types and purposes, production and distribution of writing, research to build and present knowledge, range of writing • *Speaking and listening*: Comprehension and collaboration, presentation of knowledge and ideas
Mathematics connection *(CCSS Mathematics)*	• Reason quantitatively and use units to solve problems

References

Wilensky, U. 1997. NetLogo Wolf Sheep Predation model. Evanston, IL: Center for Connected Learning and Computer-Based Modeling, Northwestern Institute on Complex Systems, Northwestern University. *http://ccl.northwestern.edu/netlogo/models/WolfSheepPredation.*

Wilensky, U. 1999. NetLogo. Evanston, IL: Center for Connected Learning and Computer-Based Modeling, Northwestern Institute on Complex Systems, Northwestern University. *http://ccl.northwestern.edu/netlogo.*

Lab 10. Predator-Prey Population Size Relationships: Which Factors Affect the Stability of a Predator-Prey Population Size Relationship?

Lab Handout

Introduction

Several factors determine the size of any population within an ecosystem. The factors that affect the size of a population are divided into two broad categories: abiotic factors, which are the nonliving components of an ecosystem, and biotic factors, which are the other living components found within an ecosystem.

Wolves (predators) surrounding a bison (prey)

Predation is an example of a biotic factor that influences the size of a population (see the figure to the right). Predation is an interaction between species in which one species (the predator) uses another species as food (the prey). Predation often leads to an increase in the population size of the predator and a decrease in the population size of the prey. However, if the size of a prey population gets too small, many of the predators may not have enough food to eat and will die. As a result, the predator population size and the population size of its prey are linked. The sizes of a predator population and a prey population often cycle over several generations (see the figure to the right, "A stable predator-prey population size relationship"), and this cyclic pattern is often described as a predator-prey population size relationship. A predator-prey population size relationship that results in both populations surviving over time, despite fluctuations in the size of each one over several generations, is described as stable. A predator-prey relationship that results in the extinction of one or more species, in contrast, is described as unstable.

A stable predator-prey population size relationship

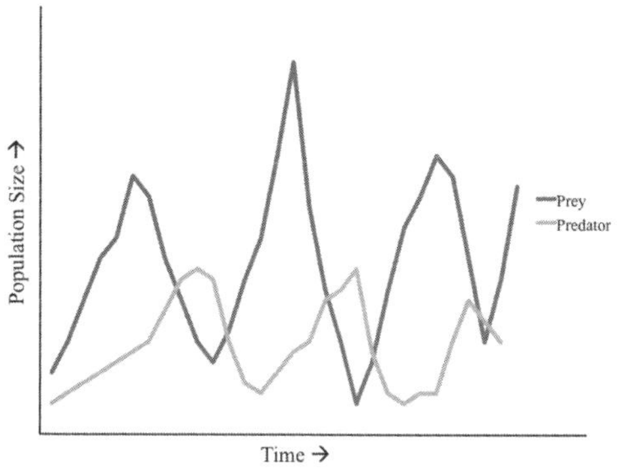

There are a number of factors that might influence the size of predator and prey populations in an ecosystem and can contribute to the overall stability of a predator-prey population size relationship. These factors include, but are not limited to, the amount of food available for the prey, the number of different prey species available for a predator, and how fast the predator and the prey species reproduce. In this investigation, you will investigate how a population of predators (wolves) and a population of its prey (sheep) interact with each other and the plant life in an environment over time.

Your Task

Determine what makes a predator-prey population size relationship stable or unstable.

The guiding question of this investigation is, **Which factors affect the stability of a predator-prey population size relationship?**

Materials

You will use an online simulation called *Wolf Sheep Predation* to conduct your investigation. You can access the simulation by going to the following website: *http://ccl.northwestern.edu/netlogo/models/WolfSheepPredation.*

Safety Precautions

1. Use caution when working with electrical equipment. Keep away from water sources in that they can cause shorts, fires, and shock hazards. Use only GFI-protected circuits.
2. Wash hands with soap and water after completing this lab.
3. Follow all normal lab safety rules.

Getting Started

The *Wolf Sheep Predation* simulation allows you to explore the stability of the predator-prey population size relationship (see the figure at the top of the next page) between a population of wolves (the predator) and a population of sheep (the prey). In the simulation, wolves and sheep wander around the landscape at random. The wolves lose energy with each step, and when they run out of energy they die. The wolves therefore must eat sheep to replenish their energy. You can set the simulation so there is an unlimited amount of food for the sheep to eat (grass off) or you can set the simulation so it includes a limited amount of grass in the ecosystem (grass on). If you decide to leave grass out of the simulation, the sheep never run out of energy and they only die when a wolf eats them. If you decide to include grass in the simulation, the sheep must eat grass to maintain their energy; when they run out of energy, they die. Once grass is eaten by a sheep it will only regrow after a fixed amount of time; you can adjust the amount of time it takes for grass to regrow. You can also set other factors such as the initial population size of the wolves and the sheep and what percentage of the wolves and sheep reproduce with each "tick" of the simulation (each tick represents a set amount of time—in this case a day).

A screen shot from the *Wolf Sheep Predation* simulation

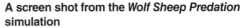

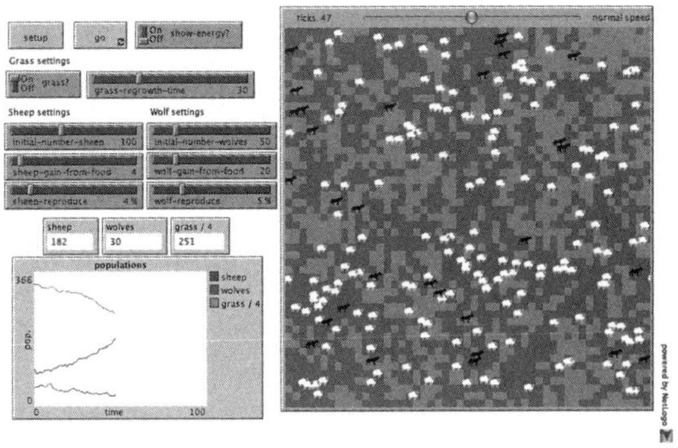

To answer the guiding question, you must determine what type of data you will need to collect, how you will collect it, and how you will analyze it. To determine *what type of data you will need to collect*, think about the following questions:

- How will you determine if a predator-prey relationship is stable?
- What will serve as your dependent variable (number of wolves, number of sheep, and so on)?
- What type of measurements or observations will you need to record during your investigation?

To determine *how you will collect your data*, think about the following questions:

- What will serve as a control (or comparison) condition?
- What types of treatment conditions will you need to set up and how will you do it?
- How often will you collect data and when will you do it?
- How will you make sure that your data are of high quality (i.e., how will you reduce error)?
- How will you keep track of the data you collect and how will you organize the data?

To determine *how you will analyze your data*, think about the following questions:

- How will you determine if there is a difference between the treatment conditions and the control condition?
- What type of calculations will you need to make?
- What type of graph could you create to help make sense of your data?

Investigation Proposal Required? ☐ Yes ☐ No

Connections to Crosscutting Concepts and to the Nature of Science and the Nature of Scientific Inquiry

As you work through your investigation, be sure to think about

- the importance of identifying patterns,
- the importance of identifying the underlying cause for observations,
- how models are used to study natural phenomena,
- how systems go through periods of stability and change,
- how social and cultural factors influence the work of scientists, and
- different methods used in scientific investigations.

Argumentation Session

Once your group has finished collecting and analyzing your data, prepare a whiteboard that you can use to share your initial argument. Your whiteboard should include all the information shown in the figure below.

Argument presentation on a whiteboard

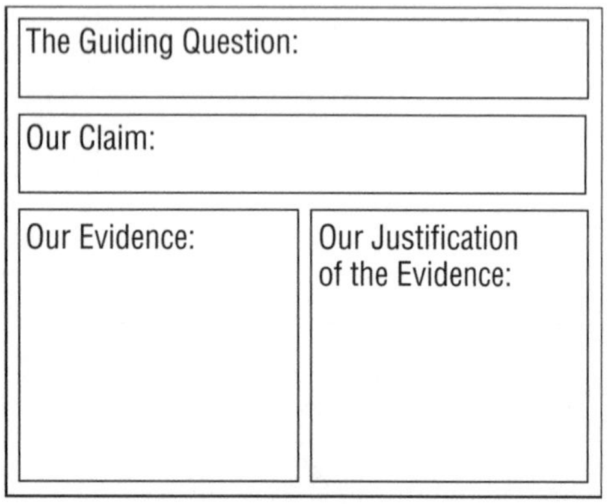

To share your argument with others, we will be using a round-robin format. This means that one member of your group will stay at your lab station to share your group's argument while the other members of your group go to the other lab stations one at a time to listen to and critique the arguments developed by your classmates.

The goal of the argumentation session is not to convince others that your argument is the best one; rather, the goal is to identify errors or instances of faulty reasoning in the arguments so these mistakes can be fixed. You will therefore need to evaluate the content of the claim, the quality of the evidence used to support the claim, and the strength of the justification of the evidence included in each argument that you see. In order to critique an argument, you will need more information than what is included on the whiteboard. You might, therefore, need to ask the presenter one or more follow-up questions, such as:

- How did you use the simulation to collect your data?
- What did you do to analyze your data? Why did you decide to do it that way? Did you check your calculations?
- Is that the only way to interpret the results of your analysis? How do you know that your interpretation of your analysis is appropriate?

- Why did your group decide to present your evidence in that manner?
- What other claims did your group discuss before you decided on that one? Why did your group abandon those alternative ideas?
- How confident are you that your claim is valid? What could you do to increase your confidence?

Once the argumentation session is complete, you will have a chance to meet with your group and revise your original argument. Your group might need to gather more data or design a way to test one or more alternative claims as part of this process. Remember, your goal at this stage of the investigation is to develop the most valid or acceptable answer to the research question!

Report

Once you have completed your research, you will need to prepare an investigation report that consists of three sections that provide answers to the following questions:

1. What question were you trying to answer and why?
2. What did you do during your investigation and why did you conduct your investigation in this way?
3. What is your argument?

Your report should answer these questions in two pages or less. This report must be typed, and any diagrams, figures, or tables should be embedded into the document. Be sure to write in a persuasive style; you are trying to convince others that your claim is acceptable or valid!

Lab 10. Predator-Prey Population Size Relationships: Which Factors Affect the Stability of a Predator-Prey Population Size Relationship?

Checkout Questions

1. In the space below, draw two graphs: the one on the left should show how the size of a predator population and the size of a prey population fluctuate over time when the predator-prey population size relationship is stable; the one on the right should show how the size of a predator population and the size of a prey population fluctuate over time when the predator-prey population size relationship is unstable.

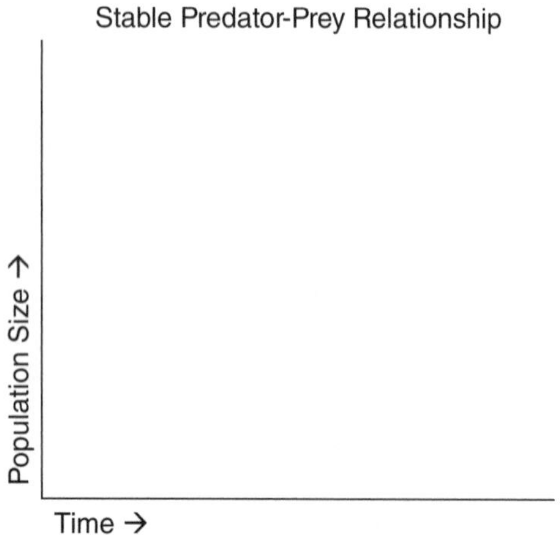

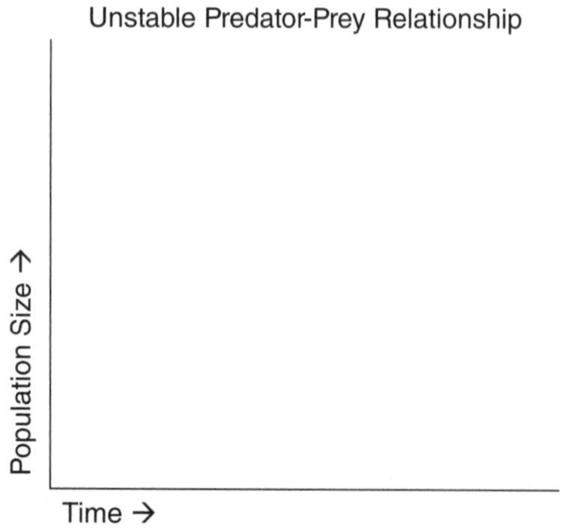

2. What are some factors that can upset the balance of a predator-prey population size relationship, and why do these factors make these relationships unstable?

3. Social and cultural values or expectations influence how an investigation is designed and the extent to which the findings are acceptable.

   a. I agree with this statement.
   b. I disagree with this statement.

   Explain your answer, using information from your investigation about predator-prey population size relationships.

4. Scientists reach true and accurate conclusions when they use the scientific method.

   a. I agree with this statement.
   b. I disagree with this statement.

   Explain your answer, using examples from your investigation about predator-prey population size relationships.

5. Scientists often look for patterns in nature. Explain why patterns are important, using an example from your investigation about predator-prey population size relationships.

6. A major goal of scientists is to identify the underlying cause for natural phenomena. Explain why it is important to learn about underlying causes, using an example from your investigation about predator-prey population size relationships.

7. Scientists often use models to study complex natural phenomenon. Explain what a model is and why models are valuable in science, using an example from your investigation about predator-prey population size relationships.

Lab 11. Ecosystems and Biodiversity: How Does Food Web Complexity Affect the Biodiversity of an Ecosystem?

Teacher Notes

Purpose

The purpose of this lab is to *introduce* students to the concepts of ecosystems, food chains, food webs, and biodiversity. This lab also gives students an opportunity to design and carry out an investigation using an online simulation called *Ecology Lab* (Annenberg Learner 2013). The simulation allows students to explore how different feeding relationships affect the biodiversity of the model ecosystem. Students will also learn about the difference between observations and inferences in science and why scientists must be creative and have a good imagination.

The Content

The nature of an ecosystem depends on the feeding relationships that exist between organisms. These feeding relationships are often described as the *trophic structure* of an ecosystem. The transfer of food energy from its source in plants and other photosynthetic organisms (producers) through the primary consumers (herbivores and omnivores) to the secondary and tertiary consumers (carnivores and omnivores) and eventually to decomposers is called a food chain. Food chains are not isolated units, however, because they are hooked together into food webs. Food webs illustrate how energy moves through an ecosystem through specific feeding relationships. The *biodiversity* of an ecosystem refers to the number of different species found in an ecosystem. Biodiversity can be measured in two ways: *species richness* and *relative abundance.* Species richness is the total number of different species in an ecosystem; relative abundance is how common each species is within the ecosystem.

Some species have a large impact on overall biodiversity because of their abundance or because they play a pivotal role in the dynamics of an ecosystem. *Dominant species* are those species in the ecosystem that are most common or have the most overall biomass. They affect the occurrence and distribution of other species through competition for resources. *Keystone species,* in contrast, are usually not common in an ecosystem but play an important role in many of the feeding relationships that occur within the ecosystem. Keystone species are often organisms that link many food chains together or help control the size of other populations of organisms within the ecosystem. It is important to note, however, that the biodiversity of an ecosystem is affected not only by the presence or absence of dominant and keystone species but also by abiotic factors such as space, temperature, and access to nutrients.

Timeline

The instructional time needed to implement this lab investigation is 130–200 minutes. Appendix 2 (p. 391) provides options for implementing this lab investigation over several class periods. Option C (200 minutes) should be used if students are unfamiliar with scientific writing because this option provides extra instructional time for scaffolding the writing process. You can scaffold the writing process by modeling, providing examples, and providing hints as students write each section of the report. Option D (130 minutes) should be used if students are familiar with scientific writing and have the skills needed to write an investigation report on their own. In option D, students complete stage 6 (writing the investigation report) and stage 8 (revising the investigation report) as homework.

Materials and Preparation

The materials needed to implement this investigation are listed in Table 11.1. The *Ecology Lab* simulation from Annenberg Learner, available at *www.learner.org/courses/envsci/interactives/ecology/ecology1.html,* is free to use and can be run online using an internet browser. You should access the simulation and learn how it works before beginning the lab investigation. In addition, it is important to check if students can access and use the simulation from a school computer, because some schools have set up firewalls and other restrictions on web browsing.

TABLE 11.1

Materials list

Item	Quantity
Computer with internet access	1 per group
Student handout	1 per student
Investigation proposal B (optional)	1 per group
Whiteboard, 2' × 3'*	1 per group
Peer-review guide and instructor scoring rubric	1 per student

* As an alternative, students can use computer and presentation software such as Microsoft PowerPoint or Apple Keynote to create their arguments.

Topics for the Explicit and Reflective Discussion

Concepts That Can Be Used to Justify the Evidence

To provide an adequate justification of their evidence, students must explain why they included the evidence in their arguments and make the assumptions underlying their analysis and interpretation of the data explicit. In this investigation, students can use the following concepts to help justify their evidence:

- How different types of organisms (producers, herbivores, carnivores) obtain the energy they need to survive
- How energy moves through an ecosystem
- How access to resources places limits on the size of a population
- Why biodiversity is important to the overall stability of an ecosystem

We recommend that you review these concepts during the explicit and reflective discussion to help students make this connection.

How to Design Better Investigations

It is important for students to reflect on the strengths and weaknesses of the investigation they designed during the explicit and reflective discussion. Students should therefore be encouraged to discuss ways to eliminate potential flaws, measurement errors, or sources of bias in their investigations. To help students be more reflective about the design of their investigation, you can ask the following questions:

- What were some of the strengths of your investigation? What made it scientific?
- What were some of the weaknesses of your investigation? What made it less scientific?
- If you were to do this investigation again, what would you do to address the weaknesses in your investigation? What could you do to make it more scientific?

Crosscutting Concepts

This investigation is well aligned with four crosscutting concepts found in *A Framework for K–12 Science Education,* and you should review these concepts during the explicit and reflective discussion.

- *Patterns:* Patterns are often used to guide the organization and classification of life on Earth. In addition, a major objective in biology is to identify the underlying cause of observed patterns, such as similarities in ecosystems with high or low levels of biodiversity.
- *Cause and Effect: Mechanism and Explanation:* One of the main objectives of science is to identify and establish relationships between a cause and an effect. It is also important to understand the mechanisms by which these causal relationships are mediated.
- *Systems and System Models:* It is critical for scientists to be able to define the system under study (e.g., the components of a habitat) and then make a model of it to understand it. Models can be physical, conceptual, or mathematical.
- *Stability and Change:* It is critical to understand what makes a system stable or unstable and what controls rates of change within a system.

The Nature of Science and the Nature of Scientific Inquiry

It is important for students to understand the *difference between observations and inferences in science.* An observation is a descriptive statement about a natural phenomenon, whereas an inference is an interpretation of an observation. Students should also understand that current scientific knowledge and the perspectives of individual scientists guide both observations and inferences. Thus, different scientists can have different but equally valid interpretations of the same observations due to differences in their perspectives and background knowledge.

It is also important for students to understand that *science requires imagination and creativity.* Students should learn that developing explanations for or models of natural phenomena and then figuring out how they can be put to the test of reality is as creative as writing poetry, composing music, or designing skyscrapers. Scientists must also use their imagination and creativity to figure out new ways to test ideas and collect or analyze data.

You should review and provide examples of these two important concepts of the nature of science (NOS) and the nature of scientific inquiry (NOSI) during the explicit and reflective discussion.

Hints for Implementing the Lab

- Learn how to use the simulation before the lab begins. It is important for you to know how to use the simulation so you can help students when they get stuck or confused.
- A group of three students per computer tends to work well.
- Allow the students to play with the simulation as part of the tool talk before they begin to design their investigation or fill out an investigation proposal. This gives students a chance to see what they can and cannot do with the simulation
- Be sure that students record actual values (e.g., the number of individuals in each population or the number of different species at a specific point in time) when they run a simulation, rather than just attempting to hand draw the graph that they see on the computer screen.

Topic Connections

Table 11.2 provides an overview of the scientific practices, crosscutting concepts, disciplinary core ideas, and support ideas at the heart of this lab investigation. In addition, it lists NOS and NOSI concepts for the explicit and reflective discussion. Finally, it lists literacy and mathematics skills (*CCSS ELA* and *CCSS Mathematics*) that are addressed during the investigation.

TABLE 11.2

Lab 11 alignment with standards

Scientific practices	• Asking questions • Developing and using models • Planning and carrying out investigations • Analyzing and interpreting data • Using mathematics and computational thinking • Constructing explanations • Engaging in argument from evidence • Obtaining, evaluating, and communicating information
Crosscutting concepts	• Patterns • Cause and effect: Mechanism and explanation • Systems and system models • Stability and change
Core idea	• LS2: Ecosystems: Interactions, energy, and dynamics
Supporting ideas	• Biodiversity • Ecosystems • Food webs • Food chains • Trophic levels • Producers • Consumers • Omnivores • Predators • Herbivores
NOS and NOSI concepts	• Observations and inferences • Imagination and creativity in science
Literacy connections *(CCSS ELA)*	• *Reading:* Key ideas and details, craft and structure, integration of knowledge and ideas • *Writing:* Text types and purposes, production and distribution of writing, research to build and present knowledge, range of writing • *Speaking and listening:* Comprehension and collaboration, presentation of knowledge and ideas
Mathematics connection *(CCSS Mathematics)*	• Reason quantitatively and use units to solve problems

Reference

Annenberg Learner. 2013. Ecology Lab. Indianapolis, IN: Annenberg Learner. *www.learner.org/courses/envsci/interactives/ecology/ecology1.html.*

Lab 11. Ecosystems and Biodiversity: How Does Food Web Complexity Affect the Biodiversity of an Ecosystem?

Lab Handout

Introduction

An ecosystem is a community of living organisms and the nonliving components of the environment. Energy flows in an ecosystem in one direction through food chains, and a food web is made up of all the food chains within a community of organisms. Food chains and food webs consist of the producers (the autotrophs of an ecosystem), the primary consumers (the herbivores and omnivores of the ecosystem), the secondary consumers (the carnivores and omnivores of the ecosystem), and the top predator. Some ecosystems have complex food webs and some do not. In ecosystems with a complex food web, herbivores and omnivores eat many different types of plants and the carnivores eat many different types of animals. The consumers in this type of ecosystem are described as generalists. Ecosystems that support consumers that rely on a single food source, in contrast, have simple food webs, because the consumers are specialists. An example of a complex food web is provided in panel (a) of the figure on the next page, and an example of a simple food web is provided in panel (b) of that figure.

Biodiversity refers to the variation in species found within an ecosystem, and it is measured in two ways: (1) species richness, which is the total number of different species in an ecosystem; and (2) relative abundance, which is a measure of how common each species is within the ecosystem. Regions that are home to many different species with a high relative abundance of those different species have high levels of biodiversity, whereas regions with only a few different types of species or that have moderate species richness but a low relative abundance of several species have a low level of biodiversity.

Notice that the food webs illustrated on the opposite page have the same amount of species richness even though the feeding relationships are different. Some of the feeding relationships illustrated in these two ecosystems, however, may or may not be sustainable over time and may result in a net decrease in biodiversity. The relative abundance of each species, for example, may change if one or more of the populations within the ecosystem grows or declines over time. The species richness of the ecosystems could also change if some of the populations disappear because of too much predation or too little access to natural resources. Given the role that biodiversity plays in ecosystem health and tolerance to ecological disturbances, it is important to understand how food web complexity is related to the biodiversity of an ecosystem.

Example of (a) a complex food web and (b) a simple food web

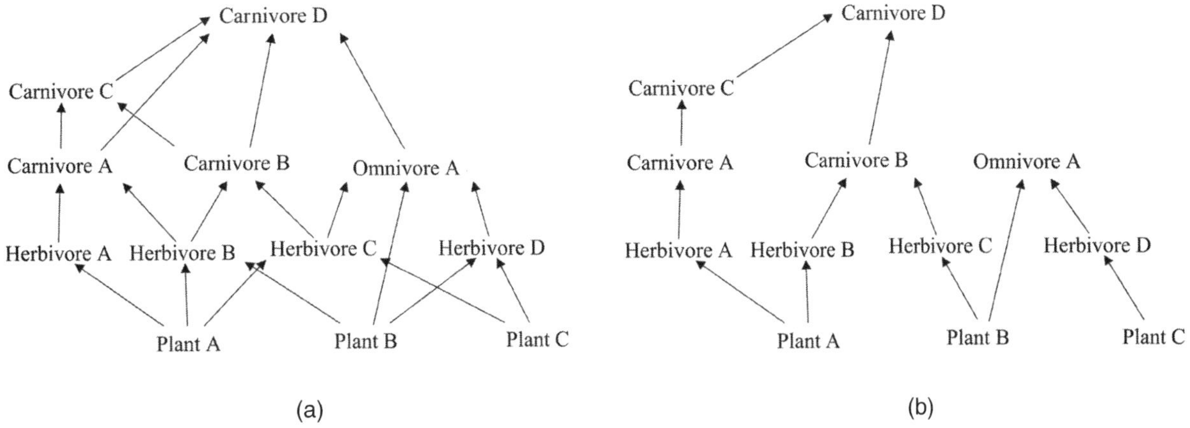

Your Task

Use the online simulation *Ecology Lab* (see the figure on p. 160), to explore the relationship between food web complexity and biodiversity in an ecosystem.

The guiding question of this investigation is, **How does food web complexity affect the biodiversity of an ecosystem?**

Materials

You will use an online simulation called *Ecology Lab* to conduct your investigation. You can access the simulation by going to the following website: *www.learner.org/courses/envsci/interactives/ecology.*

Safety Precautions

1. Use caution when working with electrical equipment. Keep away from water sources in that they can cause shorts, fires, and shock hazards. Use only GFI-protected circuits.
2. Wash hands with soap and water after completing this lab.
3. Follow all normal lab safety rules.

Getting Started

The *Ecology Lab* simulation allows you to create different food chains and webs within a model ecosystem. Once you establish the food chains and webs in the model ecosystem, you can run the simulation to determine the effect on the population of each organism (see the figure on p. 160).

LAB 11

A screen shot of the *Ecology Lab* simulation

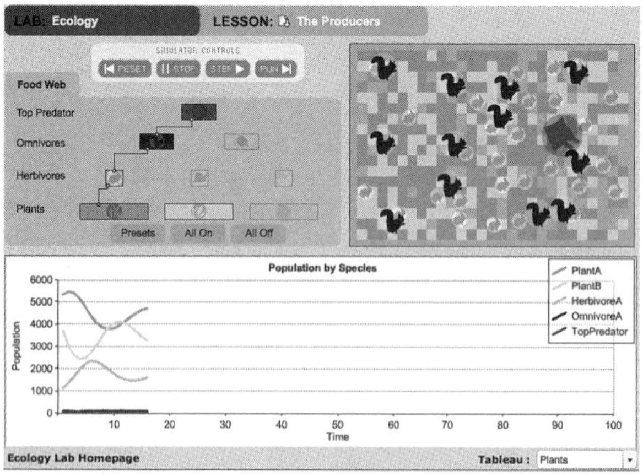

To answer the guiding question, you will need to design and conduct several experiments using the online simulation. To accomplish this task, you must determine what type of data you will need to collect during each experiment, how you will collect it, and how you will analyze it.

To determine *what type of data you will need to collect,* think about the following questions:

- What will serve as your dependent variable (population size, number of different populations, relative abundance, and so on)?
- What type of data will you need to keep a record of during your investigation?

To determine *how you will collect your data,* think about the following questions:

- What will serve as a control (or comparison) condition during each experiment?
- What types of treatment conditions will you need to set up for each experiment?
- What variables will you need to control during each experiment?
- How often will you collect data and when will you do it?
- How will you keep track of the data you collect and how will you organize the data?

To determine *how you will analyze your data,* think about the following questions:

- How will you determine if there is a difference between the conditions during each experiment?
- What type of calculations will you need to make?
- What type of table or graph could you create to help make sense of your data?

Investigation Proposal Required? ☐ Yes ☐ No

Connections to Crosscutting Concepts and to the Nature of Science and the Nature of Scientific Inquiry

As you work through your investigation, be sure to think about

- the importance of identifying patterns,

- the importance of identifying the underlying cause for observations,
- how models are used to study natural phenomena,
- how systems go through periods of stability and change,
- the importance of creativity and imagination in science, and
- the factors that influence observations and inferences in science.

Argumentation Session

Once your group has finished collecting and analyzing your data, prepare a whiteboard that you can use to share your initial argument. Your whiteboard should include all the information shown in the figure to the right.

Argument presentation on a whiteboard

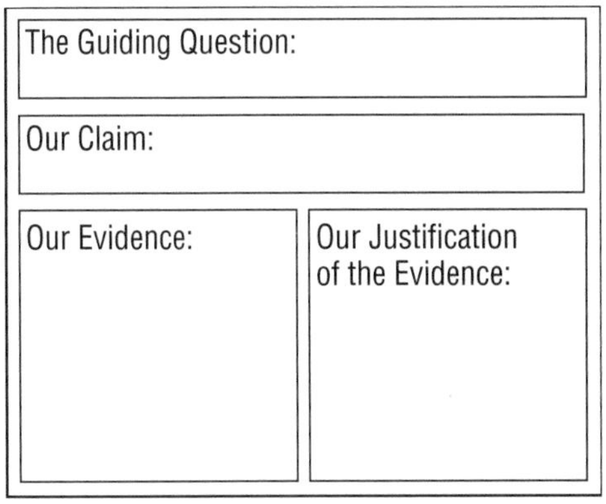

To share your argument with others, we will be using a round-robin format. This means that one member of your group will stay at your lab station to share your group's argument while the other members of your group go to the other lab stations one at a time to listen to and critique the arguments developed by your classmates.

The goal of the argumentation session is not to convince others that your argument is the best one; rather, the goal is to identify errors or instances of faulty reasoning in the arguments so these mistakes can be fixed. You will therefore need to evaluate the content of the claim, the quality of the evidence used to support the claim, and the strength of the justification of the evidence included in each argument that you see. In order to critique an argument, you will need more information than what is included on the whiteboard. You might, therefore, need to ask the presenter one or more follow-up questions such as:

- How did you use the simulation to collect your data?
- What did you do to analyze your data? Why did you decide to do it that way? Did you check your calculations?
- Is that the only way to interpret the results of your analysis? How do you know that your interpretation of your analysis is appropriate?
- Why did your group decide to present your evidence in that manner?
- What other claims did your group discuss before you decided on that one? Why did your group abandon those alternative ideas?
- How confident are you that your claim is valid? What could you do to increase your confidence?

Once the argumentation session is complete, you will have a chance to meet with your group and revise your original argument. Your group might need to gather more data or design a way to test one or more alternative claims as part of this process. Remember, your goal at this stage of the investigation is to develop the most valid or acceptable answer to the research question!

Report

Once you have completed your research, you will need to prepare an investigation report that consists of three sections that provide answers to the following questions:

1. What question were you trying to answer and why?
2. What did you do during your investigation and why did you conduct your investigation in this way?
3. What is your argument?

Your report should answer these questions in two pages or less. This report must be typed, and any diagrams, figures, or tables should be embedded into the document. Be sure to write in a persuasive style; you are trying to convince others that your claim is acceptable or valid!

Lab 11. Ecosystems and Biodiversity: How Does Food Web Complexity Affect the Biodiversity of an Ecosystem?

Checkout Questions

Use the figure below to answer questions 1 and 2. The figure illustrates the food webs of two different ecosystems. Ecosystem A has a simple food web and Ecosystem B has a complex one.

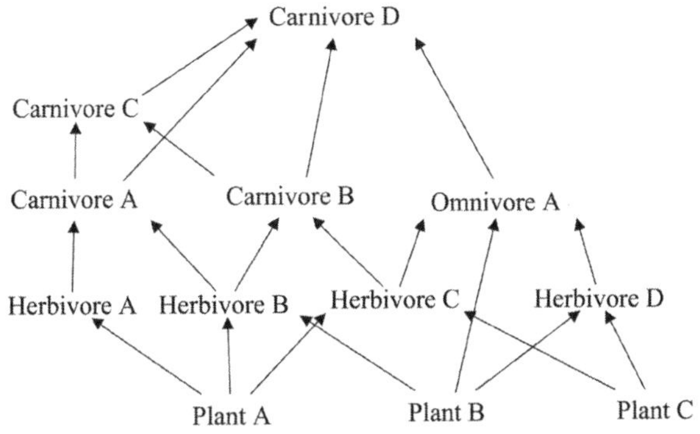

Ecosystem A

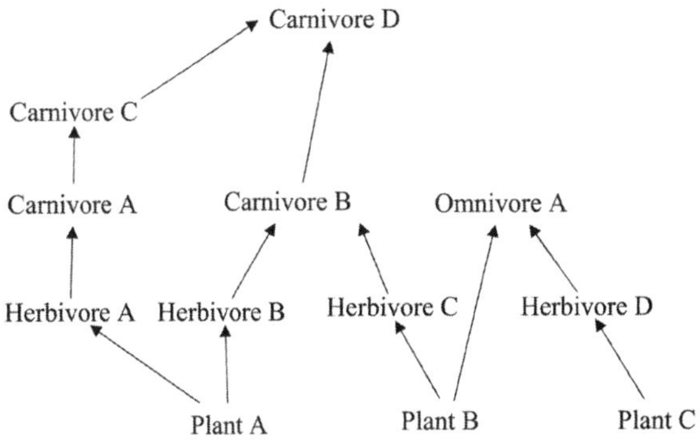

Ecosystem B

1. Which ecosystem has greater biodiversity?

   a. Ecosystem A
   b. Ecosystem B
   c. Ecosystems A and B have the same amount of biodiversity
   d. Unable to determine from the information provided

   Explain your answer.

2. Which ecosystem is most likely to sustain a greater amount of biodiversity over time?

   a. Ecosystem A
   b. Ecosystem B
   c. Ecosystems A and B will both sustain a large amount of biodiversity
   d. Unable to determine from the information provided

   Explain your answer.

3. The inferences that are made by a scientist are influenced by his or her background and past experiences, but the observations made by a scientist are not.

   a. I agree with this statement.
   b. I disagree with this statement.

   Explain your answer, using examples from your investigation about ecosystems.

4. Science requires logic and reason but not imagination or creativity.

   a. I agree with this statement.
   b. I disagree with this statement.

   Explain your answer, using information from your investigation about biodiversity.

5. Scientists often attempt to identify patterns in nature. Explain why the identification of patterns is useful in science, using an example from your investigation about ecosystems.

6. An important goal in science is to identify the underlying cause of a natural phenomenon. Explain why it is important for scientists to learn about underlying causes, using an example from your investigation about ecosystems.

7. Scientists often use models to study complex natural phenomenon. Explain what a model is and how you used models during your investigation about ecosystems.

8. Biological systems, such as ecosystems, often go through periods of stability and change. Explain what this means, using an example from your investigation about ecosystems.

Lab 12. Explanations for Animal Behavior: Why Do Great White Sharks Travel Over Long Distances?

Teacher Notes

Purpose

The purpose of this lab is to *introduce* students to many of the theories and concepts used by biologists to study and explain the behavior of animals. This lab also gives students an opportunity to design and carry out an investigation with the goal of developing an explanation for the long-range movement of great white sharks, using an online database available at the OCEARCH website. This database, called Global Shark Tracker, allows students to see the location of several great white sharks and to track their long-range movement over time. Students will also learn about the different methods used by scientists to answer research questions and how scientific knowledge can change over time.

The Content

Behavior is how an animal responds to sensory input. Behavior has both *proximate* and *ultimate* causes. Proximate mechanisms include the hormonal, nervous, and environmental stimuli that elicit a particular behavior pattern. Ultimate causes are the reasons why the behavior pattern evolved over time. Genes and the environment influence the behavior of animals. An *innate behavior* is one that occurs in all individuals of a population, regardless of individual differences in experience, whereas a *learned behavior* is one that develops only within specific individuals and stems from experience. Behavioral ecologists tend to examine behaviors such as foraging, courtship rituals, and migration through the lens of natural selection. Therefore, many of the explanations for animal behavior posed by scientists are based on the assumption that animals behave in a way that increases their fitness (or reproductive success).

Social behavior refers to the interactions that take place between two or more animals, usually of the same species. Social behaviors that are competitive in nature, such as the establishment of a dominance hierarchy or a territory, enable one animal to gain an advantage in obtaining access to limited resources (such as food or a mate). Social behaviors that are more cooperative in nature, such as pack hunting, enable animals to expend less energy to obtain the resources needed to survive. Finally, specific reproductive behaviors, such as courtship rituals or migration to a breeding ground, tend to increase the likelihood of finding a mate or to maximize the quantity of partners or the quality of a single partner. Most behaviors that animals engage in are explained by looking for ways that a behavior increases the likelihood that the animal will survive, find a mate, and produce offspring. A similar approach can be used to explain the long-range movements of the great white shark.

Timeline

The instructional time needed to implement this lab investigation is 180–250 minutes. Appendix 2 (p. 391) provides options for implementing this lab investigation over several class periods. Option E or G (250 minutes) should be used if students are unfamiliar with scientific writing because either of these options provides extra instructional time for scaffolding the writing process. You can scaffold the writing process by modeling, providing examples, and providing hints as students write each section of the report. Option F or H (180 minutes) should be used if students are familiar with scientific writing and have the skills needed to write an investigation report on their own. In options F and H, students complete stage 6 (writing the investigation report) and stage 8 (revising the investigation report) as homework.

Materials and Preparation

The materials needed to implement this investigation are listed in Table 12.1. The OCEARCH Global Shark Tracker database, available at *http://sharks-ocearch.verite.com.*, is free to use and can be run online using an internet browser. There is also a companion app for the website that can be used on mobile devices. The app can be downloaded for free from the Apple App store or Google Play. You should access the website or download the mobile app and learn how it works before beginning the lab investigation. In addition, it is important to check if students can access and use the website from a school computer because some schools have set up firewalls and other restrictions on web browsing.

TABLE 12.1
Materials list

Item	Quantity
Computer with internet access	1 per group
Student handout	1 per student
Investigation proposal C (optional)	1 per group
Whiteboard, 2' × 3'*	1 per group
Peer-review guide and instructor scoring rubric	1 per student

* As an alternative, students can use computer and presentation software such as Microsoft PowerPoint or Apple Keynote to create their arguments.

Topics for the Explicit and Reflective Discussion

Concepts That Can Be Used to Justify the Evidence

To provide an adequate justification of their evidence, students must explain why they included the evidence in their arguments and make the assumptions underlying their

analysis and interpretation of the data explicit. In this investigation, students can use the following concepts to help justify their evidence:

- Animals often engage in specific types of behaviors (e.g., foraging, migration, establishment and defense of a territory, courtship displays) because these behaviors tend to increase reproductive success (or fitness).
- Animal behavior results from both genetic and environmental factors. Some behaviors, as a result, are inherited and fixed, whereas others are learned though experience.

We recommend that you review these concepts during the explicit and reflective discussion to help students make this connection.

How to Design Better Investigations

It is important for students to reflect on the strengths and weaknesses of the investigation they designed during the explicit and reflective discussion. Students should therefore be encouraged to discuss ways to eliminate potential flaws, measurement errors, or sources of bias in their investigations. To help students be more reflective about the design of their investigation, you can ask the following questions:

- What were some of the strengths of your investigation? What made it scientific?
- What were some of the weaknesses of your investigation? What made it less scientific?
- If you were to do this investigation again, what would you do to address the weaknesses in your investigation? What could you do to make it more scientific?

Crosscutting Concepts

This investigation is well aligned with three crosscutting concepts found in *A Framework for K–12 Science Education,* and you should review these concepts during the explicit and reflective discussion.

- *Patterns:* Patterns are often used to guide the organization and classification of life on Earth. In addition, a major objective in biology is to identify the underlying cause of observed patterns, such as the long-term movements of the great white shark.
- *Cause and Effect: Mechanism and Explanation:* One of the main objectives of science is to identify and then test potential causal relationships.
- *Scale, Proportion, and Quantity:* It is critical for scientists to recognize what is relevant or important at different sizes, times, or energy scales. It is also important for scientists to think proportionally about the phenomenon they are studying and not just in absolute values. For example, in this investigation it is important (and useful) to think in proportions rather than in absolute numbers.

The Nature of Science and the Nature of Scientific Inquiry

It is important for students to understand that *scientists use different methods to answer different types of questions*. Examples of methods include experiments, systematic observations of a phenomenon, literature reviews, and analysis of existing data sets; the choice of method depends on the objectives of the research. There is no universal step-by-step scientific method that all scientists follow; rather, different scientific disciplines (e.g., biology vs. physics) and fields within a discipline (e.g., ecology vs. molecular biology) use different types of methods, use different core theories, and rely on different standards to develop scientific knowledge. For example, in this investigation the students use an existing database rather than collecting data in the field. It is also important for students to understand that *scientific knowledge can change over time.* A person can have confidence in the validity of scientific knowledge but must also accept that scientific knowledge may be abandoned or modified in light of new evidence or because existing evidence has been reconceptualized by scientists. There are many examples in the history of science of both evolutionary changes (i.e., the slow or gradual refinement of ideas) and revolutionary changes (i.e., the rapid abandonment of a well-established idea) in scientific knowledge. Biologists, for example, long worked under the assumption that great white sharks are coastal territorial predators that rarely interact with other members of the species. However, as scientists learned more about the long-range movements of the great white shark, they abandoned these views. Great white sharks are now considered to be migratory predators that spend a great deal of time in the open ocean. This is but one example of how scientific knowledge is tentative and often revised to better account for natural phenomena.

You should review and provide examples of these two important concepts of the nature of science (NOS) and the nature of scientific inquiry (NOSI) during the explicit and reflective discussion.

Hints for Implementing the Lab

- Learn how to use the online database before the lab begins. It is important for you to know how to use the database so you can help students when they get stuck or confused.
- A group of three students per computer tends to work well.
- Allow the students to play with the database as part of the tool talk before they begin to design their investigation or fill out an investigation proposal. This gives students a chance to see what they can and cannot do with the database.
- Be sure that students record actual values (e.g., number of individuals in a location or time in each location), rather than just attempting to hand draw what they see on the computer screen.
- Encourage the students to take "screen shots" of the migration patterns they observe using the database and then use the images in their reports.

LAB 12

Topic Connections

Table 12.2 provides an overview of the scientific practices, crosscutting concepts, disciplinary core ideas, and support ideas at the heart of this lab investigation. In addition, it lists NOS and NOSI concepts for the explicit and reflective discussion. Finally, it lists literacy and mathematics skills (*CCSS ELA* and *CCSS Mathematics*) that are addressed during the investigation.

TABLE 12.2

Lab 12 alignment with standards

Scientific practices	• Asking questions • Planning and carrying out investigations • Analyzing and interpreting data • Using mathematics and computational thinking • Constructing explanations • Engaging in argument from evidence • Obtaining, evaluating, and communicating information
Crosscutting concepts	• Patterns • Cause and effect: Mechanism and explanation • Scale, proportion, and quantity
Core idea	• LS2: Ecosystems: Interactions, energy, and dynamics
Supporting ideas	• Animal behavior • Foraging • Territories • Mating • Migration
NOS and NOSI concepts	• Methods used in scientific investigations • Science as a body of knowledge
Literacy connections *(CCSS ELA)*	• *Reading*: Key ideas and details, craft and structure, integration of knowledge and ideas • *Writing*: Text types and purposes, production and distribution of writing, research to build and present knowledge, range of writing • *Speaking and listening*: Comprehension and collaboration, presentation of knowledge and ideas
Mathematics connection *(CCSS Mathematics)*	• Reason quantitatively and use units to solve problems

Lab 12. Explanations for Animal Behavior: Why Do Great White Sharks Travel Over Long Distances?

Lab Handout

Introduction

Shark populations worldwide are declining in areas where they were once common. As a result, the International Union for Conservation of Nature (IUCN), has classified many species of shark as threatened with extinction. One species of shark that is currently on the IUCN "Vulnerable" list is the great white shark (*Carcharodon carcharias*). The great white shark is found in coastal surface waters of all the major oceans. It can grow up to 6 m (20 ft.) in length and weigh nearly 2,268 kg (5,000 lb). The great white shark reaches sexual maturity at around 15 years of age and can live for over 30 years. Great white sharks are apex predators (see the figure to the right). An apex predator is an animal that, as an adult, has no natural predators in its ecosystem and resides at the top of the food chain. These sharks prey on marine mammals, fish, and seabirds.

A great white shark

Great white shark conservation has become a global priority in recent years. However, our limited understanding of their behavior has hindered the development of effective conservation strategies for this species. For example, little is known about where and when great white sharks mate, where they give birth, and where they spend their time as juveniles. We also know that some great white sharks travel long distances, such as from Baja California to Hawaii or from South Africa to Australia, but we do not know why they make these journeys. There are, however, a number of potential explanations that have been suggested by scientists. For example, great white sharks might travel long distances because they need to do one or more of the following:

- Find and establish a territory (an area that they defend that contains a mating site and sufficient food resources for them and their young) once they reach sexual maturity or after losing a territory to other great white sharks.
- Migrate between a foraging site and a mating site on an annual or seasonal basis.

- Forage for food—slowly traveling over long distances allows the sharks to find, capture, and consume new sources of food along the way without expending a great deal of energy.
- Find a foraging site with other sharks in it and cooperate with them to capture prey and minimize the amount of energy required to capture and consume food.
- Follow their prey as the prey migrates on an annual or seasonal basis.
- Move between several different foraging areas because they quickly deplete their food source in a given area and must move onto new foraging areas to survive.

All of these potential explanations are plausible because they can help a great white shark survive longer or reproduce more. It is difficult, however, to determine which of these potential explanations is the most valid or acceptable because we know so little about the life history and long-range movements of the great white shark. Most research on this species has been carried out at specific aggregation sites (such as the one near Dyer Island in South Africa). Although this type of research has enabled scientists to learn a lot about the feeding behaviors and short-range movements of the great white shark, we know very little about how they act in other places. A group called OCEARCH (*www.ocearch.org*), however, is trying to facilitate more research on their life history and long-range movements so people can develop better conservation strategies to help protect the great white shark.

This group of researchers has been catching and tagging great white sharks to document where they go over time. To tag and track a great white shark, OCEARCH places a SPOT tag on the shark's dorsal fin. These tags emit a signal that is picked up by global positioning satellites. Unfortunately, the signal can only be detected when the shark's dorsal fin breaks the surface of the water and a satellite is directly overhead. Researchers at OCEARCH call these signals "pings." The time span between pings can vary a great deal (from once an hour to once in a three-week period) because of individual shark behavior and the orbit of a satellite.

OCEARCH has created the Global Shark Tracker database (*www.ocearch.org*) and a companion app for mobile devices (visit the Apple App Store or Google Play to download the free app) to share the real-time data they collect (see the figure on the opposite page). This database allows users to see the current location of all the sharks that the OCEARCH researchers have tagged. It also allows users to track the movement of each shark over time. Users can also search for sharks by name, sex (male or female), and stage of life (mature or immature).

Your Task

Use the OCEARCH Global Shark Tracker database to identify patterns in the long-range movements of the great white shark, and then develop an explanation for those patterns.

A screen shot of Global Shark Tracker from the OCEARCH website

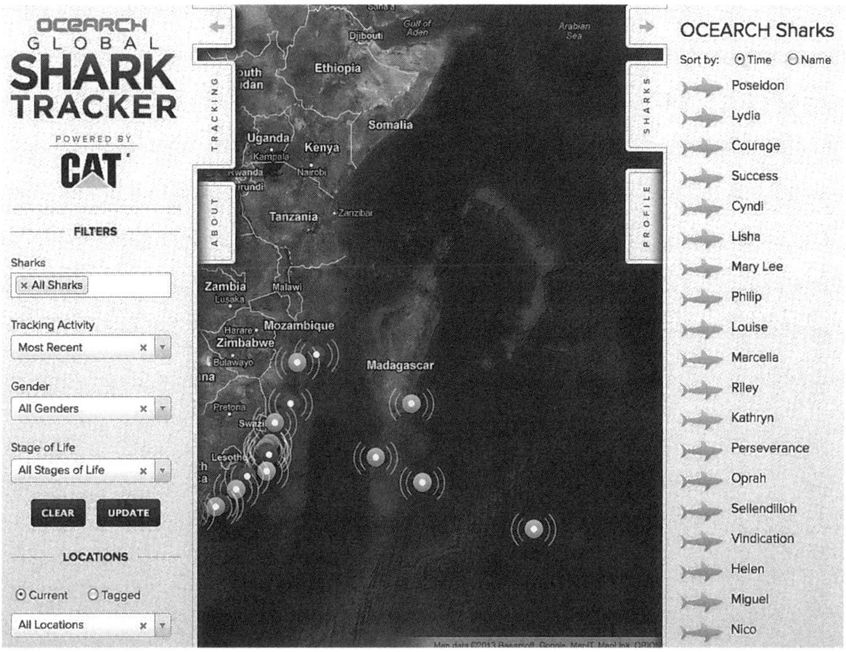

The guiding question of this investigation is, **Why do great white sharks travel over long distances?**

Materials

You will use an online database called Global Shark Tracker to conduct your investigation. You can access the database by going to the following website: *www.ocearch.org*.

Safety Precautions

1. Use caution when working with electrical equipment. Keep away from water sources in that they can cause shorts, fires, and shock hazards. Use only GFI-protected circuits.
2. Wash hands with soap and water after completing this lab.
3. Follow all normal lab safety rules.

Getting Started

Your first step in this investigation is to learn more about what is already known about the great white shark. To do this, check the following websites:

- Animal Diversity Web (*http://animaldiversity.ummz.umich.edu/accounts/Carcharodon_carcharias*)
- MarineBio (*http://marinebio.org/species.asp?id=38*)
- The Smithsonian National Museum of Natural History Ocean Portal (*http://ocean.si.edu/great-white-shark*)

You can then use the OCEARCH Global Shark Tracker database to identify patterns in the long-range movement of great white sharks. To accomplish this task, it is important for you to determine what type of data you will need to collect and how you will analyze it.

To determine *what type of data you will need to collect,* think about the following questions:

- What data will you need to determine if there are patterns in the long-range movements of great white sharks?
- What data will you need to determine if there are sex-related, age-related, or geographic region–related differences in the long-range movements of great white sharks?

To determine *how you will analyze your data,* think about the following questions:

- How can you identify a pattern in the ways great white sharks move over long distances?
- How can you determine if there are patterns in the way great white sharks move over long distances based on sex, age, or geographic region?
- What type of table or graph could you create to help make sense of your data?

Once you have identified patterns in the ways great white sharks move over long distances, you will then need to develop an explanation for those patterns. You can develop one of your own or see if one of the explanations outlined in the "Introduction" section of this investigation is consistent with the patterns you identified. These explanations stem from what scientists know about the behavior of other animals and reflect some of the theories that scientists currently use to explain animal behavior.

Investigation Proposal Required? ☐ Yes ☐ No

Connections to Crosscutting Concepts and to the Nature of Science and the Nature of Scientific Inquiry

As you work through your investigation, be sure to think about

- the importance of identifying patterns,
- the importance of identifying the underlying cause for observations,

- the importance of examining proportional relationships,
- how scientific knowledge can change over time, and
- how the methods used by scientists depend on what is being studied and the research question.

Argumentation Session

Once your group has finished collecting and analyzing your data, prepare a whiteboard that you can use to share your initial argument. Your whiteboard should include all the information shown in the figure to the right.

Argument presentation on a whiteboard

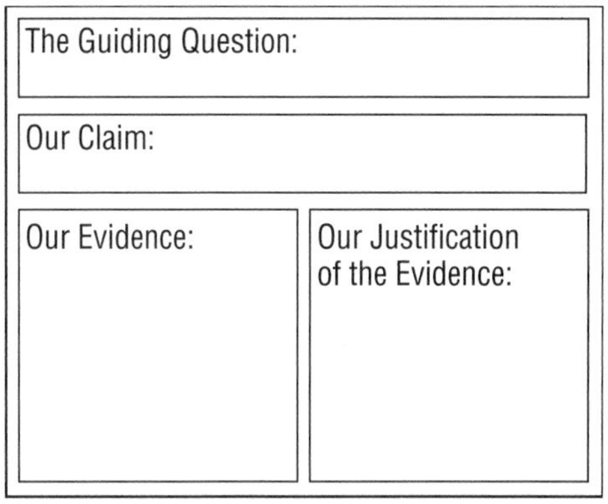

To share your argument with others, we will be using a round-robin format. This means that one member of your group will stay at your lab station to share your group's argument while the other members of your group go to the other lab stations one at a time to listen to and critique the arguments developed by your classmates.

The goal of the argumentation session is not to convince others that your argument is the best one; rather, the goal is to identify errors or instances of faulty reasoning in the arguments so these mistakes can be fixed. You will therefore need to evaluate the content of the claim, the quality of the evidence used to support the claim, and the strength of the justification of the evidence included in each argument that you see. In order to critique an argument, you will need more information than what is included on the whiteboard. You might, therefore, need to ask the presenter one or more follow-up questions, such as:

- Why did you decide to focus on those data?
- What did you do to analyze your data? Why did you decide to do it that way? Did you check your calculations?
- Is that the only way to interpret the results of your analysis? How do you know that your interpretation of your analysis is appropriate?
- Why did your group decide to present your evidence in that manner?
- What other claims did your group discuss before you decided on that one? Why did your group abandon those alternative ideas?
- How confident are you that your claim is valid? What could you do to increase your confidence?

Once the argumentation session is complete, you will have a chance to meet with your group and revise your original argument. Your group might need to gather more data or design a way to test one or more alternative claims as part of this process. Remember, your goal at this stage of the investigation is to develop the most valid or acceptable answer to the research question!

Report

Once you have completed your research, you will need to prepare an investigation report that consists of three sections that provide answers to the following questions:

1. What question were you trying to answer and why?
2. What did you do during your investigation and why did you conduct your investigation in this way?
3. What is your argument?

Your report should answer these questions in two pages or less. This report must be typed, and any diagrams, figures, or tables should be embedded into the document. Be sure to write in a persuasive style; you are trying to convince others that your claim is acceptable or valid!

Lab 12. Explanations for Animal Behavior: Why Do Great White Sharks Travel Over Long Distances?

Checkout Questions

Nowhere in the world is there a movement of animals as spectacular as the wildebeest migration that occurs from July to October each year in Africa. Over 2 million wildebeest travel from Serengeti National Park in Tanzania to the greener pastures of Maasai Mara National Reserve in Kenya. The wildebeest expend a lot of energy to migrate because of the great distance they travel. The wildebeest also have to cross the Mara River in Maasai Mara, where crocodiles will prey on them. In addition, the wildebeest will be hunted, stalked, and run down by the large carnivores found in the Maasai Mara. Many wildebeest, as a result, do not survive the migration.

1. Given the fact that wildebeest must expend a lot of energy and may even die during a migration, why would wildebeest engage in this type of behavior?

2. There is a single, universal, step-by-step scientific method that all scientists follow regardless of the type of question that they are trying to answer.

   a. I agree with this statement.
   b. I disagree with this statement.

   Explain your answer, using examples from your investigation about animal behavior.

3. Scientific knowledge may be abandoned or modified in light of new evidence or because of the reconceptualization of prior evidence and knowledge.

    a. I agree with this statement.
    b. I disagree with this statement.

    Explain your answer, using information from your investigation about animal behavior.

4. Scientists often attempt to identify patterns in nature. Explain why the identification of patterns is useful in science, using an example from your investigation about animal behavior.

5. Scientists often attempt to identify the underlying cause for the observations they make. Explain why the identification of underlying causes is so important in science, using an example from your investigation about animal behavior.

6. Scientists often need to look for proportional relationships. Explain what a proportional relationship is and why these relationships are important, using an example from your investigation about animal behavior.

Application Labs

Lab 13. Environmental Influences on Animal Behavior: How Has Climate Change Affected Bird Migration?

Teacher Notes

Purpose

The purpose of this lab is for students to *apply* what they know about animal behavior and the interactions among species and their environment to determine if bird migration patterns have been affected by climate change. This lab also gives students an opportunity to use an online database as part of their investigation. Students will also learn about the characteristics of science as a body of knowledge and the difference between data and evidence.

The Content

More than 650 species of birds nest in North America. Some are permanent residents and live in the same area year-round, but most of these species migrate during the year. Birds migrate from areas of low or decreasing resources to areas of high or increasing resources. The two most important resources that birds need are food and a nesting location. Birds that nest in the Northern Hemisphere tend to migrate northward in the spring to feed on insects or budding plants and to take advantage of the abundance of nesting locations. As winter approaches, and the number of insects and the availability of other food resources dwindle, the birds move south again. Escaping the cold of winter is also a motivating factor, but many birds can survive freezing temperatures as long they have enough food. The migration pattern of a bird usually falls into one of three categories:

- Short-distance migration: Moving only a short distance, such as from higher to lower elevations on a mountain, on a seasonal basis.
- Medium-distance migration: Traveling between one or more states.
- Long-distance migration: Traveling from the United States or Canada in the summer to Mexico or farther south in the winter.

The mechanisms that trigger the start of a migration vary from species to species. Some birds migrate in response to a change in day length or a change in temperature. Some species migrate when food becomes scarce or because of a genetic predisposition. There are some birds that migrate in response to a combination of triggers. Some of these triggers, such as temperature or food availability, may be influenced by changes in climate.

Warmer temperatures in the summer and more severe winters could lead to changes in the distances that birds migrate, where birds migrate to, and the timing of these migrations.

Timeline

The instructional time needed to implement this lab investigation is 180–250 minutes. Appendix 2 (p. 391) provides options for implementing this lab investigation over several class periods. Option E or G (250 minutes) should be used if students are unfamiliar with scientific writing because either of these options provides extra instructional time for scaffolding the writing process. You can scaffold the writing process by modeling, providing examples, and providing hints as students write each section of the report. Option F or H (180 minutes) should be used if students are familiar with scientific writing and have the skills needed to write an investigation report on their own. In options F and H, students complete stage 6 (writing the investigation report) and stage 8 (revising the investigation report) as homework.

Materials and Preparation

The materials needed to implement this investigation are listed in Table 13.1. The eBird database, available at *http://ebird.org*, is free to use and can be accessed using an internet browser; eBird is a real-time, online checklist program that was launched in 2002 by the Cornell Lab of Ornithology and the National Audubon Society. The All About Birds database (Cornell Lab of Ornithology; *www.allaboutbirds.org*), the National Weather Service database of the National Oceanic and Atmospheric Administration (NOAA; *www.weather.gov*), and the NOAA National Climatic Data Center database (*www.ncdc.noaa.gov*) are also free to use. You should access these websites and learn how they work before beginning the lab investigation. In addition, it is important to check if students can access and use the simulation from a school computer because some schools have set up firewalls and other restrictions on web browsing.

TABLE 13.1

Materials list

Item	Quantity
Computer with internet access	1 per group
Student handout	1 per student
Investigation proposal C (optional)	1 per group
Whiteboard, 2' × 3'*	1 per group
Peer-review guide and instructor scoring rubric	1 per student

* As an alternative, students can use computer and presentation software such as Microsoft PowerPoint or Apple Keynote to create their arguments.

Topics for the Explicit and Reflective Discussion

Concepts That Can Be Used to Justify the Evidence

To provide an adequate justification of their evidence, students must explain why they included the evidence in their arguments and make the assumptions underlying their analysis and interpretation of the data explicit. In this investigation, students can use the following concepts to help justify their evidence:

- Animals often engage in specific types of behaviors (such as migration) because these behaviors tend to increase reproductive success (or fitness).
- Animal behavior has both a proximate cause and an ultimate cause.
- Animal behavior can be influenced by a change in environmental conditions.

We recommend that you review these concepts during the explicit and reflective discussion to help students make this connection.

How to Design Better Investigations

It is important for students to reflect on the strengths and weaknesses of the investigation they designed during the explicit and reflective discussion. Students should therefore be encouraged to discuss ways to eliminate potential flaws, measurement errors, or sources of bias in their investigations. To help students be more reflective about the design of their investigation, you can ask the following questions:

- What were some of the strengths of your investigation? What made it scientific?
- What were some of the weaknesses of your investigation? What made it less scientific?
- If you were to do this investigation again, what would you do to address the weaknesses in your investigation? What could you do to make it more scientific?

Crosscutting Concepts

This investigation is well aligned with three crosscutting concepts found in *A Framework for K–12 Science Education,* and you should review these concepts during the explicit and reflective discussion.

- *Patterns:* Patterns are often used to guide the organization and classification of life on Earth. In addition, a major objective in biology is to identify the underlying cause of observed patterns, such as changes in the migration patterns of birds.
- *Cause and Effect: Mechanism and Explanation:* One of the main objectives of science is to identify and establish relationships between a cause and an effect. It is also important to understand the mechanisms by which these causal relationships are mediated.

- *Stability and Change:* This is perhaps the most relevant crosscutting concept to this investigation. Scientists must understand what makes a system, behavior, or an occurrence stable over time and the factors that lead to a change in the system, behavior, or occurrence.

The Nature of Science and the Nature of Scientific Inquiry

It is important for students to understand that *scientific knowledge is both tentative and durable*. A person can have confidence in the validity of scientific knowledge but must also accept that scientific knowledge may be abandoned or modified in light of new evidence or because existing evidence has been reconceptualized by scientists. There are many examples in the history of science of both evolutionary changes (i.e., the slow or gradual refinement of ideas) and revolutionary changes (i.e., the rapid abandonment of a well-established idea) in scientific knowledge. Scientific knowledge also varies in degree of certainty; some knowledge is well established and is not likely to change, whereas other knowledge represents only a conjecture. In this investigation, for example, the impact of climate change on the migration behavior of birds is not well understood and needs more research.

It is also important for students to understand the *difference between data and evidence in science*. Data are measurements, observations, and findings from other studies that are collected as part of an investigation. Evidence, in contrast, is analyzed data and an interpretation of the analysis.

You should review and provide examples of these two important concepts of the nature of science (NOS) and the nature of scientific inquiry (NOSI) during the explicit and reflective discussion.

Hints for Implementing the Lab

- Be prepared for groups to pursue different paths in completing the investigation.
- This is a very open-ended investigation, so flexibility is key.

Topic Connections

Table 13.2 provides an overview of the scientific practices, crosscutting concepts, disciplinary core ideas, and support ideas at the heart of this lab investigation. In addition, it lists NOS and NOSI concepts for the explicit and reflective discussion. Finally, it lists literacy and mathematics skills (*CCSS ELA* and *CCSS Mathematics*) that are addressed during the investigation.

TABLE 13.2

Lab 13 alignment with standards

Scientific practices	• Asking questions • Planning and carrying out investigations • Analyzing and interpreting data • Using mathematics and computational thinking • Constructing explanations • Engaging in argument from evidence • Obtaining, evaluating, and communicating information
Crosscutting concepts	• Patterns • Cause and effect: Mechanism and explanation • Stability and change
Core idea	• LS2: Ecosystems: Interactions, energy, and dynamics
Supporting ideas	• Animal behavior • Interactions • Resources
NOS and NOSI concepts	• Science as a body of knowledge • Difference between data and evidence
Literacy connections *(CCSS ELA)*	• *Reading*: Key ideas and details, craft and structure, integration of knowledge and ideas • *Writing*: Text types and purposes, production and distribution of writing, research to build and present knowledge, range of writing • *Speaking* and listening: Comprehension and collaboration, presentation of knowledge and ideas
Mathematics connection *(CCSS Mathematics)*	• Reason quantitatively and use units to solve problems

Lab 13. Environmental Influences on Animal Behavior: How Has Climate Change Affected Bird Migration?

Lab Handout

Introduction

The average temperature in the United States has increased by about 1.3°F since 1910, but the increase in average temperature has not been uniform. Some states have warmed more than others (see the figure below). The *pace* of warming in *all* regions of the United States, however, has accelerated dramatically since the 1970s. This change in pace coincides with the time when the effect of greenhouse gases began to overwhelm the other natural and human influences on climate at the global and continental scales.

A map illustrating how fast each state has been warming each decade since 1970

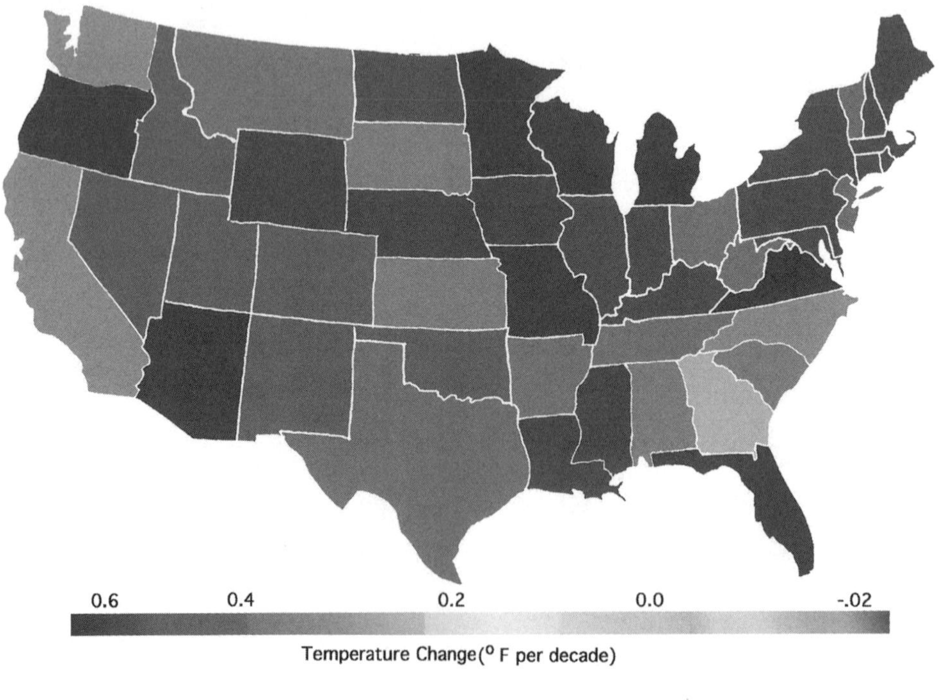

This increase in average temperature could have a negative impact on many different species of plants and animals because it could lead to changes in seasonal weather patterns, which could then lead to droughts, habitat loss, or food shortages. Migratory birds are one type of animal that may be influenced by a change in climate because birds migrate when the seasons change. Migratory birds tend to fly north in the spring to breed and return to the warmer wintering grounds of the south when temperatures get colder.

The migration of birds in response to a change of seasons is an example of animal behavior with both a proximate cause and an ultimate cause. A proximate cause is the stimulus that triggers a particular behavior (such as a change in temperature). An ultimate cause, in contrast, is the reason why the behavior exists. In this case, birds migrate because of food and because the longer days of the northern summer provide extended time for breeding birds to feed their young. Migratory birds, as a result, are often able to support larger clutches than nonmigratory species that remain in the tropics year round. This is clearly a benefit of migration.

Environmental conditions serve as both the proximate and ultimate cause of bird migration. Therefore, climate change could have drastic effects on bird migration because it changes seasonal weather patterns. For example, climate change could influence when the temperature drop that serves as the proximate cause of migration for many species of bird happens. Climate change, as noted earlier, can also lead to widespread droughts, habitat loss, and food shortages. These changes in environmental conditions could potentially eliminate the benefits associated with migration because they limit how much access birds have to the resources they need to survive and reproduce after they arrive at their destination.

Your Task

Use the All About Birds website to identify several migratory species of bird that can be found in the United States; then use the eBird online database to determine if the migration behaviors for these species have changed over the last 40 years. If you do see a change, you can then use the National Oceanic and Atmospheric Administration's (NOAA) National Weather Service and National Climatic Data Center databases to explore weather conditions and changes in climate over the same time period.

The guiding question of this investigation is, **How has climate change affected bird migration?**

Materials

You may use any of the following websites during your investigation:

- All About Birds (Cornell Lab of Ornithology): *www.allaboutbirds.org*
- *eBird: http://ebird.org*
- NOAA National Weather Service: *www.weather.gov*
- NOAA National Climatic Data Center: *www.ncdc.noaa.gov*

Safety Precautions

1. Use caution when working with electrical equipment. Keep away from water sources in that they can cause shorts, fires, and shock hazards. Use only GFI-protected circuits.
2. Wash hands with soap and water after completing this lab.
3. Follow all normal lab safety rules.

Getting Started

To answer the guiding question, you will need to design and conduct an investigation using three different online databases. Your first step in your investigation, however, is to learn more about birds, why birds migrate, the different migration patterns, and which types of birds migrate. To do this you can visit the website All About Birds, which is sponsored by the Cornell Lab of Ornithology. Your next step is to learn how to use the eBird database to find information on where and when different species of bird have been observed across the United States and over time. You will also need to learn how to use the NOAA National Weather Service database to access information about current weather conditions and the NOAA National Climatic Data Center database to access historical weather conditions for different regions of the United States.

Once you have learned how to use these databases, you will need to determine what type of data you will need to collect, how you will collect it, and how you will analyze it. To determine *what type of data you will need to collect,* think about the following questions:

- How will you determine if there has been a change in bird migration over time?
- What will serve as your dependent variable (e.g., location of breeding and winter locations, abundance of birds, arrival and departure dates in a specific area, distance traveled)?
- What information will you need to be able to link a change in a migration pattern to a change in climate?
- What type of comparisons will you need to make (e.g., different species of bird, birds in different regions, current observations vs. past observations)?

To determine *how you will collect your data,* think about the following questions:

- Where in the eBird and NOAA databases will you look to gather the information you need?
- What tools in the eBird and NOAA databases will you need to use?
- How will you keep track of the data you collect from the three different databases, and how will you organize the data?

To determine *how you will analyze your data,* think about the following questions:

- How will you demonstrate that a change in climate is or is not related to a change in the migration behaviors of bird species?
- How will you quantify a difference or amount of change?
- What type of calculations will you need to make?
- What type of graph could you create to help make sense of your data or to share the data with others?

Investigation Proposal Required? ☐ Yes ☐ No

Connections to Crosscutting Concepts and to the Nature of Science and the Nature of Scientific Inquiry

As you work through your investigation, be sure to think about

- the importance of identifying patterns,
- the importance of identifying the underlying cause for observations,
- how systems go through periods of stability and change,
- the nature of scientific knowledge, and
- the difference between data and evidence in science.

Argumentation Session

Once your group has finished collecting and analyzing your data, prepare a whiteboard that you can use to share your initial argument. Your whiteboard should include all the information shown in the figure below.

To share your argument with others, we will be using a round-robin format. This means that one member of your group will stay at your lab station to share your group's argument while the other members of your group go to the other lab stations one at a time to listen to and critique the arguments developed by your classmates.

Argument presentation on a whiteboard

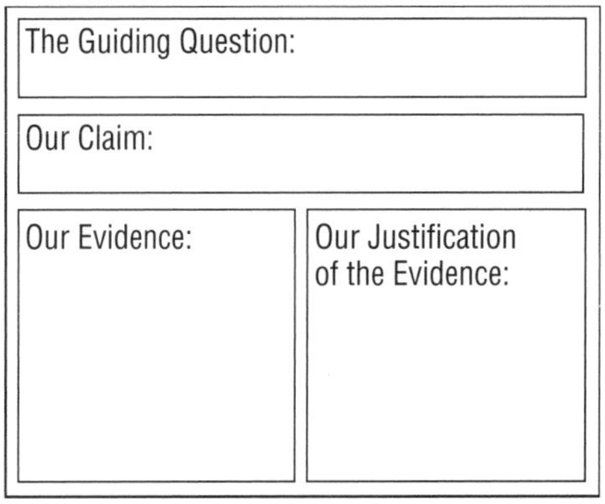

The goal of the argumentation session is not to convince others that your argument is the best one; rather, the goal is to identify errors or instances of faulty reasoning in the arguments so these mistakes can be fixed. You will therefore need to evaluate the content of the claim, the quality of the evidence used to support the claim, and the strength of the justification of the evidence included in each argument that you see. In order to critique an argument, you will need more information than what is included on the whiteboard. You might, therefore, need to ask the presenter one or more follow-up questions, such as:

- Why did you decide to focus on those data?
- What did you do to analyze your data? Why did you decide to do it that way? Did you check your calculations?
- Is that the only way to interpret the results of your analysis? How do you know that your interpretation of your analysis is appropriate?
- Why did your group decide to present your evidence in that manner?
- What other claims did your group discuss before you decided on that one? Why did your group abandon those alternative ideas?
- How confident are you that your claim is valid? What could you do to increase your confidence?

Once the argumentation session is complete, you will have a chance to meet with your group and revise your original argument. Your group might need to gather more data or design a way to test one or more alternative claims as part of this process. Remember, your goal at this stage of the investigation is to develop the most valid or acceptable answer to the research question!

Report

Once you have completed your research, you will need to prepare an investigation report that consists of three sections that provide answers to the following questions:

1. What question were you trying to answer and why?
2. What did you do during your investigation and why did you conduct your investigation in this way?
3. What is your argument?

Your report should answer these questions in two pages or less. This report must be typed, and any diagrams, figures, or tables should be embedded into the document. Be sure to write in a persuasive style; you are trying to convince others that your claim is acceptable or valid!

Lab 13. Environmental Influences on Animal Behavior: How Has Climate Change Affected Bird Migration?

Checkout Questions

Use the following information to answer questions 1–3. A biologist is interested in mealworm behavior. He sets up a box as shown below. He uses a neon lamp for light and constantly waters pieces of paper for moisture. In the center of the box he places 20 mealworms.

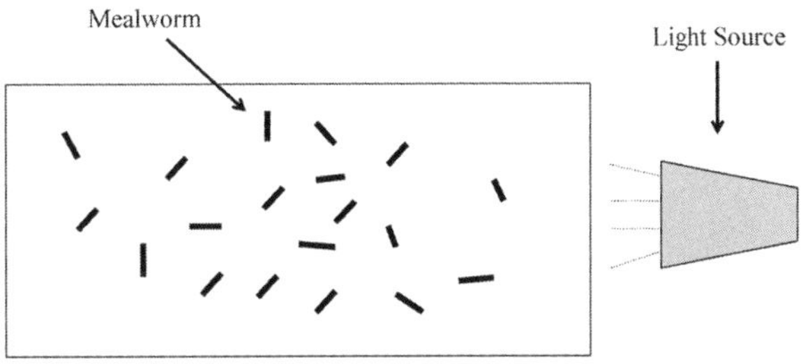

One day later he returns to see where the mealworms ended up.

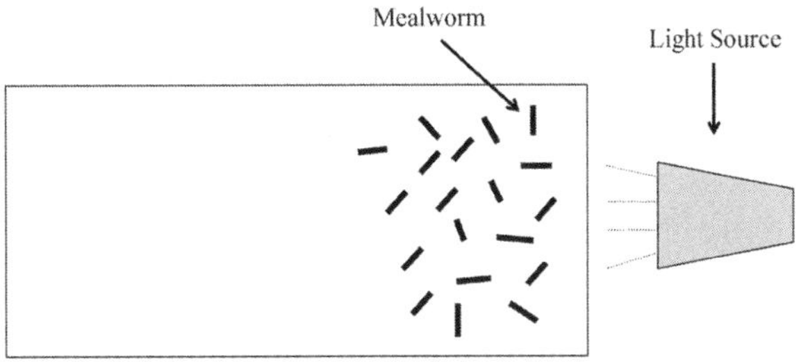

Biologists use the concepts of proximate and ultimate cause for behavior to explain this type of observation.

1. Describe the concept of a proximate cause of a behavior.

2. Describe the concept of an ultimate cause of a behavior.

3. Use the concepts of proximate and ultimate causes of a behavior to explain why the mealworms moved to one side of the box.

4. All scientific knowledge is certain and does not change.

    a. I agree with this statement.
    b. I disagree with this statement.

    Explain your answer, using examples from your investigation about animal behavior.

5. Evidence is data that are used to support a claim.

    a. I agree with this statement.
    b. I disagree with this statement.

    Explain your answer, using information from your investigation about animal behavior.

6. Scientists often attempt to identify patterns in nature. Explain why the identification of patterns is useful in science, using an example from your investigation about animal behavior.

7. Scientists often attempt to identify the underlying cause for the observations they make. Explain why the identification of underlying causes is so important in science, using an example from your investigation about animal behavior.

8. Biological systems often go through periods of stability and change. Explain what this means, using an example from your investigation about animal behavior.

Lab 14. Interdependence of Organisms: Why Is the Sport Fish Population of Lake Grace Decreasing in Size?

Teacher Notes

Purpose

The purpose of this lab is for students to *apply* what they know about food webs, nutrient cycling, and the interdependence of organisms within an ecosystem to develop an explanation for the decline of a fish population in a lake. This lab also gives students an opportunity to conduct water quality tests and use an existing data set as part of their investigation. Students will also learn about the different types of methods that scientists can use to answer a research question and the influence of society and culture on scientific research.

The Content

Water quality has an impact on the biological diversity of an aquatic ecosystem. Water high in nitrates, phosphates, and other fertilizers tends to promote algae growth. Algae growth depletes the water of dissolved oxygen (O_2), thus robbing the fish populations of O_2. Algal blooms will also block sunlight from penetrating the water, thus preventing aquatic plants from photosynthesizing and further reducing the amount of dissolved O_2 available. Without adequate O_2 supplies, small fish begin to die off, and then larger fish that depend on these smaller fish for energy also begin to die off.

Timeline

The instructional time needed to implement this lab investigation is 180–250 minutes. Appendix 2 (p. 391) provides options for implementing this lab investigation over several class periods. Option E or G (250 minutes) should be used if students are unfamiliar with scientific writing because either of these options provides extra instructional time for scaffolding the writing process. You can scaffold the writing process by modeling, providing examples, and providing hints as students write each section of the report. Option F or H (180 minutes) should be used if students are familiar with scientific writing and have the skills needed to write an investigation report on their own. In options F and H, students complete stage 6 (writing the investigation report) and stage 8 (revising the investigation report) as homework.

Materials and Preparation

The materials needed to implement this investigation are listed in Table 14.1. Be sure to prepare the water samples for students to test before the lab begins. The samples should represent a variety of locations from around the lake. Samples from around the golf course should be high in phosphate fertilizer, and samples from around the farmland should be high in bacteria and high in herbicides.

This investigation is based on a fictional scenario about Lake Grace; the locations described in the handout are not real locations, even if they have the same names as some real locations. Actual water samples from a local lake, river, or retention pond can be manipulated to represent the various areas of Lake Grace. These samples would include microorganisms that simulated samples would not contain. Follow these procedures to manipulate the samples:

- For the golf course sample, add phosphate-based fertilizer purchased from a local garden center.
- Farmland runoff can by manipulated by adding black cow fertilizer (fertilizer derived from animal manure) and generic weed killer available from a local garden center.

Water quality test kits can be ordered from science supply companies. Kits should include tests for a variety of water quality issues such as pH, nitrates, phosphates, dissolved O_2, and turbidity. The water quality test kits do not need to be professional grade for this investigation—a basic, inexpensive kit will suffice.

TABLE 14.1

Materials list

Item	Quantity
Samples of water from Lake Grace (three different locations)	1 set per class
Water quality test kit (including tests for pH, nitrates, phosphates, dissolved O_2, and turbidity)	1 per group
Information packet	1 per group
Student handout	1 per student
Investigation proposal C (optional)	1 per group
Whiteboard, 2' × 3'*	1 per group
Peer-review guide and instructor scoring rubric	1 per student

* As an alternative, students can use computer and presentation software such as Microsoft PowerPoint or Apple Keynote to create their arguments.

Topics for the Explicit and Reflective Discussion

Concepts That Can Be Used to Justify the Evidence

To provide an adequate justification of their evidence, students must explain why they included the evidence in their arguments and make the assumptions underlying their analysis and interpretation of the data explicit. In this investigation, students can use the following concepts to help justify their evidence:

- How energy moves through food chains and food webs
- How biological and geological processes move nutrients through an ecosystem
- How light and nutrient availability influences primary production in aquatic ecosystems
- How human activities often disrupt the natural cycling of nutrients in ecosystems

We recommend that you review these concepts during the explicit and reflective discussion to help students make this connection.

How to Design Better Investigations

It is important for students to reflect on the strengths and weaknesses of the investigation they designed during the explicit and reflective discussion. Students should therefore be encouraged to discuss ways to eliminate potential flaws, measurement errors, or sources of bias in their investigations. To help students be more reflective about the design of their investigation, you can ask the following questions:

- What were some of the strengths of your investigation? What made it scientific?
- What were some of the weaknesses of your investigation? What made it less scientific?
- If you were to do this investigation again, what would you do to address the weaknesses in your investigation? What could you do to make it more scientific?

Crosscutting Concepts

This investigation is well aligned with three crosscutting concepts found in *A Framework for K–12 Science Education,* and you should review these concepts during the explicit and reflective discussion.

- *Cause and Effect: Mechanism and Explanation:* One of the main objectives of science is to identify and establish relationships between a cause and an effect.
- *Scale, Proportion, and Quantity:* It is critical for scientists to recognize what is relevant or important at different sizes, times, or scales. For example, in this

investigation it is important for students to realize that even small changes in nutrient levels can have adverse effects on an entire lake.

- *Energy and Matter: Flows, Cycles, and Conservation:* This is perhaps the most relevant crosscutting concept to this investigation. Scientists must understand how energy and matter flow, into, out of, and within an ecosystem in order to understand it and to understand how human activity can disrupt the natural balance of an ecosystem.

The Nature of Science and the Nature of Scientific Inquiry

It is important for students to understand that *scientists use different methods to answer different types of questions*. Examples of methods include experiments, systematic observations of a phenomenon, literature reviews, and analysis of existing data sets; the choice of method depends on the objectives of the research. There is no universal step-by-step scientific method that all scientists follow; rather, different scientific disciplines (e.g., biology vs. physics) and fields within a discipline (e.g., ecology vs. molecular biology) use different types of methods, use different core theories, and rely on different standards to develop scientific knowledge. In this investigation, for example, the students rely on an existing data set and the results of several water quality tests to develop an explanation, rather than conducting an experiment.

It is also important for students to understand that *science is influenced by the society and culture in which it is practiced* because science is a human endeavor. Cultural values and expectations determine what scientists choose to investigate, how investigations are conducted, and how findings are interpreted. People also view some types of research as being more important than other types because of cultural values and current events. Biologists, as a result, often choose to study topics that have a direct impact on local environments or can help improve the quality of life of people.

You should review and provide examples of these two important concepts of the nature of science (NOS) and the nature of scientific inquiry (NOSI) during the explicit and reflective discussion.

Hints for Implementing the Lab

- Be prepared for groups to pursue different paths in completing the investigation.
- This is a very open-ended investigation, so flexibility is key.

Topic Connections

Table 14.2 (p. 196) provides an overview of the scientific practices, crosscutting concepts, disciplinary core ideas, and support ideas at the heart of this lab investigation. In addition, it lists NOS and NOSI concepts for the explicit and reflective discussion. Finally, it lists literacy and mathematics skills (*CCSS ELA* and *CCSS Mathematics*) that are addressed during the investigation.

TABLE 14.2

Lab 14 alignment with standards

Scientific practices	• Asking questions • Planning and carrying out investigations • Analyzing and interpreting data • Using mathematics and computational thinking • Constructing explanations • Engaging in argument from evidence • Obtaining, evaluating, and communicating information
Crosscutting concepts	• Cause and effect: Mechanism and explanation • Scale, proportion, and quantity • Energy and matter: Flows, cycles, and conservation
Core idea	• LS2: Ecosystems: Interactions, energy, and dynamics
Supporting ideas	• Ecosystems • Nutrient cycling • Energy • Food webs
NOS and NOSI concepts	• Methods used in scientific investigations • Social and cultural influences
Literacy connections *(CCSS ELA)*	• *Reading:* Key ideas and details, craft and structure, integration of knowledge and ideas • *Writing:* Text types and purposes, production and distribution of writing, research to build and present knowledge, range of writing • *Speaking and listening:* Comprehension and collaboration, presentation of knowledge and ideas
Mathematics connection *(CCSS Mathematics)*	• Reason quantitatively and use units to solve problems

Lab 14. Interdependence of Organisms: Why Is the Sport Fish Population of Lake Grace Decreasing in Size?

Lab Handout

Introduction

Lake Grace (see the figure to the right) is known as one of the best lakes for sport fishing in the United States. The Tolt and Faith rivers feed the lake, and extensive stump and grass beds provide a great habitat for sport fish, such as largemouth bass, white bass, and bluegill. Sizable populations of other fish, such as catfish, crappie, and bream, are also present. In fact, over 79 different species of fish have been found in the lake. Over the last five years, however, anglers have been catching fewer and fewer of the large sport fish that once made Lake Grace so famous.

Lake Grace

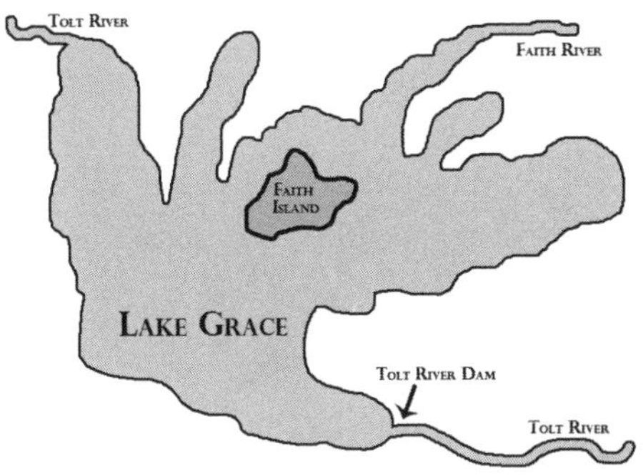

The low numbers of sport fish in the lake have led to a decrease in the number of anglers that come to the lake to fish on weekends or for a fishing vacation. As a result, there has been a downturn in the economy of the nearby town of Aidanville, and many local stores and hotels that depended on tourism have gone out of business.

Your Task

Conduct an investigation of the water quality of Lake Grace and develop an explanation for the decline in the populations of sport fish.

The guiding question of this investigation is, **Why is the sport fish population of Lake Grace decreasing in size?**

Materials

You may use any of the following materials during your investigation:

- Samples of water from Lake Grace (three different locations)
- Water quality test kit (pH, nitrates, phosphates, dissolved oxygen, turbidity)
- Information packet

Safety Precautions

1. Safety goggles, vinyl gloves, and aprons are required for this activity.
2. Wash hands with soap and water upon completing this lab.
3. Follow all normal lab safety rules.

Getting Started

To answer the guiding question, you will need to analyze an existing data set and then determine the overall quality of a water sample from Lake Grace. To accomplish this task, you must first determine what type of data you will need to collect, how you will collect it, and how you will analyze it. To determine *what type of data you will need to collect,* think about the following questions:

- What type of information do I need to collect from the existing data set found in the information packet?
- What type of tests will I need to determine the quality of the water in Lake Grace? (*Hint*: Be sure to follow all directions as given in the water quality test kits.)
- What type of measurements or observations will you need to record during your investigation?

To determine *how you will collect your data,* think about the following questions:

- What will serve as a control (or comparison) condition?
- How will you make sure that your data are of high quality (i.e., how will you reduce error)?
- How will you keep track of the data you collect and how will you organize the data?

To determine *how you will analyze your data,* think about the following questions:

- What type of calculations will you need to make?
- What type of graph could you create to help make sense of your data?

Investigation Proposal Required? ☐ Yes ☐ No

Connections to Crosscutting Concepts and to the Nature of Science and the Nature of Scientific Inquiry

As you work through your investigation, be sure to think about

- the importance of identifying the underlying cause for observations;

- why it is important to determine what is relevant at a particular scale or over a specific time frame;
- how energy and matter flow into, out of, within, and through a system;
- how the method scientists use depends on the topic under investigation and the research question; and
- how social and cultural issues influence the work of scientists.

Argumentation Session

Once your group has finished collecting and analyzing your data, prepare a whiteboard that you can use to share your initial argument. Your whiteboard should include all the information shown in the figure to the right.

Argument presentation on a whiteboard

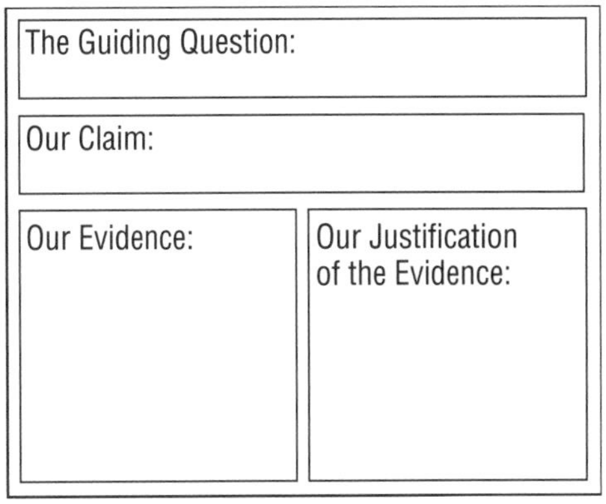

To share your argument with others, we will be using a round-robin format. This means that one member of your group will stay at your lab station to share your group's argument while the other members of your group go to the other lab stations one at a time to listen to and critique the arguments developed by your classmates.

The goal of the argumentation session is not to convince others that your argument is the best one; rather, the goal is to identify errors or instances of faulty reasoning in the arguments so these mistakes can be fixed. You will therefore need to evaluate the content of the claim, the quality of the evidence used to support the claim, and the strength of the justification of the evidence included in each argument that you see. In order to critique an argument, you will need more information than what is included on the whiteboard. You might, therefore, need to ask the presenter one or more follow-up questions, such as:

- How did you collect your data? Why did you use that method? Why did you collect those data?
- What did you do to make sure the data you collected are reliable? What did you do to decrease measurement error?
- What did you do to analyze your data? Why did you decide to do it that way? Did you check your calculations?
- Is that the only way to interpret the results of your analysis? How do you know that your interpretation of your analysis is appropriate?
- Why did your group decide to present your evidence in that manner?

- What other claims did your group discuss before you decided on that one? Why did your group abandon those alternative ideas?
- How confident are you that your claim is valid? What could you do to increase your confidence?

Once the argumentation session is complete, you will have a chance to meet with your group and revise your original argument. Your group might need to gather more data or design a way to test one or more alternative claims as part of this process. Remember, your goal at this stage of the investigation is to develop the most valid or acceptable answer to the research question!

Report

Once you have completed your research, you will need to prepare an investigation report that consists of three sections that provide answers to the following questions:

1. What question were you trying to answer and why?
2. What did you do during your investigation and why did you conduct your investigation in this way?
3. What is your argument?

Your report should answer these questions in two pages or less. This report must be typed, and any diagrams, figures, or tables should be embedded into the document. Be sure to write in a persuasive style; you are trying to convince others that your claim is acceptable or valid!

Lake Grace Information Packet

Lake Grace and the Town of Aidanville

Lake Grace is located in the southeastern United States and covers an area of 37,500 acres. Extending up the Tolt River 30 miles and up the Faith River 35 miles, Lake Grace has 376 miles of shoreline. The lake was created in 1957 when the Tolt River Dam was built. The dam produces hydroelectric power that is used by both homes and industry in the area. Aidanville was founded in 1897 and is located on the southwest side of Lake Grace (see the figure below).

Lake Grace and environs

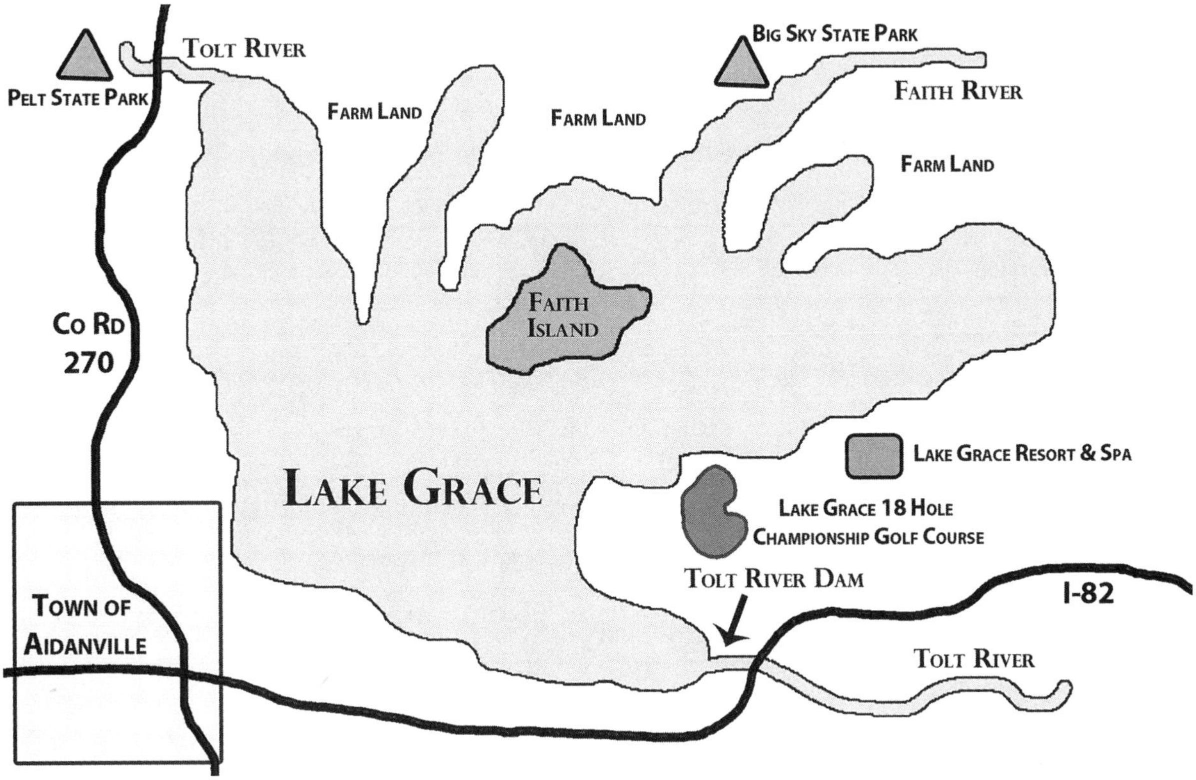

Major events in the history of Lake Grace and the town of Aidanville

Date	Event
1940	The population of Aidanville reaches 1,587, according to U.S. census data.
1947	Money to build the Tolt River Dam is authorized, and construction begins.
1952	The Tolt River Dam is completed.
1957	Lake Grace opens for public use.
1958	Pelt State Park and Big Sky State Park are completed and open for public use.
1980	The population of Aidanville reaches 2,016, according to U.S. census data.
1981	Two Rivers State Park is completed and opens for use. The park includes a public boat launch, which was built in response to the large number of anglers coming to the lake to fish.
1985	Three new hotels are built in Aidanville.
1989	Two more hotels and five more restaurants are built in Aidanville.
1990	The population of Aidanville reaches 3,287, according to U.S. census data.
1995	Aidanville City Council begins a program to monitor the water quality of Lake Grace.
1996	Lake Grace Resort and Spa completed
1998	Invasive species of water plants, such as hydrilla and water hyacinth, are found in Lake Grace for the first time.
1999	Lake Grace 18-hole championship golf course is completed and open for public use.
2000	The population of Aidanville reaches 3,824, according to U.S. census data.
2001	The farmers who own the farmland near Big Sky State Park stop raising crops, sell off part of their land to developers, and begin operating a large hog farm.
2004	The Aidanville City Council begins to use herbicides to slow the spread of invasive water plants in Lake Grace.
2011	Three hotels and four restaurants go out of business in Aidanville.

Number and size of sport fish caught annually in Lake Grace, 1995–2011

Year	Number caught			Average size of fish caught (cm)		
	Largemouth bass	White bass	Bluegill	Largemouth bass*	White bass†	Bluegill‡
2011	1,152	1,705	952	31	39	17
2010	1,287	1,830	975	29	38	19
2009	1,213	1,819	1,012	30	38	16
2008	1,284	1,962	1,204	32	39	19
2007	1,406	1,993	1,432	31	42	20
2006	1,517	2,003	1,616	30	43	21
2005	1,872	1,894	2,203	33	41	22
2004	2,411	1,752	2,106	32	45	24
2003	1,310	1,385	1,910	33	49	25
2002	1,504	1,206	1,867	34	48	23
2001	1,692	1,197	1,992	33	43	28
2000	1,825	1,151	1,845	36	45	27
1999	1,714	1,302	1,791	38	47	31
1998	1,535	1,207	1,603	39	49	29
1997	2,387	1,234	1,375	40	43	27
1996	1,747	1,750	1,402	43	48	32
1995	2,422	1,344	1,208	41	46	33

* The legal size limit for largemouth bass is 30 cm.

† The legal size limit for white bass is 40 cm.

‡ There is no legal size limit for bluegill.

Information about some of the organisms found in Lake Grace

Name	Appearance	Habitat	Size	Diet	Reproduction	Ecological importance
Largemouth bass		Shallow lakes, ponds, or rivers	Adults range in size from 26 cm to 46 cm	Young fish feed on daphnia, gammarus amphipods, and invertebrates; adults feed on small fish, frogs, and aquatic invertebrates	Male fish build nests in sand or gravel in shallow areas and attract a female to the nest. The female lays a few hundred eggs and then the male fertilizes them. The male guards the eggs until they hatch, which takes 7–10 days.	Largemouth bass are important predators in freshwater ecosystems and help maintain the population size of other primary consumers such as aquatic invertebrates and secondary consumers (such as amphibians and small fish). They are also one of the species most sought after by recreational anglers.
White bass	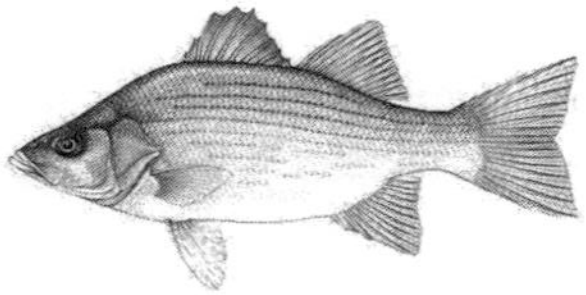	Deep, clear lakes and large rivers.	Adults range in size from 38 cm to 50 cm	Mostly daphnia, crustaceans, and other aquatic invertebrates; larger individuals feed on small fish	They only spawn in water ranging from 12 to 20°C. Females lay eggs in moving water such as a tributary stream or river. Females release 200,000 eggs, which stick to the surface of plants, submerged logs, gravel, or rocks.	White bass are important predators in freshwater ecosystems and help maintain the population size of other primary consumers such as aquatic invertebrates and secondary consumers (such as amphibians and small fish). They are also one of the species most sought after by recreational anglers.
Bluegill		Weedy, shallow, waters; does not tolerate high turbidity well	Adults range in size from 15 cm to 35 cm	Daphnia, gammarus amphipods, insects, and crustaceans	They spawn early in the spring. Females release their eggs and males then fertilize them. Eggs hatch about eight days later.	Bluegills are important aquatic predators. They also provide food for larger fish. Numerous organisms eat their eggs. For anglers, the bluegill provides considerable sport, and the flesh is firm, flaky and well flavored. Bluegills are often stocked in artificial ponds as forage for largemouth bass.
Daphnia	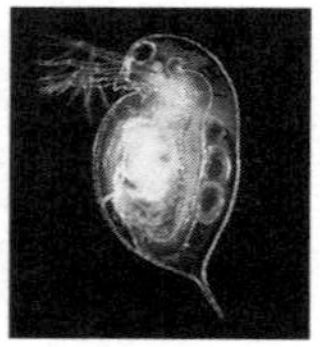	Lakes with temperatures below 20°C	1 mm long	Bacteria, protists, and algae	They produce eggs that develop without fertilization. An adult female can produce 10–15 eggs.	Daphnia are a principal food staple for fish and an important link in the food chain (fish stomach can contain 95% daphnia by volume). Daphnia also help maintain water quality by cleaning up algae blooms in lakes (daphnia can reduce the amount of algae in a lake by half in a small amount of time).

Information about some of the organisms found in Lake Grace *(continued)*

Name	Appearance	Habitat	Size	Diet	Reproduction	Ecological importance
Gammarus amphipod	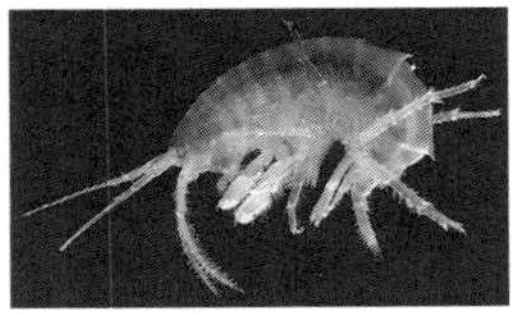	Floors of lakes and rivers that are well oxygenated and below 20°C	21 mm long	Algae and dead organic matter	Occurs during winter—females only produce one brood during their life (which lasts 1–1.5 years)	Gammarus amphipods are a main source of food for larger freshwater organisms. Gammarus amphipods are sensitive to changes in the environment—low pH levels or warm temperatures kill them.
Algae		Anywhere there is a body of water or a sufficient quantity of moisture	Can live as single cells, in colonies (groups), or as strands of attached cells (called filaments)	Photosynthetic organism	Asexual	When the concentrations of nitrates and phosphates increase in a lake, the algae population increases. The massive amount of algae gives the water a pea-green color and produces a funny smell (called an algae bloom). Many of the algae begin to die off as the population increases. Oxygen-using decomposer bacteria then increase in number, which drops the oxygen levels of the lake. As result, many fish can suffocate.
Pickerelweed		Lakes, ponds, ditches, and streams	60–90 cm tall	Photosynthetic organism	Seeds	Submerged portions of aquatic plants provide habitats for many invertebrates. These invertebrates in turn are used as food by fish and other wildlife species (e.g., amphibians, reptiles, ducks). After aquatic plants die, their decomposition by bacteria and fungi provides food for many aquatic invertebrates.
Hydrilla		Lakes, ponds, ditches, and streams	Up to 760 cm tall	Photosynthetic organism	Seeds and fragmentation	Grows into dense stands extending from the shoreline to a depth of 10 ft. Dense strands can (1) prevent light from penetrating to deeper water, (2) reduce dissolved oxygen, and (3) displace native plants and reduce biodiversity.
Water hyacinth		Lakes, ponds, ditches, and streams; floats above the water surface	Leaves are 10–20 cm and can be up to 1 m above the surface	Photosynthetic organism	Seeds	Water hyacinth will cover lakes and ponds entirely; this has a dramatic impact on water flow, blocks sunlight from reaching native aquatic plants, and starves the water of oxygen. The plants also create a prime habitat for mosquitoes.

Water quality in Lake Grace

The following table provides data from a program that was started in 1995 by the Aidanville City Council to monitor the water quality in Lake Grace. Unfortunately, the program was cut in 2005 because the city lacked the funds necessary to sustain it.

Year	pH	Dissolved oxygen (mg/L)	Nitrates* (ppm)	Phosphate† (mg/L)	Coliform bacteria	Triclopyr‡ (ppb)	Algal bloom§ observed
2005	5.8	9.5	36	0.12	Yes	11	No
2004	5.9	9.5	35	0.13	Yes	8	No
2003	5.9	9.6	33	0.12	Yes	1	No
2002	6.0	9.6	30	0.11	Yes	2	Yes
2001	6.0	9.7	12	0.12	No	2	No
2000	6.0	9.6	13	0.1	No	2	Yes
1999	6.2	9.8	12	0.09	No	2	No
1998	6.4	10.3	14	0.02	No	1	No
1997	6.6	10.2	13	0.01	No	1	No
1996	6.5	10.2	14	0.02	No	2	No
1995	6.7	10.2	12	0.01	No	1	No

* Nitrate levels over 30 ppm can inhibit growth of fish and some aquatic invertebrates and stimulate the growth of algae and other aquatic plants

† Phosphate levels of 0.01–0.03 mg/L in lake water are considered normal. Plant growth is stimulated at levels of 0.025– 0.1 mg/L.

‡ Triclopyr is a weed killer (herbicide) that targets broadleaf plants and has often been used in in lakes. Levels of triclopyr, however, must be below 2 ppb for the water to be safe for irrigation; higher doses of the chemical can be toxic to aquatic organisms. Small organisms such as gammarus amphipods, daphnia, and freshwater shrimp often ingest tiny amounts of the chemical into their bodies or absorb small amounts of it through their gills, but the small dose of the chemical usually does little harm to these organisms (although the chemical often stays in their system for long periods of time).

§ An algal bloom is a rapid increase or accumulation in the population of algae. Although there is no officially recognized threshold level, algae can be considered to be blooming at concentrations of hundreds to thousands of cells per milliliter of water. Algal bloom concentrations may reach millions of cells per milliliter of water. Algal blooms are the result of an excess of nutrients, particularly phosphorus and nitrates. The excess of nutrients may originate from fertilizers that are applied to land for agricultural or recreational purposes (such as keeping the grass on fairways healthy). These nutrients can then enter rivers and lakes through water runoff. When phosphates and nitrates are introduced into water systems, higher concentrations cause increased growth of algae and plants. Algae tend to grow very quickly under high nutrient availability, but each alga is short-lived, and the result is a high concentration of dead organic matter, which starts to decay. The decay process consumes dissolved oxygen in the water.

Average water temperature in Lake Grace

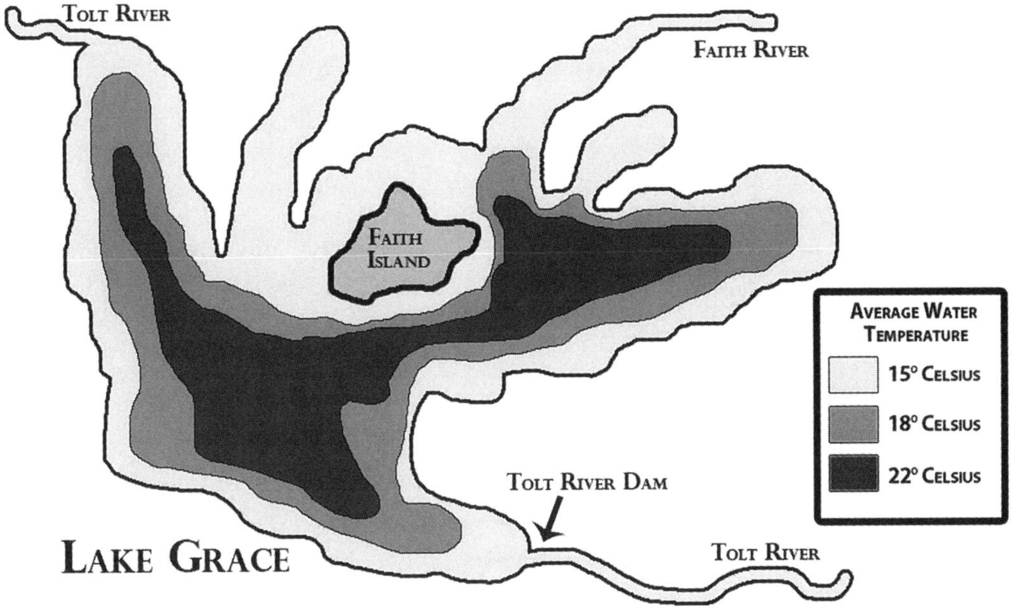

Lab 14. Interdependence of Organisms: Why Is the Sport Fish Population of Lake Grace Decreasing in Size?

Checkout Questions

1. Living organisms in an ecosystem interact with each other. If one of those organisms is removed from the ecosystem, how does that affect the remaining organisms? Use a specific example from the Lake Grace scenario as part of your explanation.

2. Scientists do not study topics or problems that are important to everyday life because science is independent of society and culture.

   a. I agree with this statement.
   b. I disagree with this statement.

   Explain your answer, using examples from your investigation about Lake Grace.

3. Scientists rely on many different types of methods such as experiments, fieldwork, systematic observations, and the analysis of an existing data set.

   a. I agree with this statement.
   b. I disagree with this statement.

   Explain your answer, using examples from your investigation about Lake Grace.

4. Scientists often attempt to identify the underlying cause for the observations they make. Explain why the identification of underlying causes is so important in science, using an example from your investigation about Lake Grace.

5. Scientists often attempt to track how energy and matter flow into, out of, and within a system during an investigation. Explain why tracking the flow of energy and matter is useful in science, using an example from your investigation about Lake Grace.

6. Scientists often need to determine what is and what is not relevant at a particular scale or during a particular time frame during an investigation. Explain why this is so important, using an example from your investigation about Lake Grace.

Lab 15. Competition for Resources: How Has the Spread of the Eurasian Collared-Dove Affected Different Populations of Native Bird Species?

Teacher Notes

Purpose

The purpose of this lab is for students to *apply* what they know about ecological communities, population growth, and the interdependence of organisms within an ecosystem to determine the impact of invasive species of native bird populations. This lab also gives students an opportunity to use an existing database as part of their investigation. Students will also learn about the difference between observations and inferences in science and the influence of society and culture on scientific investigations.

The Content

There are a number of different interspecies interactions that take place within an ecological community. Competition for resources is one example of an interaction that takes place between species. There is potential for competition between any two species that need the same limited resource. Some resources, however, are not scarce within a given area, so the species within that area do not compete for those resources. Species also do not compete for resources when they occupy different ecological niches, because they require different resources and play different roles in an ecological community.

The *competitive exclusion principle* states that two species occupying the same ecological niche cannot coexist in the same ecological community. In this situation, one species will use the resources more efficiently than the other one and thus be able to reproduce more offspring. The reproductive advantage of the one species leads to the local elimination of the other, less efficient, species. Competitive exclusion can therefore have a significant effect on the number and types of organisms found within an ecosystem.

Invasive species are organisms that are not native to an ecosystem. Invasive species can colonize a community and then spread. These organisms are able to invade areas because they can tolerate a wide variety of habitat conditions; they grow fast, reproduce often, compete aggressively for resources, and often lack natural enemies. Invasive species, as a result, can cause environmental, economic, and human harm by displacing native species through competitive exclusion, altering habitats, upsetting the balance of an ecosystem, or degrading the quality of recreation areas.

Timeline

The instructional time needed to implement this lab investigation is 180–250 minutes. Appendix 2 (p. 391) provides options for implementing this lab investigation over several class periods. Option E or G (250 minutes) should be used if students are unfamiliar with scientific writing because either of these options provides extra instructional time for scaffolding the writing process. You can scaffold the writing process by modeling, providing examples, and providing hints as students write each section of the report. Option F or H (180 minutes) should be used if students are familiar with scientific writing and have the skills needed to write an investigation report on their own. In options F and H, students complete stage 6 (writing the investigation report) and stage 8 (revising the investigation report) as homework.

Materials and Preparation

The materials needed to implement this investigation are listed in Table 15.1. The eBird database, available at *http://ebird.org*, is free to use and can be accessed using an Internet browser; eBird is a real-time, online checklist program that was launched in 2002 by the Cornell Lab of Ornithology and the National Audubon Society. You should access the database and learn how to use the visualization tools before beginning the lab investigation. In addition, it is important to check if students can access and use the simulation from a school computer because some schools have set up firewalls and other restrictions on web browsing.

TABLE 15.1
Materials list

Item	Quantity
Computer with internet access	1 per group
Student handout	1 per student
Investigation proposal C (optional)	1 per group
Whiteboard, 2' × 3'*	1 per group
Peer-review guide and instructor scoring rubric	1 per student

* As an alternative, students can use computer and presentation software such as Microsoft PowerPoint or Apple Keynote to create their arguments.

Topics for the Explicit and Reflective Discussion

Concepts That Can Be Used to Justify the Evidence

To provide an adequate justification of their evidence, students must explain why they included the evidence in their arguments and make the assumptions underlying their

analysis and interpretation of the data explicit. In this investigation, students can use the following concepts to help justify their evidence:

- Ecological niches
- The competitive exclusion principle
- Invasive species

We recommend that you review these concepts during the explicit and reflective discussion to help students make this connection.

How to Design Better Investigations

It is important for students to reflect on the strengths and weaknesses of the investigation they designed during the explicit and reflective discussion. Students should therefore be encouraged to discuss ways to eliminate potential flaws, measurement errors, or sources of bias in their investigations. To help students be more reflective about the design of their investigation, you can ask the following questions:

- What were some of the strengths of your investigation? What made it scientific?
- What were some of the weaknesses of your investigation? What made it less scientific?
- If you were to do this investigation again, what would you do to address the weaknesses in your investigation? What could you do to make it more scientific?

Crosscutting Concepts

This investigation is well aligned with two important crosscutting concepts found in *A Framework for K–12 Science Education,* and you should review these concepts during the explicit and reflective discussion.

- *Patterns:* One of the main objectives of science is to identify patterns in nature. Once these patterns are established, such as when and where specific species of birds are found, scientists often attempt to uncover the underlying reasons for them.
- *Scale, Proportion, and Quantity:* It is critical for scientists to recognize what is relevant or important at different times or scales. It is also important for scientists to examine proportional relationships and not just absolute values. For example, in this investigation it is important for students to examine how proportions of birds in a given area change over time.

The Nature of Science and the Nature of Scientific Inquiry

It is important for students to understand the *difference between observations and inferences in science.* An observation is a descriptive statement about a natural phenomenon, whereas an inference is an interpretation of an observation. In this investigation, for example, the students relied on observations included in an existing database and then needed to make inferences about the distribution and abundance of different species of bird in different locations over time. Students should also understand that current scientific knowledge and the perspectives of individual scientists guide both observations and inferences. Thus, different scientists can have different but equally valid interpretations of the same observations due to differences in their perspectives and background knowledge.

It is also important for students to understand that *science is influenced by the society and culture in which it is practiced* because science is a human endeavor. Cultural values and expectations determine what scientists choose to investigate, how investigations are conducted, how research findings are interpreted, and what people see as implications. People also view some research as being more important than others because of cultural values and current events. Biologists therefore often choose to study topics that have a direct impact on local environments or can help improve the quality of life of people.

You should review and provide examples of these two important concepts of the nature of science (NOS) and the nature of scientific inquiry (NOSI) during the explicit and reflective discussion.

Hints for Implementing the Lab

- Be prepared for groups to pursue different paths in completing the investigation.
- This is a very open-ended investigation, so flexibility is key.

Topic Connections

Table 15.2 (p. 214) provides an overview of the scientific practices, crosscutting concepts, disciplinary core ideas, and support ideas at the heart of this lab investigation. In addition, it lists NOS and NOSI concepts for the explicit and reflective discussion. Finally, it lists literacy and mathematics skills (*CCSS ELA* and *CCSS Mathematics*) that are addressed during the investigation.

TABLE 15.2

Lab 15 alignment with standards

Scientific practices	• Asking questions • Planning and carrying out investigations • Analyzing and interpreting data • Using mathematics and computational thinking • Constructing explanations • Engaging in argument from evidence • Obtaining, evaluating, and communicating information
Crosscutting concepts	• Patterns • Scale, proportion, and quantity
Core idea	• LS2: Ecosystems: Interactions, energy, and dynamics
Supporting ideas	• Community • Population • Ecological niche • Competitive exclusion • Invasive species • Interdependence of organisms
NOS and NOSI concepts	• Observations and inferences • Social and cultural influences
Literacy connections *(CCSS ELA)*	• *Reading:* Key ideas and details, craft and structure, integration of knowledge and ideas • *Writing:* Text types and purposes, production and distribution of writing, research to build and present knowledge, range of writing • *Speaking and listening:* Comprehension and collaboration, presentation of knowledge and ideas
Mathematics connection *(CCSS Mathematics)*	• Reason quantitatively and use units to solve problems

Lab 15. Competition for Resources: How Has the Spread of the Eurasian Collared-Dove Affected Different Populations of Native Bird Species?

Lab Handout

Introduction

A community is any assemblage of populations in an area or a habitat. There are a number of different interspecies interactions that take place within a community. One example of an interaction that takes place between species is competition. Organisms compete for resources, such as food, water, and space, when resources are in short supply. For example, weeds and grass compete for soil nutrients and water, grasshoppers and bison compete for grass, and lynx and foxes compete for hares. There is potential for competition between any two species populations that need the same limited resource. Resources, however, are not always scarce in every community (e.g., water in the ocean or oxygen on the Great Plains). Species therefore do not always compete for every resource they need to survive.

Species also do not compete for resources when they occupy different ecological niches. An ecological niche is the sum total of a species' use of biotic and abiotic resources in its environment. An organism's ecological niche is its ecological role or how it fits into an ecosystem. The ecological niche of a bird, for example, includes the temperature range it tolerates, the type(s) of tree it nests in, the material it uses to build its nest, the time of day it is active, and the type of insects or seeds it eats (along with numerous other components). Species with different ecological niches require different resources and play different roles in a community. Therefore, species with different ecological niches rarely compete for the same resources.

In the first half of the 20th century, a Russian ecologist named Georgii Gause formulated a law known as the competitive exclusion principle. This law states that two species occupying the same ecological niche cannot coexist in the same community because one will use the resources more efficiently and thus be able to reproduce more offspring. The reproductive advantage of one species results in the local elimination of the other one. Competitive exclusion, as a result, can have a significant effect on the number and types of organisms found within an ecosystem. It is important to note, however, that species with similar (but not identical) ecological niches can coexist in the same community if there is at least one significant difference in their niches (such as when they are active or what they eat).

Invasive species are organisms that are not native to an ecosystem. These organisms are introduced into a new environment through some type of human activity. Invasive species often colonize a community and spread rapidly. They are able to colonize and spread because they can tolerate a wide variety of habitat conditions; they grow fast, reproduce often, compete aggressively for resources, and usually lack natural enemies in the new community. Invasive species, as a result, can cause environmental, economic, and human harm by displacing native species, altering habitats, upsetting the balance of an ecosystem, or degrading the quality of recreation areas.

An example of an invasive species is the Eurasian collared-dove (see the figure to the left). This bird was introduced to the Bahamas in 1970 and spread from there to Florida in 1982. It has since spread across North America and is now found as far south as Veracruz, as far west as California, and as far north as Alaska (see the figure on the opposite page). Although the Eurasian collared-dove does not migrate, it spreads and then colonizes new areas at an alarming rate. In Arkansas, for example, it took only five years (1997–2002) for it to spread from the southeast corner of the state to the northwest corner (a distance of about 500 km).

The Eurasian collared-dove

The impact of the Eurasian collared-dove on native bird species in North America is not yet known, but it seems to occupy an ecological niche that is similar to the other members of the dove family (Columbidae). Scientists are attempting to determine if the Eurasian collared-dove will outcompete native dove species for available resources. They are also interested in the impact that this invasive species may have on other native species of nonmigratory bird. Fortunately, there are a number of databases that allow scientists to track where different species of bird can be found, when they can be found, and how common they are in a given location. One such database is eBird, which enables users to go online to access observational data submitted by bird-watchers at thousands of locations across the United States. Scientists can use these data and the visualization tools built into the website to examine the frequency and abundance of different species of birds at different locations and over time.

Your Task

Identify at least two native bird species that occupy a similar ecological niche as the Eurasian collared-dove. Then determine what has happened to these two species of birds over time as the Eurasian collared-dove spread across the United States.

The guiding question of this investigation is, **How has the spread of the Eurasian collared-dove affected different populations of native bird species?**

Materials

You may use any of the following resources during your investigation:

- eBird database: *http://ebird.org*

Range maps of the Eurasian collared-dove in the United States (shaded areas indicate a sighting during that time period)

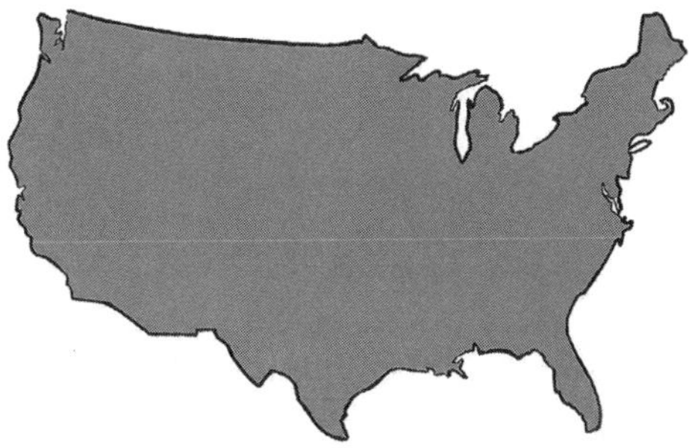

- All About Birds database: *www.allaboutbirds.org*

Safety Precautions

1. Use caution when working with electrical equipment. Keep away from water sources in that they can cause shorts, fires, and shock hazards. Use only GFI-protected circuits.
2. Wash hands with soap and water after completing this lab.
3. Follow all normal lab safety rules.

Getting Started

To answer the guiding question, you will need to design and conduct an investigation. To accomplish this task, you must determine what type of data you will need to collect, how you will collect it, and how you will analyze it. To determine *what type of data you will need to collect,* think about the following questions:

- Which native bird species will you include in your investigation?
- How will you determine if a native species of bird has been affected by the spread of the Eurasian collared-dove?
- What will serve as your dependent variable (e.g., range, frequency of sightings, abundance)?
- What type of observations will you need to record during your investigation?

To determine *how you will collect your data,* think about the following questions:

- What will you need to compare?
- How often will you collect data and when will you do it?
- How will you keep track of the data you collect and how will you organize the data?

To determine *how you will analyze your data,* think about the following questions:

- What type of calculations will you need to make?
- What type of graph could you create to help make sense of your data?

Investigation Proposal Required? ☐ Yes ☐ No

Connections to Crosscutting Concepts and to the Nature of Science and the Nature of Scientific Inquiry

As you work through your investigation, be sure to think about

- the importance of identifying and explaining patterns,
- what is relevant or important at different times and scales,
- the difference between observations and inferences in science, and
- how society and cultural values shape the work of scientists.

Argumentation Session

Once your group has finished collecting and analyzing your data, prepare a whiteboard that you can use to share your initial argument. Your whiteboard should include all the information shown in the figure below.

Argument presentation on a whiteboard

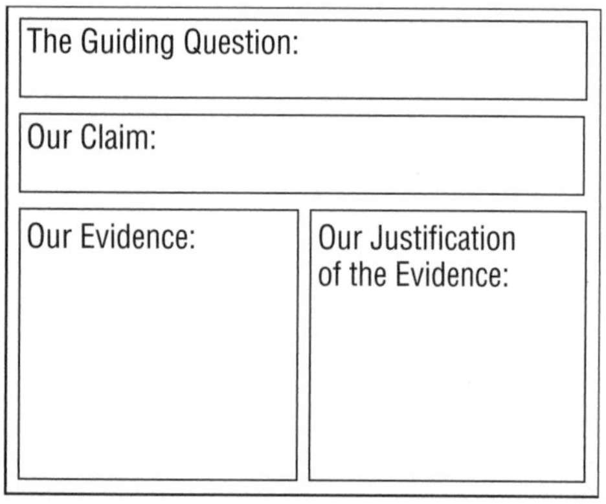

To share your argument with others, we will be using a round-robin format. This means that one member of your group will stay at your lab station to share your group's argument while the other members of your group go to the other lab stations one at a time to listen to and critique the arguments developed by your classmates.

The goal of the argumentation session is not to convince others that your argument is the best one; rather, the goal is to identify errors or instances of faulty reasoning in the arguments so these mistakes can be fixed. You will therefore need to evaluate the content of the claim, the quality of the evidence used to support the claim, and the strength of the justification of the evidence included in each argument that you see. In order to critique an argument, you will need more information than what is included on the whiteboard. You might, therefore, need to ask the presenter one or more follow-up questions, such as:

- Why did you decide to focus on those data?
- What did you do to analyze your data? Why did you decide to do it that way? Did you check your calculations?
- Is that the only way to interpret the results of your analysis? How do you know that your interpretation of your analysis is appropriate?
- Why did your group decide to present your evidence in that manner?
- What other claims did your group discuss before you decided on that one? Why did your group abandon those alternative ideas?
- How confident are you that your claim is valid? What could you do to increase your confidence?

Once the argumentation session is complete, you will have a chance to meet with your group and revise your original argument. Your group might need to gather more data or design a way to test one or more alternative claims as part of this process. Remember, your goal at this stage of the investigation is to develop the most valid or acceptable answer to the research question!

Report

Once you have completed your research, you will need to prepare an investigation report that consists of three sections that provide answers to the following questions:

1. What question were you trying to answer and why?
2. What did you do during your investigation and why did you conduct your investigation in this way?
3. What is your argument?

Your report should answer these questions in two pages or less. This report must be typed, and any diagrams, figures, or tables should be embedded into the document. Be sure to write in a persuasive style; you are trying to convince others that your claim is acceptable or valid!

Lab 15. Competition for Resources: How Has the Spread of the Eurasian Collared-Dove Affected Different Populations of Native Bird Species?

Checkout Questions

Use the following information to answer questions 1 and 2. A biologist sets up three test tubes with cultures of microorganisms: test tube A contains *Paramecium aurelia,* test tube B contains *Paramecium caudatum,* and test tube C contains both *P. aurelia* and *P. caudatum.* She then records how the size of each population changes over time in each test tube. The data she collected are provided in the figure below.

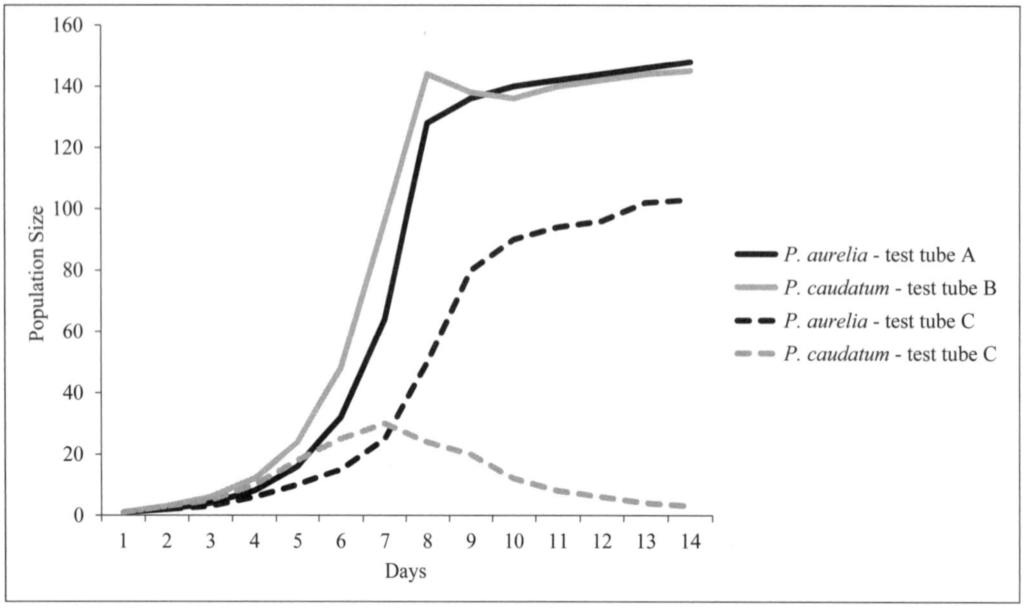

Biologists often use the competitive exclusion principle to explain these types of observations in other contexts.

1. Describe the competitive exclusion principle.

2. Use the competitive exclusion principle to explain these observations.

3. Scientists create laws.

   a. I agree with this statement.
   b. I disagree with this statement.

   Explain your answer, using information from your investigation about competition for resources.

4. Scientific research is not influenced by social and cultural values or expectations because scientists are trained to conduct unbiased studies.

   a. I agree with this statement.
   b. I disagree with this statement.

   Explain your answer, using examples from your investigation about competition for resources.

5. Scientists often attempt to identify patterns in nature. Explain why the identification of patterns is useful in science, using an example from your investigation about competition for resources.

6. Scientists often need to determine what is and what is not relevant at different times and scales during an investigation. Explain why this is important to do, using an example from your investigation about competition for resources.

SECTION 4

Life Sciences Core Idea 3:

Heredity: Inheritance and Variation of Traits

Introduction Labs

Lab 16. Mendelian Genetics: Why Are the Stem and Leaf Color Traits of the Wisconsin Fast Plant Inherited in a Predictable Pattern?

Teacher Notes

Purpose

The purpose of this lab is to *introduce* students to the underlying mechanisms that influence how traits are inherited. This lab also gives students an opportunity to design and carry out an investigation using the *Fast Plants Online Genetics Simulations*. One of these simulations allows students to cross plants with different traits and observe the traits of the offspring plants, but it does not provide students with any information about how traits are inherited. Students will also learn about the difference between theories and laws in science and why scientists must be creative and have a good imagination.

The Content

Mendelian genetics is the basis for modern research on inheritance. This important model can be broken down into four interrelated ideas. First and foremost, the fundamental unit of inheritance is the gene, and alternative versions of a gene (called alleles) account for variations in inheritable traits. Second, an organism inherits two alleles for each trait, one from each parent. Third, if the two alleles differ, then one is fully expressed and determines the nature of a specific trait (this version of the gene is called the dominant allele) while the other one has no noticeable effect (this version of the gene is called the recessive allele). Fourth, the two alleles for each trait segregate (or separate) during gamete production. Therefore, an egg or a sperm cell only gets one of the two alleles that are present in the somatic cells of the organism. This idea is known as the *law of segregation,* and it is the result of meiosis.

Timeline

The instructional time needed to implement this lab investigation is 130–200 minutes. Appendix 2 (p. 391) provides options for implementing this lab investigation over several class periods. Option C (200 minutes) should be used if students are unfamiliar with scientific writing because this option provides extra instructional time for scaffolding the writing process. You can scaffold the writing process by modeling, providing examples, and providing hints as students write each section of the report. Option D (130 minutes) should be used if students are familiar with scientific writing and have the skills needed to write an investigation report on their own. In option D, students complete stage 6 (writing the investigation report) and stage 8 (revising the investigation report) as homework.

Materials and Preparation

The materials needed to implement this investigation are listed in Table 16.1. The *Fast Plants Online Genetics Simulations* web page include three simulations, which are free to use and available at *www.fastplants.org/resources/digital_library//index.php?P=FullRecord&ID=35.* In this investigation the students will be using the third simulation, *Observing One or Two Traits in Wisconsin Fast Plants,* which is available at *www.fastplants.org/resources/digital_library//index.php?P=FullImage&ResourceId=35&FieldName=Screenshot.* The simulation can be run online using an internet browser. You should access the website and learn how the simulation works before beginning the lab investigation. In addition, it is important to check if students can access and use the simulation from a school computer because some schools have set up firewalls and other restrictions on web browsing.

TABLE 16.1

Materials list

Item	Quantity
Computer with internet access	1 per group
Student handout	1 per student
Investigation proposal C (optional)	1 per group
Whiteboard, 2' × 3'*	1 per group
Peer-review guide and instructor scoring rubric	1 per student

* As an alternative, students can use computer and presentation software such as Microsoft PowerPoint or Apple Keynote to create their arguments.

Topics for the Explicit and Reflective Discussion

Concepts That Can Be Used to Justify the Evidence

To provide an adequate justification of their evidence, students must explain why they included the evidence in their arguments and make the assumptions underlying their analysis and interpretation of the data explicit. In this investigation, students can use the following concepts to help justify their evidence:

- Biogenesis (i.e., new organisms come from existing organisms)
- Sexual and asexual forms of reproduction

- How plants and animals reproduce

We recommend that you review these concepts during the explicit and reflective discussion to help students make this connection.

How to Design Better Investigations

It is important for students to reflect on the strengths and weaknesses of the investigation they designed during the explicit and reflective discussion. Students should therefore be encouraged to discuss ways to eliminate potential flaws, measurement errors, or sources of bias in their investigations. To help students be more reflective about the design of their investigation, you can ask the following questions:

- What were some of the strengths of your investigation? What made it scientific?
- What were some of the weaknesses of your investigation? What made it less scientific?
- If you were to do this investigation again, what would you do to address the weaknesses in your investigation? What could you do to make it more scientific?

Crosscutting Concepts

This investigation is well aligned with three crosscutting concepts found in *A Framework for K–12 Science Education,* and you should review these concepts during the explicit and reflective discussion.

- *Patterns:* A major objective in biology is to identify the underlying cause of observed patterns, such as how traits are passed on from parent to offspring.
- *Cause and Effect: Mechanism and Explanation:* Another important goal in science is to identify and then test potential causal relationships. In this investigation, for example, students attempt to identify the underlying cause of the inheritance patterns they observe and then develop a model based on these causal relationships that they can use to in the future to make predictions.
- *Scale, Proportion, and Quantity:* Students need to understand that it is important for scientists to think proportionally about the phenomenon they are studying and not just in absolute values.

The Nature of Science and the Nature of Scientific Inquiry

It is important for students to understand the *difference between laws and theories in science.* A scientific law describes the behavior of a natural phenomenon or a generalized relationship under certain conditions; a scientific theory is a well-substantiated explanation of some aspect of the natural world. Theories do not become laws even with additional evidence; they explain laws. However, not all scientific laws have an accompanying explanatory theory. It is also important for students to understand that scientists do not discover laws or theories; the scientific community develops them over time.

It is also important for students to understand that *science requires imagination and creativity.* Students should learn that developing explanations for or models of natural phenomena and then figuring out how they can be put to the test of reality is as creative as writing poetry, composing music, or designing skyscrapers. Scientists must also use their imagination and creativity to figure out new ways to test ideas and collect or analyze data.

You should review and provide examples of these two important concepts of the nature of science (NOS) and the nature of scientific inquiry (NOSI) during the explicit and reflective discussion.

Hints for Implementing the Lab

- Learn how to use the simulation before the lab begins. It is important for you to know how to use the simulation so you can help students when they get stuck or confused.
- A group of three students per computer tends to work well.
- Allow the students to play with the simulation as part of the tool talk before they begin to design their investigation or fill out an investigation proposal. This gives students a chance to see what they can and cannot do with the simulation.
- Be sure to remind students that they need to quantify their observations.
- The lab can also be used to teach students about inferential statistics and statistical hypothesis testing.

Topic Connections

Table 16.2 (p. 230) provides an overview of the scientific practices, crosscutting concepts, disciplinary core ideas, and support ideas at the heart of this lab investigation. In addition, it lists NOS and NOSI concepts for the explicit and reflective discussion. Finally, it lists literacy and mathematics skills (*CCSS ELA* and *CCSS Mathematics*) that are addressed during the investigation.

TABLE 16.2

Lab 16 alignment with standards

Scientific practices	• Asking questions • Developing and using models • Planning and carrying out investigations • Analyzing and interpreting data • Using mathematics and computational thinking • Constructing explanations • Engaging in argument from evidence • Obtaining, evaluating, and communicating information
Crosscutting concepts	• Patterns • Cause and effect: Mechanism and explanation • Scale, proportion, and quantity
Core idea	• LS3: Heredity: Inheritance and variation of traits
Supporting ideas	• Patterns of inheritances • Genes • Alleles • Dominant • Recessive • Genotype • Phenotype
NOS and NOSI concepts	• Scientific theories and laws • Imagination and creativity in science
Literacy connections *(CCSS ELA)*	• *Reading:* Key ideas and details, craft and structure, integration of knowledge and ideas • *Writing:* Text types and purposes, production and distribution of writing, research to build and present knowledge, range of writing • *Speaking and listening:* Comprehension and collaboration, presentation of knowledge and ideas
Mathematics connection *(CCSS Mathematics)*	• Reason quantitatively and use units to solve problems

Lab 16. Mendelian Genetics: Why Are the Stem and Leaf Color Traits of the Wisconsin Fast Plant Inherited in a Predictable Pattern?

Lab Handout

Introduction

When dogs are bred, the result is puppies, and when racehorses are bred, the result is a foal. The same is true for plants. When one pea plant fertilizes another pea plant, each seed that is produced will become a pea plant and not a tulip, a rose, or a geranium. Species produce more of their own kind because each species passes down a specific set of traits from generation to generation. These traits make each species unique. But to anyone who has bred racehorses, dogs, or pea plants, it is abundantly clear that there are differences among members of the same species. Where do these variations come from, and how are these traits passed on from parents to offspring? These questions baffled scientists for hundreds of years, until Gregor Mendel was able to explain how traits are inherited.

Gregor Mendel identified the rules that govern heredity by crossing (breeding) individual pea plants with different versions of a trait and then documenting which version of that trait was inherited by the offspring. He also tracked the inheritance of specific versions of a trait over many generations. Once he gathered enough data, he was able to develop a set of rules that he could use to predict the traits of an offspring based on the traits of the parents. These rules are now known as Mendel's model of inheritance and are still used by scientists and medical doctors today. In this investigation, your goal will be to develop a model of inheritance that explains how traits are passed on from parent to offspring, much like Mendel did.

Your Task

Use a computer simulation to cross Wisconsin Fast Plants with different traits in order to identify patterns in the ways these traits are inherited. Once you have identified these patterns, you will need to develop a model that explains how traits are inherited in this organism. You will then need to test your model to determine how well it allows you to predict the traits of offspring.

The guiding question of this investigation is, **Why are the stem and leaf color traits of the Wisconsin Fast Plant inherited in a predictable pattern?**

Materials

You will use an online simulation called *Observing One or Two Traits in Wisconsin Fast Plants* to conduct your investigation. You can access the simulation by going to the following web page: *www.fastplants.org/legacy/genetics/Introductions/two-trait.htm.*

Safety Precautions

1. Use caution when working with electrical equipment. Keep away from water sources in that they can cause shorts, fires, and shock hazards. Use only GFI-protected circuits.
2. Wash hands with soap and water after completing this lab.
3. Follow all normal lab safety rules.

Getting Started

Your goal for this investigation is to develop a model that explains why the traits of the Wisconsin Fast Plant are inherited in a predictable pattern. Biologists determine how traits are passed from parent to offspring by (1) crossing (breeding) two individuals with specific traits (e.g., plants with purple or green stems and plants with dark green or light green leaves) and then recording the traits of their offspring in the next generation, (2) looking for patterns in the way specific traits are passed down from generation to generation, and (3) using these data to generate a model that explains why they are inherited in this manner. They then test their model to see how well it can predict the outcome of other crosses.

In the field, this type of research can be slow because a single generation can take anywhere from several weeks to several years. Fortunately, we can speed up the process of developing an explanatory model inside the classroom by using a computer simulation that allows you to breed pea plants and observe the results of your crosses in a matter of seconds.

A screen shot from the *Observing One or Two Traits in Wisconsin Fast Plants* simulation

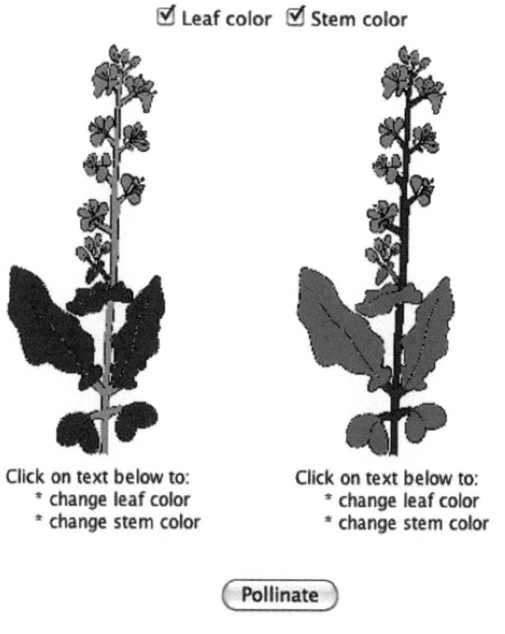

The *Observing One or Two Traits in Wisconsin Fast Plants* simulation (see the figure on the opposite page) enables you to do the following:

- Choose if you want to look at stem and/or leaf color of pea plants.
- Cross (breed) parents with different traits. (To cross the plants, click on the "Pollinate" button. You will see a bee travel between the two plants to indicate that the plants are being crossed.)
- See the 64 progeny (offspring) of the two plants that you crossed.
- Choose any two plants from the 64 progeny and cross them as well.
- Go back to any screen and repeat a cross. They will be labeled F2a, F2b, F2c, and so on.
- Perform a test cross with a parent plant and one of its offspring. A test cross involves breeding an individual of the dominant phenotype with an recessive phenotype individual to see what genotype the dominant parent is based on the trait ratios of the offspring

Remember, your first step in this investigation is to use this online simulation to identify patterns in the way the steam color and leaf color traits are inherited in Wisconsin Fast Plants. Once you have identified some patterns, you need to develop a model that you can use to explain them. Your model, like Mendel's, will likely consist of several different postulates. A postulate is a tentative claim. Mendel's model of inheritance included four postulates. The first postulate was, "Specific traits are determined by an inheritable unit that is passed down from parent to offspring." You can use the first postulate in Mendel's model of inheritance as one of the postulates in your model of inheritance.

Once you have developed your model, you will need to determine if it is valid or not by testing it with the online simulation. You will know when your model is valid because a valid model allows you to predict the traits of offspring. Your model, in other words, should enable you to predict the traits of the next generation of plants based on the traits of the parent plants. If your model allows you to make accurate predictions, then it is valid. If your model results in inaccurate predictions, then it is flawed and will need to be changed.

Investigation Proposal Required? ☐ Yes ☐ No

Connections to Crosscutting Concepts and to the Nature of Science and the Nature of Scientific Inquiry

As you work through your investigation, be sure to think about

- the importance of identifying patterns,
- how scientists attempt to uncover causal mechanisms,
- the value of looking at proportional relationships when analyzing data,

- the difference between theories and laws in science, and
- the importance of imagination and creativity in science.

Argumentation Session

Once your group has finished collecting and analyzing your data, prepare a whiteboard that you can use to share your initial argument. Your whiteboard should include all the information shown in the figure below.

Argument presentation on a whiteboard

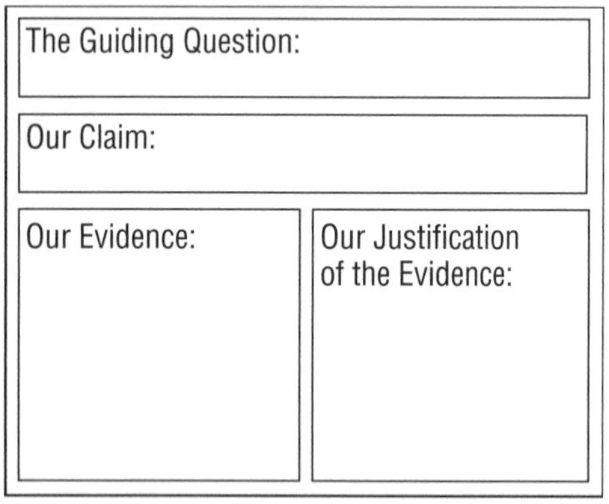

To share your argument with others, we will be using a round-robin format. This means that one member of your group will stay at your lab station to share your group's argument while the other members of your group go to the other lab stations one at a time to listen to and critique the arguments developed by your classmates.

The goal of the argumentation session is not to convince others that your argument is the best one; rather, the goal is to identify errors or instances of faulty reasoning in the arguments so these mistakes can be fixed. You will therefore need to evaluate the content of the claim, the quality of the evidence used to support the claim, and the strength of the justification of the evidence included in each argument that you see. In order to critique an argument, you will need more information than what is included on the whiteboard. You might, therefore, need to ask the presenter one or more follow-up questions, such as:

- How did you use the simulation to collect your data?
- What did you do to analyze your data? Why did you decide to do it that way? Did you check your calculations?
- Is that the only way to interpret the results of your analysis? How do you know that your interpretation of your analysis is appropriate?
- Why did your group decide to present your evidence in that manner?
- What other claims did your group discuss before you decided on that one? Why did your group abandon those alternative ideas?
- How confident are you that your claim is valid? What could you do to increase your confidence?

Once the argumentation session is complete, you will have a chance to meet with your group and revise your original argument. Your group might need to gather more data or design a way to test one or more alternative claims as part of this process. Remember, your

goal at this stage of the investigation is to develop the most valid or acceptable answer to the research question!

Report

Once you have completed your research, you will need to prepare an investigation report that consists of three sections that provide answers to the following questions:

1. What question were you trying to answer and why?
2. What did you do during your investigation and why did you conduct your investigation in this way?
3. What is your argument?

Your report should answer these questions in two pages or less. This report must be typed, and any diagrams, figures, or tables should be embedded into the document. Be sure to write in a persuasive style; you are trying to convince others that your claim is acceptable or valid!

Lab 16. Mendelian Genetics: Why Are the Stem and Leaf Color Traits of the Wisconsin Fast Plant Inherited in a Predictable Pattern?

Checkout Questions

1. Describe Mendel's model of inheritance.

2. Use Mendel's model of inheritance to explain why traits can skip a generation.

3. Scientists do not use their imagination and creativity at any time during an investigation because science is based on logic and reason.

   a. I agree with this statement.
   b. I disagree with this statement.

   Explain your answer, using examples from your investigation about Mendelian genetics.

4. A scientific law is a description of a relationship or a pattern in nature (i.e., laws describe *how* things happen).

a. I agree with this statement.
b. I disagree with this statement.

Explain your answer, using examples from your investigation about Mendelian genetics.

5. Scientists often attempt to identify patterns in nature. Explain why the identification of patterns is useful in science, using an example from your investigation about Mendelian genetics.

6. Scientists often attempt to identify the underlying cause for the observations they make. Explain why the identification of underlying causes is so important in science, using an example from your investigation about Mendelian genetics.

7. Scientists often need to look for proportional relationships. Explain what a proportional relationship is and why these relationships are important, using an example from your investigation about Mendelian genetics.

Lab 17. Chromosomes and Karyotypes: How Do Two Physically Healthy Parents Produce One Child With Down Syndrome and a Second Child With Cri Du Chat Syndrome?

Teacher Notes

Purpose

The purpose of this lab is to *introduce* students to the chromosomal basis of inheritance and the nature of chromosomal genetic disorders. This lab also gives students an opportunity to simulate the creation of a karyotype, to identify chromosomal abnormalities, and to learn about the underlying cause of two different genetic disorders. Students will also learn how social issues and cultural values influence the work of scientists and about the different methods that scientists can use during an investigation.

The Content

Physical and chemical disturbances, as well as errors during meiosis, can damage chromosomes or alter the number of chromosomes found in a cell. An example of an error that occurs during meiosis that can damage or alter the number of chromosomes found within a cell is *chromosomal nondisjunction.* Chromosomal nondisjunction can occur during the first meiotic division (meiosis I), which means one or more homologous pairs of chromosomes fail to separate, or it can occur during the second meiotic division (meiosis II), which means one or more sets of sister chromatids fail to separate. Chromosomal nondisjunction results in gametes with too many or too few chromosomes. The gametes can then result in a child with a genetic disorder. Figure 17.1 illustrates how chromosomal nondisjunction can result in gametes with extra or missing chromosomes.

Cri du chat syndrome and Down syndrome are both caused by a chromosomal abnormality. In this lab investigation, the karyotype for child 1, who was born with Down syndrome, shows an extra chromosome in the 21st pair. Neither Christopher nor Jill Miller has any abnormalities of the 21st pair on their karyotype. Therefore, during the process of meiosis a nondisjunction event occurred during meiosis I or meiosis II. The result of the nondisjunction event was an extra chromosome in the egg or sperm cell that produced child 1. The karyotype of child 2, who was born with cri du chat syndrome, shows that there is a deleted portion on top of one of the chromosomes in the 5th pair. Again, Christopher and Jill Miller's karyotypes do not show any abnormalities with the 5th chromosome. Therefore, the best explanation for the deletion is that part of the 5th chromosome was lost during the process of meiosis that formed either the sperm or egg cell that produced child 2.

Timeline

The instructional time needed to implement this lab investigation is 130–200 minutes. Appendix 2 (p. 391) provides options for implementing this lab investigation over several class periods. Option C (200 minutes) should be used if students are unfamiliar with scientific writing because this option provides extra instructional time for scaffolding the writing process. You can scaffold the writing process by modeling, providing examples, and providing hints as students write each section of the report. Option D (130 minutes) should be used if students are familiar with scientific writing and have the skills needed to write an investigation report on their own. In option D, students complete stage 6 (writing the investigation report) and stage 8 (revising the investigation report) as homework.

FIGURE 17.1

Nondisjunction of the sex chromosomes during meiosis II

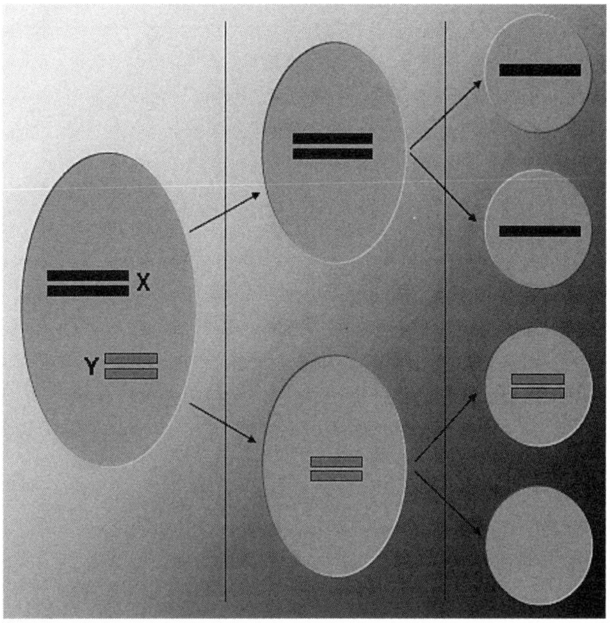

Materials and Preparation

The materials needed to implement this investigation are listed in Table 17.1 (p. 240). A number of different karyotype simulation kits can be used for this lab. Most kits provide photographs of chromosome smears that can be cut out and then arranged into a karyotype. These kits can be purchased from any biological supply company (e.g., Carolina, Flinn Scientific, or Ward's Science), but we recommend using the Karyotyping With Magnetic Chromosomes Kit from Carolina (*www.carolina.com*). This kit provides pictures of chromosomes attached to magnets, which eliminates the need for students to cut out chromosomes and then glue or tape them to a grid. One of these kits is enough to supply six groups of four students each with the materials they need to complete the lab, and it can be reused over and over.

Before the investigation begins, you will need to prepare the chromosome sets included in the karyotyping kit so they mimic the chromosomes of Christopher Miller and the two children (Emily and Andy Miller). Christopher Miller should be a normal male. Child 1 (born with Down syndrome) should be a female with three copies of chromosome 21. Child 2 (born with cri du chat) should be a male with a deletion on one chromosome from pair 5. Be sure to provide each group with a karyotype for Jill Miller (normal female) using the chromosomes from the kit. The students will need an example of a karyotype from a normal female to create the other karyotypes.

TABLE 17.1

Materials list

Item	Quantity
Karyotype simulation kit	1 per class
Karyotype for Jill Miller (normal female)	1 per group
Chromosome smear for Christopher Miller (normal male)	1 per group
Chromosome smear for child 1 (female with Down syndrome)	1 per group
Chromosome smear for child 2 (male with cri du chat syndrome)	1 per group
Karyotype placement grid	1–3 per group
Miller family pedigree	1 per group
Student handout	1 per student
Investigation proposal A (optional)	1 per group
Whiteboard, 2' × 3'*	1 per group
Peer-review guide and instructor scoring rubric	1 per student

* As an alternative, students can use computer and presentation software such as Microsoft PowerPoint or Apple Keynote to create their arguments.

Topics for the Explicit and Reflective Discussion

Concepts That Can Be Used to Justify the Evidence

To provide an adequate justification of their evidence, students must explain why they included the evidence in their arguments and make the assumptions underlying their analysis and interpretation of the data explicit. In this investigation, students can use the following concepts to help justify their evidence:

- Mendelian genetics
- Number of chromosomes (46) and pairs of chromosomes (23) in humans
- Chromosomal abnormality as an indicator of a genetic disorder

We recommend that you review these concepts during the explicit and reflective discussion to help students make this connection.

How to Design Better Investigations

It is important for students to reflect on the strengths and weaknesses of the investigation they designed during the explicit and reflective discussion. Students should therefore be encouraged to discuss ways to eliminate potential flaws, measurement errors, or sources of bias in their investigations. To help students be more reflective about the design of their investigation, you can ask the following questions:

- What were some of the strengths of your investigation? What made it scientific?
- What were some of the weaknesses of your investigation? What made it less scientific?
- If you were to do this investigation again, what would you do to address the weaknesses in your investigation? What could you do to make it more scientific?

Crosscutting Concepts

This investigation is well aligned with three crosscutting concepts found in *A Framework for K–12 Science Education,* and you should review these concepts during the explicit and reflective discussion.

- *Patterns.* A major objective in biology is to identify the underlying cause of observed patterns, such as the number of chromosomes found in humans.
- *Cause and Effect: Mechanism and Explanation:* Another important goal in science is to identify and then test potential causal relationships. In this investigation, for example, students attempt to identify the underlying cause of a genetic disorder and test three potential explanations for it.
- *Structure and Function:* Students need to understand that the way an object is shaped determines its properties and how it functions. For example, in this investigation a deletion in one chromosome from pair 5 (altered structure) is associated with a genetic disorder (altered function).

The Nature of Science and the Nature of Scientific Inquiry

It is important for students to understand that *science is influenced by the society and culture in which it is practiced* because science is a human endeavor. Cultural values and expectations determine what scientists choose to investigate, how investigations are conducted, how research findings are interpreted, and what people see as implications. People also view some research as being more important than others because of cultural values and current events. A great deal of research in science is focused on understanding the causes of and developing new treatments for illnesses and genetic disorders.

It is also important for students to understand that *scientists use different methods to answer different types of questions.* Examples of methods include experiments, systematic observations of a phenomenon, literature reviews, and analysis of existing data sets; the choice of method depends on the objectives of the research. There is no universal step-by-step scientific method that all scientists follow; rather, different scientific disciplines (e.g., biology vs. physics) and fields within a discipline (e.g., ecology vs. molecular biology) use different types of methods, use different core theories, and rely on different standards to develop scientific knowledge.

You should review and provide examples of these two important concepts of the nature of science (NOS) and the nature of scientific inquiry (NOSI) during the explicit and reflective discussion.

Hints for Implementing the Lab

- Be sure to provide a karyotype for Jill Miller using the same chromosomes found in the kit rather than using an image posted on the internet. Many karyotyping kits use illustrations of chromosomes rather than actual pictures of chromosomes, and students will not be able to create the other karyotypes if they do not have a model karyotype to use as a baseline.
- Encourage students to create the karyotype for Christopher Miller before starting on the karyotypes for the two children. This will enable the students to see that males and females have different sex chromosomes.
- Encourage students to photograph the karyotypes that they create so they can include them in their investigation reports.

Topic Connections

Table 17.2 provides an overview of the scientific practices, crosscutting concepts, disciplinary core ideas, and support ideas at the heart of this lab investigation. In addition, it lists NOS and NOSI concepts for the explicit and reflective discussion. Finally, it lists literacy skills (*CCSS ELA*) that are addressed during the investigation.

TABLE 17.2

Lab 17 alignment with standards

Scientific practices	• Asking questions • Planning and carrying out investigations • Analyzing and interpreting data • Constructing explanations • Engaging in argument from evidence • Obtaining, evaluating, and communicating information
Crosscutting concepts	• Patterns • Cause and effect: Mechanism and explanation • Structure and function
Core idea	• LS3: Heredity: Inheritance and variation of traits
Supporting ideas	• Chromosomal basis of inheritance • Chromosomes • Meiosis • Nondisjunction
NOS and NOSI concepts	• Social and cultural influences • Methods used in scientific investigations
Literacy connections *(CCSS ELA)*	• *Reading:* Key ideas and details, craft and structure, integration of knowledge and ideas • *Writing:* Text types and purposes, production and distribution of writing, research to build and present knowledge, range of writing • *Speaking and listening:* Comprehension and collaboration, presentation of knowledge and ideas

Lab 17. Chromosomes and Karyotypes: How Do Two Physically Healthy Parents Produce a Child With Down Syndrome and a Second Child With Cri Du Chat Syndrome?

Lab Handout

Introduction

Mendel's model of inheritance is the basis for modern genetics. This important model can be broken down into four main ideas. First, and foremost, the fundamental unit of inheritance is the gene and alternative versions of a gene (alleles) account for the variation in inheritable characters. Second, an organism inherits two alleles for each character, one from each parent. Third, if the two alleles differ, then one is fully expressed and determines the nature of the specific trait (this version of the gene is called the dominant allele) while the other one has no noticeable effect (this version of the gene is called the recessive allele). Fourth, the two alleles for each character segregate (or separate) during gamete production. Therefore, an egg or a sperm cell only gets one of the two alleles that are present in the somatic cells of the organism. This idea is known as the law of segregation.

It was brilliant (or lucky) that Mendel chose plant traits that turned out to have a relatively simple genetic basis. Each trait that he studied is determined by only one gene, and each of these genes only consists of two alleles. These conditions, however, are not met by all inheritable traits. The relationship between traits and genes is not always a simple one. In this investigation, you will use what you know about the relationship between traits and genes to explain how two children from the same family inherited two different genetic disorders.

The first child is Emily. She was born with Down syndrome. Children with Down syndrome have developmental delays, a characteristic facial appearance, and weak muscle tone. In addition, these children have an increased risk of heart defects, digestive problems such as gastroesophageal reflux, and hearing loss. The second child is Andy, Emily's younger brother. He was born with cri du chat syndrome. Children with cri du chat syndrome have severe physical and mental developmental delays, distinctive facial features, a small head (microcephaly), a low birth weight, and weak muscle tone (hypotonia).

Christopher and Jill Miller are the parents of Emily and Andy and have been married for 15 years. Although the Millers were in their early forties when they had their first child, both of them were in excellent health. They both eat a well-balanced diet and exercise on a regular basis, and they do not smoke. The Millers therefore want to know why their daughter was born with Down syndrome and their son was born with cri du chat syndrome. Here are three potential explanations:

1. Down syndrome and cri du chat syndrome are both recessive genetic disorders. Christopher and Jill Miller each carried a recessive allele for these syndromes, and they each passed it down to their children.
2. Down syndrome and cri du chat syndrome are both caused by a chromosomal abnormality. Either the sperm cell from Christopher Miller or the egg from Jill Miller had a damaged, missing, or additional chromosome.
3. Down syndrome and cri du chat syndrome are both caused by toxins in the environment that alter genes. The children were exposed to these toxins before they were born.

Your Task

Determine which one of these explanations is most valid or acceptable.

The guiding question for this investigation is, **How do two physically healthy parents produce a child with Down syndrome and a second child with cri du chat syndrome?**

Materials

You may use any of the following materials during your investigation:

- Karyotype for Jill Miller
- Chromosome smear for Christopher Miller
- Chromosome smear for Emily Miller (born with Down syndrome)
- Chromosome smear for Andy Miller (born with cri du chat syndrome)
- 1–3 Karyotype placement grids
- Miller family pedigree

Safety Precautions

1. Wash hands with soap and water after completing this lab.
2. Follow all normal lab safety rules.

Getting Started

Unlike diseases that are transmitted from person to person, such as the flu or strep throat, people are born with cri du chat syndrome or Down syndrome. These syndromes therefore may have a genetic basis. One way to determine the underlying cause of a syndrome with a genetic basis is to produce a karyotype and then look for chromosomal abnormalities that may explain it.

A lab technician can create a karyotype by collecting a sample of cells from an individual. The sample of cells is then stained a dye that makes the chromosomes easier to see (see the figure on p. 244). Next, the chromosomes are photographed using a microscope

Chromosomes in a cell

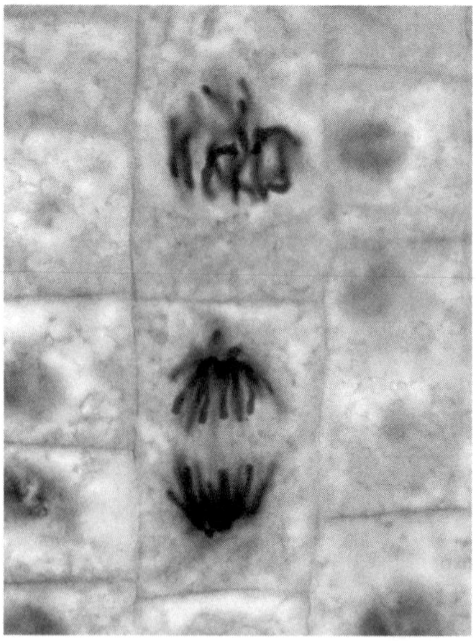

camera. The pictures of the chromosomes are organized onto a grid by size, shape, and banding pattern. Medical professionals can then use the karyotype to look for chromosomal abnormalities such as a missing chromosome or the presence of too many chromosomes. A chromosomal abnormality can also be found on a single chromosome; for example, a chromosome might be shorter or longer than it should.

To create a karyotype for Christopher Miller and the two children, you will need to sort images of chromosomes taken from their cells according to length, pair any matching sets of chromosomes, and place them onto a grid. The final product is a karyotype (a picture of an individual's chromosomes). Your teacher will provide a karyotype from Jill Miller so you can see what a normal female karyotype looks like.

Your teacher will also provide you with a pedigree for the Miller family. This pedigree will provide you with important information about the extended Miller family. It will also show the members of the Miller family that were born with either Down syndrome or cri du chat syndrome. You can use the pedigree to determine if a recessive gene could have caused one or both of these syndromes.

Investigation Proposal Required? ☐ Yes ☐ No

Connections to Crosscutting Concepts and to the Nature of Science and the Nature of Scientific Inquiry

As you work through your investigation, be sure to think about

- the importance of identifying patterns,
- how scientists attempt to uncover causal mechanisms,
- how structure is related to function in living things,
- how the work of scientists is influenced by social and culral values, and
- the different methods that scientists can use to answer a research question.

Argumentation Session

Once your group has finished collecting and analyzing your data, prepare a whiteboard that you can use to share your initial argument. Your whiteboard should include all the information shown in the figure on the opposite page.

To share your argument with others, we will be using a round-robin format. This means that one member of your group will stay at your lab station to share your group's argument while the other members of your group go to the other lab stations one at a time to listen to and critique the arguments developed by your classmates.

Argument presentation on a whiteboard

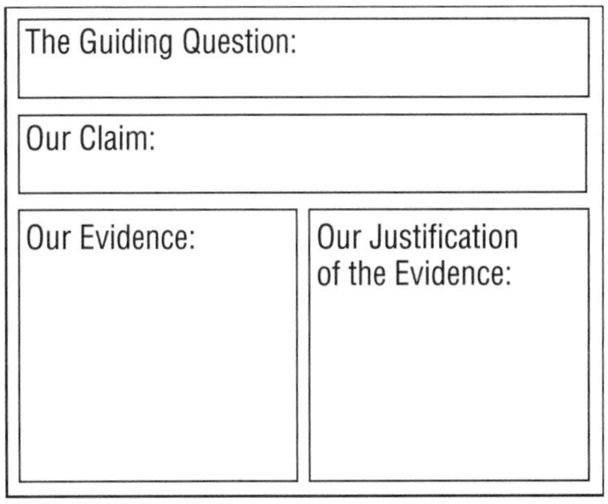
The Guiding Question:
Our Claim:
Our Evidence:
Our Justification of the Evidence:

The goal of the argumentation session is not to convince others that your argument is the best one; rather, the goal is to identify errors or instances of faulty reasoning in the arguments so these mistakes can be fixed. You will therefore need to evaluate the content of the claim, the quality of the evidence used to support the claim, and the strength of the justification of the evidence included in each argument that you see. In order to critique an argument, you will need more information than what is included on the whiteboard. You might, therefore, need to ask the presenter one or more follow-up questions, such as:

- Is that the only way to interpret the results of your analysis? How do you know that your interpretation of your analysis is appropriate?
- Why did your group decide to present your evidence in that manner?
- Why did your group abandon the other alternative explanations?
- How confident are you that your claim is valid? What could you do to increase your confidence?

Once the argumentation session is complete, you will have a chance to meet with your group and revise your original argument. Your group might need to gather more data or design a way to test one or more alternative claims as part of this process. Remember, your goal at this stage of the investigation is to develop the most valid or acceptable answer to the research question!

Report

Once you have completed your research, you will need to prepare an investigation report that consists of three sections that provide answers to the following questions:

1. What question were you trying to answer and why?
2. What did you do during your investigation and why did you conduct your investigation in this way?
3. What is your argument?

Your report should answer these questions in two pages or less. This report must be typed, and any diagrams, figures, or tables should be embedded into the document. Be sure to write in a persuasive style; you are trying to convince others that your claim is acceptable or valid!

Miller family pedigree

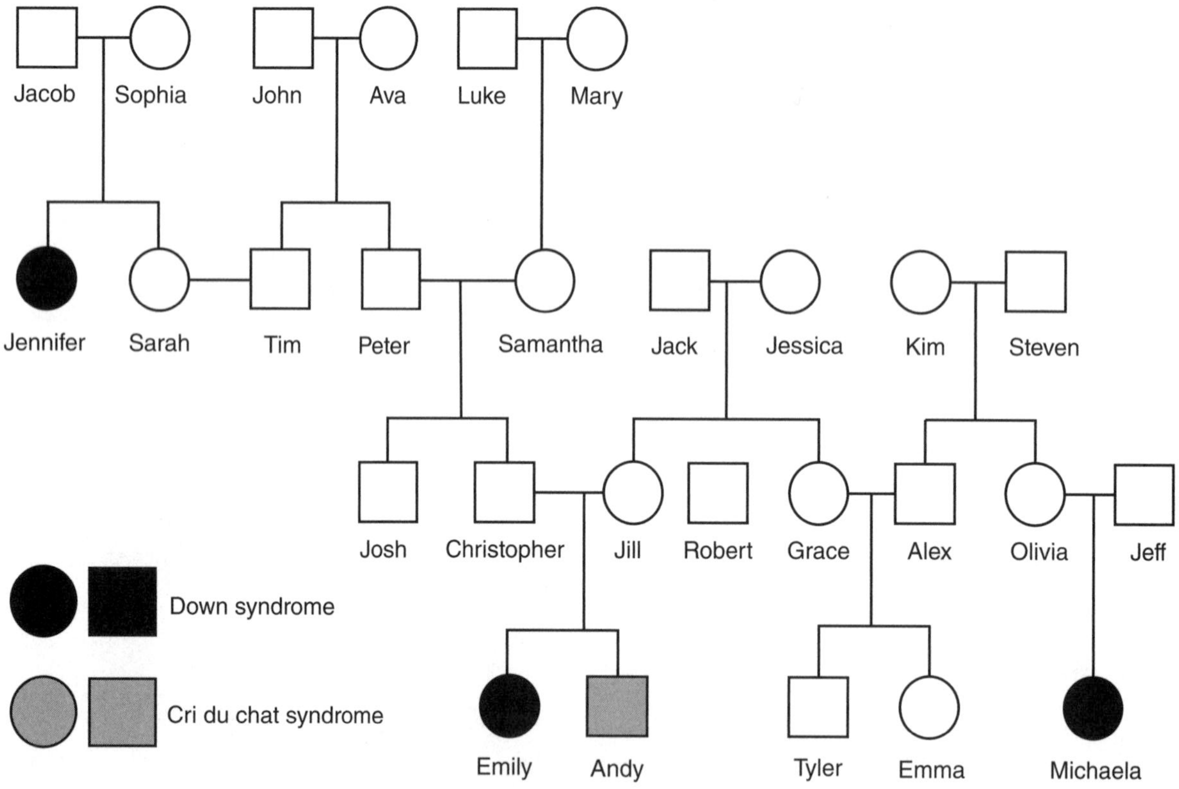

Lab 17. Chromosomes and Karyotypes: How Do Two Physically Healthy Parents Produce a Child With Down Syndrome and a Second Child With Cri Du Chat Syndrome?

Checkout Questions

Use the picture below to answer questions 1–3.

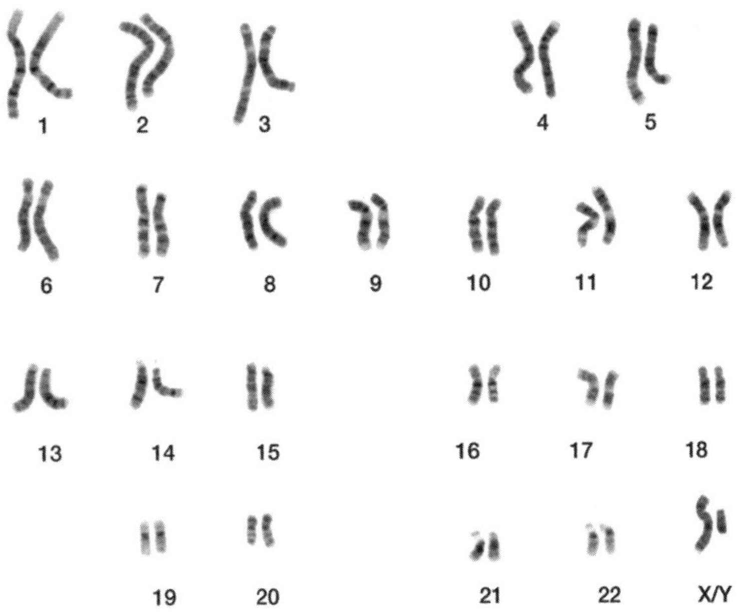

1. Is this karyotype from a male or a female?

   a. Male

   b. Female

   How do you know?

2. Does this person have Down syndrome?

   a. Yes
   b. No

   How do you know?

3. Does this person have cri du chat syndrome?

   a. Yes
   b. No

   How do you know?

4. Social issues and cultural values can influence the work of scientists.

   a. I agree with this statement.
   b. I disagree with this statement.

   Explain your answer, using examples from your investigation about chromosomes and karyotypes.

5. All scientific investigations follow the same step-by-step procedure.

   a. I agree with this statement.
   b. I disagree with this statement.

   Explain your answer, using information from your investigation about chromosomes and karyotypes.

6. Scientists often attempt to identify patterns in nature. Explain why the identification of patterns is useful in science, using an example from your investigation about chromosomes and karyotypes.

7. An important goal of science is to undercover the underlying cause of observations. Explain why the identification of underlying causes is so important in science, using an example from your investigation about chromosomes and karyotypes.

8. Structure and function are related in living things. Explain what this means and why this is an important concept to keep in mind during an investigation, using an example from your investigation about chromosomes and karyotypes.

Lab 18. DNA Structure: What Is the Structure of DNA?

Teacher Notes

Purpose

The purpose of this lab is to *introduce* the concept of deoxyribonucleic acid (DNA) structure as a means for explaining how genetic information is stored, transferred, and conserved. This lab also gives students an opportunity to develop an explanatory model based on an existing data set. Students will also learn about the development of science as a body of knowledge and the different methods used in different types of scientific investigations.

FIGURE 18.1

Structural components of a DNA molecule.

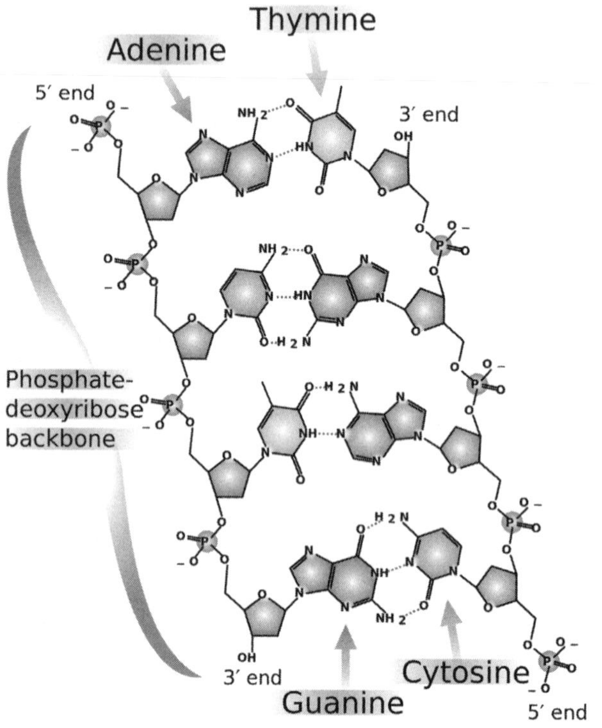

The Content

DNA is a large molecule that consists of several smaller molecules called nucleotides. Each nucleotide is composed of three parts: (1) a nitrogenous base, (2) a five-carbon sugar called deoxyribose, and (3) a phosphate group. There are two families of nitrogenous bases: pyrimidines and purines. A pyrimidine has a six-member ring of carbon and nitrogen atoms; the members of the pyrimidine family are cytosine (C) and thymine (T). Purines are larger than pyrimidines and have a six-member ring fused to a five-member ring of carbon and nitrogen. The members of the purine family are adenine (A) and guanine (G). A nucleotide is formed when a nitrogenous base is joined to a deoxyribose, which in turn is connected to a phosphate group. Nucleotides are joined together in a DNA molecule by covalent bonds between the phosphate group of one nucleotide and the deoxyribose of the next. The bonding of nucleotides together in this manner results in a backbone with a repeating pattern of sugar-phosphate units. Figure 18.1 provides an illustration of a DNA molecule.

Figure 18.2 illustrates two models that are valid based on the information provided in the fact sheet given to the students. One is the model developed by Watson and Crick (model A); the other includes a base pair in the sides of the ladder between each nucleotide

FIGURE 18.2

Acceptable DNA models (based on the information in the fact sheet)

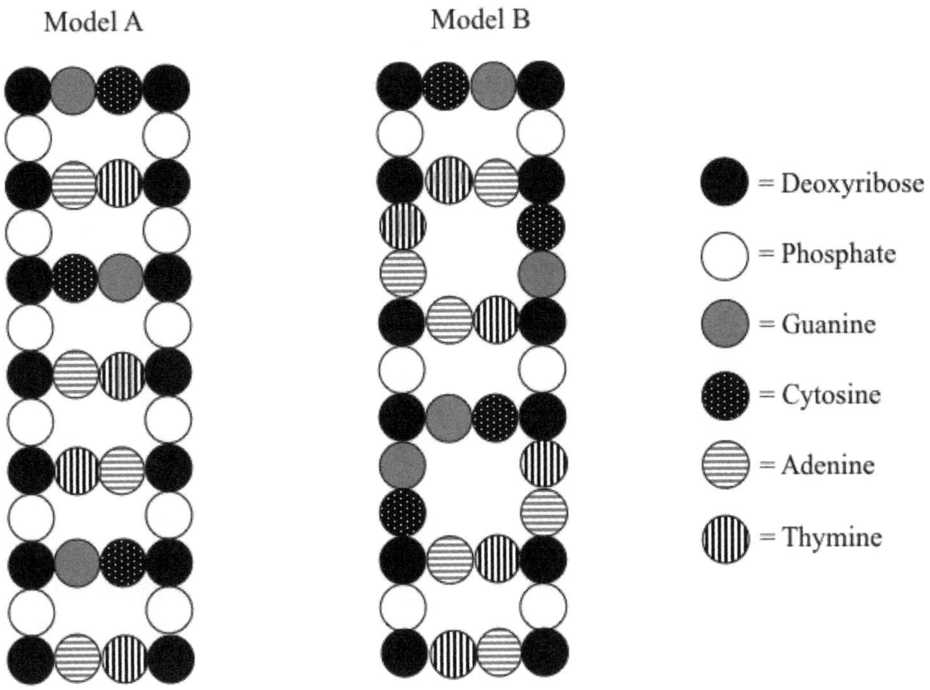

(model B). Both of these models are acceptable explanations for this investigation, even though one is known to be the correct one. Please take note of the following:

- Although the pairing of the nitrogen bases is important, the order in which they appear in the figure is not. The length is also arbitrary; however, it is recommended that the models not be any shorter than depicted.
- There is information on the fact sheet about the binding of the nitrogen bases (A to T and G to C) based on Chargaff's rules. A valid model should display both these properties.
- It is NOT clear from the fact sheet that DNA is twisted (double helix). If students twist their model, be sure to ask them if they have any evidence to support it.

Timeline

The instructional time needed to implement this lab investigation is 130–200 minutes. Appendix 2 (p. 391) provides options for implementing this lab investigation over several class periods. Option C (200 minutes) should be used if students are unfamiliar with scientific writing because this option provides extra instructional time for scaffolding the writing process. You can scaffold the writing process by modeling, providing examples, and providing hints as students write each section of the report. Option D (130 minutes) should be used if students are familiar with scientific writing and have the skills needed to write an investigation report on their own. In option D, students complete stage 6 (writing the investigation report) and stage 8 (revising the investigation report) as homework.

Materials and Preparation

The materials needed to implement this investigation are listed in Table 18.1. Pop bead kits for making models of DNA can be purchased from any biological supply company (e.g., Carolina, Flinn Scientific, or Ward's Science). Be sure to purchase a kit that includes six different colors of pop beads, with one color of bead that has five holes, and pop bead connectors. The materials in these kits can also be purchased separately. Each group will need enough materials to make a 6″ model molecule. Each group should therefore have at least 50 beads of each color and at least 20 pop bead connectors. We recommend that you split up the pop beads and put them into individual containers. One container can then be given to each group.

TABLE 18.1

Materials list

Item	Quantity
Container of pop-beads (six different colors, one color with five holes, at least 50 beads of each color, and at least 20 pop bead connectors)	1 per group
DNA fact sheet	1 per group
Student handout	1 per student
Whiteboard, 2' × 3'*	1 per group
Peer-review guide and instructor scoring rubric	1 per student

* As an alternative, students can use computer and presentation software such as Microsoft PowerPoint or Apple Keynote to create their arguments.

Topics for the Explicit and Reflective Discussion

Concepts That Can Be Used to Justify the Evidence

To provide an adequate justification of their evidence, students must explain why they included the evidence in their arguments and make the assumptions underlying their analysis and interpretation of the data explicit. In this investigation, students can use the following concepts to help justify their evidence:

- Genes are composed of DNA.
- DNA must be able to store, transfer, and conserve genetic information.

- Molecules are composed of smaller subunits, and the subunits of molecules can be rearranged to form different molecules.

We recommend that you review these concepts during the explicit and reflective discussion to help students make this connection.

How to Design Better Investigations

It is important for students to reflect on the strengths and weaknesses of the investigation they designed during the explicit and reflective discussion. Students should therefore be encouraged to discuss ways to eliminate potential flaws, measurement errors, or sources of bias in their investigations. To help students be more reflective about the design of their investigation, you can ask the following questions:

- What were some of the strengths of your investigation? What made it scientific?
- What were some of the weaknesses of your investigation? What made it less scientific?
- If you were to do this investigation again, what would you do to address the weaknesses in your investigation? What could you do to make it more scientific?

Crosscutting Concepts

This investigation is well aligned with three crosscutting concepts found in *A Framework for K–12 Science Education,* and you should review these concepts during the explicit and reflective discussion.

- *Patterns:* A major objective in biology is to identify the underlying cause of observed patterns, such as the repeating nature of the sugar-phosphate backbone found in a molecule of DNA.
- *Scale, Proportion, and Quantity:* When developing explanatory models, it is often important for scientists to look for and recognize proportional relationships in natural phenomena. In this investigation, for example, students must recognize that the ratio of adenine to thymine and the ratio of guanine and cytosine are the same in a molecule of DNA and then use this information to infer that adenine binds to thymine and guanine binds to cytosine.
- *Structure and Function:* Students need to understand that a way an object is shaped determines its properties and how it functions. For example, in this investigation students should see that the unique structure of the DNA molecule makes it possible for it to store, transfer, and conserve genetic information.

The Nature of Science and the Nature of Scientific Inquiry

It is important for students to understand that *science as a body of knowledge develops over time.* A person can have confidence in the validity of scientific knowledge but must also accept that scientific knowledge may be abandoned or modified in light of new evidence or because existing evidence has been reconceptualized by scientists. For example, in the mid-1800s, Gregor Mendel suggested the idea of a gene based on his research with the inheritance of traits in peas. In the early 1900s, Walter Sutton, Theodor Boveri and others helped show that genes are located on chromosomes. Frederick Griffith, Oswald Avery (with MacLeod and McCarty), and many others then went on to demonstrate that it was the DNA in chromosomes that carries genetic information. James Watson and Francis Crick, again aided by the work of many others, provided a model for the molecular structure of DNA in 1953. In the 1960s, Marshall Nirenberg, Heinrich Matthaei, and others deciphered the molecular code that allows DNA to code for proteins. Students, however, should realize that all scientific knowledge, including the findings from studies that have been published in peer-reviewed journals or the knowledge that is used to guide current investigations, is subject to ongoing testing and revision.

It is also important for students to understand that *scientists use different methods to answer different types of questions.* Examples of methods include experiments, systematic observations of a phenomenon, literature reviews, and analysis of existing data sets; the choice of method depends on the objectives of the research. There is no universal step-by-step scientific method that all scientists follow; rather, different scientific disciplines (e.g., biology vs. physics) and fields within a discipline (e.g., ecology vs. molecular biology) use different types of methods, use different core theories, and rely on different standards to develop scientific knowledge. In this investigation, the students do not need to design their own experiment or collect any data; instead they rely on the findings of others to develop a model for the structure of DNA.

You should review and provide examples of these two important concepts of the nature of science (NOS) and the nature of scientific inquiry (NOSI) during the explicit and reflective discussion.

Hints for Implementing the Lab

- Students may need more than one class period to complete their DNA model. If the majority of the class is not done at the end of the first day, adjust the timeline accordingly.
- Resist the urge to help students interpret the fact sheet. Instead, ask them to provide evidence for certain connections. If they reread the fact sheet, they often catch their own mistakes.
- Incorrect models are great! Don't feel like all the groups must have the "correct" model *before* the argumentation session. It is important that students learn to

question models and demand (in a respectful manner) quality evidence for that model.

- Encourage students to take pictures of their models and use them in their reports. Alternatively, students can draw their models in a presentation application such as PowerPoint or Keynote using "basic shapes" and save the image as a picture. These pictures can then be embedded into their reports.

Topic Connections

Table 18.2 provides an overview of the scientific practices, crosscutting concepts, disciplinary core ideas, and support ideas at the heart of this lab investigation. In addition, it lists NOS and NOSI concepts for the explicit and reflective discussion. Finally, it lists literacy skills (*CCSS ELA*) that are addressed during the investigation.

TABLE 18.2

Lab 18 alignment with standards

Scientific practices	• Asking questions • Developing and using models • Planning and carrying out investigations • Analyzing and interpreting data • Constructing explanations • Engaging in argument from evidence • Obtaining, evaluating, and communicating information
Crosscutting concepts	• Patterns • Scale, proportion, and quantity • Structure and function
Core ideas	• LS1: From molecules to organisms: Structures and processes • LS3: Heredity: Inheritance and variation of traits
Supporting ideas	• Chromosome • Nitrogen base • Phosphate • Sugar (deoxyribose and ribose) • Nucleotide • Double helix
NOS and NOSI concepts	• Science as a body of knowledge • Methods used in scientific investigations
Literacy connections *(CCSS ELA)*	• *Reading*: Key ideas and details, craft and structure, integration of knowledge and ideas • *Writing*: Text types and purposes, production and distribution of writing, research to build and present knowledge, range of writing • *Speaking and listening*: Comprehension and collaboration, presentation of knowledge and ideas

Lab 18. DNA Structure: What Is the Structure of DNA?

Lab Handout

Introduction

We know that genes are made of DNA because scientists were able to demonstrate that DNA and proteins are found in the nucleus of cells, and, more importantly, that DNA (and not protein) is able to transform the traits of organisms. Oswald Avery, Colin MacLeod, and Maclyn McCarty made this discovery in 1944. Their research showed that it is possible to transform harmless bacteria into infectious ones with pure DNA. They also provided further support for their claim by demonstrating that it is possible to prevent this "'trans-formation" with a DNA-digesting enzyme called DNase.

However, knowing that genes are made of DNA and that DNA is able to store the genetic information of an individual is a little like having a parts list to a 747 jumbo jet. It tells what is important, but it tells you little about how it works. To figure out how DNA works—that is, how it is able to store genetic information—scientists had to figure out its structure. In this investigation, you will duplicate the work of the two scientists who first figured out the structure of DNA—James Watson and Francis Crick.

Your Task

Use the available data to develop a model that explains the structure of DNA.

The guiding question of this investigation is, **What is the structure of DNA?**

Materials

You may use any of the following materials during your investigation:

- Pop beads (DNA kit)
- Fact sheet about DNA

Safety Precautions

1. Safety goggles or glasses are required for this lab.
2. Wash hands with soap and water after completing this lab.
3. Follow all normal lab safety rules.

Getting Started

To answer the guiding question, you will need to develop a model for the structure of DNA. In science, models are explanations for how things work or how they are structured. Scientists often need to develop models to explain a complex phenomenon or to understand the structure of things that are too small to see (such as the structure of an atom or the structure of a molecule of DNA). Scientists use drawings, graphs, equations, three-dimensional representations, or words to communicate their models to others, but scientists only use these physical objects as a way to illustrate the major components of the model.

You will need to create a three-dimensional representation of your model for the structure of DNA using pop beads. Remember that more than one model may be an acceptable explanation for the same phenomenon. It is not always possible to exclude all but one model—and also not always desirable. For example, physicists think about light as a wave and as a particle, and each model of light's behavior is used to think about and account for phenomena differently.

Investigation Proposal Required? ☐ Yes ☐ No

Connections to Crosscutting Concepts and to the Nature of Science and Scientific Inquiry

As you work through your investigation, be sure to think about

- the importance of identifying patterns;
- the importance of examining proportional relationships;
- how the way an object is shaped or structured determines many of its properties or functions;
- how science, as a body of knowledge, changes over time; and
- the different methods that scientists can use to answer a research question.

Argumentation Session

Once your group has finished collecting and analyzing your data, prepare a whiteboard that you can use to share your initial argument. Your whiteboard should include all the information shown in the figure to the right.

Argument presentation on a whiteboard

The Guiding Question:	
Our Claim:	
Our Evidence:	Our Justification of the Evidence:

To share your argument with others, we will be using a round-robin format. This means that one member of your group will stay at your lab station to share your group's argument while the other members of your group go to the other lab stations one at a time to listen to and critique the arguments developed by your classmates.

The goal of the argumentation session is not to convince others that your argument is the best one; rather, the goal is to identify errors or instances of faulty reasoning in the arguments so these mistakes can be fixed. You will therefore need to evaluate the content of the claim, the quality of the evidence used to support the claim, and the strength of the justification of the evidence included in each argument that you see. In order to critique an argument, you will need more information than what is included on the whiteboard. You might, therefore, need to ask the presenter one or more follow-up questions, such as:

- What did you do to develop your model?
- Is that the only way to interpret the results of your analysis? How do you know that your interpretation of your analysis is appropriate?
- Why did your group decide to present your evidence in that manner?
- What other models did your group discuss before you decided on that one? Why did your group abandon those alternative ideas?
- How confident are you that your model is valid? What could you do to increase your confidence?

Once the argumentation session is complete, you will have a chance to meet with your group and revise your original argument. Your group might need to gather more data or design a way to test one or more alternative claims as part of this process. Remember, your goal at this stage of the investigation is to develop the most valid or acceptable answer to the research question!

Report

Once you have completed your research, you will need to prepare an investigation report that consists of three sections that provide answers to the following questions:

1. What question were you trying to answer and why?
2. What did you do during your investigation and why did you conduct your investigation in this way?
3. What is your argument?

Your report should answer these questions in two pages or less. This report must be typed, and any diagrams, figures, or tables should be embedded into the document. Be sure to write in a persuasive style; you are trying to convince others that your claim is acceptable or valid.

DNA Fact Sheet

1. DNA is a very long molecule composed of smaller molecules called subunits. You can use the different colored beads to represent the different subunits in your physical representation of DNA.
2. DNA is composed of six different subunits (or smaller molecules):

Guanine (a base)	Phosphate group	Thymine (a base)
Deoxyribose (a sugar)	Adenine (a base)	Cytosine (a base)

3. DNA consists of two chains that are bonded (connected) together. A subunit from one strand bonds to a subunit on the other.
4. The diameter of DNA is the same along its entire length (exactly four molecules or subunits wide). Rosalind Franklin made this discovery in 1952 by using x-ray diffraction (see the figure below).

X-rays show that DNA has the same diameter along its entire length.

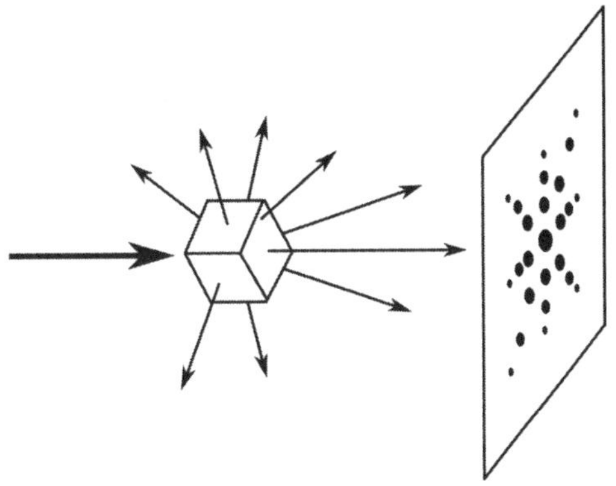

X-ray diffraction

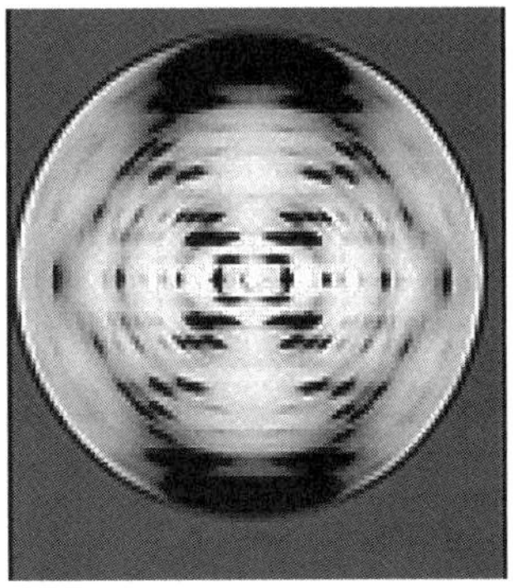

DNA x-ray

5. A sugar subunit can only bind with two other subunits: a base subunit and a phosphate group subunit.
6. A base subunit can only bind with two other subunits: a sugar subunit and a base subunit.
7. A phosphate group subunit can only bind with a sugar subunit.
8. In 1950, biochemist Erwin Chargaff examined the proportion of adenine (A), thymine (T), guanine (G), and cytosine (C) molecules in DNA from different types of organisms. His findings, which are shown below, were so important that it led

to a fundamental principle about the relative proportion of bases found in the DNA of all organisms; this principle is now known as Chargaff's rules.

Relative proportions (%) of bases in DNA				
Organism	**A**	**T**	**G**	**C**
Human	30.9	29.4	19.9	19.8
Chicken	28.8	29.2	20.5	21.5
Grasshopper	29.3	29.3	20.5	20.7
Sea urchin	32.8	32.1	17.7	17.3
Wheat	27.3	27.1	22.7	22.8
Yeast	31.3	32.9	18.7	17.1
E. coli	24.7	23.6	26.0	25.7

Lab 18. DNA Structure: What Is the Structure of DNA?

Checkout Questions

1. In the space below, draw a picture that illustrates the structure of DNA. Be sure to include and label the four different bases, the phosphate group, and the deoxyribose.

2. All scientific knowledge, including the findings from studies that have been published in peer-reviewed journals, is subject to ongoing testing and revision.

    a. I agree with this statement.
    b. I disagree with this statement.

    Explain your answer, using information from your investigation about DNA structure.

3. When conducting a new investigation, scientists can use data previously gathered by other scientists.

    a. I agree with this statement.
    b. I disagree with this statement.

    Explain your answer, using examples from your investigation about DNA structure.

4. Scientists often attempt to identify patterns in nature. Explain why the identification of patterns is useful in science, using an example from your investigation about DNA structure.

5. Scientists often need to look for proportional relationships when analyzing data. Explain why it is often useful to look for these relationships in science, using an example from your investigation about DNA structure.

6. Scientists often attempt to determine the structure of molecules that are too small to see. Explain why this is important for scientists to do, using an example from your investigation about DNA structure.

Lab 19. Meiosis: How Does the Process of Meiosis Reduce the Number of Chromosomes in Reproductive Cells?

Teacher Notes

Purpose

The purpose of this lab is to *introduce* students to the process of meiosis at the chromosomal level. This lab also gives students an opportunity to develop an explanatory model based on an existing data set. Students will also learn about the difference between theories and laws in science and the important role imagination and creativity play in science.

The Content

Reproductive cells go from *diploid* (2n) to *haploid* (n) and have half the number of chromosomes as body cells because of the process of meiosis. Meiosis consists of two phases of cell division: meiosis I and meiosis II (see Figure 19.1). Meiosis I is described as reduction

FIGURE 19.1

The process of meiosis

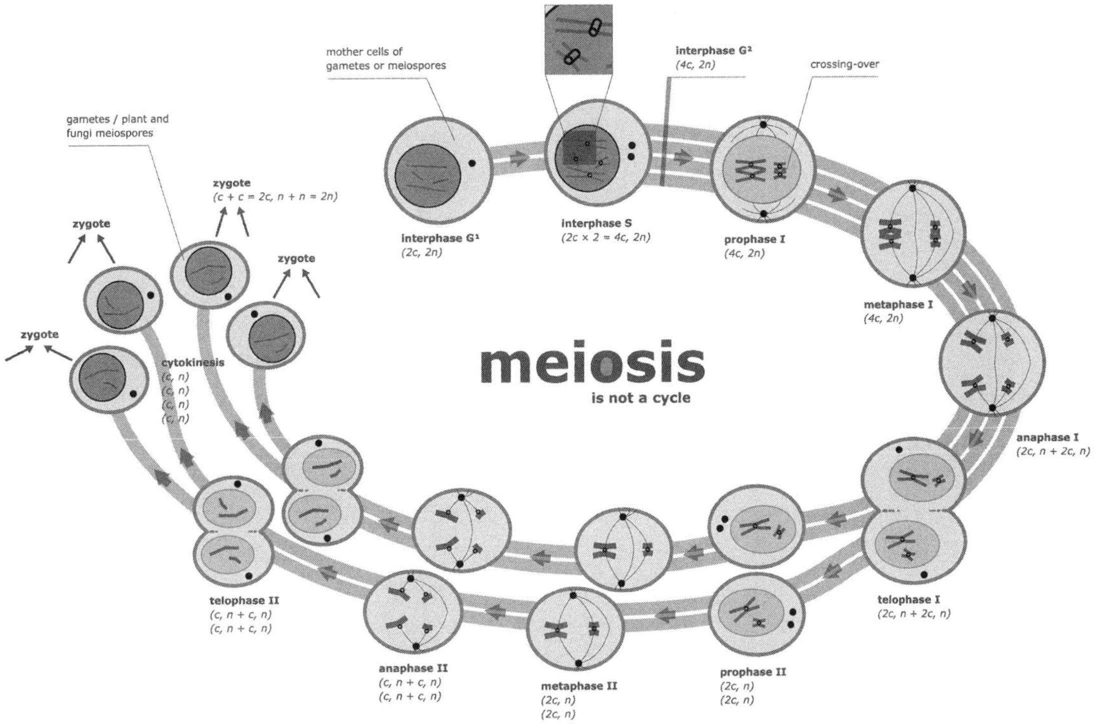

division because homologous chromosomes separate and this separation reduces the cell from diploid to haploid. The cell in Figure 19.1 contains four chromosomes at the beginning of the process of meiosis and is diploid (2n) because it contains two pairs of homologous chromosomes. After meiosis I, the two daughter cells are haploid (n) because there are no pairs of chromosomes (although each daughter cell contains four chromatids). In meiosis II, the sister chromatids separate (which is similar to what takes place during mitosis). The result is four haploid (n) cells, two from each daughter cell from the first division, with each of the four cells containing half the number of chromosomes as the original cell. The haploid cells will not contain any homologous pairs of chromosomes. The two daughter cells in Figure 19.1, for example, have two sets of sister chromatids at the beginning of meiosis II. The sister chromatids then separate during anaphase II. When the four reproductive cells form after telophase II, each cell contains two chromosomes (half the original number) and each cell has no homologous pairs of chromosomes.

Timeline

The instructional time needed to implement this lab investigation is 130–200 minutes. Appendix 2 (p. 391) provides options for implementing this lab investigation over several class periods. Option C (200 minutes) should be used if students are unfamiliar with scientific writing because this option provides extra instructional time for scaffolding the writing process. You can scaffold the writing process by modeling, providing examples, and providing hints as students write each section of the report. Option D (130 minutes) should be used if students are familiar with scientific writing and have the skills needed to write an investigation report on their own. In option D, students complete stage 6 (writing the investigation report) and stage 8 (revising the investigation report) as homework.

FIGURE 19.2

Pop bead chromosomes

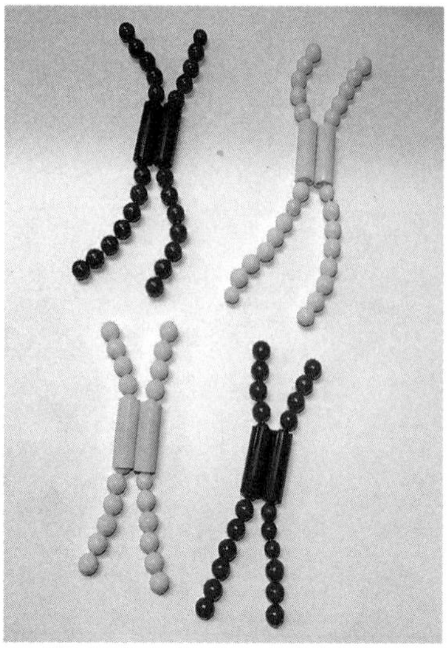

Materials and Preparation

The materials needed to implement this investigation are listed in Table 19.1. Kits for making chromosomes out of pop beads can be purchased from any biological supply company (e.g., Carolina, Flinn Scientific, or Ward's Science). Be sure to purchase a kit that includes magnetic centromeres and at least two different colors of pop beads. The materials in these kits can also be purchased separately.

Each group will need at least eight pop bead chromosomes. We recommend that you create in advance two long chromosomes using red beads, two long chromosomes using yellow beads, two short chromosomes using blue beads, and two short chromosomes using pink beads. The chromosomes should be put together in this manner so the students can combine the chromosomes that are the same length and color to make four sister chromatids (see Figure 19.2). Once assembled, the eight pop bead chromosomes can be put into individual containers so each group has access to their own container of chromosomes. The containers should also include extra pop beads and magnetic centromeres so the groups can create more chromosomes if needed.

Print the PowerPoint file called Images of Cells Going Through Meiosis (available at *www.nsta.org/publications/press/extras/argument.aspx*), then copy the images on card stock so there is one set of images per group. These images can also be cut out and laminated so they can be used in several different class periods. The images of the cells in the various stages of meiosis included in the PowerPoint file can also be shown to the entire class as needed.

TABLE 19.1

Materials list

Item	Quantity
Container with eight pop bead model chromosomes (that can be combined to make four sister chromatids)	1 per group
Images of the stages of meiosis	1 per group
Student handout	1 per student
Whiteboard, 2' × 3'*	1 per group
Peer-review guide and instructor scoring rubric	1 per student

* Students can use the whiteboard to draw an outline of the cell as they work to develop their models. Students can also use computer and presentation software such as Microsoft PowerPoint or Apple Keynote to create their arguments.

Topics for the Explicit and Reflective Discussion

Concepts That Can Be Used to Justify the Evidence

To provide an adequate justification of their evidence, students must explain why they included the evidence in their arguments and make the assumptions underlying their analysis and interpretation of the data explicit. In this investigation, students can use the following concepts to help justify their evidence:

- Basic cell structure and function.
- Cells divide during the process of mitosis.
- Meiosis is the process in which chromosomes are duplicated and then separated into four reproductive cells that have exactly half the number of chromosomes of the original organism.
- There is only one copy of each chromosome in reproductive cells instead of two.
- During fertilization, chromosomes from the male and female combine to form homologous pairs.

We recommend that you review these concepts during the explicit and reflective discussion to help students make this connection.

How to Design Better Investigations

It is important for students to reflect on the strengths and weaknesses of the investigation they designed during the explicit and reflective discussion. Students should therefore be encouraged to discuss ways to eliminate potential flaws, measurement errors, or sources of bias in their investigations. To help students be more reflective about the design of their investigation, you can ask the following questions:

- What were some of the strengths of your investigation? What made it scientific?
- What were some of the weaknesses of your investigation? What made it less scientific?
- If you were to do this investigation again, what would you do to address the weaknesses in your investigation? What could you do to make it more scientific?

Crosscutting Concepts

This investigation is well aligned with two crosscutting concepts found in *A Framework for K–12 Science Education,* and you should review these concepts during the explicit and reflective discussion.

- *Patterns:* A major objective in biology is to identify the underlying cause of observed patterns, such as the sequence of stages that are observed during meiosis.
- *Systems and System Models:* Scientists often need to develop explanatory models to understand complex phenomena, and these models must be consistent with the phenomenon under investigation for the model to be valid. In this investigation, for example, students need to determine if their model is valid by comparing it with the images of cells going through meiosis and what they know about the process of mitosis.

The Nature of Science and the Nature of Scientific Inquiry

It is important for students to understand the *difference between laws and theories in science.* A scientific law describes the behavior of a natural phenomenon or a generalized relationship under certain conditions; a scientific theory is a well-substantiated explanation of some aspect of the natural world. Theories do not become laws even with additional evidence; they explain laws. Meiosis is a theory because it explains how cells divide. It is considered a theory because it explains something, not because it lacks empirical support. It should be noted that not all scientific laws have an accompanying explanatory theory. It is also important for students to understand that scientists do not discover laws or theories; the scientific community develops them over time.

It is also important for students to understand that science requires imagination and creativity. Students should learn that developing explanations for or models of natural phenomena and then figuring out how they can be put to the test of reality is as creative as writing poetry, composing music, or designing skyscrapers. Scientists must also use their imagination and creativity to figure out new ways to test ideas and collect or analyze data.

You should review and provide examples of these two important concepts of the nature of science (NOS) and the nature of scientific inquiry (NOSI) during the explicit and reflective discussion.

Hints for Implementing the Lab

- Students *should not* learn about meiosis prior to this lab! In fact, if students focus more on the information found in the "Introduction," "Your Task," and the "Getting Started" sections of the handout, they can develop a better understanding of the *big picture* of meiosis (the goal of it) and can reason through the stages rather than memorizing them.
- It is helpful, however, if students know about the process of mitosis before they begin this lab. Students can then be encouraged to use what they know about mitosis to develop their model of meiosis.
- Students often take apart the pop bead chromosomes during the investigation as they develop their model of meiosis. Be sure to have students reassemble the chromosomes before they leave class so the chromosomes are ready for the next class period.
- At the end of class, have the students shuffle the picture cards so they are in random order for the next period.
- Encourage students to take pictures of their models and use them in their reports.

Topic Connections

Table 19.2 (p. 270) provides an overview of the scientific practices, crosscutting concepts, disciplinary core ideas, and support ideas at the heart of this lab investigation. In addition, it lists NOS and NOSI concepts for the explicit and reflective discussion. Finally, it lists literacy skills (*CCSS ELA*) that are addressed during the investigation.

TABLE 19.2

Lab 19 alignment with standards

Scientific practices	• Asking questions • Developing and using models • Planning and carrying out investigations • Analyzing and interpreting data • Constructing explanations • Engaging in argument from evidence • Obtaining, evaluating, and communicating information
Crosscutting concepts	• Patterns • Systems and system models
Core ideas	• LS1: From molecules to organisms: Structures and processes • LS3: Heredity: Inheritance and variation of traits
Supporting ideas	• Chromosomes • Meiosis • Cells • Sexual reproduction
NOS and NOSI concepts	• Scientific theories and laws • Imagination and creativity in science
Literacy connections *(CCSS ELA)*	• *Reading*: Key ideas and details, craft and structure, integration of knowledge and ideas • *Writing*: Text types and purposes, production and distribution of writing, research to build and present knowledge, range of writing • *Speaking and listening*: Comprehension and collaboration, presentation of knowledge and ideas

Lab 19. Meiosis: How Does the Process of Meiosis Reduce the Number of Chromosomes in Reproductive Cells?

Lab Handout

Introduction

Sexual reproduction is a process that creates a new organism by combining the genetic material of two organisms. There are two main steps in sexual reproduction: (1) the production of reproductive cells and (2) fertilization. Fertilization is the fusion of two reproductive cells to form a new individual. During fertilization, chromosomes from the male and female combine to form homologous pairs (see the figure below). The number of chromosomes donated from the male and female are equal, and offspring have the same number of chromosomes as each of the parents.

A human karyotype depicting 23 homologous pairs of chromosomes.

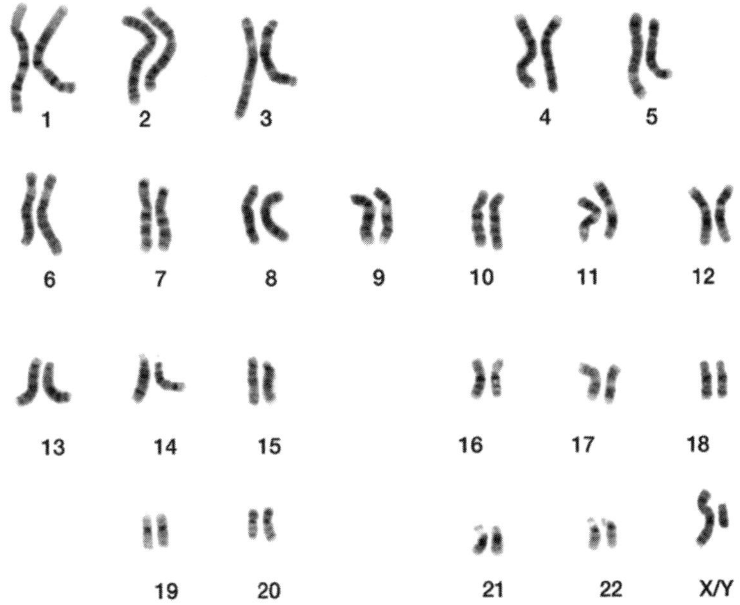

If the reproductive cell from a male and the reproductive cell from a female each donate the same number of chromosomes that are found in a typical cell to the new embryo, then the chromosome number of the species would double with each generation. Yet that doesn't happen; the chromosome number within a species stays constant from one generation to the next. Therefore, a mechanism that reduces the number of chromosomes found in reproductive cells is needed to prevent the chromosome number from doubling as the result of fertilization. This mechanism is called meiosis.

It took many years of research and contributions from several different scientists to uncover what happens inside a cell during the complex process of meiosis. The German biologist Oscar Hertwig made the first major contribution in 1876, when he documented the stages of meiosis by examining the formation of eggs in sea urchins. The Belgian zoologist Edouard Van Beneden made the next major contribution in 1883. He was the first to describe the basic behavior of chromosomes during meiosis by studying the formation of eggs in an intestinal worm (Ascaris). Finally, the German biologist August Weismann highlighted the potential significance of meiosis for reproduction and inheritance in 1890. Weismann was the first one to publish an article that suggested that meiosis could half the number of chromosomes in reproductive cells and, as a result, keep the chromosome number within a species constant from one generation to the next. In this investigation, you will attempt to build on the work of these scientists by developing a model that explains how this type of cell division results in the production of reproductive cells that contain halve the number of chromosomes that are found in the other cells of that organism.

Your Task

Meiosis is the process in which chromosomes are duplicated and then separated into four reproductive cells that have exactly half the number of chromosomes of the original organism. In addition, this process ensures that there are no pairs of chromosomes found in the reproductive cells. In other words, there is only one copy of each chromosome in reproductive cells instead of two. Then during fertilization, a reproductive cell from a male (i.e., a sperm) and a reproductive cell from a female (i.e., an egg) will fuse to form an embryo that has the same number of chromosomes as the original organism. This process happens in all animals, plants, and fungi that reproduce sexually. Your goal is to develop a model that explains what happens to the chromosomes within a cell during each stage of meiosis.

The guiding question of this investigation is, **How does the process of meiosis reduce the number of chromosomes in reproductive cells?**

Materials

You may use any of the following materials:

- 8 Pop bead chromosomes (and extra pop beads if needed)
- Images of the stages of meiosis

Safety Precautions

1. Safety goggles or glasses are required for this lab.

2. Wash hands with soap and water after completing this lab.
3. Follow all normal lab safety rules.

Getting Started

To answer the guiding question, you will need to develop a model that explains the process of meiosis. Your first step is to learn more about what a cell looks like as it goes through meiosis. You will therefore be given a series of pictures that show the different stages of meiosis as seen through a microscope. Your next step will be to figure out (a) the correct order of stages and (b) what you think may be going on during each stage. Use what you know about the stages of mitosis and how cells divided during mitosis to accomplish this task. From there, you can use pop bead chromosomes (see the figure to the right) to attempt to make sense of what is happening with the individual chromosomes during each stage of meiosis.

Pop bead chromosomes

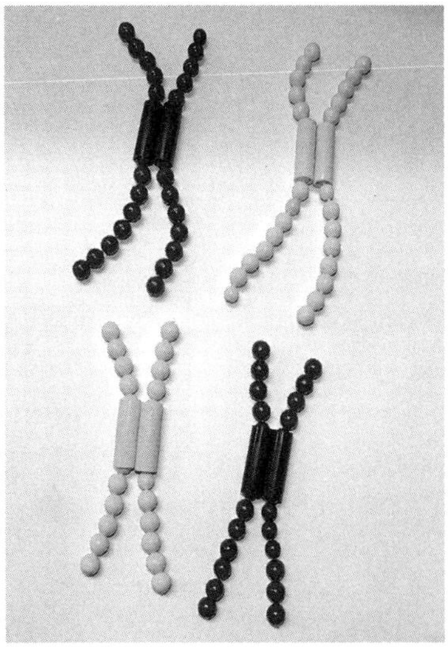

Your model, once complete, should be able to explain (a) what happens to the chromosomes inside a cell as it goes though meiosis, (b) why reproductive cells have half the number of chromosomes of the individuals who produce them, and (c) why there are no pairs of chromosomes in reproductive cells. To be valid, your model must be able to explain all three of these issues.

Investigation Proposal Required? ☐ Yes ☐ No

Connections to Crosscutting Concepts and to the Nature of Science and Scientific Inquiry

As you work through your investigation, be sure to think about

- the importance of identifying and explaining patterns,
- how scientists develop and use models,
- the difference between theories and laws in science, and
- the role of creativity and imagination in science.

Argumentation Session

Once your group has finished collecting and analyzing your data, prepare a whiteboard that you can use to share your initial argument. Your whiteboard should include all the information shown in the figure on p. 272.

Argument presentation on a whiteboard

The Guiding Question:	
Our Claim:	
Our Evidence:	Our Justification of the Evidence:

To share your argument with others, we will be using a round-robin format. This means that one member of your group will stay at your lab station to share your group's argument while the other members of your group go to the other lab stations one at a time to listen to and critique the arguments developed by your classmates.

The goal of the argumentation session is not to convince others that your argument is the best one; rather, the goal is to identify errors or instances of faulty reasoning in the arguments so these mistakes can be fixed. You will therefore need to evaluate the content of the claim, the quality of the evidence used to support the claim, and the strength of the justification of the evidence included in each argument that you see. In order to critique an argument, you will need more information than what is included on the whiteboard. You might, therefore, need to ask the presenter one or more follow-up questions, such as:

- Is that the only way to interpret the results of your analysis? How do you know that your interpretation of your analysis is appropriate?
- Why did your group decide to present your evidence in that manner?
- What other models did your group discuss before you decided on that one? Why did your group abandon those alternative ideas?
- How confident are you that your model is valid? What could you do to increase your confidence?

Once the argumentation session is complete, you will have a chance to meet with your group and revise your original argument. Your group might need to gather more data or design a way to test one or more alternative claims as part of this process. Remember, your goal at this stage of the investigation is to develop the most valid or acceptable answer to the research question!

Report

Once you have completed your research, you will need to prepare an investigation report that consists of three sections that provide answers to the following questions:

1. What question were you trying to answer and why?
2. What did you do during your investigation and why did you conduct your investigation in this way?
3. What is your argument?

Your report should answer these questions in two pages or less. This report must be typed, and any diagrams, figures, or tables should be embedded into the document. Be sure to write in a persuasive style; you are trying to convince others that your claim is acceptable or valid!

Lab 19. Meiosis: How Does the Process of Meiosis Reduce the Number of Chromosomes in Reproductive Cells?

Checkout Questions

1. Describe the process and products of meiosis.

2. The idea that genes are found on chromosomes and that there is the process of meiosis are theories and not laws.

   a. I agree with this statement.
   b. I disagree with this statement.

   Explain your answer, using information from your investigation about meiosis.

3. Creativity and imagination are an important part of this investigation.

   a. I agree with this statement.
   b. I disagree with this statement.

   Explain your answer, using examples from your investigation about meiosis.

4. Scientists often attempt to identify and explain the patterns in nature. Explain why the identification of patterns is useful in science, using an example from your investigation about meiosis.

5. Scientists often attempt to develop a conceptual model to explain complex phenomena. Explain what a model is and why models are useful in science, using an example from your investigation about meiosis.

Application Labs

Lab 20. Inheritance of Blood Type: Are All of Mr. Johnson's Children His Biological Offspring?

Teacher Notes

Purpose

The purpose of this lab is to give students an opportunity to *apply* what they know about the inheritance of traits to solve a problem. This lab also gives students an opportunity to use an explanatory model, in this case the multiple allele model of inheritance, as a way to make sense of a natural phenomenon. Students will also learn about the differences between observations and inferences and between data and evidence in science.

The Content

The ABO blood group includes four types of blood: A, B, AB, and O. The differences in blood types are due to the presence or absence of certain types of *antigens* and *antibodies.* Antigens are molecules that are located on the surface of the red blood cells (RBCs), and antibodies are molecules that are located in the blood plasma. Individuals have different types and combinations of these molecules. Figure 20.1 shows which antigens and antibodies are associated with each type of blood.

FIGURE 20.1

Surface antigens and antibodies associated with each blood type in the ABO blood group

	Type A	Type B	Type AB	Type O
Red blood cell type	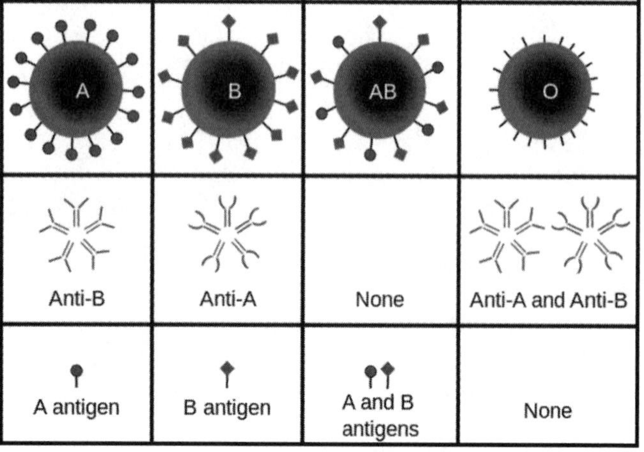 A	B	AB	O
Antibodies in Plasma	Anti-B	Anti-A	None	Anti-A and Anti-B
Antigens in Red Blood Cell	A antigen	B antigen	A and B antigens	None

A single gene that consists of three different versions (or *alleles*) determines the four blood types in the ABO group. Allele A codes for the synthesis of RBCs that have the type A antigens on their surface, Allele B codes for the synthesis of RBCs that have the type B antigens on their surface, and allele O codes for RBCs that lack surface antigens. The A and B alleles are codominant to each other, and both the A and B alleles are dominant over the O allele. Although there are three different alleles associated with the ABO blood group gene, each individual only inherits two copies of it—one copy comes from the mother and one copy comes from the father. The ABO blood type therefore follows a *multiple allele model of inheritance.*

To illustrate the inheritance of blood type, consider the family illustrated in Figure 20.2. In this family the father has blood type A but is heterozygous and therefore carries the A allele and the O allele. The mother has type B blood and is heterozygous as well, so she carries the B allele and the O allele. The father can pass down the A allele or the O allele and the mother can pass down the B allele or the O allele. As a result, their children can inherit any of the four blood types in the ABO blood group. The first child in this family inherited an A allele from his father and an O allele from his mother. He therefore has type A blood. The second child has type AB blood because she inherited an A allele from her father and a B allele from her mother. The third child inherited an O allele from his father and a B allele from his mother. He therefore has type B blood. Finally, the fourth child has type O blood because she inherited an O allele from both her father and her mother.

FIGURE 20.2

The inheritance of ABO blood type in a fictional family

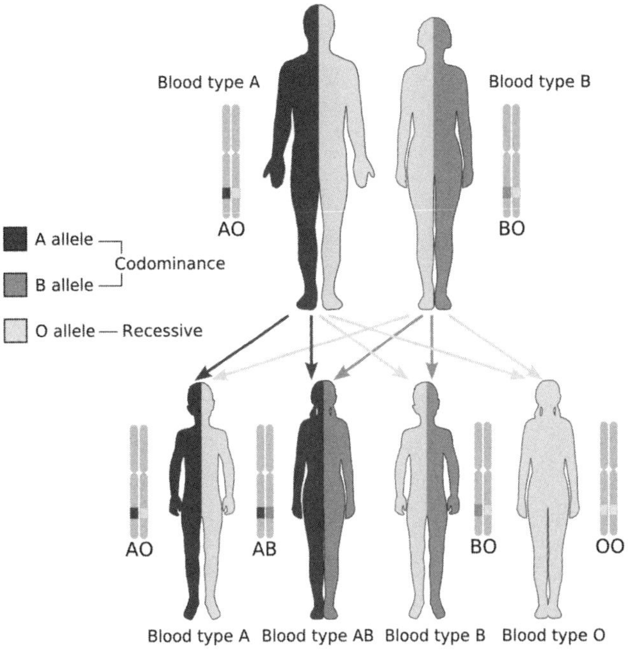

Timeline

The instructional time needed to implement this lab investigation is 130–200 minutes. Appendix 2 (p. 391) provides options for implementing this lab investigation over several class periods. Option C (200 minutes) should be used if students are unfamiliar with scientific writing because this option provides extra instructional time for scaffolding the writing process. You can scaffold the writing process by modeling, providing examples, and providing hints as students write each section of the report. Option D (130 minutes) should be used if students are familiar with scientific writing and have the skills needed to write an investigation report on their own. In option D, students complete stage 6 (writing the investigation report) and stage 8 (revising the investigation report) as homework.

Materials and Preparation

The materials needed to implement this investigation are listed in Table 20.1. Blood typing kits that include simulated blood samples, antiserums, and blood-typing slides can be purchased from any biological supply company (e.g., Boreal Science, Carolina, or Ward's Science). The materials in these kits can also be purchased separately.

TABLE 20.1

Materials list

Item	Quantity
Blood samples from Mrs. Johnson, Mr. Johnson, Mr. Wilson, child 1, child 2, and child 3 in disposable Beral pipettes	1 per group
Samples of type A, type B, type AB, and type O blood in disposable Beral pipettes	1 per group
Anti-A serum in disposable Beral pipette	1 per group
Anti-B serum in disposable Beral pipette	1 per group
Blood-typing slide	6 per group
Toothpicks	12 per group
Student handout	1 per student
Whiteboard, 2' × 3'*	1 per group
Peer-review guide and instructor scoring rubric	1 per student

* Students can also use computer and presentation software such as Microsoft PowerPoint or Apple Keynote to create their arguments.

The samples of blood from each individual can be placed in disposable Beral pipettes to facilitate the distribution of materials to groups and to limit the amount of blood each group used during the investigation. Label each pipette with the name of the individual being studied, not with the blood type. Fill each pipette with about 2 ml of blood, as follows:

- Mrs. Johnson is blood type O.
- Mr. Johnson is blood type A.
- Mr. Wilson is blood type B.
- Child 1 is blood type A.
- Child 2 is blood type B.
- Child 3 is blood type O.

Fill enough pipettes so each group has one from each individual. Then place a set of pipettes (i.e., one from each individual) into a beaker bulb end down to prevent leakage and cross contamination. Provide each group with a beaker of blood samples.

It is also important to set up a station where each group can come to collect *known* blood samples for each blood type. Fill the pipettes in the same way but label these by blood type, not by the name of an individual. The known samples serve as a positive control so students can see agglutination. If there are sufficient supplies, a representative sample of each blood type can be assembled and provided to each group in a beaker and provided to each group along with the unknown blood samples.

Topics for the Explicit and Reflective Discussion

Concepts That Can Be Used to Justify the Evidence

To provide an adequate justification of their evidence, students must explain why they included the evidence in their arguments and make the assumptions underlying their analysis and interpretation of the data explicit. In this investigation, students must use the multiple allele model of inheritance to help justify their evidence. We recommend that you review this concept during the explicit and reflective discussion to help students make this connection.

How to Design Better Investigations

It is important for students to reflect on the strengths and weaknesses of the investigation they designed during the explicit and reflective discussion. Students should therefore be encouraged to discuss ways to eliminate potential flaws, measurement errors, or sources of bias in their investigations. To help students be more reflective about the design of their investigation, you can ask the following questions:

- What were some of the strengths of your investigation? What made it scientific?
- What were some of the weaknesses of your investigation? What made it less scientific?
- If you were to do this investigation again, what would you do to address the weaknesses in your investigation? What could you do to make it more scientific?

Crosscutting Concepts

This investigation is well aligned with two crosscutting concepts found in *A Framework for K–12 Science Education,* and you should review these concepts during the explicit and reflective discussion.

- *Systems and System Models:* Scientists often need to use explanatory models to understand complex phenomena. In this investigation, for example, students need to use the multiple allele model of inheritance to interpret the results of the blood test.
- *Structure and Function:* Students should be reminded that, in nature, the way an object is shaped or structured determines many of its properties and functions. In this investigation, for example, the structure of the blood cells and the structure

of the antibodies determine whether agglutination occurs when the blood sample and an antiserum are mixed. This relationship between structure and function enables us to easily identify blood types.

The Nature of Science and the Nature of Scientific Inquiry

It is important for students to understand the *difference between observations and inferences in science.* An observation is a descriptive statement about a natural phenomenon, whereas an inference is an interpretation of an observation. Students should also understand that current scientific knowledge and the perspectives of individual scientists guide both observations and inferences. In this investigation, for example, students look for clumping because of what is known about the behavior of blood when it is mixed with antiserum. Then they infer a blood type based on this clumping. Both their observations and their inferences are based on current scientific knowledge.

It is also important for students to understand the *difference between data and evidence in science.* Data are measurements, observations, and findings from other studies that are collected as part of an investigation. Evidence, in contrast, is analyzed data and an interpretation of the analysis. In this investigation, for example, students collect observations about the clumping behavior of the blood samples—this is their data. They then have to analyze their data and interpret their analysis to generate evidence that they can use to support their answer to the guiding question.

Hints for Implementing the Lab

- Encourage students to test the known blood sample to see what agglutination reactions look like if they are having trouble distinguishing between positive and negative test results.
- The members of the fictional family can be assigned different blood types during different class periods so the results are not the same in each class period. Be sure to make the mother's blood type fit with the children's blood type (e.g., don't have the mother be AB and one of the children be O).
- If supplies are limited, you can slightly decrease the blood-typing students do (e.g., provide the adult blood types and have the students just test the blood types of the children).

Topic Connections

Table 20.2 provides an overview of the scientific practices, crosscutting concepts, disciplinary core ideas, and support ideas at the heart of this lab investigation. In addition, it lists NOS and NOSI concepts for the explicit and reflective discussion. Finally, it lists literacy skills (*CCSS ELA*) that are addressed during the investigation.

TABLE 20.2

Lab 20 alignment with standards

Scientific practices	• Asking questions • Developing and using models • Planning and carrying out investigations • Analyzing and interpreting data • Constructing explanations • Engaging in argument from evidence • Obtaining, evaluating, and communicating information
Crosscutting concepts	• Systems and system models • Structure and function
Core ideas	• LS1: From molecules to organisms: Structures and processes • LS3: Heredity: Inheritance and variation of traits
Supporting ideas	• Multiple allele traits • Genotypes • Phenotypes • Blood typing • Pedigrees
NOS and NOSI concepts	• Observations and inferences • Difference between data and evidence
Literacy connections *(CCSS ELA)*	• *Reading*: Key ideas and details, craft and structure, integration of knowledge and ideas • *Writing*: Text types and purposes, production and distribution of writing, research to build and present knowledge, range of writing • *Speaking and listening*: Comprehension and collaboration, presentation of knowledge and ideas

Lab 20. Inheritance of Blood Type: Are All of Mr. Johnson's Children His Biological Offspring?

Lab Handout

Introduction

Karl Landsteiner identified the ABO blood group in 1901. The ABO blood group includes four types of blood (A, B, AB, and O). The differences in blood types are due to the presence or absence of certain types of antigens and antibodies. Antigens are molecules that are located on the surface of the red blood cells (RBCs), and antibodies are molecules that are located in the blood plasma. Individuals have different types and combinations of these molecules. The figure below shows which antigens and antibodies are associated with each blood type in the ABO blood group.

Blood types and red blood cell surface antigens

	Type A	Type B	Type AB	Type O
Red blood cell type	A	B	AB	O
Antibodies in Plasma	Anti-B	Anti-A	None	Anti-A and Anti-B
Antigens in Red Blood Cell	A antigen	B antigen	A and B antigens	None

A single gene that consists of three different versions (or alleles) determines the four blood types in the ABO group. Allele A codes for the synthesis of RBCs that have the type A antigens on their surface. Allele B codes for the synthesis of RBCs that have the type B antigens on their surface, and allele O codes for RBCs that lack surface antigens. The A and B alleles are codominant to each other, and both the A and B alleles are dominant over the O allele. Although there are three different alleles associated with the ABO blood group gene, each individual only inherits two copies of it. One copy of the gene comes from the mother and one copy of the gene comes from the father. The ABO blood type therefore follows the multiple allele model of inheritance.

Although blood type is an inherited trait, the U.S. judicial system does not recognize ABO blood typing as an acceptable way to determine paternity because many individuals can have the same blood type. In the United States, for example, approximately 44% of the population has type O blood, 42% has type A blood, 10% has type B blood, and 4% has type AB blood. ABO blood-typing, however, can be used to exclude a man from being a child's father. Therefore, it is sometimes useful to conduct a quick and inexpensive test for ABO blood type to determine if further testing using a DNA analysis is warranted.

Your Task

Mr. and Mrs. Johnson have been married for eight years. During this time, Mrs. Johnson has had three children. Recently Mr. Johnson found out that Mrs. Johnson has been secretly dating another man, Mr. Wilson, throughout their marriage. Mr. Johnson now questions if he is truly the biological father of the three children. Your goal is to use what you know about the inheritance of ABO blood types to determine if Mr. Johnson can be excluded as the father of any of Mrs. Johnson's children.

The guiding question of this investigation is, **Are all of Mr. Johnson's children his biological offspring?**

Materials

You may use any of the following materials during your investigation:

- Type A blood sample
- Type B blood sample
- Type AB blood sample
- Type O blood sample
- Blood sample from Mr. Wilson
- Blood sample from Mr. Johnson
- Blood sample from Mrs. Johnson
- Blood sample from child 1
- Blood sample from child 2
- Blood sample from child 3
- Anti-A serum
- Anti-B serum
- 6 blood-typing slides
- Toothpicks

Safety Precautions

1. Safety goggles, gloves, and aprons are required for this lab.
2. Under no circumstances is human or animal blood to be used or tested. Only use commercially prepared simulated blood products.
3. Wash hands with soap and water after completing the lab.
4. Follow all normal lab safety rules.

LAB 20

Getting Started

To test a person's blood type, you can mix a sample of blood with an antiserum that has high levels of anti-A or anti-B antibodies. The simple test is performed as follows:

1. Add two drops of a blood sample to well A and to well B of a blood-typing slide.
2. Add two drops of the appropriate antiserum to each of the samples.
3. Stir each sample for 20 seconds with a toothpick.

If the blood cells have the appropriate antigens on their surface, agglutination (clumping of the blood) will occur. For example, if anti-A serum is added to a sample of blood and agglutination occurs, that means the blood contains cells that have the type A antigens on their surface. The figure below illustrates the reaction of each antiserum with each blood type. Be sure to test known samples first before the unknown samples to see what the agglutination reactions look like.

Investigation Proposal Required? ☐ Yes ☐ No

Connections to Crosscutting Concepts and to the Nature of Science and Scientific Inquiry

As you work through your investigation, be sure to think about

- how scientists develop and use explanatory models to make sense of their observations,

Reaction of different blood types with antiserum

Antiserum	Reaction when blood is mixed with antiserum			
	Type A	Type B	Type AB	Type O
Anti-B	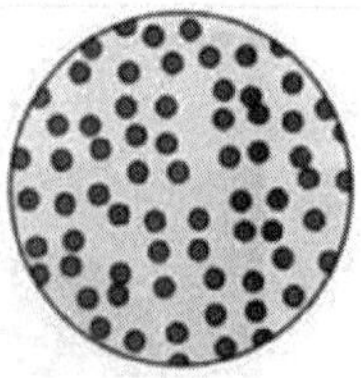	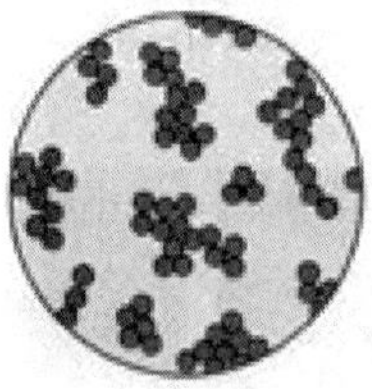	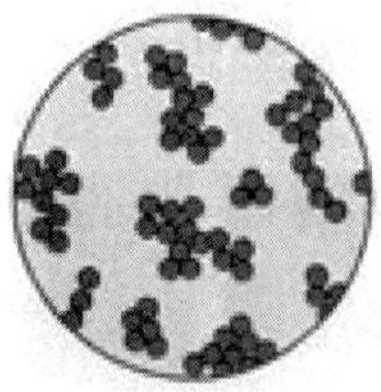	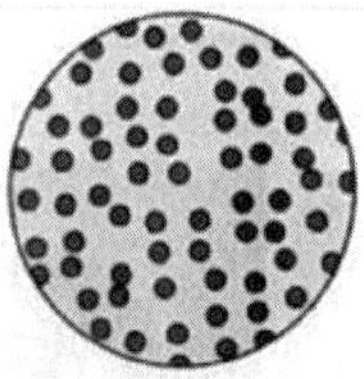
Anti-A	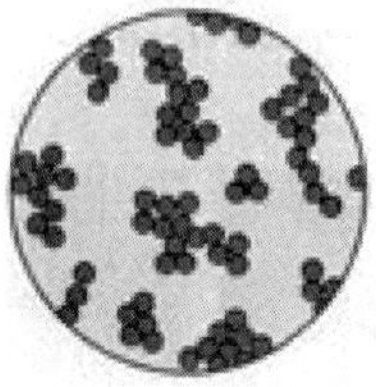	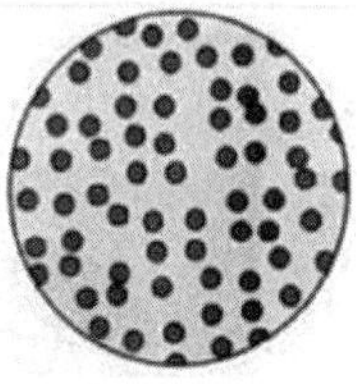	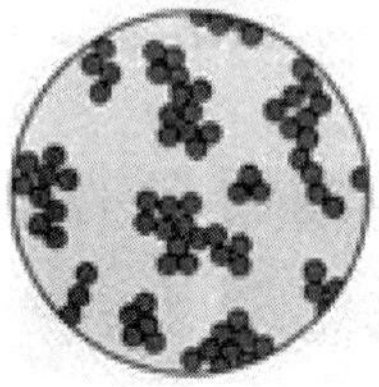	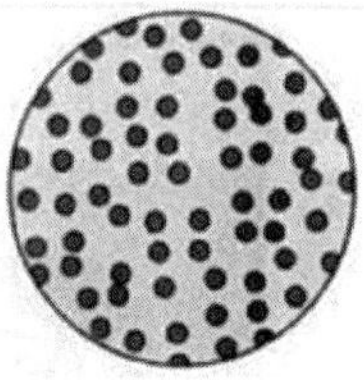

- the relationship between structure and function,
- the relationship between observations and inferences in science, and
- the difference between data and evidence.

Argumentation Session

Once your group has finished collecting and analyzing your data, prepare a whiteboard that you can use to share your initial argument. Your whiteboard should include all the information shown in the figure to the right.

Argument presentation on a whiteboard

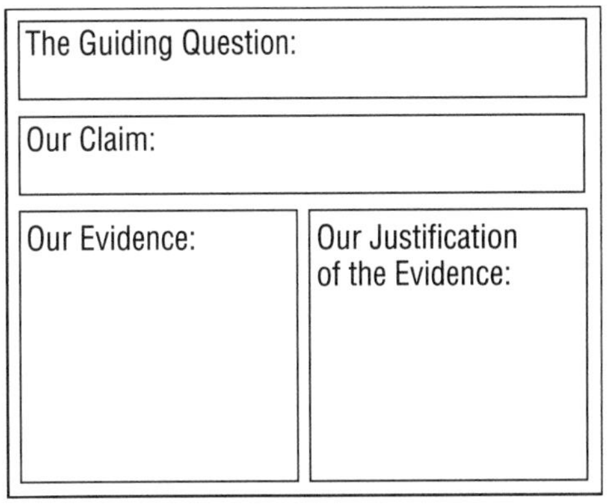

To share your argument with others, we will be using a round-robin format. This means that one member of your group will stay at your lab station to share your group's argument while the other members of your group go to the other lab stations one at a time to listen to and critique the arguments developed by your classmates.

The goal of the argumentation session is not to convince others that your argument is the best one; rather, the goal is to identify errors or instances of faulty reasoning in the arguments so these mistakes can be fixed. You will therefore need to evaluate the content of the claim, the quality of the evidence used to support the claim, and the strength of the justification of the evidence included in each argument that you see. In order to critique an argument, you will need more information than what is included on the whiteboard. You might, therefore, need to ask the presenter one or more follow-up questions, such as:

- How did you collect your data? Why did you use that method? Why did you collect those data?
- What did you do to make sure the data you collected are reliable? What did you do to decrease measurement error?
- What did you do to analyze your data? Why did you decide to do it that way?
- Is that the only way to interpret the results of your analysis? How do you know that your interpretation of your analysis is appropriate?
- Why did your group decide to present your evidence in that manner?
- What other claims did your group discuss before you decided on that one? Why did your group abandon those alternative ideas?
- How confident are you that your claim is valid? What could you do to increase your confidence?

Once the argumentation session is complete, you will have a chance to meet with your group and revise your original argument. Your group might need to gather more data or design a way to test one or more alternative claims as part of this process. Remember, your goal at this stage of the investigation is to develop the most valid or acceptable answer to the research question!

Report

Once you have completed your research, you will need to prepare an investigation report that consists of three sections that provide answers to the following questions:

1. What question were you trying to answer and why?
2. What did you do during your investigation and why did you conduct your investigation in this way?
3. What is your argument?

Your report should answer these questions in two pages or less. This report must be typed, and any diagrams, figures, or tables should be embedded into the document. Be sure to write in a persuasive style; you are trying to convince others that your claim is acceptable or valid!

Lab 20. Inheritance of Blood Type: Are All of Mr. Johnson's Children His Biological Offspring?

Checkout Questions

1. Two tall pea plants are cross-fertilized and produce four offspring. Three of the four offspring are tall plants, and one of the offspring is short.

Parents:		Tall Plant	×	Tall Plant
Offspring:	Tall Plant	Tall Plant	Tall Plant	Short Plant

Use Mendel's model of inheritance to explain how two tall plants can produce tall plants and short plants.

2. In science the terms *data* and *evidence* have the same meaning.

   a. I agree with this statement.
   b. I disagree with this statement.

   Explain your answer, using examples from your investigation about inheritance of blood type.

3. Scientists will always make the same observations and inferences during an investigation.

   a. I agree with this statement.
   b. I disagree with this statement.

   Explain your answer, using information from your investigation about inheritance of blood type.

4. Scientists often use models to explain a complex phenomenon. Explain why models are useful in science, using an example from your investigation about inheritance of blood type.

5. Structure and function are related in nature. Explain how this principle influenced how you collected data and how you made sense of the data you collected during your investigation about inheritance of blood type.

Lab 21. Models of Inheritance: Which Model of Inheritance Best Explains How a Specific Trait Is Inherited in Fruit Flies?

Teacher Notes

Purpose

The purpose of this lab is to give students an opportunity to *apply* what they know about the inheritance of traits to solve a problem. This lab also gives students an opportunity to use several explanatory models, in this case the dominant-recessive, sex-linked, codominance, incomplete dominance, and multiple alleles models of inheritance, as a way to make sense of a natural phenomenon. Students will also learn about the difference between theories and laws and how laws are developed in science.

The Content

The principles of Mendelian genetics encompass several different models of inheritance. These models include dominant-recessive, incomplete dominance, codominance, multiple allele, and sex-linked. All of these models are based on two fundamental ideas. The first and most important idea is the gene. The gene is the fundamental unit of inheritance, and alternative versions of a gene (*alleles*) account for variations in inheritable traits. The gene for a particular inherited trait, such as eye color in fruit flies, resides at a specific locus (position) on a specific chromosome. Second, an organism inherits two alleles for each trait, one from each parent. This occurs because individuals inherit one chromosome for each homologous pair from each parent. What makes these models of inheritance different from each other is the nature of the interaction that takes place between alleles, the number of alleles that are associated with a gene, and whether or not a gene is located on a sex chromosome.

The *dominant-recessive* model of inheritance is the model developed by Mendel. In this model, an individual inherits two alleles. When the two alleles differ, one is fully expressed and determines the nature of the trait (this version of the gene is called the dominant allele) while the other one has no noticeable effect (this version of the gene is called the recessive allele).

In contrast to the dominant-recessive model, the *incomplete dominance* model of inheritance suggests that alleles interact with each other to produce a trait that is a hybrid phenotype of the two parental varieties. A well-known example of incomplete dominance in humans is hair texture. When an individual inherits the allele for curly hair from one parent and the allele for straight hair from the other parent, that individual will have a hair texture that is a blend of the two, or wavy hair.

In the *codominance* model of inheritance, both alleles affect the phenotype of the individual in separate and distinguishable ways; the coat color of Shorthorn cattle is an example of this model. Shorthorn cattle that are homozygous for the R allele have red hair, and individuals that are homozygous for the W allele have white hair. Individuals that inherit a copy of the R allele and the W allele have intermingled red and white hair (not pink hair).

The *multiple allele* model of inheritance simply means that there are more than two versions of a gene for a given trait with a population. The ABO blood type in humans is an example of a trait that follows the multiple allele model of inheritance because there are three alleles in the population: A, B, and O (A and B are codominant, O is recessive to both A and B).

Finally, the *sex-linked* model of inheritance only involves genes that are located on sex chromosomes, called sex-linked genes. Females and males differ in the number of genes they inherit when the gene is found on the sex chromosome; one gender inherits two copies of the gene and the other gender inherits only one (in humans, females inherit two copies of a sex-linked gene because they inherit two X chromosomes, whereas men inherit only one because they inherit an X chromosome and a Y chromosome).

Timeline

The instructional time needed to implement this lab investigation is 180–250 minutes. Appendix 2 (p. 391) provides options for implementing this lab investigation over several class periods. Option E or G (250 minutes) should be used if students are unfamiliar with scientific writing because either of these options provides extra instructional time for scaffolding the writing process. You can scaffold the writing process by modeling, providing examples, and providing hints as students write each section of the report. Option F or H (180 minutes) should be used if students are familiar with scientific writing and have the skills needed to write an investigation report on their own. In options F and H, students complete stage 6 (writing the investigation report) and stage 8 (revising the investigation report) as homework.

Materials and Preparation

The materials needed to implement this investigation are listed in Table 21.1. The *Drosophila* simulation, created by the Virtual Courseware for Inquiry-Based Science Education (VCISE) project at California State University, Los Angeles (see *www.sciencecourseware.org/vcise*), is free to use and can be run online using an internet browser. You should access the website and learn how the simulation works before beginning the lab investigation. In addition, it is important to check if students can access and use the simulation from a school computer because some schools have set up firewalls and other restrictions on web browsing.

There are two options for using this simulation: (1) you can have students use the simulation as a guest or (2) you can create an account and be given access codes for each class. The access codes allow students to save their work. If you choose to create a login for yourself and your classes, you will need to follow this procedure:

1. Go to the VCISE website (*www.sciencecourseware.org/vcise*) and create a free teacher account.
2. Log in to your new teacher account and register your classes (click "Add a New Class").
3. Provide the class code you are given to your students so they can use it when they register to use the simulation.

TABLE 21.1
Materials list

Item	Quantity
Computer with internet access	1 per group
Student handout	1 per student
Investigation proposal A or B (optional)	1 per group
Whiteboard, 2' × 3'*	1 per group
Peer-review guide and instructor scoring rubric	1 per student

* Students can also use computer and presentation software such as Microsoft PowerPoint or Apple Keynote to create their arguments.

Topics for the Explicit and Reflective Discussion

Concepts That Can Be Used to Justify the Evidence

To provide an adequate justification of their evidence, students must explain why they included the evidence in their arguments and make the assumptions underlying their analysis and interpretation of the data explicit. In this investigation, students must use various models of inheritance to help justify their evidence:

- Dominant-recessive
- Codominance
- Incomplete dominance
- Multiple allele
- Sex-linked

We recommend that you review this concept during the explicit and reflective discussion to help students make this connection.

How to Design Better Investigations

It is important for students to reflect on the strengths and weaknesses of the investigation they designed during the explicit and reflective discussion. Students should therefore be encouraged to discuss ways to eliminate potential flaws, measurement errors, or sources of bias in their investigations. To help students be more reflective about the design of their investigation, you can ask the following questions:

- What were some of the strengths of your investigation? What made it scientific?
- What were some of the weaknesses of your investigation? What made it less scientific?
- If you were to do this investigation again, what would you do to address the weaknesses in your investigation? What could you do to make it more scientific?

Crosscutting Concepts

This investigation is well aligned with two crosscutting concepts found in *A Framework for K–12 Science Education,* and you should review these concepts during the explicit and reflective discussion.

- *Systems and System Models:* Scientists often need to use explanatory models to understand complex phenomena. In this investigation, for example, students need to use the various models of inheritance to interpret the results of the test crosses that they performed using the online simulation.
- *Patterns:* Students should be reminded that, in nature, patterns have underlying causes and observed patterns can help us understand natural phenomena. In this investigation, for example, the students need to use the observed patterns in the ratio of offspring with specific traits after conducting a test cross to test their ideas about how a specific trait is inherited.

The Nature of Science and the Nature of Scientific Inquiry

It is important for students to understand the *difference between laws and theories in science.* A scientific law describes the behavior of a natural phenomenon or a generalized relationship under certain conditions; a scientific theory is a well-substantiated explanation of some aspect of the natural world. Theories do not become laws even with additional evidence; they explain laws. However, not all scientific laws have an accompanying explanatory theory. It is also important for students to understand that scientists do not discover laws or theories; the scientific community develops them over time.

You should review and provide examples of this important concept of the nature of science (NOS) and the nature of scientific inquiry (NOSI) during the explicit and reflective discussion.

Hints for Implementing the Lab

- Students should have a good understanding of the different models of inheritance before beginning this investigation. They should also know how to perform a test cross and how to set up and interpret a Punnett square.
- To learn more about the simulation, take the "tour of the simulation" when you log in as a guest or consult the simulation manual, which can be found on the tabs on the left-hand side of the window when you log in to a teacher account on the VCISE homepage (*www.sciencecourseware.org/vcise*).
- Remind students to keep detailed records of their data, and encourage the use of charts and tables!
- If you have limited access to computers (either number or time allotted), have students familiarize themselves with the simulation by taking the simulation tour outside of class time. They can access the simulation tour at home or at a library if needed.
- You can also show students how to use a chi-square test as part of this investigation. This is an excellent opportunity to introduce statistics and then teach students about statistical hypothesis testing.

Topic Connections

Table 21.2 (p. 296) provides an overview of the scientific practices, crosscutting concepts, disciplinary core ideas, and support ideas at the heart of this lab investigation. In addition, it lists NOS and NOSI concepts for the explicit and reflective discussion. Finally, it lists literacy and mathematics skills (*CCSS ELA* and *CCSS Mathematics*) that are addressed during the investigation.

TABLE 21.2

Lab 21 alignment with standards

Scientific practices	• Asking questions • Developing and using models • Planning and carrying out investigations • Analyzing and interpreting data • Using mathematics and computational thinking • Constructing explanations • Engaging in argument from evidence • Obtaining, evaluating, and communicating information
Crosscutting concepts	• Systems and system models • Patterns
Core ideas	• LS1: From molecules to organisms: Structures and processes • LS3: Heredity: Inheritance and variation of traits
Supporting ideas	• Multiple allele traits • Dominant-recessive • Incomplete dominance • Codominance • Sex-linked traits • Genotypes • Phenotypes • Test cross • Punnett squares
NOS and NOSI concept	• Scientific theories and laws
Literacy connections *(CCSS ELA)*	• Reading: Key ideas and details, craft and structure, integration of knowledge and ideas • Writing: Text types and purposes, production and distribution of writing, research to build and present knowledge, range of writing • Speaking and listening: Comprehension and collaboration, presentation of knowledge and ideas
Mathematics connections *(CCSS Mathematics)*	• Create equations that describe numbers or relationships • Solve equations and inequalitities in one variable • Reason quantitatively and use units to solve problems

Lab 21. Models of Inheritance: Which Model of Inheritance Best Explains How a Specific Trait Is Inherited in Fruit Flies?

Lab Handout

Introduction

The principles of Mendelian genetics encompass several different models of inheritance. These models include dominant-recessive, incomplete dominance, codominance, multiple allele, and sex-linked. All these models share two key ideas. First, inherited genes determine specific traits and alternative versions of a gene (called alleles) are responsible for the variation we see in traits. Second, an organism inherits two alleles for each trait, one from each parent. What makes these models different from each other is in the nature of the interactions that occur between alleles, the number of types of alleles that are associated with a gene, or which chromosome carries the gene for a trait.

The dominant-recessive model of inheritance suggests that when an individual inherits two alleles and the two alleles differ, then one is fully expressed and determines the nature of a trait (this version of the gene is called the dominant allele) while the other one has no noticeable effect (this version of the gene is called the recessive allele). The incomplete dominance model of inheritance suggests that the interaction that occurs between two different alleles results in a hybrid with an appearance somewhere between the phenotypes of the two parental varieties. The codominance model of inheritance is similar to the incomplete dominance model, but in the codominance model both alleles affect the phenotype of the individual in separate and distinguishable ways. The multiple allele model of inheritance simply means that there are more than two versions of a gene for a given trait within a population, and each allele can be either dominant, recessive, incomplete dominant, or codominant to the other alleles. Finally, the sex-linked model of inheritance only applies to genes located on the sex chromosomes. Females and males differ in the number of genes they inherit when the gene is found on the sex chromosome; one gender inherits two copies of the gene and the other gender inherits only one.

In this investigation, you will use what you have learned about these different models of inheritance to determine how fruit flies inherit a specific trait. Fruit flies are very common. Most fruit flies have six legs, two wings, and two antennae (see the figure on p. 296). Most fruit flies also have an orange-yellow body and red eyes. Scientists call flies with these traits the "wild type." Every once in a while, however, you might see a fruit fly with body and/or eyes that are different colors, such as black or yellow body and sepia (brown) or white eyes.

Male and female fruit flies

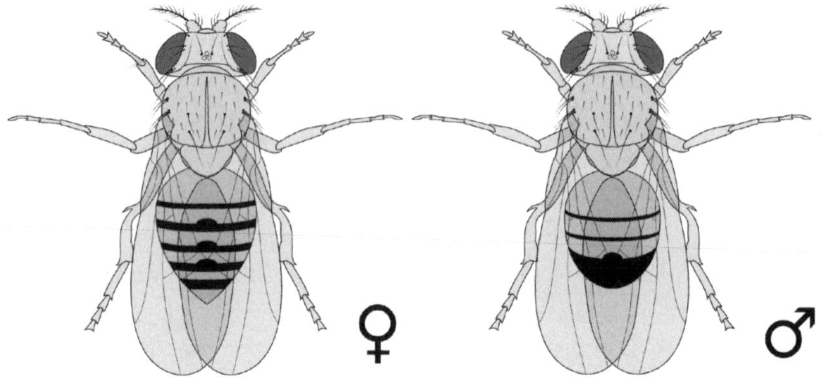

Your Task

Pick two fruit fly traits (e.g., eye color, body color, wing shape). Then you will need to determine which model of inheritance (dominant-recessive, incomplete dominance, codominance, multiple allele, or sex-linked) best explains the inheritance pattern of these two specific traits in fruit flies. To accomplish this goal, you will use an online simulation that allows you to "order" fruit flies with specific traits from a supply company and then "breed" them to see how a trait is passed down from parent to offspring.

The guiding question of this investigation is, **Which model of inheritance best explains how a specific trait is inherited in fruit flies?**

Materials

You will use an online simulation called *Drosophila* to conduct your investigation. You can access the simulation by going to the following website: *www.sciencecourseware.org/vcise/drosophila* .

Safety Precautions

1. Use caution when working with electrical equipment. Keep away from water sources in that they can cause shorts, fires, and shock hazards. Use only GFI-protected circuits.
2. Wash hands with soap and water after completing this lab.
3. Follow all normal lab safety rules.

Getting Started

Your teacher will show you how to use the Drosophila online simulation and the types of traits you will be able to investigate before you begin designing your investigation.

To answer the guiding question, you will need to determine what type of data you will need to collect using the online simulation, how you will collect these data, and how you will analyze the data. To determine *what type of data you will need to collect,* think about the following questions:

- What types of flies will you need to work with during your investigation (e.g., males or females, flies with a specific eye color, flies with a specific wing shape)?
- What type of measurements or observations will you need to record during your investigation?
- How will you determine which model of inheritance is the best explanation for a particular trait?

To determine *how you will collect your data,* think about the following questions:

- How many times will you need to breed the flies?
- How many generations of flies will you need to follow?
- How often will you collect data and when will you do it?
- How will you keep track of the data you collect and how will you organize the data?

To determine *how you will analyze your data,* think about the following questions:

- How will you determine if the results of your cross tests match your predictions? (Hint: Your teacher will show you how to use a statistical method called a chi-square test to help determine if your observations match your prediction once you have collected all your data.)
- What type of graph could you create to help make sense of your data?

Investigation Proposal Required? ☐ Yes ☐ No

Connections to Crosscutting Concepts and to the Nature of Science and Scientific Inquiry

As you work through your investigation, be sure to think about

- the importance of uncovering causes for patterns observed in nature,
- how scientists develop and use explanatory models to make sense of their observations, and
- the nature of theories and laws in science.

Argumentation Session

Once your group has finished collecting and analyzing your data, prepare a whiteboard that you can use to share your initial argument. Your whiteboard should include all the information shown in the figure below.

Argument presentation on a whiteboard

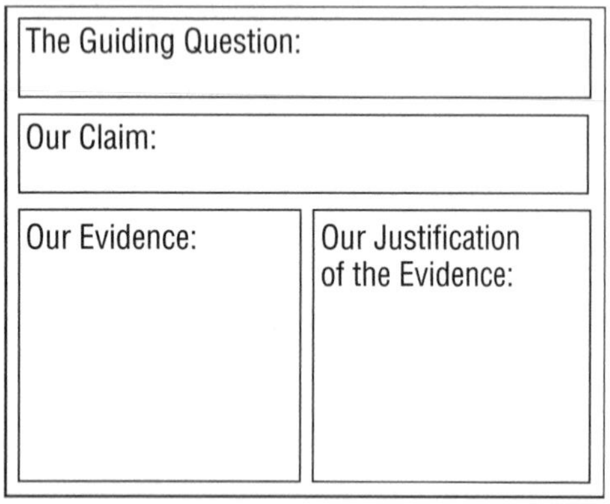

To share your argument with others, we will be using a round-robin format. This means that one member of your group will stay at your lab station to share your group's argument while the other members of your group go to the other lab stations one at a time to listen to and critique the arguments developed by your classmates.

The goal of the argumentation session is not to convince others that your argument is the best one; rather, the goal is to identify errors or instances of faulty reasoning in the arguments so these mistakes can be fixed. You will therefore need to evaluate the content of the claim, the quality of the evidence used to support the claim, and the strength of the justification of the evidence included in each argument that you see. In order to critique an argument, you will need more information than what is included on the whiteboard. You might, therefore, need to ask the presenter one or more follow-up questions, such as:

- How did you use the simulation to collect your data?
- What did you do to analyze your data? Why did you decide to do it that way? Did you check your calculations?
- Is that the only way to interpret the results of your analysis? How do you know that your interpretation of your analysis is appropriate?
- Why did your group decide to present your evidence in that manner?
- What other claims did your group discuss before you decided on that one? Why did your group abandon those alternative ideas?
- How confident are you that your claim is valid? What could you do to increase your confidence?

Once the argumentation session is complete, you will have a chance to meet with your group and revise your original argument. Your group might need to gather more data or design a way to test one or more alternative claims as part of this process. Remember, your goal at this stage of the investigation is to develop the most valid or acceptable answer to the research question!

Report

Once you have completed your research, you will need to prepare an investigation report that consists of three sections that provides answers to the following questions:

1. What question were you trying to answer and why?
2. What did you do during your investigation and why did you conduct your investigation in this way?
3. What is your argument?

Your report should answer these questions in two pages or less. This report must be typed, and any diagrams, figures, or tables should be embedded into the document. Be sure to write in a persuasive style; you are trying to convince others that your claim is acceptable or valid!

Lab 21. Models of Inheritance: Which Model of Inheritance Best Explains How a Specific Trait Is Inherited in Fruit Flies?

Checkout Questions

1. Color blindness is a sex-linked trait in humans. Both mother and father have normal color vision. Is it possible for their children to be color-blind?

   a. Yes
   b. No

   Explain why.

2. Scientific laws are theories that have been proven true.

   a. I agree with this statement.
   b. I disagree with this statement.

   Explain your answer, using information from your investigation about models of inheritance.

3. Mendelian genetics is based on the idea that gametes (reproductive cells) only get one of the two alleles that are present in the somatic (body) cells of the organism. Is this idea an example of a theory or a law?

   a. This idea is an example of a theory.
   b. This idea is an example of a law.

Explain your answer, using information from your investigation about models of inheritance.

4. Scientists often attempt to explain observed patterns in nature. Explain why they do this, using an example from your investigation about models of inheritance.

5. Scientists develop and or use models to explain complex phenomena. Explain what models are and why scientists view them as valuable, using an example from your investigation about models of inheritance.

SECTION 5

Life Sciences Core Idea 4:

Biological Evolution: Unity and Diversity

Introduction Labs

Lab 22. Biodiversity and the Fossil Record: How Has Biodiversity on Earth Changed Over Time?

Teacher Notes

Purpose

The purpose of this lab is to *introduce* students to the history of life on Earth. This lab also gives students an opportunity to use an existing data set and mathematics to answer a guiding question. Students will also learn about the difference between data and evidence and the various methods that scientists can use during an investigation.

The Content

The fossil record provides the historical archives that biologists use to study the history of life on Earth. The fossil record is a substantial but incomplete account of life on Earth because species that existed for a long period of time, were abundant and widespread, and had hard shells or skeletons are more likely to be preserved in the fossil record than species with soft bodies or ones that lived in specific locations. The *relative age* of fossils is determined using sedimentary strata, and the *absolute age* of fossils is determined using radiometric dating techniques.

The history of life involves enormous change. A variety of life forms have appeared, prospered, and gone extinct. At some points in Earth's history there were mass extinctions, when many different species went extinct in a short amount of time. Overall, life on Earth has become more diverse over time, even though extinction is so common.

In this investigation, students are asked to use a large data set to determine if the number and types of families found on Earth have changed over time; the data set includes the number of different families found in the fossil record at different points in time. This data set is a simplified version of a more comprehensive one compiled by Benton (1993, 1995) and published online at *www.fossilrecord.net*. The data set clearly illustrates how the number of types of families on Earth has, in general, increased over time. However, mass extinctions that decreased the overall number and types of families found on Earth are also evident in the data set. An example of one such mass extinction is the one that marked the end of the Triassic period (~200 million years ago).

Timeline

The instructional time needed to implement this lab investigation is 130–200 minutes. Appendix 2 (p. 391) provides options for implementing this lab investigation over several class periods. Option C (200 minutes) should be used if students are unfamiliar with scientific writing because this option provides extra instructional time for scaffolding the writing process. You can scaffold the writing process by modeling, providing examples, and providing hints as students write each section of the report. Option D (130 minutes) should be used if students are familiar with scientific writing and have the skills needed to write an investigation report on their own. In option D, students complete stage 6 (writing the investigation report) and stage 8 (revising the investigation report) as homework.

Materials and Preparation

The materials needed to implement this investigation are listed in Table 22.1. The "Diversity in the Fossil Record Data" Excel file (available at *www.nsta.org/publications/press/extras/argument.aspx*) can be loaded onto student computers before the investigation, e-mailed to students, or uploaded to a class website that students can access. It is important that Excel be available on the computers that students will use so they can analyze the data set using the tools built into the spreadsheet application. It is also important for you to look over the file before the investigation begins so you can learn how the data in the file are organized. This will enable you to give students suggestions on how to analyze the data.

TABLE 22.1

Materials list

Item	Quantity
Computer with Excel application	1 per group
Student handout	1 per student
Investigation proposal B*	1 per group
Whiteboard, 2' × 3'†	1 per group
Peer-review guide and instructor scoring rubric	1 per student

*We highly recommend that students fill out an investigation proposal for this lab, because of the unique nature of the data and the three hypotheses.

† Students can also use computer and presentation software such as Microsoft PowerPoint or Apple Keynote to create their arguments.

Topics for the Explicit and Reflective Discussion

Concepts That Can Be Used to Justify the Evidence

To provide an adequate justification of their evidence, students must explain why they included the evidence in their arguments and make the assumptions underlying their analysis and interpretation of the data explicit. In this investigation, students can use the following concepts to help justify their evidence:

- Biodiversity
- The nature of the biological classification scheme
- The characteristics of the fossil record

We recommend that you review these concepts during the explicit and reflective discussion to help students make this connection.

How to Design Better Investigations

It is important for students to reflect on the strengths and weaknesses of the investigation they designed during the explicit and reflective discussion. Students should therefore be encouraged to discuss ways to eliminate potential flaws, measurement errors, or sources of bias in their investigations. To help students be more reflective about the design of their investigation, you can ask the following questions:

- What were some of the strengths of your investigation? What made it scientific?
- What were some of the weaknesses of your investigation? What made it less scientific?
- If you were to do this investigation again, what would you do to address the weaknesses in your investigation? What could you do to make it more scientific?

Crosscutting Concepts

This investigation is well aligned with two crosscutting concepts found in *A Framework for K–12 Science Education*, and you should review these concepts during the explicit and reflective discussion.

- *Patterns:* Students should be reminded that, in nature, patterns have underlying causes and observed patterns can help us understand natural phenomena. In this investigation, for example, the students need to look for patterns in the fossil record to determine how biodiversity has changed over time.
- *Scale, Proportion, and Quantity:* In science, it is important to think about what is relevant and what is irrelevant at different time scales and to look for proportional relationships across scales.

The Nature of Science and the Nature of Scientific Inquiry

It is important for students to understand the *difference between data and evidence in science.* Data are measurements, observations, and findings from other studies that are collected as part of an investigation. Evidence, in contrast, is analyzed data and an interpretation of the analysis. In this investigation, students are provided with data (presence or absence of different families at different times in the fossil record) and need to transform the data into evidence. To accomplish this task, students have to analyze the data and then interpret the results of that analysis.

It is also important for students to understand that *scientists use different methods to answer different types of questions.* Examples of methods include experiments, systematic observations of a phenomenon, literature reviews, and analysis of existing data sets; the choice of method depends on the objectives of the research. There is no universal step-by step scientific method that all scientists follow; rather, different scientific disciplines (e.g., biology vs. physics) and fields within a discipline (e.g., ecology vs. molecular biology) use different types of methods, use different core theories, and rely on different standards to develop scientific knowledge. In this investigation, for example, students conduct an analysis of an existing data set to test the merits of the alternative hypotheses; they do not design and carry out an experiment.

You should review and provide examples of these two important concepts of the nature of science (NOS) and the nature of scientific inquiry (NOSI) during the explicit and reflective discussion.

Hints for Implementing the Lab

- When introducing the investigation, show the students what the data set looks like and explain how it is set up. Be sure to indicate and review what each column shows (e.g., the far-left column represents families, *not* species). A "1" indicates that there is at least one representative fossil from that family in that time period. It is also important to show students how to use Excel to fill in missing values, use the formula tools, and create graphs.
- Even if students have written an investigation proposal before, they will most likely struggle to write an investigation proposal for this investigation. Make sure they understand that they must make predictions about what the fossil record should include based on the assumption that each hypothesis is valid.
- Students' evidence should not only support the hypothesis they think is most valid but also falsify the other hypotheses.
- Because there is limited information in the data set, you may want students to use outside sources as well. If you decide to do that, be sure to review what good sources include and discuss how you would like them to cite their sources (e.g., *Publication Manual of the American Psychological Manual* [American Psychological Association 2010] is frequently used in science).

Topic Connections

Table 22.2 provides an overview of the scientific practices, crosscutting concepts, disciplinary core ideas, and support ideas at the heart of this lab investigation. In addition, it lists NOS and NOSI concepts for the explicit and reflective discussion. Finally, it lists literacy and mathematics skills (*CCSS ELA* and *CCSS Mathematics*) that are addressed during the investigation.

TABLE 22.2

Lab 22 alignment with standards

Scientific practices	• Asking questions • Planning and carrying out investigations • Analyzing and interpreting data • Using mathematics and computational thinking • Constructing explanations • Engaging in argument from evidence • Obtaining, evaluating, and communicating information
Crosscutting concepts	• Patterns • Scale, proportion, and quantity
Core idea	• LS4: Biological evolution: Unity and diversity
Supporting ideas	• History of life • Biodiversity • Biological classification • Fossil record
NOS and NOSI concepts	• Difference between data and evidence • Methods used in scientific investigations
Literacy connections *(CCSS ELA)*	• *Reading*: Key ideas and details, craft and structure, integration of knowledge and ideas • *Writing*: Text types and purposes, production and distribution of writing, research to build and present knowledge, range of writing • *Speaking and listening*: Comprehension and collaboration, presentation of knowledge and ideas
Mathematics connection *(CCSS Mathematics)*	• Reason quantitatively and use units to solve problems

References

American Psychological Association (APA). 2010. *Publication manual of the American Psychological Association.* 6th ed. Washington, DC: APA.

Benton, M. J. 1993. *The fossil record 2.* London: Chapman & Hall.

Benton, M. J. 1995. Diversification and extinction in the history of life. *Science* 268: 52–58.

Lab 22. Biodiversity and the Fossil Record: How Has Biodiversity on Earth Changed Over Time?

Lab Handout

Introduction

Biodiversity refers to the variation in life forms found on Earth. Biodiversity can be measured in two different ways. The first is richness, which refers to the total number of different life forms. The second is relative abundance, which is a measure of how common each type of life form is in a given area. In terms of richness, Earth is high in biodiversity—biologists have identified approximately 1.5 million different types of life forms, and some biologists think that the actual number of different life forms on Earth is at least 7 million.

To help organize and make sense of this biodiversity, biologists use a nested classification scheme. This system (see the figure to the right) starts with species as the foundational unit of classification. A species is often defined as a group of organisms capable of interbreeding and producing fertile offspring. Each species can then be placed into a larger group called a genus, based on similarities in traits. Each genus can then be placed into a larger group called a family. Families, in turn, can be grouped together to create an order; and so on.

The biological classification scheme

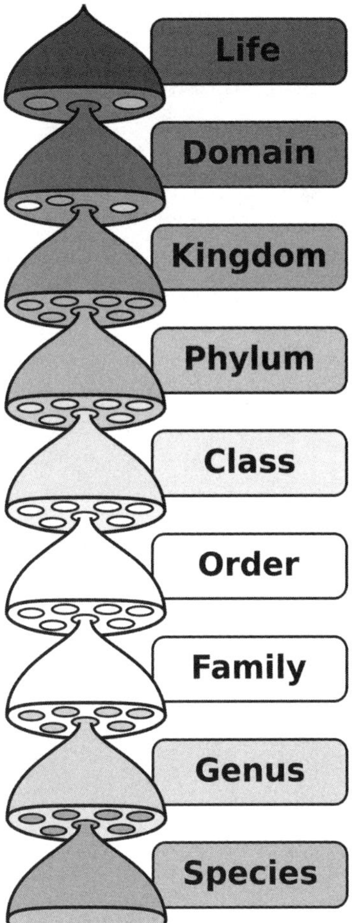

There have been several different hypotheses offered to explain the source of all the biodiversity on Earth and the amount of biodiversity found on Earth over time. Here are three of these hypotheses:

1. All life on Earth appeared at the same time in Earth's history. As a result, biodiversity has remained the same throughout Earth's history.
2. Present-day forms of life arose from other forms of life over a considerable amount of time. As a result, biodiversity has increased throughout Earth's history.
3. All life on Earth appeared at the same time in Earth's history. However, current life forms are the survivors of one or more catastrophic events that wiped out many of the other life forms that once inhabited the Earth. As a result, biodiversity has decreased throughout Earth's history.

You can evaluate the merits of these three hypotheses by determining if they are consistent with what is found in the fossil record. Scientists, over many years, have collected data about the history of life on Earth. These data include the collection, classification, and dating of fossils. This information allows scientists to determine what the conditions were like on Earth in the past and when major events occurred in the history of life. It is important to note, however, that the fossil record provides only an incomplete picture of what life on Earth was like in the past. Although the fossil record is substantial, it is incomplete because life forms that are abundant, widespread, and have hard shells or skeletons are more likely to be preserved as fossils than are life forms that are rare, live in only specific locations, or have soft bodies. The fossil record, therefore, can only provide limited information about the history of life on Earth.

Your Task

Determine if the fossil record supports any of the three hypotheses listed above.

The guiding question of this investigation is, **How has biodiversity on Earth changed over time?**

Materials

You will use an Excel file called "Diversity in the Fossil Record Data," which can be found at *www.nsta.org/publications/press/extras/argument.aspx*, in your investigation.

Safety Precautions

1. Use caution when working with electrical equipment. Keep away from water sources in that they can cause shorts, fires and shock hazards. Use only GFI protected circuits.
2. Wash hands with soap and water after completing this lab.
3. Follow all normal lab safety rules.

Getting Started

The data file that you will use during this investigation comes from the Fossil Record website (*www.fossilrecord.net*). The Excel data file is a simplified version of the original Fossil Record 2 Excel file, which can be downloaded from the website. The Fossil Record 2 is a near-complete listing of the diversity of life through time, compiled at the level of the family by Mary Benton and originally published as a book in 1993. In biology, the term family refers to a taxonomic rank that falls between order and genus. The levels of classification include species, genus, family, order, class, phylum, and kingdom. For example, the Bonobo (*Pan paniscus*) is a part of the genus Pan, the family Hominidae, the order Primates, the class Mammalia, the phylum Chordata, and the kingdom Animalia. Many different species make up a particular family.

In the data file, there are tabs for 10 different classes of organisms (Mammalia, Reptilia, Amphibia, and so on). Each tab includes information about all the families within that class that have been found in the fossil record. The dates represent the midpoint of different geologic stages. For example, 0.001 mya is the midpoint of the Holocene stage and 0.8 mya is the midpoint of the Pleistocene stage. The number 1 in a cell indicates that a fossil belonging to that particular family has been found for that time period. A question mark (?) in a cell indicates that a fossil is likely to be found for a specific time period (because there are fossils from that family in earlier and later time periods) but has not been discovered yet. Cells that are blank indicate that there are no fossils from that family in that time period.

Investigation Proposal Required? ☐ Yes ☐ No

Connections to Crosscutting Concepts and to the Nature of Science and the Nature of Scientific Inquiry

As you work through your investigation, be sure to think about

- the importance of looking for patterns in nature,
- the importance of considering what is and what is not relevant at different scales of time,
- the difference between data and evidence in science, and
- the different types of methods that scientists use to answer questions.

Argumentation Session

Once your group has finished collecting and analyzing your data, prepare a whiteboard that you can use to share your initial argument. Your whiteboard should include all the information shown in the figure to the right.

Argument presentation on a whiteboard

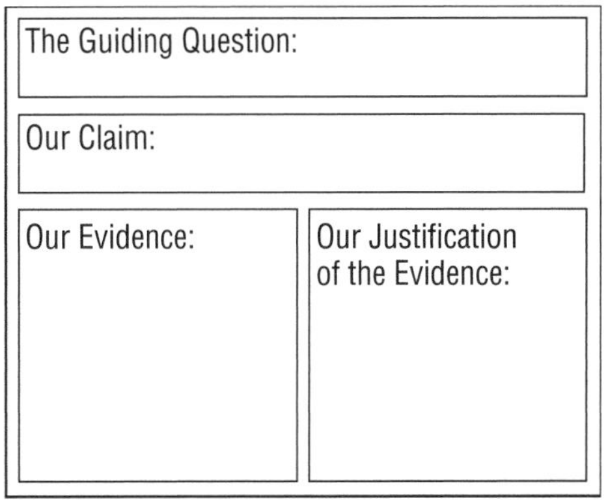

To share your argument with others, we will be using a round-robin format. This means that one member of your group will stay at your lab station to share your group's argument while the other members of your group go to the other lab stations one at a time to listen to and critique the arguments developed by your classmates.

The goal of the argumentation session is not to convince others that your argument is the best one;

rather, the goal is to identify errors or instances of faulty reasoning in the arguments so these mistakes can be fixed. You will therefore need to evaluate the content of the claim, the quality of the evidence used to support the claim, and the strength of the justification of the evidence included in each argument that you see. In order to critique an argument, you will need more information than what is included on the whiteboard. You might, therefore, need to ask the presenter one or more follow-up questions, such as:

- Why did you decide to focus on those data?
- What did you do to analyze your data? Why did you decide to do it that way? Did you check your calculations?
- Is that the only way to interpret the results of your analysis? How do you know that your interpretation of your analysis is appropriate?
- Why did your group decide to present your evidence in that manner?
- What other claims did your group discuss before you decided on that one? Why did your group abandon those alternative ideas?
- How confident are you that your claim is valid? What could you do to increase your confidence?

Once the argumentation session is complete, you will have a chance to meet with your group and revise your original argument. Your group might need to gather more data or design a way to test one or more alternative claims as part of this process. Remember, your goal at this stage of the investigation is to develop the most valid or acceptable answer to the research question!

Report

Once you have completed your research, you will need to prepare an investigation report that consists of three sections that provide answers to the following questions:

1. What question were you trying to answer and why?
2. What did you do during your investigation and why did you conduct your investigation in this way?
3. What is your argument?

Your report should answer these questions in two pages or less. This report must be typed, and any diagrams, figures, or tables should be embedded into the document. Be sure to write in a persuasive style; you are trying to convince others that your claim is acceptable or valid!

Lab 22. Biodiversity and the Fossil Record: How Has Biodiversity on Earth Changed Over Time?

Checkout Questions

1. What does the fossil record suggest about how biodiversity on Earth has changed over time?

2. Evidence is data that have been collected by a scientist.

    a. I agree with this statement.
    b. I disagree with this statement.

    Explain your answer, using examples from your investigation about the fossil record.

3. Using an existing data set to test several hypotheses is an example of an experiment.

    a. I agree with this statement.
    b. I disagree with this statement.

    Explain your answer, using information from your investigation about the fossil record.

4. Scientists often need to determine what is and what is not relevant at different time scales. Explain why this is important in science, using an example from your investigation about the fossil record.

5. Scientists often attempt to identify patterns in nature. Explain why the identification of patterns is useful in science, using an example from your investigation about the fossil record.

Lab 23. Mechanisms of Evolution: Why Will the Characteristics of a Bug Population Change in Different Ways in Response to Different Types of Predation?

Teacher Notes

Purpose

The purpose of this lab is to *introduce* students to the effects of predation on the characteristics of a population and the basic principles of natural selection. This lab also gives students an opportunity to use a simulation to develop an explanation for a natural phenomenon. The simulation, called *Bug Hunt Speeds* (Novak and Wilensky 2005), was created using NetLogo, a multiagent programmable modeling environment developed at the Center for Connected Learning and Computer-Based Modeling at Northwestern University (Wilensky 1999). Students will also learn about the difference between observations and inferences and the various methods that scientists can use during an investigation.

The Content

Natural selection is a mechanism that drives the change in the characteristics of a population. The basic tenets of natural selection are as follows (Lawson 1995):

- Only a fraction of the individuals that make up a population survive long enough to reproduce.
- The individuals in a population are not all the same. Individuals have traits that make them unique.
- Much, but not all, of this variation in traits is inheritable and can therefore be passed down from parent to offspring.
- The environment, including both abiotic (e.g., temperature, amount of water available) and biotic (e.g., amount of food, presence of predators) factors, determines which traits are favorable or unfavorable because some traits increase an individual's chance of survival and others do not.
- Individuals with favorable traits tend to produce more offspring than those with unfavorable traits. Therefore, over time, favorable traits become more common within a population found in a particular environment (and unfavorable traits become less common).

To learn more about natural selection and the role it plays in evolution, we recommend visiting the Understanding Evolution website at *http://evolution.berkeley.edu/evolibrary/home.*

php. This website was created by the University of California Museum of Paleontology and is an excellent resource for teachers and students.

Timeline

The instructional time needed to implement this lab investigation is 130–200 minutes. Appendix 2 (p. 391) provides options for implementing this lab investigation over several class periods. Option C (200 minutes) should be used if students are unfamiliar with scientific writing because this option provides extra instructional time for scaffolding the writing process. You can scaffold the writing process by modeling, providing examples, and providing hints as students write each section of the report. Option D (130 minutes) should be used if students are familiar with scientific writing and have the skills needed to write an investigation report on their own. In option D, students complete stage 6 (writing the investigation report) and stage 8 (revising the investigation report) as homework.

Materials and Preparation

The materials needed to implement this investigation are listed in Table 23.1. The *Bug Hunt Speeds* simulation, available at *http://ccl.northwestern.edu/netlogo/models/BugHuntSpeeds*, is free to use and can be run online using an internet browser. You should access the simulation and learn how it works before beginning the lab investigation. In addition, it is important to check if students can access and use the simulation from a school computer because some schools have set up firewalls and other restrictions on web browsing.

Since this is an "introduction" lab, students do not have any formal instruction about evolution or the mechanisms of evolution before the lab.

TABLE 23.1
Materials list

Item	Quantity
Computer with internet access	At least 1 per group
Student handout	1 per student
Investigation proposal A*	1 per group
Whiteboard, 2' × 3'†	1 per group
Peer-review guide and instructor scoring rubric	1 per student

* We highly recommend that students fill out an investigation proposal for this lab.

† Students can also use computer and presentation software such as Microsoft PowerPoint or Apple Keynote to create their arguments.

Topics for the Explicit and Reflective Discussion

Concepts That Can Be Used to Justify the Evidence

To provide an adequate justification of their evidence, students must explain why they included the evidence in their arguments and make the assumptions underlying their analysis and interpretation of the data explicit. In this investigation, students can use the following concepts to help justify their evidence:

- Population dynamics
- Predation
- Genetic basis of inheritance

We recommend that you review these concepts during the explicit and reflective discussion to help students make this connection.

How to Design Better Investigations

It is important for students to reflect on the strengths and weaknesses of the investigation they designed during the explicit and reflective discussion. Students should therefore be encouraged to discuss ways to eliminate potential flaws, measurement errors, or sources of bias in their investigations. To help students be more reflective about the design of their investigation, you can ask the following questions:

- What were some of the strengths of your investigation? What made it scientific?
- What were some of the weaknesses of your investigation? What made it less scientific?
- If you were to do this investigation again, what would you do to address the weaknesses in your investigation? What could you do to make it more scientific?

Crosscutting Concepts

This investigation is well aligned with two crosscutting concepts found in *A Framework for K–12 Science Education*, and you should review these concepts during the explicit and reflective discussion.

- *Patterns:* Students should be reminded that patterns in nature have underlying causes, and observed patterns can help us understand natural phenomena. In this investigation, for example, the students needed to look for patterns in the ways the bug populations change over time.
- *Cause and Effect: Mechanism and Explanation:* An important goal of science is to uncover the underlying cause for a natural phenomenon.

The Nature of Science and the Nature of Scientific Inquiry

It is important for students to understand the *difference between observations and inferences in science*. An observation is a descriptive statement about a natural phenomenon, whereas an inference is an interpretation of an observation. Students should also understand that current scientific knowledge and the perspectives of individual scientists guide both observations and inferences. Thus, different scientists can have different but equally valid interpretations of the same observations due to differences in their perspectives and background knowledge. In this investigation, for example, different groups decide to make different observations and then interpret them in different ways based on what they know.

It is also important for students to understand that *scientists use different methods to answer different types of questions*. Examples of methods include experiments, systematic observations of a phenomenon, literature reviews, and analysis of existing data sets; the choice of method depends on the objectives of the research. There is no universal step-by-step scientific method that all scientists follow; rather, different scientific disciplines (e.g., biology vs. physics) and fields within a discipline (e.g., ecology vs. molecular biology) use different types of methods, use different core theories, and rely on different standards to develop scientific knowledge. In this investigation, for example, students conduct an analysis of an existing data set to test the merits of the alternative hypotheses; they do not design and carry out an experiment.

You should review and provide examples of these two important concepts of the nature of science (NOS) and the nature of scientific inquiry (NOSI) during the explicit and reflective discussion.

Hints for Implementing the Lab

- Learn how to use the simulation before the lab begins. It is important for you to know how to use the simulation so you can help students when they get stuck or confused.
- A group of three students per computer tends to work well.
- Allow the students to play with the simulation as part of the tool talk before they fill out an investigation proposal. This gives students a chance to see what they can and cannot do with the simulation.
- Be sure that students record actual values (e.g., number of bugs with specific traits at a given point in time) when they run a simulation, rather than just attempting to hand draw the graph that they see on the computer screen.
- This investigation provides a great introduction to natural selection. We recommend that you explain this important concept after this lab is complete and then use this investigation to illustrate each of the major tenets of natural selection.

Topic Connections

Table 23.2 provides an overview of the scientific practices, crosscutting concepts, disciplinary core ideas, and support ideas at the heart of this lab investigation. In addition, it lists NOS and NOSI concepts for the explicit and reflective discussion. Finally, it lists literacy and mathematics skills (*CCSS ELA* and *CCSS Mathematics*) that are addressed during the investigation.

TABLE 23.2

Lab 23 alignment with standards

Scientific practices	• Asking questions • Developing and using models • Planning and carrying out investigations • Analyzing and interpreting data • Using mathematics and computational thinking • Constructing explanations • Engaging in argument from evidence • Obtaining, evaluating, and communicating information
Crosscutting concepts	• Patterns • Cause and effect: Mechanisms and explanation
Core ideas	• LS2: Ecosystems: Interactions, energy, and dynamics • LS3: Heredity: Inheritance and variation of traits • LS4: Biological evolution: Unity and diversity
Supporting ideas	• Ecosystems • Predation • Predators • Prey • Population • Natural selection
NOS and NOSI concepts	• Observations and inferences • Methods used in scientific investigations
Literacy connections *(CCSS ELA)*	• *Reading*: Key ideas and details, craft and structure, integration of knowledge and ideas • *Writing*: Text types and purposes, production and distribution of writing, research to build and present knowledge, range of writing • *Speaking and listening*: Comprehension and collaboration, presentation of knowledge and ideas
Mathematics connection *(CCSS Mathematics)*	• Reason quantitatively and use units to solve problems

References

Lawson, A. 1995. *Science teaching and the development of thinking*. Belmont, CA: Wadsworth.

Novak, M., and U. Wilensky. 2005. NetLogo Bug Hunt Speeds model. Evanston, IL: Center for Connected Learning and Computer-Based Modeling, Northwestern Institute on Complex Systems, Northwestern University. *http://ccl.northwestern.edu/netlogo/models/BugHuntSpeeds.*

Wilensky, U. 1999. NetLogo. Evanston, IL: Center for Connected Learning and Computer-Based Modeling, Northwestern Institute on Complex Systems, Northwestern University. *http://ccl.northwestern.edu/netlogo.*

Lab 23. Mechanisms of Evolution: Why Will the Characteristics of a Bug Population Change in Different Ways in Response to Different Types of Predation?

Lab Handout

Introduction

The various components of an ecosystem are all connected. Plants depend on the abiotic resources of an ecosystem to produce the food they need to grow, herbivores eat these plants, and carnivores eat the herbivores. Thus, a change in the amount of abiotic resources available or a change in the size of any one of these populations of organisms can influence the size of the other populations found in that ecosystem. A drought, for example, could reduce the size of the plant population. A decrease in the size of the plant population results in less food for the herbivores. When herbivores do not have enough food to eat, the death rate of the population increases, which, in turn, results in fewer herbivores. The size of the carnivore population, as a result, begins to shrink because there is not enough food available.

In addition to influencing the size of a population, the interactions that take place between the organisms found within an ecosystem can actually change the characteristics of some populations. Some of the characteristics that can be influenced by these interactions include the ratio of males to females in a population or the ratio of juveniles to adults in the population. Other characteristics that can be influenced by population interactions include the proportion of individuals within a population that have a specific trait or the average height or weight of the members of that population. It is therefore important for biologists to understand how different types of interactions can result in a change in the characteristics of a population.

One type of interaction that can result in a change in the characteristics of a population is predation. Predation often has a strong influence on the characteristics of a prey population. For example, a population of herbivores that lives in an area with a lot of predators will often have different characteristics than a population of herbivores that lives in an area with few or no predators. The hunting strategy used by the predator will also have an influence on the characteristics of a prey population. For example, a herbivore population that is eaten by a predator that chases its prey and a herbivore population that is eaten by a predator that hunts by sitting and waiting for its prey will often have different characteristics. Biologists often study how the characteristics of a specific prey population change in response to a specific type of predation, to understand how different types of interactions can result in a change in the characteristics of a population.

LAB 23

Your Task

Use a computer simulation called *Bug Hunt Speed* to explore how a population of a "bug" responds to the influence of two different types of predators. You will then develop an explanation for the changes you observe in the bug population. Your explanation must outline a mechanism that will cause the characteristics of a prey population to change in different ways in response to different types of predation.

The guiding question of this investigation is, **Why will the characteristics of a bug population change in different ways in response to different types of predation?**

Materials

You will use an online simulation called *Bug Hunt Speed* to conduct your investigation. You can access the simulation by going to the following website: *http://ccl.northwestern.edu/netlogo/models/BugHuntSpeeds.*

Safety Precautions

1. Use caution when working with electrical equipment. Keep away from water sources in that they can cause shorts, fires and shock hazards. Use only GFI protected circuits.
2. Wash hands with soap and water after completing this lab.
3. Follow all normal lab safety rules.

Getting Started

Bug Hunt Speed simulates a population of bugs that all belong to the same species. All the bugs in this population, however, are different, even though they belong to the same species. The bugs vary in terms of color, how fast they move, if they wiggle or not, and if they flee from predators when one is nearby.

In this simulation, you will act as the predator. You are able to eat the bugs (your prey) by clicking on them. You can act as a "hunting" predator by moving the mouse around to catch the bugs, or you can act as a "sit and wait" predator by keeping the mouse in one place and then catching the bugs that come to you. When a bug is eaten, it is replaced through reproduction by a bug in the simulated ecosystem. The new bug, therefore, will have the same characteristics as a bug that has not been eaten yet. Remember, all of the bugs in the ecosystem are from the same species.

The simulation also allows you to adjust the characteristics of the bugs. You can use the menus on the left of the screen to determine the color scheme for the bugs, the initial number of bugs in the habitat, if the bugs wiggle or not, and if they "flee" from a predator or not (see the figure on the opposite page).

A screen shot from the *Bug Hunt Speed* simulation

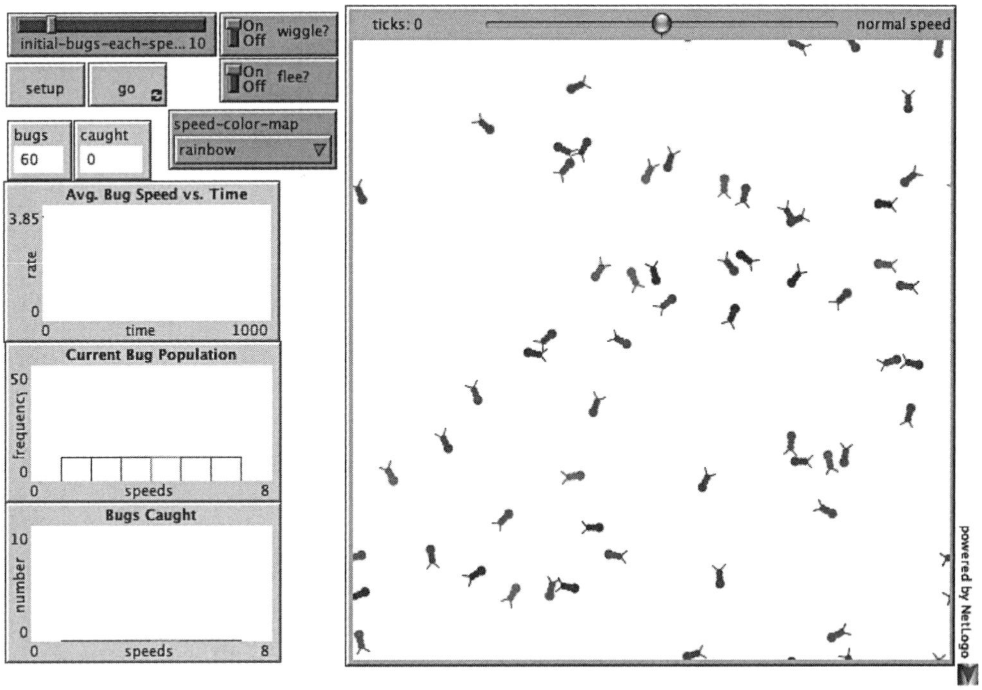

To answer the guiding question, you must determine what type of data you will need to collect, how you will collect it, and how you will analyze it. To determine *what type of data you will need to collect,* think about the following questions:

- How will you determine if the characteristics of the bug population change over time?
- How will you test your explanation for the changes you observe in the population of bugs?
- What will serve as your dependent variable (e.g., color, speed, number of bugs caught)?
- What type of measurements or observations will you need to record during your investigation?

To determine *how you will collect your data,* think about the following questions:

- What will serve as a control condition (e.g., no predation)?
- What types of treatment conditions will you need to set up and how will you do it?
- How many trials will you need to conduct?
- How long will you need to run the simulation during each trial (e.g., for three minutes or until 60 bugs are caught)?

- How often will you collect data and when will you do it?
- How will you keep track of the data you collect and how will you organize the data?

To determine *how you will analyze your data,* think about the following questions:

- How will you determine if there is a difference between the different treatment conditions and the control condition?
- What type of calculations will you need to make?
- What type of graph could you create to help make sense of your data?

Investigation Proposal Required? ☐ Yes ☐ No

Connections to Crosscutting Concepts and to the Nature of Science and the Nature of Scientific Inquiry

As you work through your investigation, be sure to think about

- the importance of looking for patterns in nature,
- the importance of developing causal explanations for natural phenomena,
- the different types of methods that scientists use to answer questions, and
- the difference between observations and inferences.

Argumentation Session

Once your group has finished collecting and analyzing your data, prepare a whiteboard that you can use to share your initial argument. Your whiteboard should include all the information shown in the figure below.

Argument presentation on a whiteboard

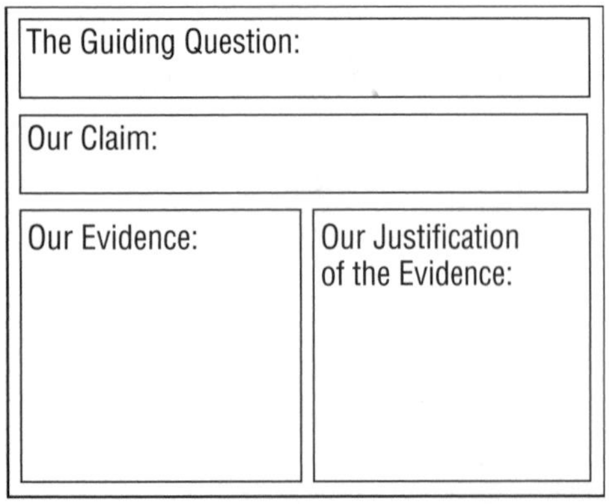

To share your argument with others, we will be using a round-robin format. This means that one member of your group will stay at your lab station to share your group's argument while the other members of your group go to the other lab stations one at a time to listen to and critique the arguments developed by your classmates.

The goal of the argumentation session is not to convince others that your argument is the best one; rather, the goal is to identify errors or instances of faulty reasoning in the arguments so these mistakes can be fixed. You will therefore need to evaluate the content of the claim, the quality of the evidence used to support the claim, and the strength of the justification of the evidence included in each argument that you see. In order to critique an argument, you will need more information than what is included on the whiteboard. You might, therefore, need to ask the presenter one or more follow-up questions, such as:

- How did you use the simulation to collect your data?
- What did you do to analyze your data? Why did you decide to do it that way? Did you check your calculations?
- Is that the only way to interpret the results of your analysis? How do you know that your interpretation of your analysis is appropriate?
- Why did your group decide to present your evidence in that manner?
- What other claims did your group discuss before you decided on that one? Why did your group abandon those alternative ideas?
- How confident are you that your claim is valid? What could you do to increase your confidence?

Once the argumentation session is complete, you will have a chance to meet with your group and revise your original argument. Your group might need to gather more data or design a way to test one or more alternative claims as part of this process. Remember, your goal at this stage of the investigation is to develop the most valid or acceptable answer to the research question!

Report

Once you have completed your research, you will need to prepare an investigation report that consists of three sections that provide answers to the following questions:

1. What question were you trying to answer and why?
2. What did you do during your investigation and why did you conduct your investigation in this way?
3. What is your argument?

Your report should answer these questions in two pages or less. This report must be typed, and any diagrams, figures, or tables should be embedded into the document. Be sure to write in a persuasive style; you are trying to convince others that your claim is acceptable or valid!

Lab 23. Mechanisms of Evolution: Why Will the Characteristics of a Bug Population Change in Different Ways in Response to Different Types of Predation?

Checkout Questions

1. There are two varieties of moles, brown and white, living on an island. They are a source of food for the owls. The island recently had a volcanic eruption and is now covered with dark ash, dark volcanic rock, and some soil. What will be the effect on the mole population over time?

2. Scientists often make different inferences based on the same observations.

   a. I agree with this statement.
   b. I disagree with this statement.

   Explain your answer, using information from your investigation about the mechanisms of evolution.

3. All scientists use the same method to test their ideas.

   a. I agree with this statement.

b. I disagree with this statement.

Explain your answer, using examples from your investigation about the mechanisms of evolution.

4. Scientists often attempt to identify patterns in nature. Explain why the identification of patterns is useful in science, using an example from your investigation about the mechanisms of evolution.

5. An important goal in science is to develop explanations for natural phenomena. Explain why the development of explanations is so important in science, using an example from your investigation about the mechanisms of evolution.

Application Labs

Lab 24. Descent With Modification: Does Mammalian Brain Structure Support or Refute the Theory of Descent With Modification?

Teacher Notes

Purpose

The purpose of this lab is for students to *apply* what they have learned about the theory of descent with modification to explain similarities in mammalian brain structure. This lab also gives students an opportunity to use an online database to test a fundamental idea in biology. Students will also learn about how science as a body of knowledge develops over time and the various methods that scientists can use during an investigation.

The Content

Biological evolution is defined as descent with modification. This definition includes both *small-scale evolution,* which refers to a change in gene frequency from one generation to the next, and *large-scale evolution,* which refers to the descent of different species from a common ancestor over many generations. The central idea of descent with modification is that all life on Earth shares a common ancestor. All organisms on Earth, as a result, share some features. Organisms also have *shared derived characters*. A shared derived character is one that developed or appeared at some point in the evolutionary history of an organism and is shared by other closely related organisms but not by distantly related organisms. Shared derived characteristics, such as the folds found on the surface of some mammalian brains or a large cerebellum, allow biologists to determine how closely related an organism is to other organisms. Two organisms that have many shared derived characters in common are considered to be more closely related than two organisms that have few shared derived characters in common.

Timeline

The instructional time needed to implement this lab investigation is 180–250 minutes. Appendix 2 (p. 391) provides options for implementing this lab investigation over several class periods. Option G (250 minutes) should be used if students are unfamiliar with scientific writing because this option provides extra instructional time for scaffolding the writing process. You can scaffold the writing process by modeling, providing examples, and providing hints as students write each section of the report. Option H (180 minutes) should be used if students are familiar with scientific writing and have the skills needed to write an investigation report on their own. In option H, students complete stage 6 (writing the investigation report) and stage 8 (revising the investigation report) as homework.

Materials and Preparation

The materials needed to implement this investigation are listed in Table 24.1. The online database Comparative Mammalian Brain Collections, which is sponsored by the University of Wisconsin, Michigan State University, and the National Museum of Health and Medicine, is free to use and available online at *http://brainmuseum.org*. You should access the database and learn how it works before beginning the lab investigation. In addition, it is important to check if students can access and use the database from a school computer, because some schools have set up firewalls and other restrictions on web browsing.

TABLE 24.1

Materials list

Item	Quantity
Computer with internet access	At least 1 per group
Student handout	1 per student
Investigation proposal A*	1 per group
Whiteboard, 2' × 3'†	1 per group
Peer-review guide and instructor scoring rubric	1 per student

* We highly recommend that students fill out an investigation proposal for this lab.

† Students can also use computer and presentation software such as Microsoft PowerPoint or Apple Keynote to create their arguments.

Topics for the Explicit and Reflective Discussion

Concepts That Can Be Used to Justify the Evidence

To provide an adequate justification of their evidence, students must explain why they included the evidence in their arguments and make the assumptions underlying their analysis and interpretation of the data explicit. Students will therefore need to highlight specific predictions that are consistent with the theory of descent with modification to justify their evidence.

How to Design Better Investigations

It is important for students to reflect on the strengths and weaknesses of the investigation they designed during the explicit and reflective discussion. Students should therefore be encouraged to discuss ways to eliminate potential flaws, measurement errors, or sources of bias in their investigations. To help students be more reflective about the design of their investigation, you can ask the following questions:

- What were some of the strengths of your investigation? What made it scientific?
- What were some of the weaknesses of your investigation? What made it less scientific?
- If you were to do this investigation again, what would you do to address the weaknesses in your investigation? What could you do to make it more scientific?

Crosscutting Concepts

This investigation is well aligned with two crosscutting concepts found in *A Framework for K–12 Science Education*, and you should review these concepts during the explicit and reflective discussion.

- *Scale, Proportion, and Quantity:* When analyzing data, it is often important for scientists to look for and recognize proportional relationships in natural phenomena. In this investigation, for example, students need to compare the ratio of a brain structure to overall brain size rather than absolute size in order to make fair comparisons across different-size mammals.
- *Structure and Function:* Students need to understand that a way an object is shaped determines its properties and how it functions. For example, in this investigation students should understand that brain size and shape provide information about the behavior of different mammals.

The Nature of Science and the Nature of Scientific Inquiry

It is important for students to understand how *science as a body of knowledge develops over time*. A person can have confidence in the validity of scientific knowledge but must also accept that scientific knowledge may be abandoned or modified in light of new evidence or because existing evidence has been reconceptualized by scientists. There are many examples in the history of science of both evolutionary changes (i.e., the slow or gradual refinement of ideas) and revolutionary changes (i.e., the rapid abandonment of a well-established idea) in scientific knowledge. Some scientific ideas, however, are so well established and supported by so many lines of evidence that they are unlikely to be completely overturned. An example of such a theory is descent with modification.

It is also important for students to understand that *scientists use different methods to answer different types of questions*. Examples of methods include experiments, systematic observations of a phenomenon, literature reviews, and analysis of existing data sets; the choice of method depends on the objectives of the research. There is no universal step-by-step scientific method that all scientists follow; rather, different scientific disciplines (e.g., biology vs. physics) and fields within a discipline (e.g., ecology vs. molecular biology) use different types of methods, use different core theories, and rely on different standards to develop scientific knowledge. In this investigation, for example, students conduct an analysis of an existing data set to test the validity of descent with modification; they do not design and carry out an experiment.

You should review and provide examples of these two important concepts of the nature of science (NOS) and the nature of scientific inquiry (NOSI) in the explicit and reflective discussion.

Hints for Implementing the Lab

- Be sure to allow each group to play around with the online database as part of the tool talk before they design their investigation. Students will be able to design a better investigation if they understand what information they can and cannot access from the database.
- Many suggestions for student data collection are found on the student handout. Encourage students to use those suggestions.
- If students are struggling with types of measurements, here are some suggestions (in addition to those found on the handout):
    - Size, location of brainstem
    - Size of cerebellum (length:width ratio)
    - Size of frontal lobe (If students are struggling with this, you can have a class discussion to determine the "lobes"; you should also point out that when scientists have issues, they consult with their peers.)

Topic Connections

Table 24.2 (p. 334) provides an overview of the scientific practices, crosscutting concepts, disciplinary core ideas, and support ideas at the heart of this lab investigation. In addition, it lists NOS and NOSI concepts for the explicit and reflective discussion. Finally, it lists literacy and mathematics skills (*CCSS ELA* and *CCSS Mathematics*) that are addressed during the investigation.

TABLE 24.2

Lab 24 alignment with standards

Scientific practices	• Asking questions • Planning and carrying out investigations • Analyzing and interpreting data • Using mathematics and computational thinking • Constructing explanations • Engaging in argument from evidence • Obtaining, evaluating, and communicating information
Crosscutting concepts	• Scale, proportion, and quantity • Structure and function
Core ideas	• LS3: Heredity: Inheritance and variation of traits • LS4: Biological evolution: Unity and diversity
Supporting ideas	• Descent with modification • Homologous structures • Brain anatomy
NOS and NOSI concepts	• Science as a body of knowledge • Methods used in scientific investigations
Literacy connections *(CCSS ELA)*	• *Reading*: Key ideas and details, craft and structure, integration of knowledge and ideas • *Writing*: Text types and purposes, production and distribution of writing, research to build and present knowledge, range of writing • *Speaking and listening*: Comprehension and collaboration, presentation of knowledge and ideas
Mathematics connection *(CCSS Mathematics)*	• Reason quantitatively and use units to solve problems

Lab 24. Descent With Modification: Does Mammalian Brain Structure Support or Refute the Theory of Descent With Modification?

Lab Handout

Introduction

One of Darwin's most revolutionary ideas was that all living things are related. According to Darwin, all life on Earth today is actually related because all life on Earth shares a common ancestor. This ancestor, he argued, lived on Earth sometime in the distant past but is now extinct. As a result of this common ancestor, all organisms now share some common features. An example of how organisms share common features can be seen in the figure below. The figure illustrates how the limbs of mammals have a similar internal structure. These limbs are examples of homologous structures because they have a similar internal structure but serve different functions (such as walking, swimming, or grasping).

Bones found in the limbs of seven different mammals

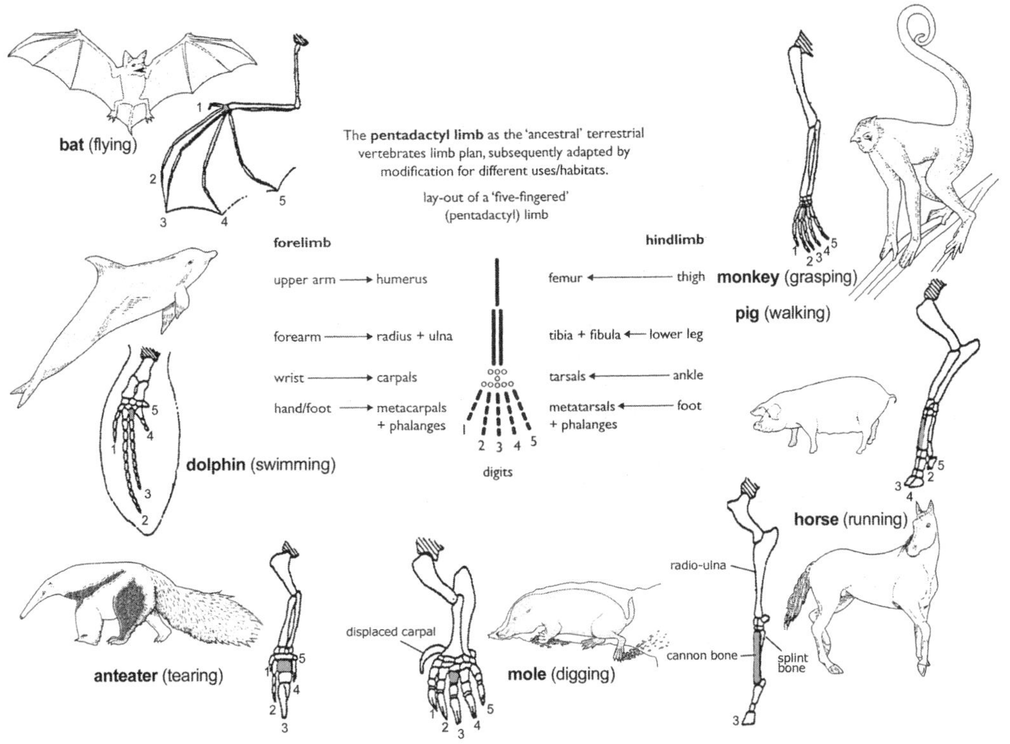

To explain the similar internal bone structure in these mammals, Darwin said that they must be descendants of the same ancestor that had a limb that consisted of the same set of bones. He reasoned that the difference in the shape of the bones was a result of gradual modifications that made the organisms better adapted to survive in a particular environment. He called this idea descent with modification. He argued that environmental factors, over time, could slowly select for or against subtle variations in the basic shape of the bones in the limbs of organisms but could not completely change the basic body plan. This selection process would gradually result in whale fins and bat wings that had fingers similar to the fingers of a lizard, a frog, or a monkey. These variations would give their owners an advantage in a particular environment, such as the ocean in the case of the whale or the air in the case of the bat.

According to this theory, all species will share some physical features because all species share a common ancestor. This theory, however, also predicts that two species that have diverged from one another relatively recently in time will share more features than species that diverged from one another earlier. This prediction is based on the assumption that the longer it has been since two species separated from the same ancestral species, the more time there will be for differences to accumulate in each independent line.

The theory of descent with modification certainly seems reasonable. However, like all theories in science, the principles of descent with modification must be tested in many different ways before it can be considered valid or acceptable by the scientific community. In this investigation, you will determine if mammalian brain structure is consistent with the principles of descent with modification.

Your Task

Collect data about the brain structure of at least 10 different mammals. Then use the data you collect to test the theory of descent with modification.

The guiding question of this investigation is, **Does mammalian brain structure support or refute the theory of descent with modification?**

Materials

You will use an online database called Comparative Mammalian Brain Collections to conduct your investigation. You can access the database by going to the following website: *http://brainmuseum.org*.

Safety Precautions

1. Use caution when working with electrical equipment. Keep away from water sources in that they can cause shorts, fires, and shock hazards. Use only GFI-protected circuits.

2. Wash hands with soap and water after completing this lab.
3. Follow all normal lab safety rules.

Getting Started

To answer the guiding question, you will need to compare and contrast the brains from a sample of at least 10 different mammals. You MUST include the polar bear, the domestic dog, the domestic guinea pig, and the gorilla in your sample. To compare and contrast these brains, you will need to access the online database Comparative Mammalian Brain Collections, which is sponsored by the University of Wisconsin, Michigan State University, and the National Museum of Health and Medicine.

Once you have accessed the database, you must determine what type of data you will need to collect, how you will collect it, and how you will analyze it. To determine *what type of data you will need to collect,* think about the following questions:

- What would you expect mammalian brains to look like if the theory of descent with modification is valid? What would you expect mammalian brains to look like if the theory of descent with modification is not valid? (Hint: Think about what the brains of mammals would look like if mammals did not share a common ancestor.)
- How will you be able to identify the major structures of the mammalian brain, and how will you determine the function of each structure? (Hint: The database includes information about the structure and function of mammalian brains. You can access this information at *http://brainmuseum.org/functions/index.html.*)
- Which characteristics of the mammalian brain will you examine?
- How many different characteristics of the mammalian brain will you need to examine? (Hint: You should examine at least four different characteristics of each brain.)

To determine *how you will collect the data you need,* think about the following questions:

- How will you quantify differences and similarities in brain characteristics? (Hint: If you decide to examine the texture of the brain, you could look at the presence or absence of folds on the surface of the brain. If you decide to examine the shape of the brain, you could calculate the height-to-length ratio. If you decide to examine the size of different structures found in the brain, you could calculate a ratio between the length of a particular structure and the overall length of the brain.)
- How will you make sure that your data are of high quality (i.e., what will you do to help reduce measurement error)?
- What will you do with the data you collect?

To determine *how you will analyze your data,* think about the following questions:

- How will you compare and contrast the various brains?
- What type of graph or table could you create to help make sense of your data?

Investigation Proposal Required? ☐ Yes ☐ No

Connections to Crosscutting Concepts and to the Nature of Science and the Nature of Scientific Inquiry

As you work through your investigation, be sure to think about

- the importance of looking at proportional relationships in science,
- the relationship between structure and function in nature,
- how science as a body of knowledge develops over time, and
- the different types of methods that scientists use to answer questions.

Argumentation Session

Once your group has finished collecting and analyzing your data, prepare a whiteboard that you can use to share your initial argument. Your whiteboard should include all the information shown in the figure below.

Argument presentation on a whiteboard

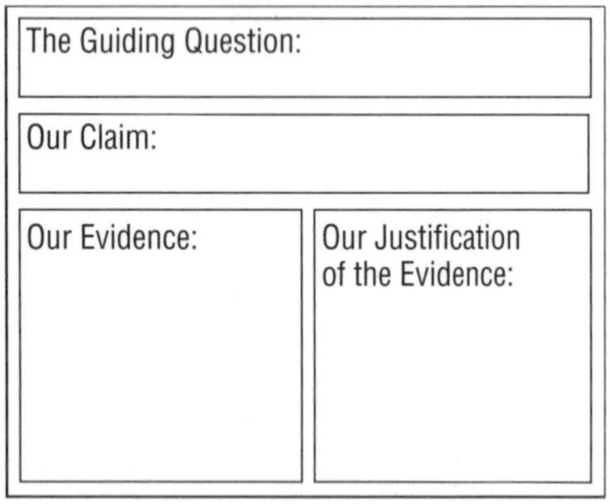

To share your argument with others, we will be using a round-robin format. This means that one member of your group will stay at your lab station to share your group's argument while the other members of your group go to the other lab stations one at a time to listen to and critique the arguments developed by your classmates.

The goal of the argumentation session is not to convince others that your argument is the best one; rather, the goal is to identify errors or instances of faulty reasoning in the arguments so these mistakes can be fixed. You will therefore need to evaluate the content of the claim, the quality of the evidence used to support the claim, and the strength of the justification of the evidence included in each argument that you see. In order to critique an argument, you will need more information than what is included on the whiteboard. You might, therefore, need to ask the presenter one or more follow-up questions, such as:

- How did you use the database to collect your data? Why did you decide to do it that way? Why did you focus on those features of the brain?
- What did you do to make sure the data you collected are reliable? What did you do to decrease measurement error?

- What did you do to analyze your data? Why did you decide to do it that way? Did you check your calculations?
- Is that the only way to interpret the results of your analysis? How do you know that your interpretation of your analysis is appropriate?
- Why did your group decide to present your evidence in that manner?
- What other claims did your group discuss before you decided on that one? Why did your group abandon those alternative ideas?
- How confident are you that your claim is valid? What could you do to increase your confidence?

Once the argumentation session is complete, you will have a chance to meet with your group and revise your original argument. Your group might need to gather more data or design a way to test one or more alternative claims as part of this process. Remember, your goal at this stage of the investigation is to develop the most valid or acceptable answer to the research question!

Report

Once you have completed your research, you will need to prepare an investigation report that consists of three sections that provide answers to the following questions:

1. What question were you trying to answer and why?
2. What did you do during your investigation and why did you conduct your investigation in this way?
3. What is your argument?

Your report should answer these questions in two pages or less. This report must be typed, and any diagrams, figures, or tables should be embedded into the document. Be sure to write in a persuasive style; you are trying to convince others that your claim is acceptable or valid!

Lab 24. Descent With Modification: Does Mammalian Brain Structure Support or Refute the Theory of Descent With Modification?

Checkout Questions

1. What are the basic principles of the theory of descent with modification?

2. Use the theory of descent with modification to explain why the number of neck vertebrae is the same in all mammals. The neck of a giraffe, for example, is made of seven long bones, and the neck of the whale is made of seven short bones.

3. All scientific investigations must follow the same step-by-step method to be considered scientific.

   a. I agree with this statement.
   b. I disagree with this statement.

   Explain your answer, using examples from your investigation about descent with modification.

4. Scientific knowledge does not change.

   a. I agree with this statement.
   b. I disagree with this statement.

   Explain your answer, using information from your investigation about descent with modification.

5. Scientists often need to look for proportional relationships when they analyze data or make comparisons. Explain why proportional relationships are useful in science, using an example from your investigation about descent with modification.

6. Structure and function are related in nature. Explain why, using an example from your investigation about descent with modification.

Lab 25. Mechanisms of Speciation: Why Does Geographic Isolation Lead to the Formation of a New Species?

Teacher Notes

Purpose

The purpose of this lab is to have students *apply* what they know about natural selection to explain the process of allopatric speciation. This lab also gives students an opportunity to use an online simulation to develop an explanation for how the characteristics of different subpopulations can potentially change enough over time so that the members of one subpopulation no longer interbreed with members of the other subpopulations. The simulation, called *Bug Hunt Camouflage* (Novak and Wilensky 2005), was created using NetLogo, a multiagent programmable modeling environment developed at the Center for Connected Learning and Computer-Based Modeling at Northwestern University (Wilensky 1999). Students will also learn how theories are developed rather than discovered and the different ways to test scientific ideas.

The Content

Speciation is the process whereby a single species diverges into two or more new species. Speciation has been observed multiple times under controlled laboratory conditions and in nature. In sexually reproducing organisms, speciation results from reproductive isolation followed by genealogical divergence. One of the most common types of speciation in animals is *allopatric speciation*. Allopatric speciation occurs when a subpopulation is initially isolated geographically from another subpopulation, such as by habitat fragmentation or migration. The geographic isolation then leads to the formation of a new species by preventing interbreeding and the mixing of genetic material over many generations. Over time, selective pressures unique to each subpopulation's environment may alter the subpopulations so much that the organisms would no longer be able to interbreed successfully should they come in contact with one another.

Timeline

The instructional time needed to implement this lab investigation is 130–200 minutes. Appendix 2 (p. 391) provides options for implementing this lab investigation over several class periods. Option C (200 minutes) should be used if students are unfamiliar with scientific writing because this option provides extra instructional time for scaffolding the writing process. You can scaffold the writing process by modeling, providing examples, and providing hints as students write each section of the report. Option D (130 minutes) should be used if students are familiar with scientific writing and have the skills needed to write an investigation report on their own. In option D, students complete stage 6 (writing the investigation report) and stage 8 (revising the investigation report) as homework.

Materials and Preparation

The materials needed to implement this investigation are listed in Table 25.1 The *Bug Hunt Camouflage* simulation, available at *http://ccl.northwestern.edu/netlogo/models/BugHuntCamouflage*, is free to use and can be run online using an internet browser. You should access the online simulation and learn how it works before beginning the lab investigation. In addition, it is important to check if students can access and use the simulation from a school computer, because some schools have set up firewalls and other restrictions on web browsing.

TABLE 25.1
Materials list

Item	Quantity
Computer with internet access	At least 1 per group
Student handout	1 per student
Natural Selection and Species Concept Fact Sheet	1 per group
Investigation proposal A (optional)	1 per group
Whiteboard, 2' × 3'*	1 per group
Peer-review guide and instructor scoring rubric	1 per student

* Students can also use computer and presentation software such as Microsoft PowerPoint or Apple Keynote to create their arguments.

Topics for the Explicit and Reflective Discussion

Concepts That Can Be Used to Justify the Evidence

To provide an adequate justification of their evidence, students must explain why they included the evidence in their arguments and make the assumptions underlying their analysis and interpretation of the data explicit. In this investigation, students can use the following concepts to help justify their evidence:

- Allopatric speciation
- Species definition
- Natural selection

We recommend that you review these concepts during the explicit and reflective discussion to help students make this connection.

How to Design Better Investigations

It is important for students to reflect on the strengths and weaknesses of the investigation they designed during the explicit and reflective discussion. Students should therefore be encouraged to discuss ways to eliminate potential flaws, measurement errors, or sources of bias in their investigations. To help students be more reflective about the design of their investigation, you can ask the following questions:

- What were some of the strengths of your investigation? What made it scientific?
- What were some of the weaknesses of your investigation? What made it less scientific?
- If you were to do this investigation again, what would you do to address the weaknesses in your investigation? What could you do to make it more scientific?

Crosscutting Concepts

This investigation is well aligned with three crosscutting concepts found in *A Framework for K–12 Science Education*, and you should review these concepts during the explicit and reflective discussion.

- *Cause and Effect: Mechanism and Explanation:* One of the main objectives of science is to identify and establish relationships between a cause and an effect. It is also important to understand the mechanisms by which these causal relationships are mediated.
- *Scale, Proportion, and Quantity:* When analyzing data, it is often important for scientists to look for and recognize proportional relationships in natural phenomena. In this investigation, for example, students need to compare the ratio of different colors of bugs in different environments.
- *Systems and System Models:* It is critical for scientists to be able to define the system under study (e.g., the elements of an environment) and then make a model of it to understand it. Models can be physical, conceptual, or mathematical.

The Nature of Science and the Nature of Scientific Inquiry

A scientific theory is a well-substantiated explanation of some aspect of the natural world. It is important for students to understand that *theories are developed, not discovered*. Scientists develop theories over time through numerous investigations and their interactions with other scientists. In this investigation, for example, each group develops an explanation for the mechanism that drives allopatric speciation through an iterative process that includes testing their ideas with the computer simulation and discussing them with others.

It is also important for students to understand that *scientists do not always use experiments to test their ideas*. There are actually many ways to test a scientific idea. Some scientists test ideas by setting up a controlled experiment in the lab, some scientists test ideas by making detailed observations of the natural world, and some scientists create computer simulations. In this investigation, for example, students test their ideas about the mechanism underlying allopatric speciation by using a computer simulation.

You should review and provide examples of these two important concepts of the nature of science (NOS) and the nature of scientific inquiry (NOSI) during the explicit and reflective discussion.

Hints for Implementing the Lab

- Be sure to allow each group to play around with the simulation as part of the tool talk before they design their investigation. Students will be able to design a better investigation if they understand what they can and cannot do with the simulation.
- Actively monitor students as they collect their data by asking the following questions:
  - What do you think may cause a population to become two or more species? How long might it take to form a new species (months, years, thousands of years)?
  - What evidence have you collected to support this?
  - How do you plan to present the data in your investigation report?
- It is important that students "make sense" of the data as they go along to ensure that they are actually getting quality data, as opposed to just playing with the simulation.
- In this investigation, the task is very open (no supplied explanations, hypotheses, and so on). It is important that students remain focused on explaining how new species can form under the allopatric speciation model.

Topic Connections

Table 25.2 provides an overview of the scientific practices, crosscutting concepts, disciplinary core ideas, and support ideas at the heart of this lab investigation. In addition, it lists NOS and NOSI concepts for the explicit and reflective discussion. Finally, it lists literacy and mathematics skills (*CCSS ELA* and *CCSS Mathematics*) that are addressed during the investigation.

TABLE 25.2

Lab 25 alignment with standards

Scientific practices	• Asking questions • Developing and using models • Planning and carrying out investigations • Analyzing and interpreting data • Using mathematics and computational thinking • Constructing explanations • Engaging in argument from evidence • Obtaining, evaluating, and communicating information
Crosscutting concepts	• Cause and effect: Mechanism and explanation • Scale, proportion, and quantity • Systems and system models
Core ideas	• LS2: Ecosystems: Interactions, energy, and dynamics • LS3: Heredity: Inheritance and variation of traits • LS4: Biological evolution: Unity and diversity
Supporting ideas	• Descent with modification • Natural selection • Speciation • Population dynamics
NOS and NOSI concepts	• Scientific theories and laws • Nature and role of experiments
Literacy connections *(CCSS ELA)*	• *Reading*: Key ideas and details, craft and structure, integration of knowledge and ideas • *Writing*: Text types and purposes, production and distribution of writing, research to build and present knowledge, range of writing • *Speaking and listening*: Comprehension and collaboration, presentation of knowledge and ideas
Mathematics connection *(CCSS Mathematics)*	• Reason quantitatively and use units to solve problems

References

Novak, M., and U. Wilensky. 2005. NetLogo Bug Hunt Camouflage model. Evanston, IL: Center for Connected Learning and Computer-Based Modeling, Northwestern Institute on Complex Systems, Northwestern University. *http://ccl.northwestern.edu/netlogo/models/BugHuntCamouflage.*

Wilensky, U. 1999. NetLogo. Evanston, IL: Center for Connected Learning and Computer-Based Modeling, Northwestern Institute on Complex Systems, Northwestern University. *http://ccl.northwestern.edu/netlogo.*

Lab 25. Mechanisms of Speciation: Why Does Geographic Isolation Lead to the Formation of a New Species?

Lab Handout

Introduction

There have been a number of models that have been proposed to explain the process of speciation (i.e., the formation of a new species). One of these models, called allopatric speciation, suggests that new species can arise when a population is divided into two or more subpopulations by some type of geographic barrier (such as a mountain range or an ocean). The two isolated subpopulations then diverge into different species over time (see the figure to the right). This explanation of the model, however, is incomplete because it only suggests that two or more subpopulations can become separate species when a geographic barrier separates them; it does not explain what causes the two subpopulations to diverge into different species over time.

The model of allopatric speciation

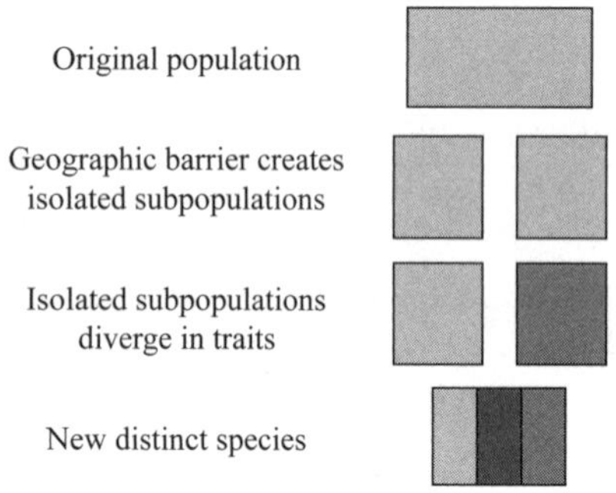

Your Task

Use a computer simulation called *Bug Hunt Camouflage* to develop an explanation for how geographic isolation could lead to the formation of a new species. Your goal is to identify an underlying mechanism that can cause a physical characteristic (such as body color) found in two different populations of the same species to diverge when they live in different environments (seashore, glacier, or poppy field). This mechanism must be able to change a characteristic in the two populations enough so the individual members of one population will no longer interbreed with members of the other population.

The guiding question of this investigation is, **Why does geographic isolation lead to the formation of a new species?**

Materials

You will use the following materials during your investigation:

- An online simulation called *Bug Hunt Camouflage*, which can be accessed at *http://ccl.northwestern.edu/netlogo/models/BugHuntCamouflage.*
- Natural Selection and Species Concept Fact Sheet

Safety Precautions

1. Use caution when working with electrical equipment. Keep away from water sources in that they can cause shorts, fires and shock hazards. Use only GFI protected circuits.
2. Wash hands with soap and water after completing this lab. Follow all normal lab safety rules.

Getting Started

Bug Hunt Camouflage simulates a population of bugs that all belong to the same species. However, the bugs in this population are not all the same color. You will be acting as a predator by using the mouse to eat the bugs (your prey) by clicking on them. When a bug is eaten, it is replaced through reproduction by a bug in the simulated environment. The new bug will appear near the parent bug and will start out as a small dot and then grow after a few seconds. The new bug will usually have the same characteristics as one of the bugs that have not been eaten yet. Some offspring, however, will have a slightly different coloration than the parent it came from because the simulation will allow the pigment genes to drift (to simulate the effect of random mutation). You can also create an entire new generation of bugs at any time by clicking the "Make a Generation" button. When you click this button, all of the bugs in the environment produce one offspring.

The simulation also allows you to adjust the following factors (see the figure on p. 350):

- The number of bugs in the environment (0 bugs to 100 bugs),
- The size of bugs in the environment (0.5 to 5),
- The nature of the environment (seashore, glacier, or poppy field), and
- How much the pigment gene can drift from the parent value when a new bug is produced (0 to 98).

The simulation also allows you to keep track of a number of characteristics of the bugs and the environment over time:

- How many bugs you have caught (total-caught).
- How many bugs are in the world (bugs in world).
- Your progress and performance as a predator (bugs caught vs. time).
- How the average values for the hue, saturation, and brightness of the bugs change over time (average HSB values).
- The distribution of hues in the starting population (initial hues).
- The distribution of hues in the current population (current hues).

A screen shot from the *Bug Hunt Camouflage* simulation.

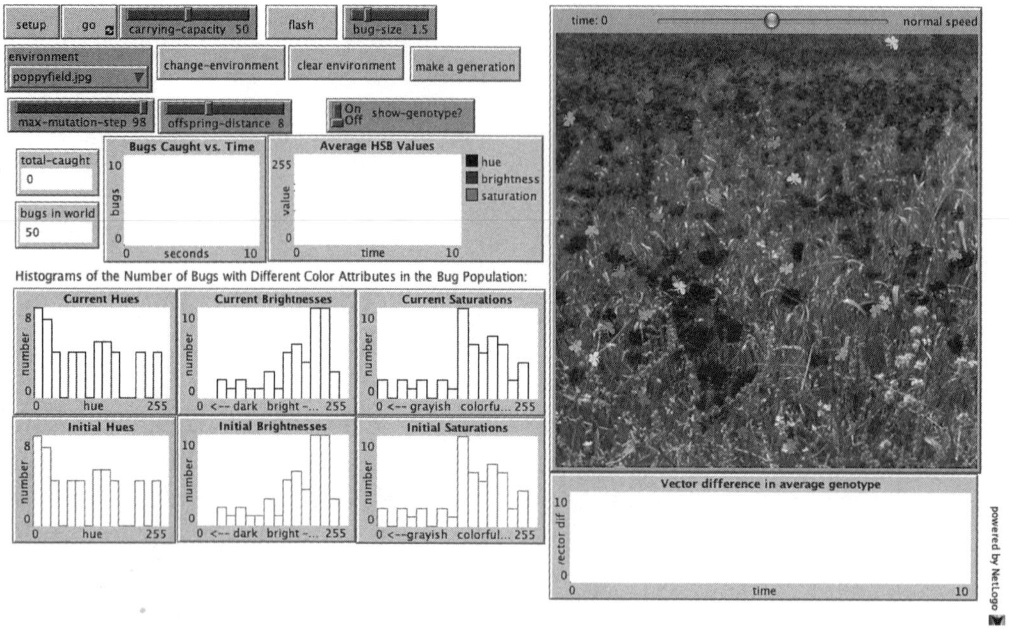

- The distribution of saturations (of colors) in the current population (current saturation) and starting populations (initial saturation). Low values represent "grayish" colorations and high values represent "vivid" colorations.
- The distribution of brightness (of colors) in the current (current brightness) and starting (initial brightness) populations. Low values represent "dark" colorations and high values represent "light" colorations.
- How the average values of the genotype of the population change over time (vector difference in average genotype). The plot shows the vector difference between the average value of red gene frequency, green gene frequency, and blue gene frequency for the current population compared with the initial population.

To answer the guiding question using this computer simulation, you must determine what type of data you will need to collect, how you will collect it, and how you will analyze it. To determine *what type of data you will need to collect*, think about the following questions:

- How will you determine if the characteristics of a bug population change over time?
- What will serve as your dependent variable (e.g., number of bugs caught, hues, brightness, saturation)?
- What type of measurements or observations will you need to record during your investigation?

To determine *how you will collect your data,* think about the following questions:

- What will serve as a control condition (glacier, poppy field, seashore)?
- What types of treatment conditions will you need to set up and how will you do it?
- What factors will you need to keep constant during each simulation?
- What should the characteristics of the initial population of bugs be at the beginning of each simulation?
- How long will you need to run the simulation (e.g., for three minutes or until 60 bugs are caught)?
- How many trials will you need to conduct for each treatment?
- How often will you collect data and when will you do it?
- How will you keep track of the data you collect and how will you organize the data?

To determine *how you will analyze your data,* think about the following questions:

- How will you determine if the environment affected the characteristics of a bug population?
- What type of calculations will you need to make?
- What type of graph could you create to help make sense of your data?

Investigation Proposal Required? ☐ Yes ☐ No

Connections to Crosscutting Concepts and to the Nature of Science and the Nature of Scientific Inquiry

As you work through your investigation, be sure to think about

- the importance of identifying causal relationships in science,
- the importance of looking at proportional relationships in science,
- how scientists use models,
- how theories are developed rather than discovered, and
- the different types of methods that scientists use to test ideas.

Argumentation Session

Once your group has finished collecting and analyzing your data, prepare a whiteboard that you can use to share your initial argument. Your whiteboard should include all the information shown in the figure on p. 350.

To share your argument with others, we will be using a round-robin format. This means that one member of your group will stay at your lab station to share your group's argument while the other members of your group go to the other lab stations one at a time

Argument presentation on a whiteboard

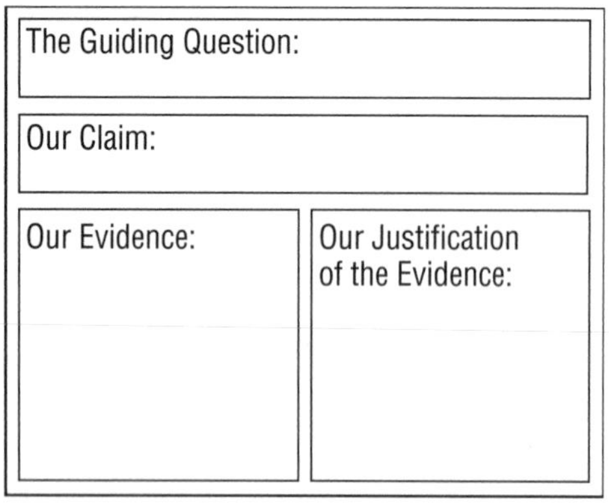

to listen to and critique the arguments developed by your classmates.

The goal of the argumentation session is not to convince others that your argument is the best one; rather, the goal is to identify errors or instances of faulty reasoning in the arguments so these mistakes can be fixed. You will therefore need to evaluate the content of the claim, the quality of the evidence used to support the claim, and the strength of the justification of the evidence included in each argument that you see. In order to critique an argument, you will need more information than what is included on the whiteboard. You might, therefore, need to ask the presenter one or more follow-up questions, such as:

- How did you use the simulation to collect your data?
- What did you do to analyze your data? Why did you decide to do it that way? Did you check your calculations?
- Is that the only way to interpret the results of your analysis? How do you know that your interpretation of your analysis is appropriate?
- Why did your group decide to present your evidence in that manner?
- What other claims did your group discuss before you decided on that one? Why did your group abandon those alternative ideas?
- How confident are you that your claim is valid? What could you do to increase your confidence?

Once the argumentation session is complete, you will have a chance to meet with your group and revise your original argument. Your group might need to gather more data or design a way to test one or more alternative claims as part of this process. Remember, your goal at this stage of the investigation is to develop the most valid or acceptable answer to the research question!

Report

Once you have completed your research, you will need to prepare an investigation report that consists of three sections that provide answers to the following questions:

1. What question were you trying to answer and why?
2. What did you do during your investigation and why did you conduct your investigation in this way?
3. What is your argument?

Your report should answer these questions in two pages or less. This report must be typed, and any diagrams, figures, or tables should be embedded into the document. Be sure to write in a persuasive style; you are trying to convince others that your claim is acceptable or valid!

Natural Selection and Species Concept Fact Sheet

The Theory of Natural Selection

The fossil record provides convincing evidence that species evolve. In other words, the number of species found on Earth and the characteristics of these species have changed over time. However, these observations tell us little about the natural processes that drive evolution. A number of different explanations have been offered by scientists in an effort to explain why (or if) evolution occurs. One of these explanations is called natural selection. The basic tenets of natural selection are as follows (Lawson 1995):

- Only a fraction of the individuals that make up a population survive long enough to reproduce.
- The individuals in a population are not all the same. Individuals have traits that make them unique.
- Much, but not all, of this variation in traits is inheritable and can therefore be passed down from parent to offspring.
- The environment, including both abiotic (e.g., temperature, amount of water available) and biotic (e.g., amount of food, presence of predators) factors, determines which traits are favorable or unfavorable, because some traits increase an individual's chance of survival and others do not.
- Individuals with favorable traits tend to produce more offspring than those with unfavorable traits. Therefore, over time, favorable traits become more common within a population found in a particular environment (and unfavorable traits become less common).

How Biologists Define a Species

A species can be defined as "a population or group of populations whose members have the potential to interbreed with one another in nature to produce viable, fertile offspring, but who cannot produce viable, fertile offspring with members of other species" (Campbell and Reece 2002, p. 465). This definition is known as the biological species concept. A group of individuals can therefore be classified as a species when there are one or more factors that will prevent them from interbreeding with individuals from another group.

In nature, however, the biological species concept does not always work well. A bacterium, for example, reproduces by copying its genetic material and then splitting (this is called binary fission). Therefore, defining a species as a group of interbreeding individuals only works with organisms that do not use an asexual form of reproduction. Most plants (and some animals) that use sexual reproduction can also self-fertilize, which makes it difficult to determine the boundaries of a species. Biologists are also unable to check for the ability to interbreed in extinct forms of organisms found in the fossil record.

Therefore, many other "species concepts" have been proposed by scientists, such as the ecological species concept (which means a species is defined by its ecological niche or its role in a biological community), the morphological species concept (which means a species is defined using a unique set of shared structural features), and the genealogical species concept (which means a species is a set of organisms with a unique genetic history). The species concept that a scientist chooses to use will often reflect his or her research focus. All scientists, however, are expected to decide on a species concept, provide a rationale for doing so, and then use it consistently.

References

Benton, M. J. 1995. Diversification and extinction in the history of life. *Science* 268 (5207): 52–58.

Campbell, N., and J. Reece. 2002. *Biology*. 6th ed. San Francisco: Benjamin Cummings.

Lawson, A. 1995. *Science teaching and the development of thinking*. Belmont, CA: Wadsworth.

Lab 25. Mechanisms of Speciation: Why Does Geographic Isolation Lead to the Formation of a New Species?

Checkout Questions

1. How can geographic isolation result in the formation of a new species?

2. Experiments are a necessary part of the scientific process. Without an experiment, a study is not rigorous or scientific.

   a. I agree with this statement.
   b. I disagree with this statement.

   Explain your answer, using information from your investigation about the mechanisms of speciation.

3. Scientific theories exist in the natural world and are uncovered through scientific investigations (i.e., scientists discover theories).

   a. I agree with this statement.
   b. I disagree with this statement.

Explain your answer, using examples from your investigation about the mechanisms of speciation.

4. Scientists often need to look for proportional relationships when they analyze data or make comparisons. Explain why this is important for scientists to do, using an example from your investigation about the mechanisms of speciation.

5. Structure and function are related in nature. How did this principle play a role in your investigation about the mechanisms of speciation?

Lab 26. Human Evolution: How Are Humans Related to Other Members of the Family Hominidae?

Teacher Notes

Purpose

The purpose of this lab is for students to *apply* their understanding of evolutionary relationships or phylogeny to the family Hominidae. This lab provides students with an opportunity to analyze the features of seven different Hominidae skulls and then use this information to create a phylogenetic tree for seven members of the Hominidae family. Students will also learn about the difference between data and evidence and the various methods scientists use to answer questions.

The Content

The Hominidae, also known as the great apes, are a taxonomic family of primates. This family includes four extant genera:

- *Pongo* (orangutans)
- *Gorilla* (gorillas)
- *Pan* (chimpanzees)
- *Homo* (humans)

In addition to these extant genera, archaeologists, paleontologists, and anthropologists have identified at least seven other genera of Hominidae that are extinct. They have also identified several different extinct species within each of these extant and extinct genera.

Scientists have learned a great deal about human evolution by examining the fossils of extinct members of the Hominidae family. Figure 26.1 provides a phylogenetic tree for the seven Hominidae species that students will study as part of this lab investigation. It is important to note, however, that this phylogenetic tree is not complete because it does not include many of the extinct hominid lineages that are known to have once walked the Earth. The complete phylogenetic tree for hominids will also change in the future as new hominid fossils are discovered and as scientists reinterpret current specimens in light of theoretical advances. To learn more about human evolution, visit the Becoming Human website sponsored by the Institute of Human Origins (*www.becominghuman.org*) or the What Does It Mean to Be Human? website sponsored by the Smithsonian Institution's Human Origins Program (*http://humanorigins.si.edu*).

FIGURE 26.1

A phylogenetic tree for the seven members of the family Hominidae (MYA = million years ago)

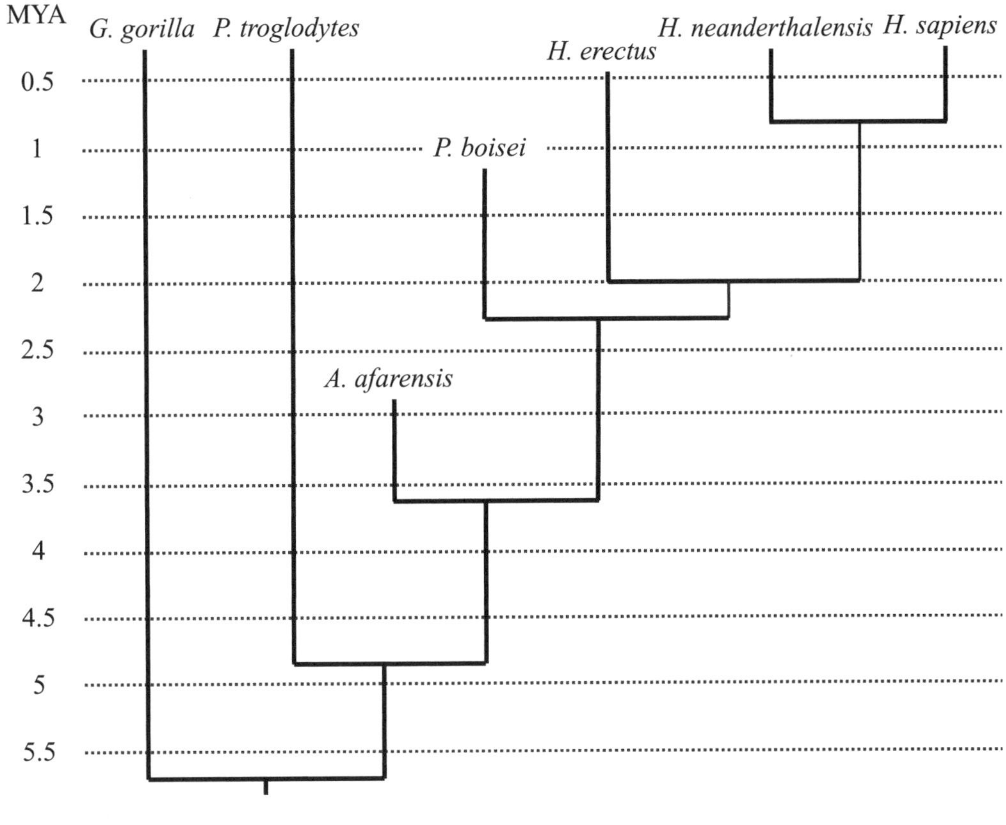

Timeline

The instructional time needed to implement this lab investigation is 180–250 minutes. Appendix 2 (p. 391) provides options for implementing this lab investigation over several class periods. Option E (250 minutes) should be used if students are unfamiliar with scientific writing because this option provides extra instructional time for scaffolding the writing process. You can scaffold the writing process by modeling, providing examples, and providing hints as students write each section of the report. Option F (180 minutes) should be used if students are familiar with scientific writing and have the skills needed to write an investigation report on their own. In option F, students complete stage 6 (writing the investigation report) and stage 8 (revising the investigation report) as homework.

Materials and Preparation

The materials needed to implement this investigation are listed in Table 26.1 (p. 260). Full-size skulls can be purchased from companies such as Skulls Unlimited International (Hominid & Ape Comparison Set) or Educational Biofacts. You can also purchase a half-size replica set from Ward's Science (Hominid/Great Ape Skull Replica Series) at a lower price. One skull set per class is all that is needed to implement this lab because each group can be given one skull at a time. Once the group is done measuring the various features of one skull, they can pass it on to the next group. The Smithsonian Institution's Human Origins Program website also has a 3-D collection of hominid fossils available at *http://humanorigins.si.edu/evidence/3d-collection/fossil*. Students can view, rotate, and interact with the 3-D models online for free. However, it is difficult to measure many of the different features of the skulls using the 3-D collection, so we recommend using actual skulls.

TABLE 26.1

Materials list

Item	Quantity
Paranthropus boisei skull	1 per class
Australopithecus afarensis skull	1 per class
Pan troglodytes (chimpanzee) skull	1 per class
Gorilla gorilla (gorilla) skull	1 per class
Homo erectus skull	1 per class
Homo neanderthalensis skull	1 per class
Homo sapiens skull	1 per class
Caliper or ruler	1 per group
Protractor	1 per group
Computer with internet access (optional)	1 per group
Student handout	1 per student
Whiteboard, 2' × 3'*	1 per group
Peer-review guide and instructor scoring rubric	1 per student

* Students can also use computer and presentation software such as Microsoft PowerPoint or Apple Keynote to create their arguments.

Topics for the Explicit and Reflective Discussion

Concepts That Can Be Used to Justify the Evidence

To provide an adequate justification of their evidence, students must explain why they included the evidence in their arguments and make the assumptions underlying their analysis and interpretation of the data explicit. In this investigation, students can use the following concepts to help justify their evidence:

- Descent with modification
- Phylogenetic trees and the assumptions underlying their construction

We recommend that you review these concepts during the explicit and reflective discussion to help students make this connection.

How to Design Better Investigations

It is important for students to reflect on the strengths and weaknesses of the investigation they designed during the explicit and reflective discussion. Students should therefore be encouraged to discuss ways to eliminate potential flaws, measurement errors, or sources of bias in their investigations. To help students be more reflective about the design of their investigation, you can ask the following questions:

- What were some of the strengths of your investigation? What made it scientific?
- What were some of the weaknesses of your investigation? What made it less scientific?
- If you were to do this investigation again, what would you do to address the weaknesses in your investigation? What could you do to make it more scientific?

Crosscutting Concepts

This investigation is well aligned with two crosscutting concepts found in *A Framework for K–12 Science Education*, and you should review these concepts during the explicit and reflective discussion.

- *Patterns:* Observed patterns in nature guide many classification systems in biology. For example, it has been observed that all living things share common features and certain shared derived characteristics can be used to determine evolutionary relationships.
- *Structure and Function:* In nature, the way a living thing is structured or shaped determines how it functions and places limits on what it can and cannot do. The features of a Hominidae skull, for example, can tell us a great deal about its diet and how it lived.

The Nature of Science and the Nature of Scientific Inquiry

It is important for students to understand the *difference between data and evidence in science.* Data are measurements, observations, and findings from other studies that are collected as part of an investigation. Evidence, in contrast, is analyzed data and an interpretation of the analysis. In this investigation, for example, each group collects measurements about the features of the primate skulls. These measurements are data. The students then analyze and interpret their analysis to create a phylogenetic tree that they can use as evidence to support their claims.

It is also important for students to understand that *scientists use different methods to answer different types of questions*. Examples of methods include experiments, systematic observations of a phenomenon, literature reviews, and analysis of existing data sets; the choice of method depends on the objectives of the research. There is no universal step-by step scientific method that all scientists follow; rather, different scientific disciplines (e.g., biology vs. physics) and fields within a discipline (e.g., ecology vs. molecular biology) use different types of methods, use different core theories, and rely on different standards to develop scientific knowledge.

You should review and provide examples of these two important concepts of the nature of science (NOS) and the nature of scientific inquiry (NOSI) during the explicit and reflective discussion.

Hints for Implementing the Lab

- Encourage students to think of ways to limit measurement error before they begin collecting their data.
- This lab can be made more challenging by requiring students to examine a larger sample of Hominidae skulls at the website sponsored by the Smithsonian Institution's Human Origins Program (*http://humanorigins.si.edu/evidence/3d-collection/fossil*). Students can view, rotate, and interact with the 3-D collection of hominid fossils.

Topic Connections

Table 26.2 provides an overview of the scientific practices, crosscutting concepts, disciplinary core ideas, and support ideas at the heart of this lab investigation. In addition, it lists NOS and NOSI concepts for the explicit and reflective discussion. Finally, it lists literacy and mathematics skills (*CCSS ELA* and *CCSS Mathematics*) that are addressed during the investigation.

TABLE 26.2

Lab 26 alignment with standards

Scientific practices	• Asking questions • Planning and carrying out investigations • Analyzing and interpreting data • Using mathematics and computational thinking • Constructing explanations • Engaging in argument from evidence • Obtaining, evaluating, and communicating information
Crosscutting concepts	• Patterns • Structure and function
Core idea	• LS4: Biological evolution: Unity and diversity
Supporting ideas	• Descent with modification • Phylogenetic trees • Human evolution
NOS and NOSI concepts	• Difference between data and evidence • Methods used in scientific investigations
Literacy connections *(CCSS ELA)*	• *Reading*: Key ideas and details, craft and structure, integration of knowledge and ideas • *Writing*: Text types and purposes, production and distribution of writing, research to build and present knowledge, range of writing • *Speaking and listening*: Comprehension and collaboration, presentation of knowledge and ideas
Mathematics connection *(CCSS Mathematics)*	• Reason quantitatively and use units to solve problems

Lab 26. Human Evolution: How Are Humans Related to Other Members of the Family Hominidae?

Lab Handout

Introduction

The central idea of biological evolution is that all life on Earth shares a common ancestor. All organisms found on Earth are therefore related, and their unique features are the result of the process of descent with modification. Scientists can determine which species are most closely related by studying the unique inheritable characteristics these species share and other historical information.

Biologists use phylogenetic trees to represent evolutionary relationships between organisms. A phylogenetic tree is a branching diagram that shows the inferred evolutionary relationships among various biological entities based on similarities and differences in their physical and/or genetic characteristics. The root of the phylogenetic tree represents the common ancestor, and the tips of the branches represent all the descendants (see the left figure below). As you move from the tips to the root of the tree, you are moving backward in time. The branches on the tree represent speciation events (see the right figure below). When a speciation event occurs, a single species (ancestral lineage) gives rise to two or more new species (daughter lineages).

The root of a phylogenetic tree represents the common ancestor (left), and the branches represent speciation events (right).

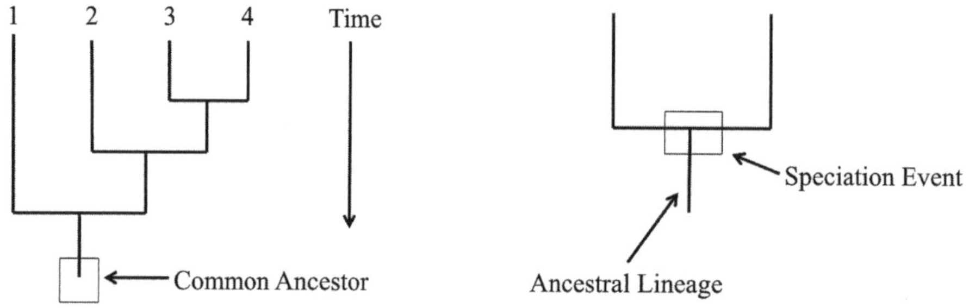

Phylogenetic trees are used to show common ancestry. Each species has a part of its history that is unique to it alone and parts that are shared with other species (see the top left figure on the opposite page). Similarly, each species has ancestors that are unique to that species and ancestors that are shared with other species (see the top right figure on the opposite page).

Each species has both unique and shared histories (left) and unique and shared ancestors (left).

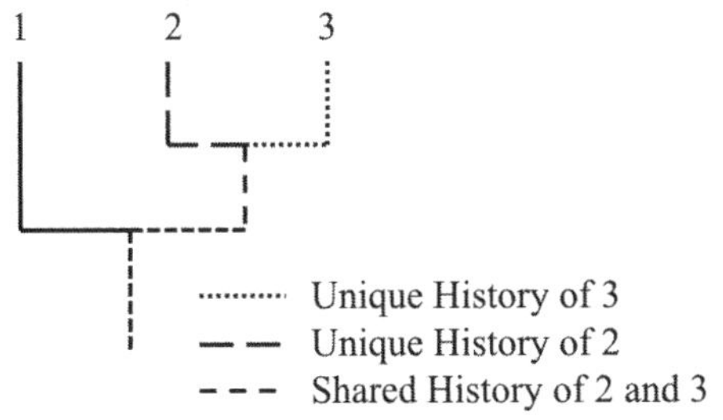

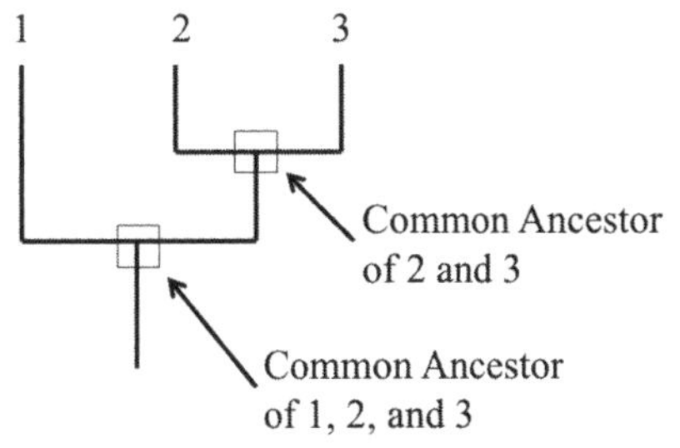

A clade is a grouping that includes a common ancestor and all the descendants (living and extinct) of that ancestor. Clades are nested within one another—scientists call this a nested hierarchy. A clade may include thousands of species or just a few. Some examples of clades at different levels are marked in the phylogenetic tree shown in the figure on the left below. Notice how clades are nested within larger clades. Biologists often represent time on phylogenies by drawing the branch lengths in proportion to the amount of time that has passed since that lineage arose. The figure on the right below provides an example of how a phylogenetic tree can be used to illustrate when different lineages arose or went extinct in the history of life on Earth (MYA in this figure stands for "million years ago," so [for example] "100" means "100 million years ago").

A clade (left) includes a common ancestor and all of its descendants. Phylogenetic trees can show when different species arose or went extinct.

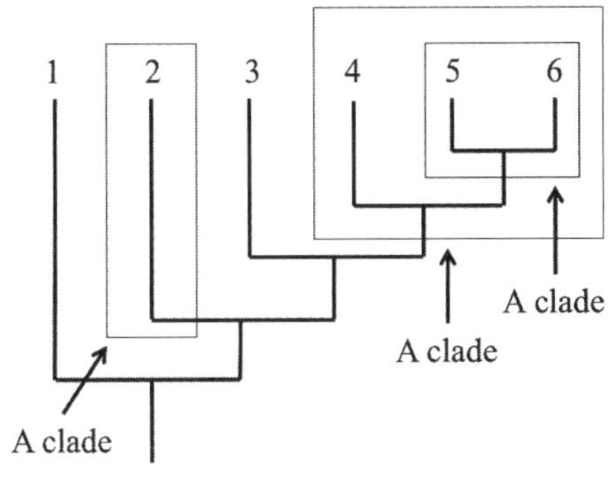

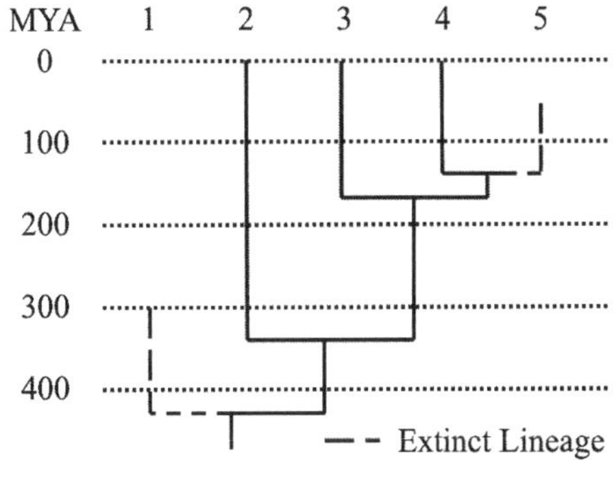

Humans and other members of the family Hominidae are notable among the rest of the primates for their bipedal locomotion, slow rate of maturation, and large brain size. Our current understanding of the evolutionary history of Hominidae is derived largely from the findings of paleontology and anthropology. Thousands of fossils of human ancestors and extinct relatives have been unearthed. Each fossil, whether it is a complete skeleton or a single tooth, contributes significantly to our understanding of the origins of humans. In this investigation, you will have an opportunity to explore the evolutionary history of Hominidae.

Your Task

Develop a phylogenetic tree for the living and extinct members of the family Hominidae and then use this information to draw inferences about the evolutionary history of humans.

The guiding question for this investigation is, **How are humans related to other members of the family Hominidae?**

Materials

You will be supplied with a set of seven skulls. The table below provides some information about them.

Information about the Hominidae skulls

Name	Oldest Specimen	Youngest Specimen	Where found
Paranthropus boisei	2.3 MYA	1.2 MYA	Ethiopia, Tanzania, Kenya
Australopithecus afarensis	3.6 MYA	2.9 MYA	Ethiopia
Pan troglodytes (chimpanzee)	4.9 MYA	Today	Africa
Gorilla gorilla (gorilla)	5.9 MYA	Today	Africa
Homo erectus	2 MYA	400 TYA	Africa, Asia, and Europe.
Homo neanderthalensis	250 TYA	45 TYA	Europe and the Middle East
Homo sapiens	200 TYA	Today	Worldwide

Key: MYA = million years ago; TYA = thousand years ago.

Safety Precautions

1. Use caution when working with electrical equipment. Keep away from water sources in that they can cause shorts, fires and shock hazards. Use only GFI protected circuits.
2. Use caution when handling skulls—sharp edges can cut skin.
3. Wash hands with soap and water after completing this lab.
4. Follow all normal lab safety rules.

Getting Started

Your first step is to carefully examine the seven Hominidae skulls to identify the similarities and differences between them. The figure below lists 13 features that scientists use to describe a hominid skull. You should collect data about all 13 of these features for each skull.

Features of Hominidae skulls

Aspect of the skull	Location
Braincase and face: • Presence or absence of a supraorbital browridge • Continuous or divided supraorbital browridge • Size of the braincase • Presence or absence of a sagittal crest • Flat or protruding mastoid process • Raised or flat nasal bones • Maximum height of the nasal opening (in millimeters) • Length of the mandible (in millimeters) • Slope of the face (in degrees)	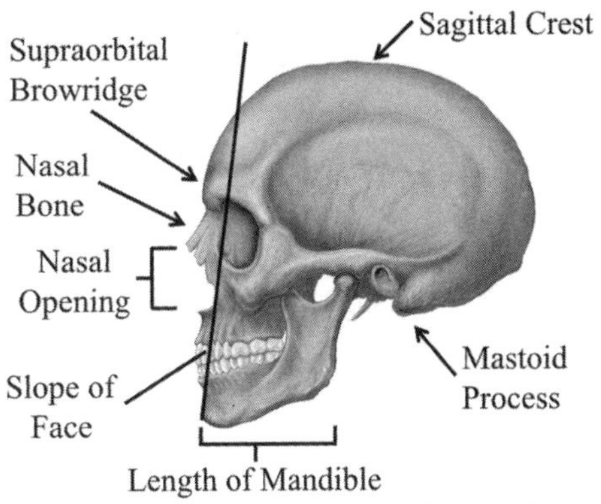
Dentition: • Combined width or breadth of the four incisors (in millimeters) • Canine tooth that protrudes above the chewing surfaces of the other teeth • Presence or absence of a canine diastema (a space between the canine tooth and the incisors) • Combined length of the two premolars and the three molars (in millimeters)	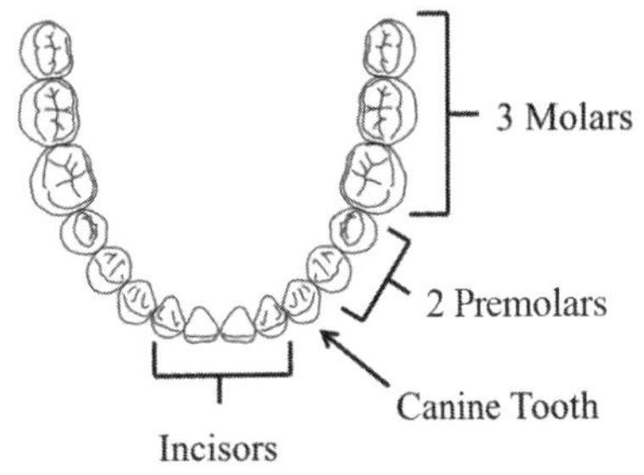

Once you have collected your data, you will need to analyze it. One way to accomplish this goal is to create a phylogenetic tree. Biologists begin the process of constructing a phylogenetic tree by collecting data about heritable traits that can be compared across species (such as the 13 skull features listed in the figure above). Biologists then determine which species have a shared derived character and which do not. A shared derived character is one that two species have in common and that has appeared in the lineage leading up to a clade. As a result, the character sets members of a clade apart from other individuals not in the clade. It is important to note, however, that a shared derived character does not need to be a new feature or a feature that has increased in size; a shared derived character can also be a feature that has gotten smaller or has disappeared completely. For example, the absence of a sagittal crest might be a shared derived character in hominids that sets the members of a clade apart from other clades. One way to keep track of the presence or absence of the shared derived characters for each hominid is to create a chart such as the one shown in the "Features of the hominidae skull" figure.

Biologists then create the phylogenetic tree by grouping species into clades based on the number of shared derived characters they have. The figure to the right shows an example of a phylogenetic tree that is based on the number of derived characters shared by species 1–6 in Table 2. Notice that species 1 has the fewest number of shared derived characters (only A) and species 3–6 have the most (A, B, C, and D or A, B, C, and E). Species 3 and 4 share different characters (A, B, C, and D) than 5 and 6 (A, B, C, and E)—this means that species 3 and 4 share more of their evolutionary history than species 5 and 6 do, even though they have the same number of shared derived characters.

Presence of shared derived characters for each species

	Shared derived character					
Species	**A**	**B**	**C**	**D**	**E**	**Total**
1	Y	N	N	N	N	1
2	Y	Y	N	N	N	2
3	Y	Y	Y	Y	N	4
4	Y	Y	Y	Y	N	4
5	Y	Y	Y	N	Y	4
6	Y	Y	Y	N	Y	4

A phylogenetic tree.

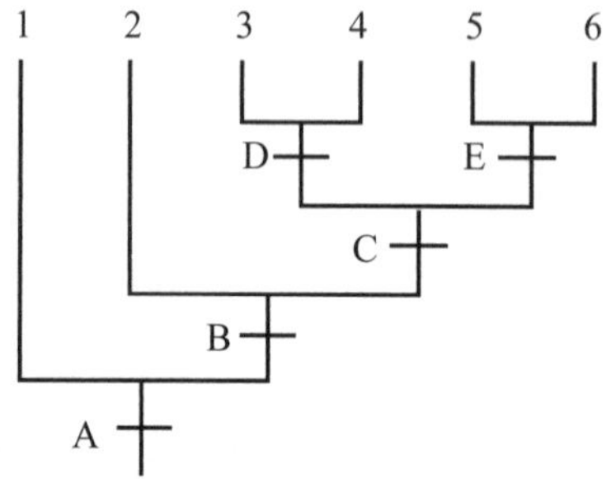

Once you have created your phylogenetic tree, you will use it as evidence to support your answer to the guiding question.

Investigation Proposal Required? ☐ Yes ☐ No

Connections to Crosscutting Concepts and to the Nature of Science and the Nature of Scientific Inquiry

As you work through your investigation, be sure to think about

- the importance of identifying and explaining patterns in science,
- the relationship between structure and function in nature,
- the difference between data and evidence in science, and
- the different types of methods that scientists use to answer questions.

Argumentation Session

Once your group has finished collecting and analyzing your data, prepare a whiteboard that you can use to share your initial argument. Your whiteboard should include all the information shown in the figure to the right.

To share your argument with others, we will be using a round-robin format. This means that one member of your group will stay at your lab station to share your group's argument while the other members of your group go to the other lab stations one at a time to listen to and critique the arguments developed by your classmates.

Argument presentation on a whiteboard

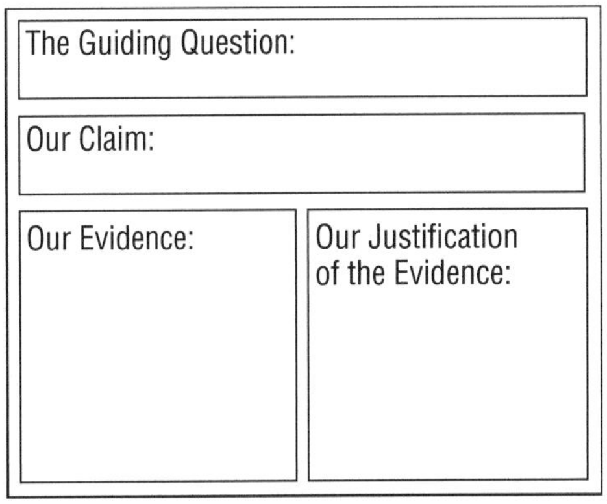

The goal of the argumentation session is not to convince others that your argument is the best one; rather, the goal is to identify errors or instances of faulty reasoning in the arguments so these mistakes can be fixed. You will therefore need to evaluate the content of the claim, the quality of the evidence used to support the claim, and the strength of the justification of the evidence included in each argument that you see. In order to critique an argument, you will need more information than what is included on the whiteboard. You might, therefore, need to ask the presenter one or more follow-up questions, such as:

- How did you collect your data? Why did you decide to use that method? Why did you collect those data?
- What did you do to make sure the data you collected are reliable? What did you do to decrease measurement error?
- What did you do to analyze your data? Why did you decide to do it that way? Did you check your calculations?
- Is that the only way to interpret the results of your analysis? How do you know that your interpretation of your analysis is appropriate?
- Why did your group decide to present your evidence in that manner?
- What other claims did your group discuss before you decided on that one? Why did your group abandon those alternative ideas?
- How confident are you that your claim is valid? What could you do to increase your confidence?

Once the argumentation session is complete, you will have a chance to meet with your group and revise your original argument. Your group might need to gather more data or design a way to test one or more alternative claims as part of this process. Remember, your

goal at this stage of the investigation is to develop the most valid or acceptable answer to the research question!

Report

Once you have completed your research, you will need to prepare an investigation report that consists of three sections that provide answers to the following questions:

1. What question were you trying to answer and why?
2. What did you do during your investigation and why did you conduct your investigation in this way?
3. What is your argument?

Your report should answer these questions in two pages or less. This report must be typed, and any diagrams, figures, or tables should be embedded into the document. Be sure to write in a persuasive style; you are trying to convince others that your claim is acceptable or valid!

Lab 26. Human Evolution: How Are Humans Related to Other Members of the Family Hominidae?

Checkout Questions

1. Explain how humans and chimpanzees are related to members of the family Hominidae.

2. Evidence is data that have been analyzed and then interpreted by scientists.

   a. I agree with this statement.
   b. I disagree with this statement.

   Explain your answer, using examples from your investigation about human evolution.

3. All scientific investigations are experiments.

   a. I agree with this statement.
   b. I disagree with this statement.

   Explain your answer, using information from your investigation about evolution.

4. An important aspect of science is identifying and the explaining patterns in nature. Explain why this is important for scientists to do, using an example from your investigation about human evolution.

5. Scientists often need to think about how structure is related to function in nature when they analyze data or make comparisons. Explain why this is important for scientists to do, using an example from your investigation about human evolution.

Lab 27. Whale Evolution: How Are Whales Related to Other Mammals?

Teacher Notes

Purpose

The purpose of this lab is for students to *apply* their understanding of protein synthesis, descent with modification, and cladograms to identify the evolutionary relationship of whales to other mammal species. Students also have an opportunity to access and use an online database as part of the investigation. Students will also learn about the differences between data and evidence and how science, as a body of knowledge, develops over time.

The Content

The original explanation for cetacean evolution was that whales were related to the mesonychids, which belonged to an extinct order (Mesonychia) of carnivorous ungulates (hoofed animals). Mesonychids resembled wolves with hooves (see Figure 27.1). These animals had unusual triangular teeth similar to those of whales. This is why scientists long believed that whales evolved from a form of mesonychid. Recent research in molecular phylogeny, however, suggests that whales are more closely related to artiodactyls and that the closest living relative of the whale is the hippopotamus. The phylogeny developed using molecular similarities is also supported by the discovery of *Pakicetus*, the earliest proto-whale (see Figure 27.2, p. 374). The *Pakicetus* skeletons support the idea that whales did not derive directly from mesonychids. Instead, they are artiodactyls that began to take to the water soon after artiodactyls split from mesonychids. Proto-whales retained aspects of their mesonychid ancestry (such as the triangular teeth), which modern artiodactyls have lost. Figure 27.3 (p. 374) shows the evolutionary history of whales.

FIGURE 27.1

Synoplotherium Vorax, a Mesonychid from the middle Eocene

FIGURE 27.2

Pakicetus Inachus, a whale ancestor from the early Eocene of Pakistan

FIGURE 27.3

Current view of the evolutionary history of whales

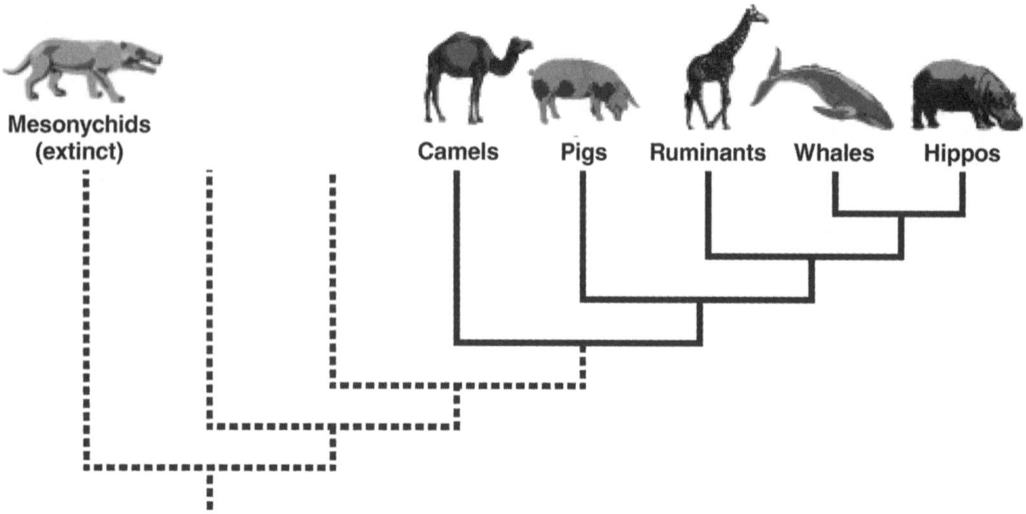

Timeline

The instructional time needed to implement this lab investigation is 130–200 minutes. Appendix 2 (p. 391) provides options for implementing this lab investigation over several class periods. Option C (200 minutes) should be used if students are unfamiliar with scientific writing because this option provides extra instructional time for scaffolding the writing process. You can scaffold the writing process by modeling, providing examples, and providing hints as students write each section of the report. Option D (130 minutes) should be used if students are familiar with scientific writing and have the skills needed to write an investigation report on their own. In option D, students complete stage 6 (writing the investigation report) and stage 8 (revising the investigation report) as homework.

Materials and Preparation

The materials needed to implement this investigation are listed in Table 27.1. The UniProt database, is free to use and available online at *www.uniprot.org*. You should access the database and learn how it works before beginning the lab investigation. In addition, it is important to check if students can access and use the database from a school computer, because some schools have set up firewalls and other restrictions on web browsing.

TABLE 27.1

Materials list

Item	Quantity
Computer with internet access	At least 1 per group
Student handout	1 per student
Mammal Classification Fact Sheet	1 per group
Investigation proposal A (optional)	1 per group
Whiteboard, 2' × 3'*	1 per group
Peer-review guide and instructor scoring rubric	1 per student

* Students can also use computer and presentation software such as Microsoft PowerPoint or Apple Keynote to create their arguments.

Topics for the Explicit and Reflective Discussion

Concepts That Can Be Used to Justify the Evidence

To provide an adequate justification of their evidence, students must explain why they included the evidence in their arguments and make the assumptions underlying their analysis and interpretation of the data explicit. In this investigation, students can use the following concepts to help justify their evidence:

- Protein structure, composition, and synthesis
- Effect of gene mutation on amino acid sequence
- The theory of descent with modification
- The assumptions underlying the construction of a phylogenetic tree

We recommend that you review these concepts during the explicit and reflective discussion to help students make this connection.

How to Design Better Investigations

It is important for students to reflect on the strengths and weaknesses of the investigation they designed during the explicit and reflective discussion. Students should therefore be encouraged to discuss ways to eliminate potential flaws, measurement errors, or sources of bias in their investigations. To help students be more reflective about the design of their investigation, you can ask the following questions:

- What were some of the strengths of your investigation? What made it scientific?
- What were some of the weaknesses of your investigation? What made it less scientific?
- If you were to do this investigation again, what would you do to address the weaknesses in your investigation? What could you do to make it more scientific?

Crosscutting Concepts

This investigation is well aligned with two crosscutting concepts found in *A Framework for K–12 Science Education,* and you should review these concepts during the explicit and reflective discussion.

- *Patterns:* Observed patterns in nature guide many classification systems and the design of investigations in biology. For example, it has been observed that all living things share common features and certain shared derived characteristics can be used to determine evolutionary relationships.
- *Structure and Function:* In nature, the way a living thing is structured or shaped determines how it functions and places limits on what it can and cannot do. The amino acid sequence of a protein, for example, determines the function of that protein.

The Nature of Science and the Nature of Scientific Inquiry

It is important for students to understand the *difference between data and evidence in science.* Data are measurements, observations, and findings from other studies that are collected as part of an investigation. Evidence, in contrast, is analyzed data and an interpretation of the analysis. In this investigation, for example, students access a database containing amino acid sequences for a specific protein. This information is data. The students then use the tools built into the database to analyze the amino acid sequences. Once analyzed, the students have to interpret their analysis to produce the evidence they need to support their claim.

It is also important for students to understand that *scientific knowledge is durable but also tentative.* A person can have confidence in the validity of scientific knowledge but must also accept that scientific knowledge may be abandoned or modified in light of new evidence or because existing evidence has been reconceptualized by scientists. There are many examples in the history of science of both evolutionary changes (i.e., the slow or gradual refinement of ideas) and revolutionary changes (i.e., the rapid abandonment of a well-established idea) in scientific knowledge. For example, for many years biologists worked under the assumption that whales were related to the mesonychids, but they abandoned this view as they learned more about molecular similarities between whales and hippopotamuses.

You should review and provide examples of these two important concepts of the nature of science (NOS) and the nature of scientific inquiry (NOSI) during the explicit and reflective discussion.

Hints for Implementing the Lab

- Learn how to use the database before the lab begins. It is important for you to know how to use it so you can help students when they get stuck or confused.
- A group of three students per computer tends to work well.
- Allow the students to play with the database as part of the tool talk before they begin to design their investigation. This gives students a chance to see what they can and cannot do with the database.
- Be sure that students record the phylogenetic trees that they created using UniProt. They will need to use these trees as evidence in their arguments.

Topic Connections

Table 27.2 (p. 378) provides an overview of the scientific practices, crosscutting concepts, disciplinary core ideas, and support ideas at the heart of this lab investigation. In addition, it lists NOS and NOSI concepts for the explicit and reflective discussion. Finally, it lists literacy skills (*CCSS ELA*) that are addressed during the investigation.

TABLE 27.2

Lab 27 alignment with standards

Scientific practices	• Asking questions • Planning and carrying out investigations • Analyzing and interpreting data • Constructing explanations • Engaging in argument from evidence • Obtaining, evaluating, and communicating information
Crosscutting concepts	• Patterns • Structure and function
Core ideas	• LS1: From molecules to organisms: Structures and processes • LS3: Heredity: Inheritance and variation of traits • LS4: Biological evolution: Unity and diversity
Supporting ideas	• Descent with modification • Phylogenetic trees • Protein synthesis
NOS and NOSI concepts	• Difference between data and evidence • Science as a body of knowledge
Literacy connections *(CCSS ELA)*	• *Reading*: Key ideas and details, craft and structure, integration of knowledge and ideas • *Writing*: Text types and purposes, production and distribution of writing, research to build and present knowledge, range of writing • *Speaking and listening*: Comprehension and collaboration, presentation of knowledge and ideas

Lab 27. Whale Evolution: How Are Whales Related to Other Mammals?

Lab Handout

Introduction

You have learned about the different categories of large molecules that play an important role in the bodies of organisms. One category of large molecule is called protein. A protein is made up of a chain of amino acids, and a specific gene determines the sequence of amino acids in the chain. Enzymes are examples of proteins that are very important to the function of an organism, and these proteins have very specific structures.

Protein structure levels

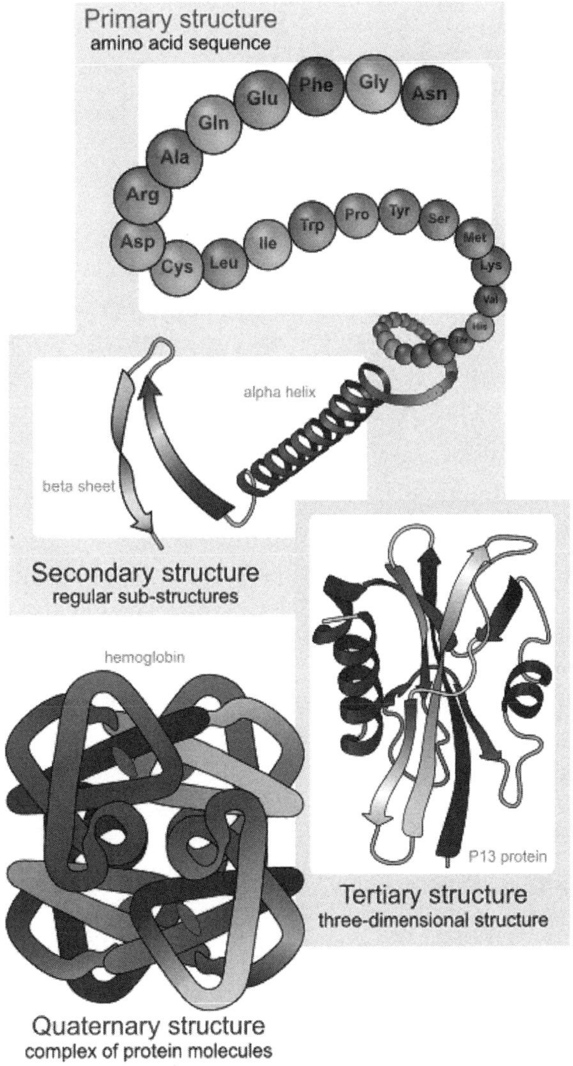

Scientists are often interested in the amino acid sequence of proteins for a number of reasons. Scientists, for example, often want to identify the amino acid sequence of a protein because the sequence determines the structure of a protein (see the figure to the right). Scientists can also use amino acid sequences to examine evolutionary relationships, because all life on Earth shares a common ancestor.

The central idea of biological evolution is that through a process of descent with modification, the common ancestor of all life on Earth gave rise to the biodiversity we see today (see the figure on p. 378). This idea is important in biology because it enables scientists to study the evolutionary history of life on Earth. The process of descent with modification, for example, suggests that two species that diverged from one another relatively recently in the history

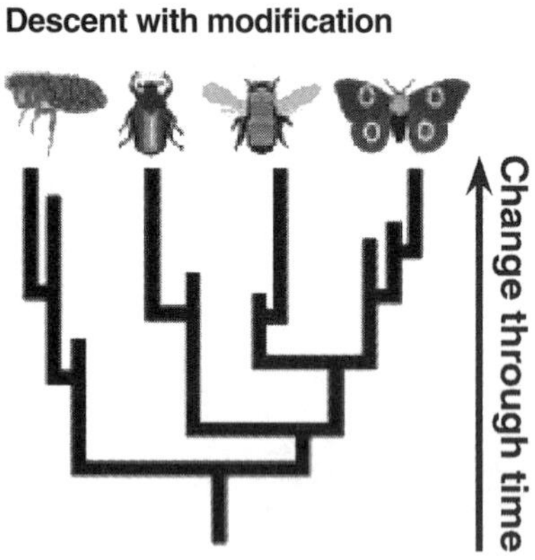

of life on Earth will share more genetic similarities than two species that diverged from one another further back in time. Species that share many genetic similarities, as a result, are considered to be more closely related than two species that have many differences. Scientists, therefore, can compare an amino acid sequence for a specific protein to determine the evolutionary history of a group of organisms. In this investigation you will use an online database called UniProt that contains information about amino acid sequences to determine how whales are related to other mammals.

Your Task

Use the UniProt online database to examine the amino acid sequence for a protein found in all mammals. The protein you will examine is called hemoglobin subunit alpha (HBA); it enables red blood cells to transport oxygen. You will then choose several mammals that you think may be closely related to whales and use the UniProt database to create a phylogenetic tree that illustrates the evolutionary history of this group of mammals based on similarities and differences in the amino acid sequence of the HBA protein. You will then need to explain (1) how whales are related to other mammals and (2) how the phylogenetic tree you created supports your claim.

The guiding question of this investigation is, **How are whales related to other mammals?**

Materials

You will use the following materials during your investigation:

- An online database called UniProt, which can be accessed at *www.uniprot.org*
- Mammal Classification Fact Sheet

Safety Precautions

1. Use caution when working with electrical equipment. Keep away from water sources in that they can cause shorts, fires, and shock hazards. Use only GFI-protected circuits.
2. Wash hands with soap and water after completing this lab.
3. Follow all normal lab safety rules.

Getting Started

To answer the guiding question, you will need to use the UniProt database. This database is a collection of amino acid sequences that have been submitted by scientists from all over the world, and it is free for anyone to use. You will use this database to examine the HBA amino acid sequence found in whales and then compare it with the HBA amino acid sequence found in other mammals.

Once you access the UniProt database, follow these directions:

- In the "Query" box at the top of the page type in "HBA Whale" and click "Search."
    - Click on the first box to select "Sperm Whale."
    - Your selection should appear in a green toolbar at the bottom of the window.
- Go back up to the "Query" box at the top of the page and type in "HBA" and click "Search."
- Click on the boxes at the left of the page to make "checks" next to the organisms you want to compare with the sperm whale. Make sure you select animals with the gene HBA listed (not HBA1 or HBA2).
- Once you have made your selections, click on the "Align" button at the bottom of the page. It will take a few seconds to run, so be patient. You are running an application called ALIGN that compares the amino acid sequence of the organisms you selected. The application will provide you with the HBA amino acid sequence for all the organisms you selected, a phylogenetic tree based on differences in the sequence (which are shared derived characteristics), and a key that will tell you which entry belongs to which animal.

Once you know how to use the UniProt database to compare the amino acid sequences of different mammals, you need to think about what data you will need to collect and what you will do with the results of the analysis. To determine what type of data you need to collect, think about the following questions:

- Which mammals will you need to include in the analysis?
- How many mammals will you need to include?
- Will you choose mammals to represent different orders or to represent different families?

To determine what to do with the results of the analysis, think about the following questions:

- How will you keep track of the information you collect and how will you organize it?

- What would you expect to see in the amino acid sequence of a mammal that is closely related to the sperm whale? How about a mammal that is not very closely related to the sperm whale?
- Will you be able to use the results of your analysis as your claim, or are the results of your analysis part of the evidence you will use to support your claim?
- How can you share the results of your analysis with others?

Investigation Proposal Required? ☐ Yes ☐ No

Connections to Crosscutting Concepts and to the Nature of Science and the Nature of Scientific Inquiry

As you work through your investigation, be sure to think about

- the importance of identifying and explaining patterns in science,
- the relationship between structure and function in nature,
- the difference between data and evidence, and
- how science, as a body of knowledge, develops over time.

Argumentation Session

Once your group has finished collecting and analyzing your data, prepare a whiteboard that you can use to share your initial argument. Your whiteboard should include all the information shown in the figure below.

Argument presentation on a whiteboard

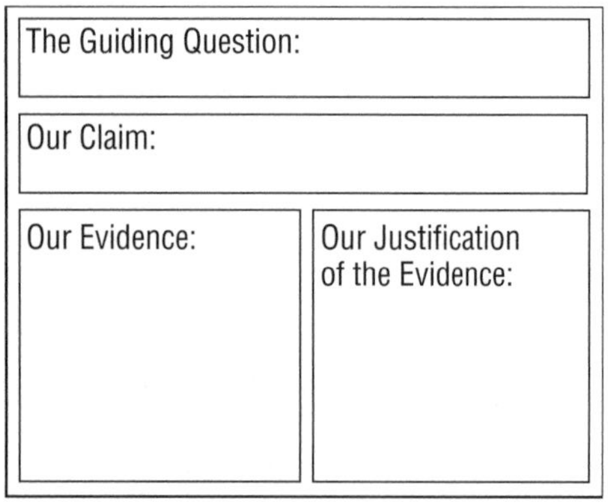

To share your argument with others, we will be using a round-robin format. This means that one member of your group will stay at your lab station to share your group's argument while the other members of your group go to the other lab stations one at a time to listen to and critique the arguments developed by your classmates.

The goal of the argumentation session is not to convince others that your argument is the best one; rather, the goal is to identify errors or instances of faulty reasoning in the arguments so these mistakes can be fixed. You will therefore need to evaluate the content of the claim, the quality of the evidence used to support the claim, and the strength of the justification of the evidence included in each argument that you see. In order to critique an argument, you will need more information than what is included on the whiteboard. You might, therefore, need to ask the presenter one or more follow-up questions, such as:

- How did you use the database to collect your data? Why did you decide to focus on those mammals?
- What did you do to analyze your data? Why did you decide to do it that way? Did you check your calculations?
- Is that the only way to interpret the results of your analysis? How do you know that your interpretation of your analysis is appropriate?
- Why did your group decide to present your evidence in that manner?
- What other claims did your group discuss before you decided on that one? Why did your group abandon those alternative ideas?
- How confident are you that your claim is valid? What could you do to increase your confidence?

Once the argumentation session is complete, you will have a chance to meet with your group and revise your original argument. Your group might need to gather more data or design a way to test one or more alternative claims as part of this process. Remember, your goal at this stage of the investigation is to develop the most valid or acceptable answer to the research question!

Report

Once you have completed your research, you will need to prepare an investigation report that consists of three sections that provide answers to the following questions:

1. What question were you trying to answer and why?
2. What did you do during your investigation and why did you conduct your investigation in this way?
3. What is your argument?

Your report should answer these questions in two pages or less. This report must be typed, and any diagrams, figures, or tables should be embedded into the document. Be sure to write in a persuasive style; you are trying to convince others that your claim is acceptable or valid!

Mammal Classification Fact Sheet

Phylum	Class	Order*	Families†	Example
Chordata	Mammalia	Didelphimorphia	Didelphidae	Opossum
		Diprotodontia	Phascolarctidae	Koala
			Vombatidae	Wombat
			Macropodidae	Kangaroo
		Chiroptera	Pteropodidae	Fruit bat
			Emballonuridae	Sac-winged bat
			Vespertilionidae	Evening bat
		Primates	Lemuridae	Lemur
			Hominidae	Great ape
			Hylobatidae	Gibbon
		Carnivora	Felidae	Cat
			Canidae	Dog
			Ursidae	Bear
			Phocidae	Seal
			Odobenidae	Walrus
			Mustelidae	Weasel
		Cetacea	Balaenopteridae	Humpback whale
			Eschrichtiidae	Grey whale
			Physeteridae	Sperm whale
			Delphinidae	Dolphin
			Monodontidae	Beluga whale
			Phocoenidae	Porpoise
		Sirenia	Dugongidae	Dugong
			Trichechidae	Manatee
		Proboscidea	Elephantidae	Elephant
		Perissodactyla	Equidae	Horse
			Tapiridae	Tapir
			Rhinocerotidae	Rhinoceros
		Artiodactyla	Hippopotamidae	Hippopotamus
			Camelidae	Camel
			Giraffidae	Giraffe
			Cervidae	Deer
			Bovidae	Cow
		Rodentia	Castoridae	Beaver
			Caviidae	Guinea pig
			Cricetidae	Rat
			Sciuridae	Squirrel
		Lagomorpha	Leporidae	Rabbit

* Some orders have been omitted.

† Many of the families within each order have been omitted.

Lab 27. Whale Evolution: How Are Whales Related to Other Mammals?

Checkout Questions

1. How do the branches of a phylogenetic tree demonstrate the relatedness of species?

2. All evidence is data, but all data are not evidence.

   a. I agree with this statement.
   b. I disagree with this statement.

   Explain your answer, using examples from your investigation about whale evolution.

3. Scientific knowledge may be abandoned or modified in light of new evidence or due to the reconceptualization of prior evidence and knowledge.

   a. I agree with this statement.
   b. I disagree with this statement.

   Explain your answer, using information from your investigation about whale evolution.

4. An important aspect of science is identifying and explaining patterns in nature. Explain why this is important for scientists to do, using an example from your investigation about whale evolution.

5. Scientists often need to think about how structure is related to function in nature when they analyze data or make comparisons. Explain why this is important for scientists to do, using an example from your investigation about whale evolution.

SECTION 6

Appendixes

APPENDIX 1

Standards Alignment Matrixes

Alignment of the Argument-Driven Inquiry Lab Investigations With the Scientific Practices, Crosscutting Concepts, and Core Ideas in *A Framework for K–12 Science Education* (NRC 2012)

Aspect of the NRC *Framework*	Lab Investigation																										
	Osmosis and Diffusion	Cell Structure	Cell Cycle	Normal and Abnormal Cell Division	Photosynthesis	Cellular Respiration	Transpiration	Enzymes	Population Growth	Predator-Prey Relationships	Ecosystems and Biodiversity	Explanations for Animal Behavior	Environmental Influences on Animal Behavior	Interdependence of Organisms	Competition for Resources	Mendelian Genetics	Chromosomes and Karyotypes	DNA Structure	Meiosis	Inheritance of Blood Type	Models of Inheritance	Biodiversity and the Fossil Record	Mechanisms of Evolution	Descent With Modification	Mechanisms of Speciation	Human Evolution	Whale Evolution
Scientific practices																											
Asking questions	□	□	□	□	□	□	□	□	□	□	□	□	□	□	□	□	□	□	□	□	□	□	□	□	□	□	□
Developing and using models	■	□			■	■	■		■	■	■	■				■		■	■	■	■		■		■		
Planning and carrying out investigations	■	■	■	■	■	■	■	■	■	■	■	■	■	■	■	■	■	■	■	■	■	■	■	■	■	■	■
Analyzing and interpreting data	■	■	■	■	■	■	■	■	■	■	■	■	■	■	■	■	■	■	■	■	■	■	■	■	■	■	■
Using mathematics and computational thinking	■		■	■	■	■	■	■	■	■	■	□	□	□	□	■					■	■	■	■	■	■	
Constructing explanations	■	■	■	■	■	■	■	■	■	■	■	■	■	■	■	■	■	■	■	■	■	■	■	■	■	■	■
Engaging in argument from evidence	■	■	■	■	■	■	■	■	■	■	■	■	■	■	■	■	■	■	■	■	■	■	■	■	■	■	■
Obtaining, evaluating, and communicating information	■	■	■	■	■	■	■	■	■	■	■	■	■	■	■	■	■	■	■	■	■	■	■	■	■	■	■
Crosscutting concepts																											
Patterns		■	■	■					■	■	■	■	■		■	■	■	■	■		■	■	■			■	■
Cause and effect: Mechanism and explanation	■				■	■	■	■		■	■	■	■	■		■	■						■		■		

Strong alignment ■; moderate alignment □

Aspect of the NRC *Framework*	Lab Investigation																										
	Osmosis and Diffusion	Cell Structure	Cell Cycle	Normal and Abnormal Cell Division	Photosynthesis	Cellular Respiration	Transpiration	Enzymes	Population Growth	Predator-Prey Relationships	Ecosystems and Biodiversity	Explanations for Animal Behavior	Environmental Influences on Animal Behavior	Interdependence of Organisms	Competition for Resources	Mendelian Genetics	Chromosomes and Karyotypes	DNA Structure	Meiosis	Inheritance of Blood Type	Models of Inheritance	Biodiversity and the Fossil Record	Mechanisms of Evolution	Descent With Modification	Mechanisms of Speciation	Human Evolution	Whale Evolution
Scale, proportion, and quantity			■	■			■					■		■	■	■		■				■		■	■		
Systems and system models	■				■				■	■	■								■	■	■				■		
Energy and matter: Flows, cycles, and conservation	■				■	■	■	■						■													
Structure and function		■		■		■	■	■									■	■		■				■		■	■
Stability and change			■						■	■	■		■														
Core ideas																											
LS1: From molecules to organisms: Structures and processes	■	■	■	■	■	■	■	■									□	□	□	□	□						■
LS2: Ecosystems: Interactions, energy and dynamics					■	■	□	□	■	■	■	■	■	■	■								■		■		
LS3: Heredity: Inheritance and variation of traits																■	■	■	■	■	■		■	□	■		■
LS4: Biological evolution: Unity and diversity																						■	■	■	■	■	■

Strong alignment ■; moderate alignment □

Alignment of the Argument-Driven Inquiry Lab Investigations With the *Common Core State Standards,* for English Language Arts and Mathematics (NGAC and CCSSO 2010)

Standard	Lab Investigation																										
	Osmosis and Diffusion	Cell Structure	Cell Cycle	Normal and Abnormal Cell Division	Photosynthesis	Cellular Respiration	Transpiration	Enzymes	Population Growth	Predator-Prey Relationships	Ecosystems and Biodiversity	Explanations for Animal Behavior	Environmental Influences on Animal Behavior	Interdependence of Organisms	Competition for Resources	Mendelian Genetics	Chromosomes and Karyotypes	DNA Structure	Meiosis	Inheritance of Blood Type	Models of Inheritance	Biodiversity and the Fossil Record	Mechanisms of Evolution	Descent With Modification	Mechanisms of Speciation	Human Evolution	Whale Evolution
Reading																											
Key ideas and details	■	■	■	■	■	■	■	■	■	■	■	■	■	■	■	■	■	■	■	■	■	■	■	■	■	■	■
Craft and structure	■	■	■	■	■	■	■	■	■	■	■	■	■	■	■	■	■	■	■	■	■	■	■	■	■	■	■
Integration of knowledge and ideas	■	■	■	■	■	■	■	■	■	■	■	■	■	■	■	■	■	■	■	■	■	■	■	■	■	■	■
Writing																											
Text types and purposes	■	■	■	■	■	■	■	■	■	■	■	■	■	■	■	■	■	■	■	■	■	■	■	■	■	■	■
Production and distribution of writing	■	■	■	■	■	■	■	■	■	■	■	■	■	■	■	■	■	■	■	■	■	■	■	■	■	■	■
Research to build and present knowledge	■	■	■	■	■	■	■	■	■	■	■	■	■	■	■	■	■	■	■	■	■	■	■	■	■	■	■
Range of writing	■	■	■	■	■	■	■	■	■	■	■	■	■	■	■	■	■	■	■	■	■	■	■	■	■	■	■
Speaking and listening																											
Comprehension and collaboration	■	■	■	■	■	■	■	■	■	■	■	■	■	■	■	■	■	■	■	■	■	■	■	■	■	■	■
Presentation of knowledge and ideas	■	■	■	■	■	■	■	■	■	■	■	■	■	■	■	■	■	■	■	■	■	■	■	■	■	■	■
Mathematics																											
Create equations that describe numbers or relationships			■	■	■	■	■	■													□						
Solve equations and inequalities in one variable			■	■	■	■	■	■													□						
Reason quantitatively and use units to solve problems	■		■	■	■	■	■	■	■	■	■	■	■	■	■	■					■	■	■	■	■	■	

Strong alignment ■; moderate alignment □

Alignment of the Argument-Driven Inquiry Lab Investigations With the Nature of Science (NOS) and the Nature of Scientific Inquiry (NOSI) Concepts*

NOS or NOSI concept	Lab Investigation																										
	Osmosis and Diffusion	Cell Structure	Cell Cycle	Normal and Abnormal Cell Division	Photosynthesis	Cellular Respiration	Transpiration	Enzymes	Population Growth	Predator-Prey Relationships	Ecosystems and Biodiversity	Explanations for Animal Behavior	Environmental Influences on Animal Behavior	Interdependence of Organisms	Competition for Resources	Mendelian Genetics	Chromosomes and Karyotypes	DNA Structure	Meiosis	Inheritance of Blood Type	Models of Inheritance	Biodiversity and the Fossil Record	Mechanisms of Evolution	Descent With Modification	Mechanisms of Speciation	Human Evolution	Whale Evolution
Observations and inferences			■	■	■		■				■				■					■			■				
Science as a body of knowledge			■	■				■				■	■					■						■			■
Scientific theories and laws						■										■			■		■				■		
Social and cultural influences										■				■	■		■										
Difference between data and evidence	■								■				■							■		■				■	■
Methods used in scientific investigations		■					■		■	■		■		■			■	■				■	■	■		■	
Imagination and creativity in science		■				■					■					■			■								
Nature and role of experiments	■				■			■																	■		

*The NOS/NOSI concepts listed in this matrix are based on the work of Abd-El-Khalick and Lederman 2000; Akerson, Abd-El-Khalick, and Lederman 2000; Lederman et al. 2002, 2014; and Schwartz, Lederman, and Crawford 2004.

References

Abd-El-Khalick, F., and N. G. Lederman. 2000. Improving science teachers' conceptions of nature of science: A critical review of the literature. *International Journal of Science Education* 22: 665–701.

Akerson, V., F. Abd-El-Khalick, and N. Lederman. 2000. Influence of a reflective explicit activity-based approach on elementary teachers' conception of nature of science. *Journal of Research in Science Teaching* 37 (4): 295–317.

Lederman, N. G., F. Abd-El-Khalick, R. L. Bell, and R. S. Schwartz. 2002. Views of nature of science questionnaire: Toward a valid and meaningful assessment of learners' conceptions of nature of science. *Journal of Research in Science Teaching* 39 (6): 497–521.

Lederman, J., N. Lederman, S. Bartos, S. Bartels, A. Meyer, and R. Schwartz. 2014. Meaningful assessment of learners' understanding about scientific inquiry: The Views About Scientific Inquiry (VASI) questionnaire. *Journal of Research in Science Teaching* 51 (1): 65–83.

National Governors Association Center for Best Practices and Council of Chief State School Officers (NGAC and CCSSO). 2010. *Common core state standards.* Washington, DC: NGAC and CCSSO.

National Research Council (NRC). 2012. *A framework for K–12 science education: Practices, crosscutting concepts, and core ideas.* Washington, DC: National Academies Press.

Schwartz, R. S., N. Lederman, and B. Crawford. 2004. Developing views of nature of science in an authentic context: An explicit approach to bridging the gap between nature of science and scientific inquiry. *Science Education* 88: 610–645.

APPENDIX 2

Options for Implementing ADI Lab Investigations

Option A

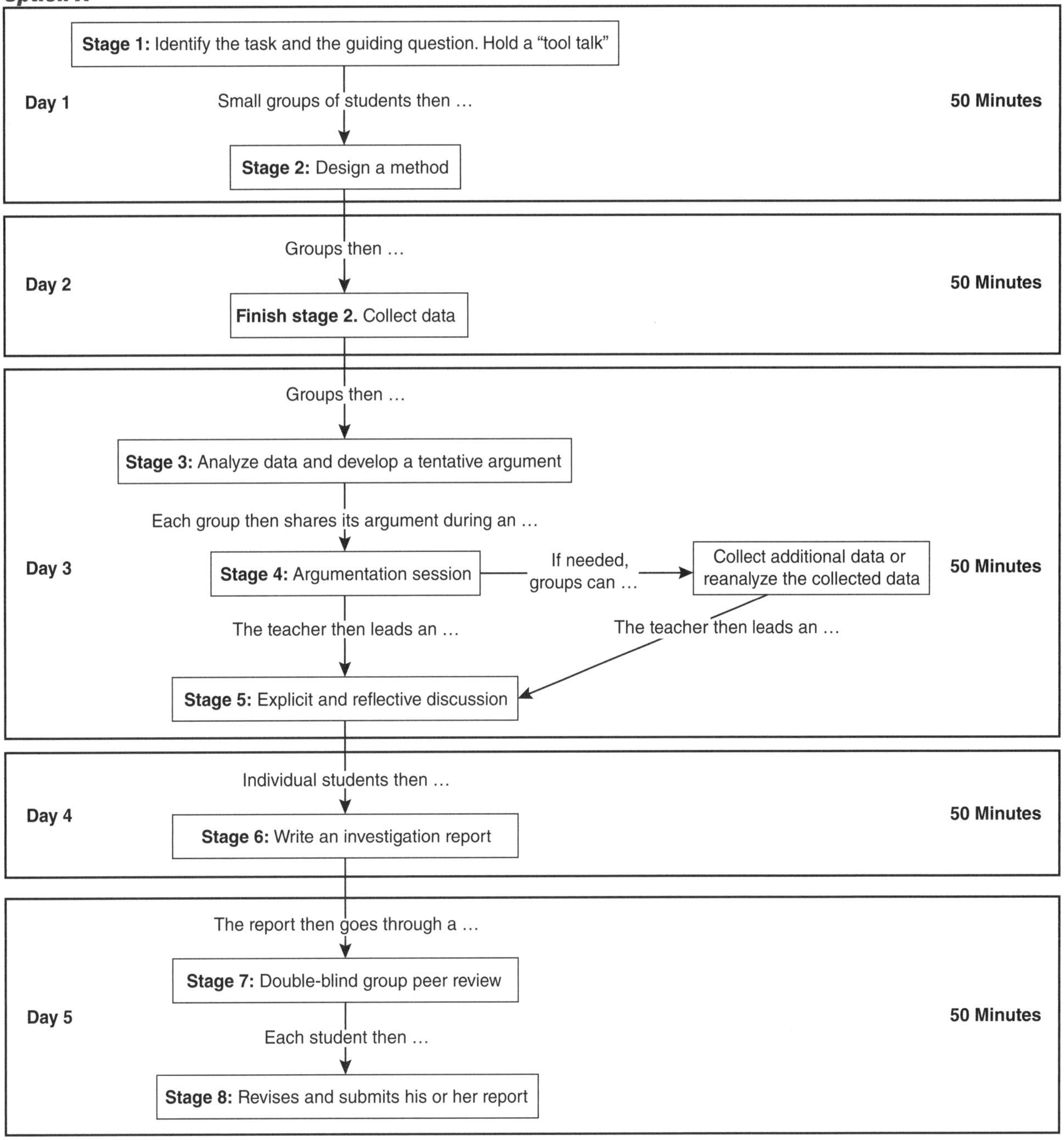

Option B

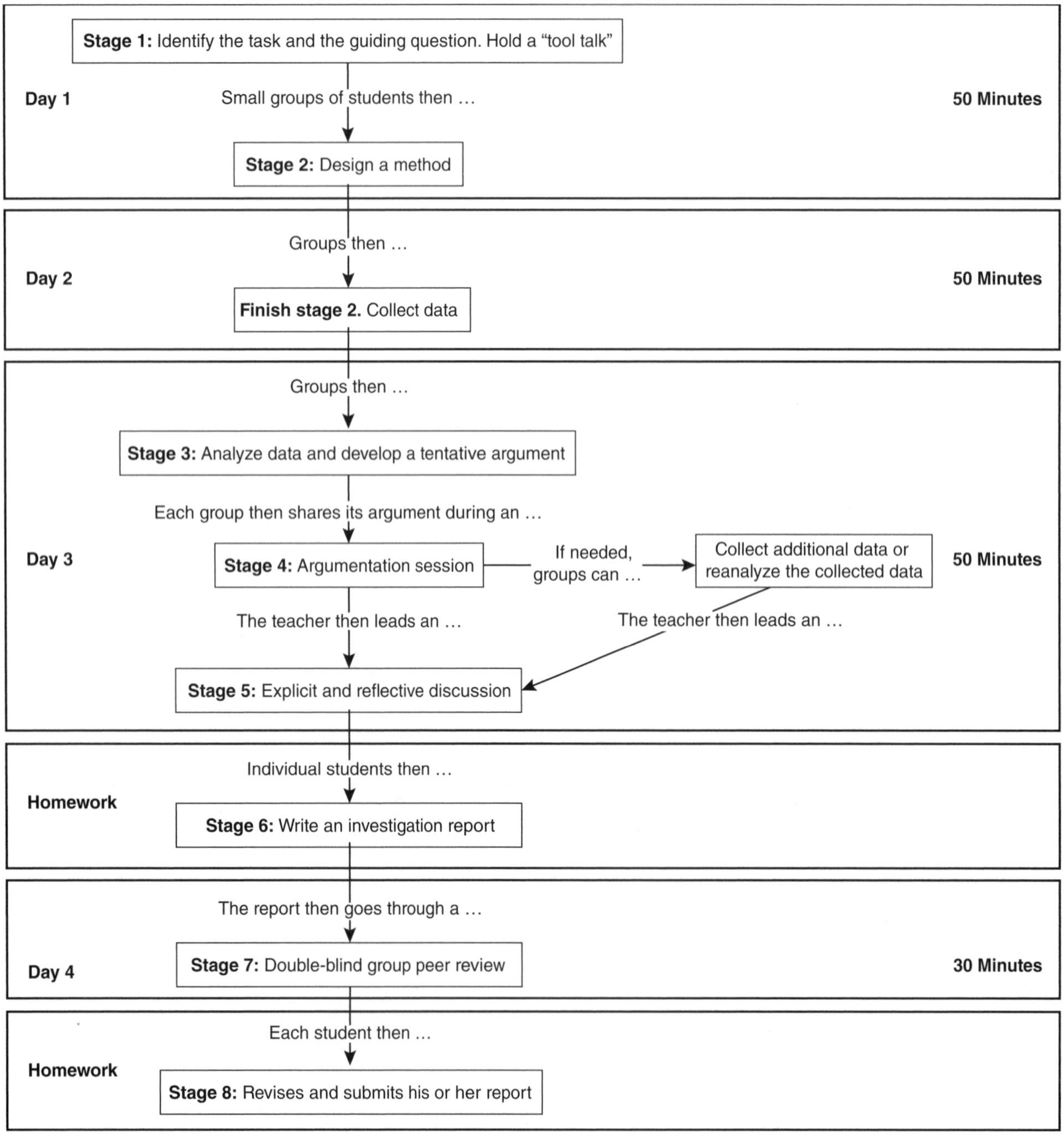
Day 1
Stage 1: Identify the task and the guiding question. Hold a "tool talk"
Small groups of students then …
Stage 2: Design a method
50 Minutes
Day 2
Groups then …
Finish stage 2. Collect data
50 Minutes
Day 3
Groups then …
Stage 3: Analyze data and develop a tentative argument
Each group then shares its argument during an …
Stage 4: Argumentation session
If needed, groups can …
Collect additional data or reanalyze the collected data
The teacher then leads an …
The teacher then leads an …
Stage 5: Explicit and reflective discussion
50 Minutes
Homework
Individual students then …
Stage 6: Write an investigation report
Day 4
The report then goes through a …
Stage 7: Double-blind group peer review
30 Minutes
Homework
Each student then …
Stage 8: Revises and submits his or her report

Option C

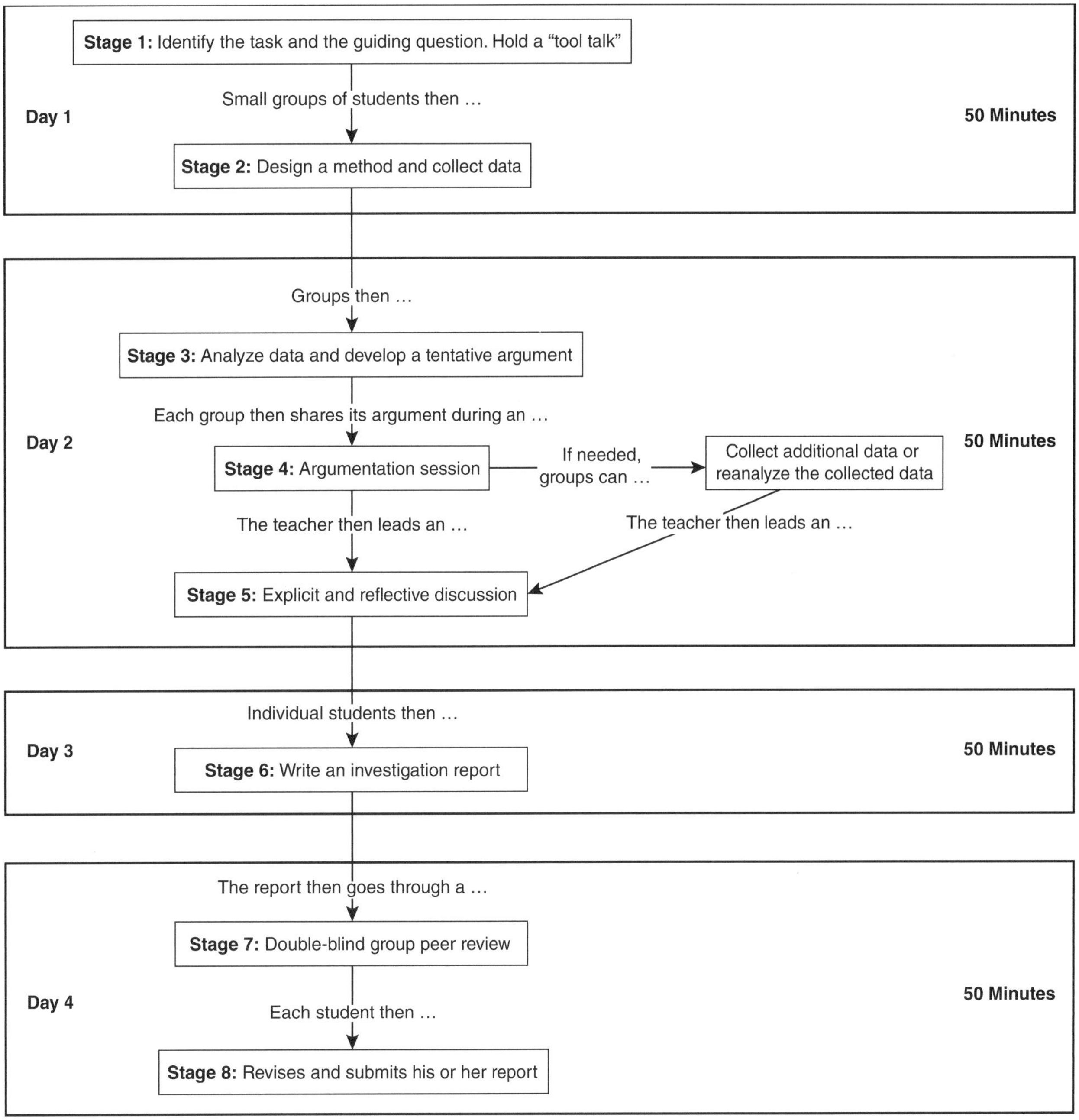
Stage 1: Identify the task and the guiding question. Hold a "tool talk"
Small groups of students then …
Day 1
50 Minutes
Stage 2: Design a method and collect data
Groups then …
Stage 3: Analyze data and develop a tentative argument
Each group then shares its argument during an …
Day 2
50 Minutes
Stage 4: Argumentation session
If needed, groups can …
Collect additional data or reanalyze the collected data
The teacher then leads an …
The teacher then leads an …
Stage 5: Explicit and reflective discussion
Individual students then …
Day 3
50 Minutes
Stage 6: Write an investigation report
The report then goes through a …
Stage 7: Double-blind group peer review
Day 4
50 Minutes
Each student then …
Stage 8: Revises and submits his or her report

Option D

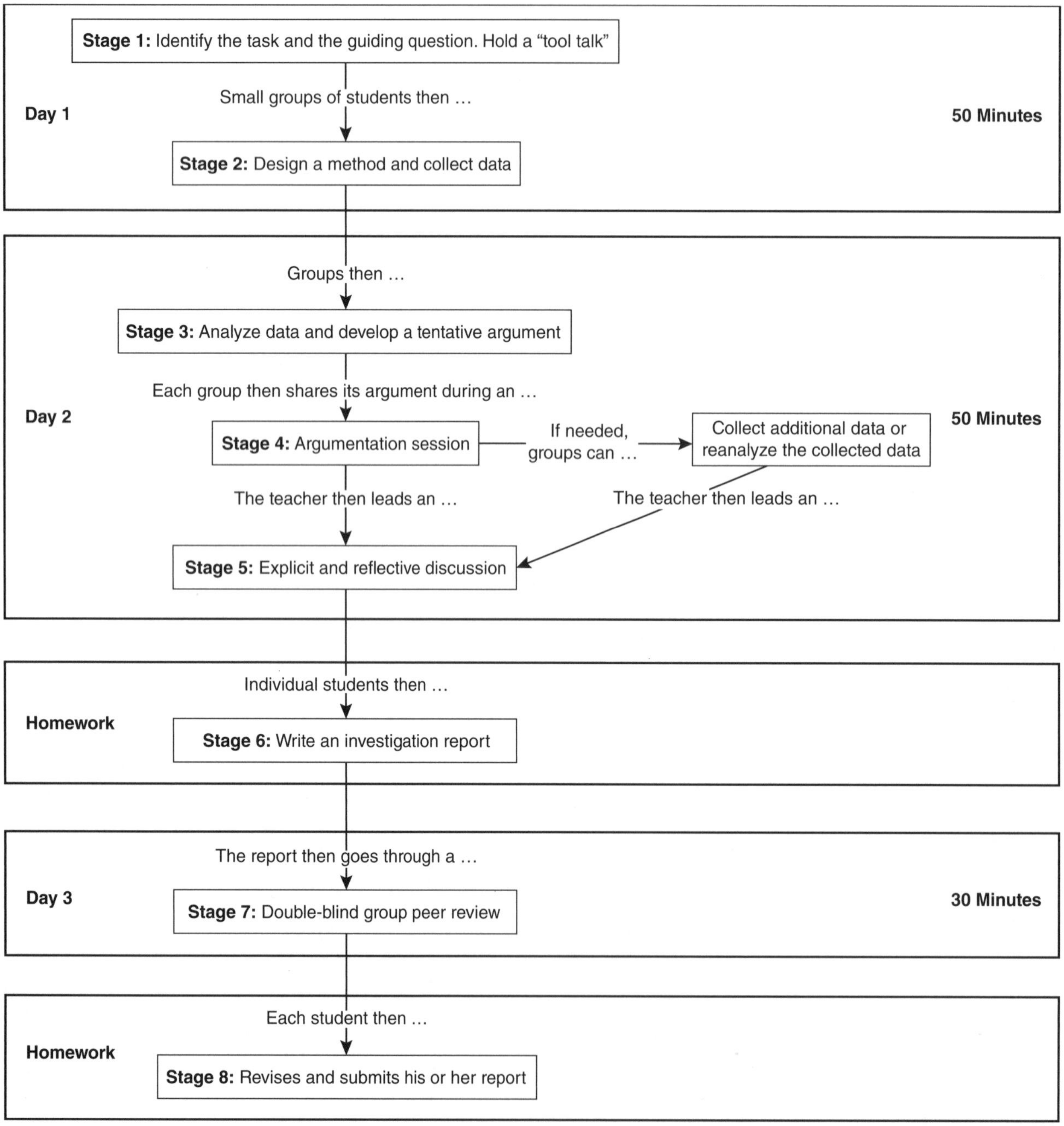
Stage 1: Identify the task and the guiding question. Hold a "tool talk"
Small groups of students then …
Day 1
50 Minutes
Stage 2: Design a method and collect data
Groups then …
Stage 3: Analyze data and develop a tentative argument
Each group then shares its argument during an …
Day 2
50 Minutes
Stage 4: Argumentation session
If needed, groups can …
Collect additional data or reanalyze the collected data
The teacher then leads an …
The teacher then leads an …
Stage 5: Explicit and reflective discussion
Individual students then …
Homework
Stage 6: Write an investigation report
The report then goes through a …
Day 3
30 Minutes
Stage 7: Double-blind group peer review
Each student then …
Homework
Stage 8: Revises and submits his or her report

Option E

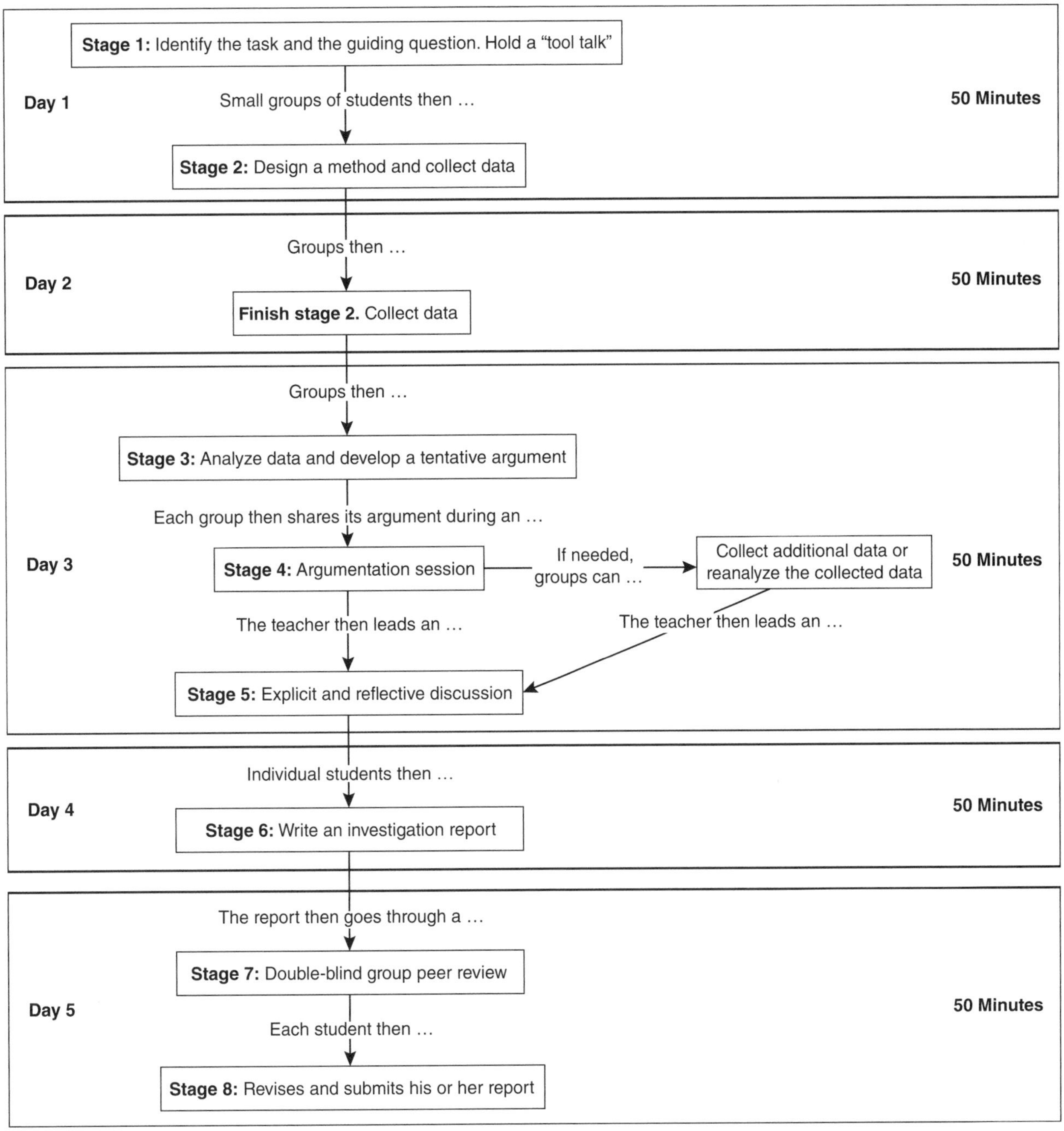
Day 1
Stage 1: Identify the task and the guiding question. Hold a "tool talk"
Small groups of students then …
Stage 2: Design a method and collect data
50 Minutes
Day 2
Groups then …
Finish stage 2. Collect data
50 Minutes
Day 3
Groups then …
Stage 3: Analyze data and develop a tentative argument
Each group then shares its argument during an …
Stage 4: Argumentation session
If needed, groups can …
Collect additional data or reanalyze the collected data
The teacher then leads an …
The teacher then leads an …
Stage 5: Explicit and reflective discussion
50 Minutes
Day 4
Individual students then …
Stage 6: Write an investigation report
50 Minutes
Day 5
The report then goes through a …
Stage 7: Double-blind group peer review
Each student then …
Stage 8: Revises and submits his or her report
50 Minutes

Option F

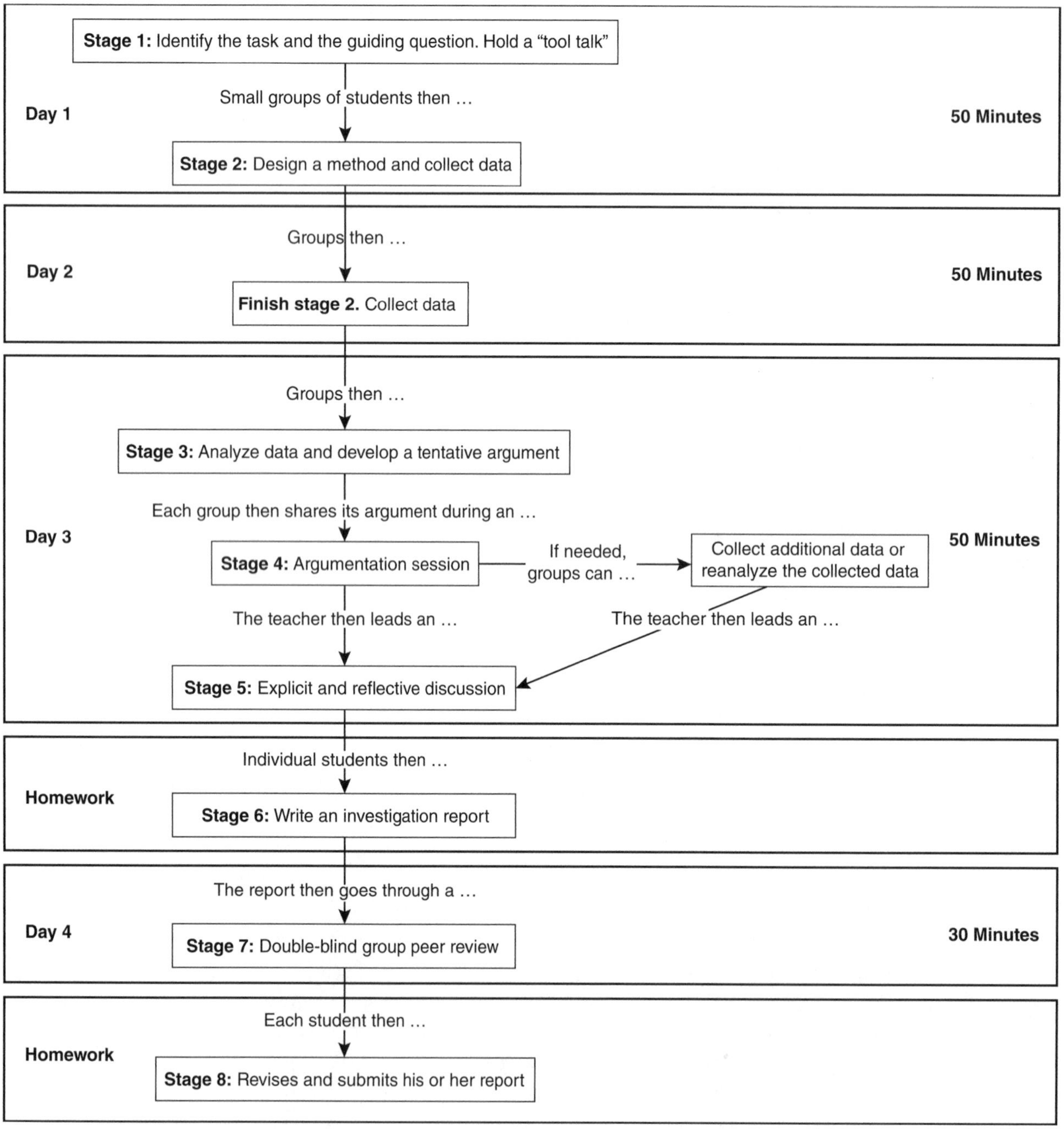
Day 1
50 Minutes
Stage 1: Identify the task and the guiding question. Hold a “tool talk”
Small groups of students then …
Stage 2: Design a method and collect data
Day 2
50 Minutes
Groups then …
Finish stage 2. Collect data
Day 3
50 Minutes
Groups then …
Stage 3: Analyze data and develop a tentative argument
Each group then shares its argument during an …
Stage 4: Argumentation session
If needed, groups can …
Collect additional data or reanalyze the collected data
The teacher then leads an …
The teacher then leads an …
Stage 5: Explicit and reflective discussion
Homework
Individual students then …
Stage 6: Write an investigation report
Day 4
30 Minutes
The report then goes through a …
Stage 7: Double-blind group peer review
Homework
Each student then …
Stage 8: Revises and submits his or her report

Option G

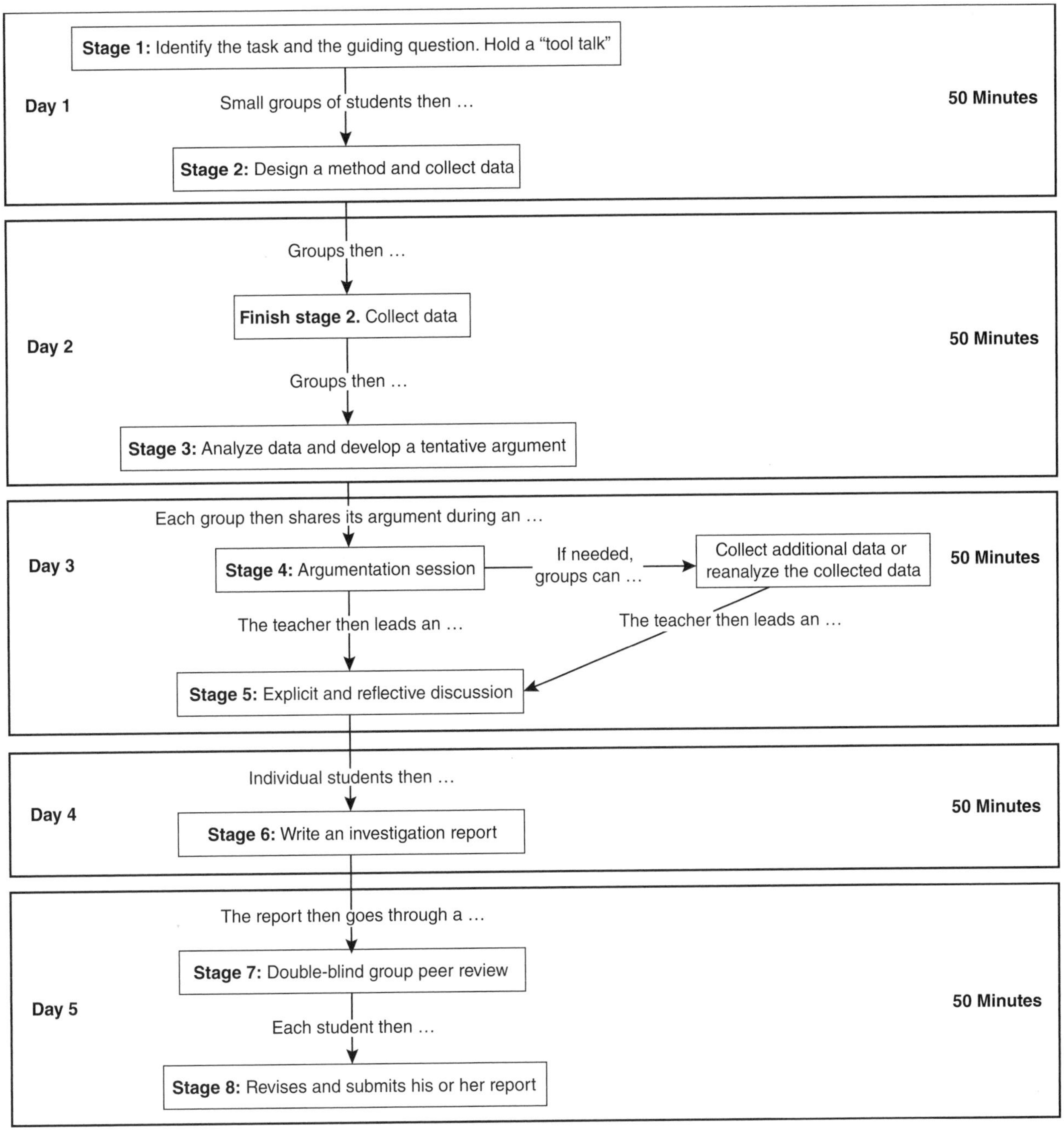
Day 1
Stage 1: Identify the task and the guiding question. Hold a "tool talk"
Small groups of students then …
Stage 2: Design a method and collect data
50 Minutes
Day 2
Groups then …
Finish stage 2. Collect data
Groups then …
Stage 3: Analyze data and develop a tentative argument
50 Minutes
Day 3
Each group then shares its argument during an …
Stage 4: Argumentation session
If needed, groups can …
Collect additional data or reanalyze the collected data
The teacher then leads an …
The teacher then leads an …
Stage 5: Explicit and reflective discussion
50 Minutes
Day 4
Individual students then …
Stage 6: Write an investigation report
50 Minutes
Day 5
The report then goes through a …
Stage 7: Double-blind group peer review
Each student then …
Stage 8: Revises and submits his or her report
50 Minutes

Option H

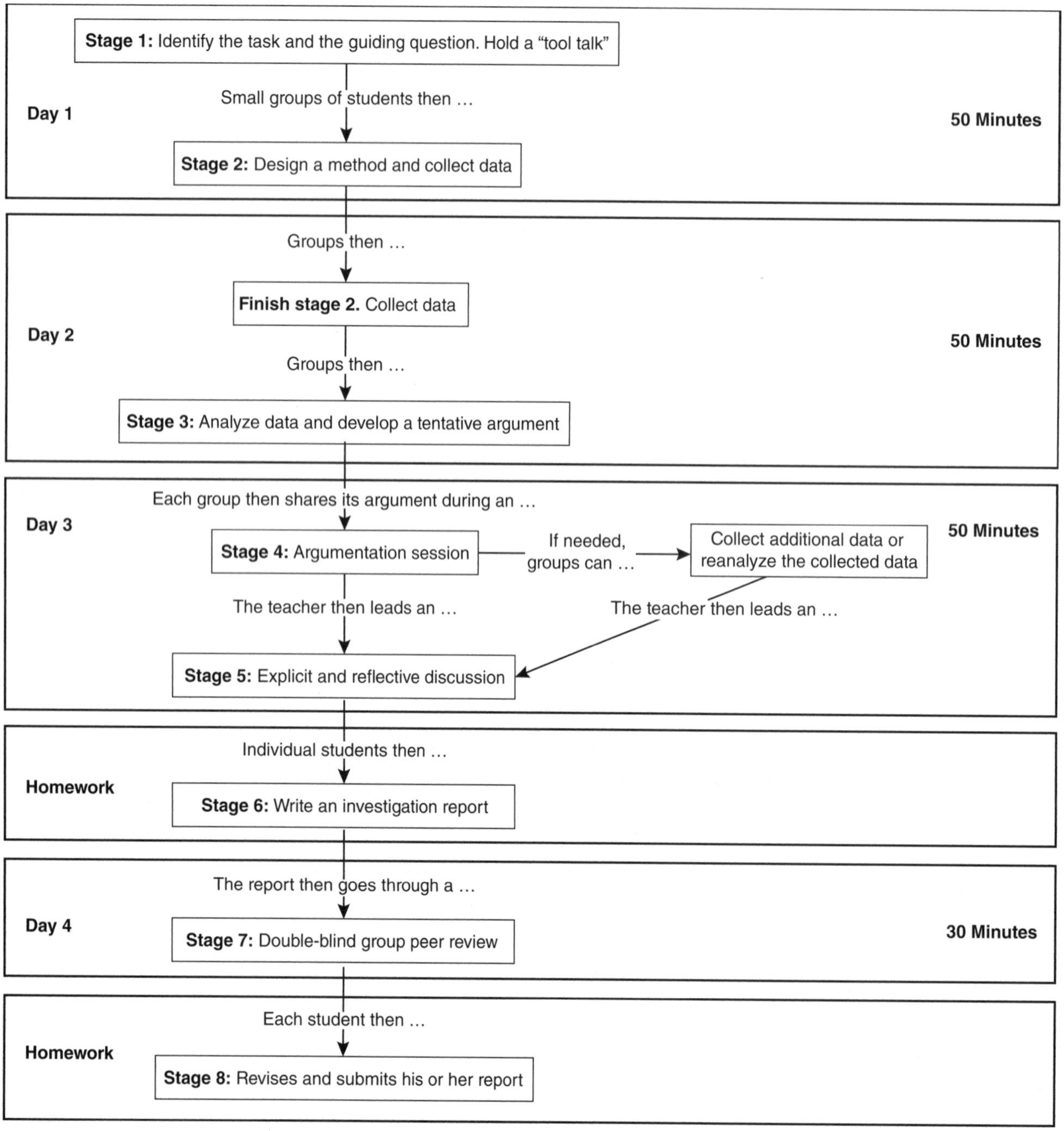

Day 1
Stage 1: Identify the task and the guiding question. Hold a "tool talk"
Small groups of students then …
Stage 2: Design a method and collect data
50 Minutes
Day 2
Groups then …
Finish stage 2. Collect data
Groups then …
Stage 3: Analyze data and develop a tentative argument
50 Minutes
Day 3
Each group then shares its argument during an …
Stage 4: Argumentation session
If needed, groups can …
Collect additional data or reanalyze the collected data
The teacher then leads an …
The teacher then leads an …
Stage 5: Explicit and reflective discussion
50 Minutes
Homework
Individual students then …
Stage 6: Write an investigation report
Day 4
The report then goes through a …
Stage 7: Double-blind group peer review
30 Minutes
Homework
Each student then …
Stage 8: Revises and submits his or her report

APPENDIX 3

Investigation Proposal Options

This appendix presents three investigation proposals that may be used in most labs. The development of these proposals was supported by the Institute of Education Sciences, U.S. Department of Education, through grant R305A100909 to Florida State University.

The format of investigation proposals A and B is modeled after a hypothetical deductive-reasoning guide described in *Exploring the Living World* (Lawson 1995) and modified from an investigation guide described in an article by Maguire, Myerowitz, and Sampson (2010).

References

Lawson, A. E. 1995. *Exploring the living world: A laboratory manual for biology*. McGraw-Hill College.

Maguire, L., L. Myerowitz, and V. Sampson. 2010. Diffusion and osmosis in cells: A guided inquiry activity. *The Science Teacher* 77 (8): 55–60.

Investigation Proposal A

The Guiding Question ...

Hypothesis 1

IF ...

Hypothesis 2

IF ...

The Test

AND ...

Procedure

What data will you collect?

How will you analyze the data??

What safety precautions will you follow?

Predicted Result if hypothesis 1 is valid

THEN ...

Predicted Result if hypothesis 2 is valid

THEN ...

The Actual Results

AND ...

I approve of this investigation. ______________________ ____________

Instructor's Signature Date

The development of this investigation proposal was supported by the Institute of Education Sciences, U.S. Department of Education, through Grant R305A100909 to the Florida State University. The format of the proposal is modeled after a hypothetical deductive-reasoning guide described in Exploring the Living World (Lawson 1995) and modified from an investigation guide described in Macquire, Myerowitz, and Sampson (2010).

Investigation Proposal B

The Guiding Question …

Hypothesis 1	**Hypothesis 2**	**Hypothesis 3**
IF …	IF …	IF …

The Test

AND …

Procedure

What data will you collect?

How will you analyze the data??

What safety precautions will you follow?

Predicted Result if hypothesis 1 is valid	**Predicted Result** if hypothesis 2 is valid	**Predicted Result** if hypothesis 3 is valid
THEN …	THEN …	THEN …

The Actual Results

AND …

I approve of this investigation. ______________________ Instructor's Signature ____________ Date

The development of this investigation proposal was supported by the Institute of Education Sciences, U.S. Department of Education, through Grant R305A100909 to the Florida State University. The format of the proposal is modeled after a hypothetical deductive-reasoning guide described in Exploring the Living World (Lawson 1995) and modified from an investigation guide described in Macquire, Myerowitz, and Sampson (2010).

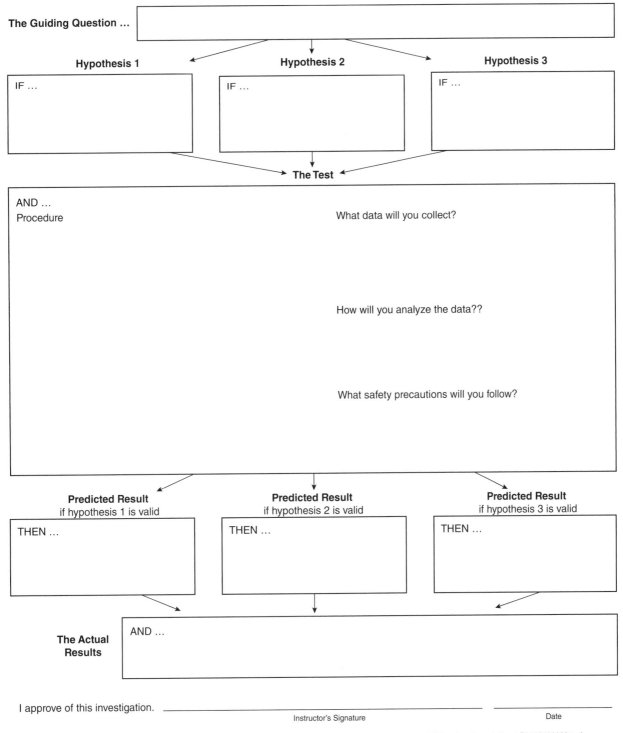

Investigation Proposal C

The Guiding Question ...	
What data will you collect?	
How will you collect your data?	Your Procedure / What safety precautions will you follow?
How will you analyze your data?	
Your actual data	

I approve of this investigation. ______________________ Instructor's Signature ____________ Date

The development of this investigation proposal was supported by the Institute of Education Sciences, U.S. Department of Education, through Grant R305A100909 to the Florida State University.

APPENDIX 4

Peer-Review Guide and Instructor Scoring Rubric

Report By: ____________________ Author: Did the reviewers do a good job? 1 2 3 4 5

ID Number — Rate the overall quality of the peer review

Reviewed By: ____________ ____________ ____________ ____________

ID Number — ID Number — ID Number — ID Number

Section 1: Introduction and Guiding Question	Reviewer Rating			Instructor Score
1. Did the author provide enough *background information* about the concept, theory, law, or model underlying the investigation?	☐ No	☐ Partially	☐ Yes	0 1 2
2. Did the author *describe the goal* of the study?	☐ No	☐ Partially	☐ Yes	0 1 2
3. Did the author make the *guiding question* explicit and explain how the guiding question is related to the background information?	☐ No	☐ Partially	☐ Yes	0 1 2

Reviewers: If your group made any "No" or "Partially" marks in this section, please **explain how the author could improve** this part of his or her report.	**Author:** What revisions did you make in your report? Is there anything you decided to keep the same even though the reviewers suggested otherwise? Be sure to explain why.

Section 2: Method	Reviewer Rating			Instructor Score
1. Did the author describe the *procedure* he/she used to gather data and then explain why he/she used this procedure?	☐ No	☐ Partially	☐ Yes	0 1 2
2. Did the author explain *what data* (quantitative or qualitative) was collected (or used) and why that data was collected (or used)?	☐ No	☐ Partially	☐ Yes	0 1 2
3. Did the author describe *how* he or she *analyzed the data* and explain why the analysis helped him/her answer the guiding question?	☐ No	☐ Partially	☐ Yes	0 1 2
4. Did the author use the *correct term* to describe his/her investigation (i.e., experiment, systematic observation, interpretation of a data set)?	☐ No	☐ Partially	☐ Yes	0 1 2

Reviewers: If your group made any "No" or "Partially" marks in this section, please **explain how the author could improve** this part of his or her report.	**Author:** What revisions did you make in your report? Is there anything you decided to keep the same even though the review-ers suggested otherwise? Be sure to explain why.

Section 3: The Argument	Reviewer Rating			Instructor Score
1. Did the author include a *claim* that answers the guiding question?	☐ No	☐ Partially	☐ Yes	0 1 2
2. Did the author support his or her claim with *high-quality evidence*? ▪ Was the analysis of the data appropriate and free from errors? ▪ Was the author's interpretation of the analysis valid? ▪ Is there enough evidence to support the claim?	 ☐ No ☐ No ☐ No	 ☐ Partially ☐ Partially ☐ Partially	 ☐ Yes ☐ Yes ☐ Yes	 0 1 2 0 1 2 0 1 2
3. Did the author *present the evidence* in an appropriate manner by: ▪ Using a correctly formatted and labeled graph (or table); ▪ Including correct metric units (e.g., m/s, g, ml, and so on); and, ▪ Referencing the graph or table in the body of the text?	 ☐ No ☐ No ☐ No	 ☐ Partially ☐ Partially ☐ Partially	 ☐ Yes ☐ Yes ☐ Yes	 0 1 2 0 1 2 0 1 2
4. Did the author include a *justification of the evidence* that: ▪ Explains why the evidence is important? ▪ Defends the inclusion of the evidence with a specific science concept or by discussing an underlying assumption?	 ☐ No ☐ No	 ☐ Partially ☐ Partially	 ☐ Yes ☐ Yes	 0 1 2 0 1 2
5. Did the author *discuss the arguments* made by other groups by: ▪ Describing some of the claims made by other groups? ▪ Describing how well the other claims align with his or her claim? ▪ Critiquing the evidence provided for the other claims?	 ☐ No ☐ No ☐ No	 ☐ Partially ☐ Partially ☐ Partially	 ☐ Yes ☐ Yes ☐ Yes	 0 1 2 0 1 2 0 1 2
6. Did the author use *scientific terms* (hypothesis vs. prediction, data vs. evidence) and phrases (supports vs. proves) correctly?	☐ No	☐ Partially	☐ Yes	0 1 2
Reviewers: If your group made any "No" or "Partially" marks in this section, please **explain how the author could improve** this part of his or her report.	**Author:** What revisions did you make in your report? Is there anything you decided to keep the same even though the reviewers suggested otherwise? Be sure to explain why.			

Mechanics	Reviewer Rating			Instructor Score
1. *Organization:* Is each section easy to follow? Do paragraphs include multiple sentences? Do paragraphs begin with a topic sentence?	☐ No	☐ Partially	☐ Yes	0 1 2
2. *Grammar:* Are the sentences complete? Is there proper subject-verb agreement in each sentence? No run-on sentences.	☐ No	☐ Partially	☐ Yes	0 1 2
3. *Conventions:* Did the author use appropriate spelling, punctuation, paragraphing and capitalization?	☐ No	☐ Partially	☐ Yes	0 1 2
4. *Word Choice:* Did the author use the appropriate word (there vs. their, to vs. too, and so on)	☐ No	☐ Partially	☐ Yes	0 1 2

Instructor Comments:	
Was the investigation rigorous and appropriate given the nature of the guiding question?	0 1 2

Total: ________/50

IMAGE CREDITS

CHAPTER 1

p. 8: Victor Sampson

p. 9: Victor Sampson

LAB 1

p. 31: Richard Wheeler, Wikimedia Commons, CC BY-SA 3.0. *http://commons.wikimedia.org/wiki/File:Human_Erythrocytes_OsmoticPressure_PhaseContrast_Plain.svg*

p. 33: Victor Sampson

LAB 2

p. 44: User:kaibara87, Wikimedia Commons, CC BY 2.0. *http://commons.wikimedia.org/wiki/File%3AMouth_cells.jpg*

LAB 3

p. 54: Plant: Luis Fernбndez Garcнa, Wikimedia Commons, CC BY-SA 2.5 ES. *http://commons.wikimedia.org/wiki/File:Meristemo_apical_1.jpg*; Animal: User:Staticd, Wikimedia Commons, CC BY-SA 3.0. *http://commons.wikimedia.org/wiki/File:Onion_root_mitosis.jpg*

LAB 4

pp. 61 and 66: Photo by Pat Kenny (National Cancer Institute, National Institutes of Health, Wikimedia Commons, Public domain. *http://commons.wikimedia.org/wiki/File:Normal_and_cancer_cells_%28labeled%29_illustration.jpg*

LAB 5

pp. 74 and 81: Victor Sampson

LAB 6

p. 88: Victor Sampson

p.93 (left): Wikimedia Commons, Public domain. *http://commons.wikimedia.org/wiki/File:Alpha-D-glucose-2D-skeletal-hexagon.png;* (center) Wikimedia Commons, Public domain. *http://commons.wikimedia.org/wiki/File:Lactose_Haworth.svg;* (right) Wikimedia Commons, Public domain. *http://commons.wikimedia.org/wiki/File:Amylopektin_Haworth.svg.*

p. 94 (a): Wolfgang Schaefer, Wikimedia Commons, Public domain. *http://commons.wikimedia.org/wiki/File:Fat_triglyceride_shorthand_formula.png;* (b) Sten Andrй, Wikimedia Commons, Public domain. *http://commons.wikimedia.org/wiki/File:Lysine_simple.png*

p. 95: Victor Sampson

LAB 7

p. 107: H. McKenna, Wikimedia Commons, CC BY 2.5. *http://commons.wikimedia.org/wiki/File:Leaf_anatomy.svg*

p. 108: Victor Sampson

LAB 8

p. 118: Magnus Manske, Wikimedia Commons, CC BY-SA 3.0, GFDL 1.2. *http://upload.wikimedia.org/wikipedia/commons/5/56/Enzyme_activation_energy.png*

p. 119: User:Aejahnke, Wikimedia Commons, CC BY-SA 3.0. *http://upload.wikimedia.org/wikipedia/commons/f/fc/Enzyme_mechanism_1.jpg*

LAB 9

p. 131: National Archives of Australia, Wikimedia Commons, Public domain. *http://commons.wikimedia.org/wiki/File:Rabbits_MyxomatosisTrial_WardangIsland_1938.jpg*

p. 133: *http://ccl.northwestern.edu/netlogo/models/RabbitsGrassWeeds*

LAB 10

p. 145 (top): Doug Smith (National Park Service), Wikimedia Commons, Public domain. *http://commons.wikimedia.org/wiki/File:Canis_lupus_pack_surrounding_Bison.jpg;* (bottom): Victor Sampson

p. 147: *http://ccl.northwestern.edu/netlogo/models/WolfSheepPredation* via Victor Sampson

LAB 11

pp. 159 and 163: Victor Sampson

p. 160: *www.learner.org/courses/envsci/interactives/ecology/ecology1.html*

LAB 12

p. 171: Terry Goss, Wikimedia Commons, CC BY-SA 3.0, GFDL. *http://commons.wikimedia.org/wiki/File:White_shark.jpg*

p. 173: *www.ocearch.org* via Victor Sampson

LAB 13

p. 184: Victor Sampson

LAB 14

p. 197: Victor Sampson

LAKE GRACE INFORMATION PACKET

p. 201: Victor Sampson

p. 204:

Largemouth bass: User:Solrman, Wikimedia Commons, CC0. *http://commons.wikimedia.org,wiki,File%3ALargemouth-bass.jpg*

white bass: Wikimedia Commons , Public domain , *http://commons.wikimedia.org/wiki/File%3AWhite_Bass.jpg*

Bluegill: National Oceanic and Atmospheric Administration, Wikimedia Commons , Public domain. *http://commons.wikimedia.org/wiki/File%3ABlue_gill.jpg*

Daphnia: Photo by Paul Hebert. Gewin, V. 2005. PLoS Biology 3 (6): e219, Wikimedia Commons, CC BY 2.5. *http://commons.wikimedia.org/wiki/File%3ADaphnia_pulex.png*

p. 205:

Gammarus amphipod: Michal Manas, Wikimedia Commons, CC BY 2.5. *http://commons.wikimedia.org/wiki/File%3AGammarus_roeselii.jpg*

algae: Vera Buhl, Wikimedia Commons, CC BY-SA 3.0, GFDL. *http://commons.wikimedia.org/wiki/File%3A2009-08-19_(47)_Lake%2C_See.jpg*

pickerelweed: Russ Pollanen / Wikimedia Commons / CC BY 2.5 / *http://commons.wikimedia.org/wiki/File:Pickler-2-s.jpg*

hydrilla: United States Geological Survey, Wikimedia Commons, Public domain. *http://en.wikipedia.org/wiki/File:Hydrilla_USGS.jpg*

water hyacinth: Ted Center (USDA), Wikimedia Commons, Public domain. *http://commons.wikimedia.org/wiki/File%3AWater_hyacinth.jpg.*

p. 207: Victor Sampson

LAB 15

p. 216: Mahesh Iyer, Wikimedia Commons, CC BY-SA 3.0, GFDL. *http://commons.wikimedia.org/wiki/File:Eurasian_Collared_Dove.svg*

p. 217: Victor Sampson

LAB 16

p. 230: *www.fastplants.org/resources/digital_library//index.php?P=FullImage&ResourceId=35&FieldName=Screenshot* via Victor Sampson

LAB 17

p. 237: User:Dracocephalus, Wikimedia Commons, Public Domain. *http://upload.wikimedia.org/wikipedia/commons/f/ff/Meiosis_II_Non_Disjunction.jpg*

p. 244: Thomas Geier (Fachgebiet Botanik der Forschungsanstalt Geisenheim), Wikimedia Commons, CC BY-SA 3.0. *http://commons.wikimedia.org/wiki/File%3AAllium-Mitose06-DM100x_BL28.jpg*

LAB 18

p. 250: Madeleine Price Ball, Wikimedia Commons, CC0, CC BY-SA 3.0, CC BY 2.5, GFDL 1.2. *http://commons.wikimedia.org/wiki/File:DNA_chemical_structure.svg*

p. 257: Victor Sampson

DNA FACT SHEET

p. 259: User:cdang, Wikimedia Commons, CC BY-SA 3.0, GFDL. http://commons.wikimedia.org/wiki/File%3ACliche_de_laue_principe.svg; National Institutes of Health, Wikimedia Commons, Public domain. *http://commons.wikimedia.org/wiki/File%3AXray_DNA.gif*

LAB 19

p. 263: Marek Kultys, Wikimedia Commons, CC BY-SA 3.0. *http://commons.wikimedia.org/wiki/File:Meiosis_diagram.jpg*

pp. 264 and 271: Victor Sampson

p. 269: National Human Genome Research Institute, Wikimedia Commons, Public domain. *http://commons.wikimedia.org/wiki/File:DNA_human_male_chromosomes.gif*

LAB 20

p. 276: User:InvictaHOG, Wikimedia Commons, Public domain, *http://en.wikipedia.org/wiki/File:ABO_blood_type.svg*

p. 277: National Institutes of Health, Wikimedia Commons, Public domain. *http://en.wikipedia.org/wiki/File:ABO_system_codominance.svg*

p. 282: Modified by Victor Sampson from User:InvictaHOG, Wikimedia Commons, Public domain. *http://en.wikipedia.org/wiki/File:ABO_blood_type.svg*

p. 284: Victor Sampson

LAB 21

p. 296: User:Madboy74, Wikimedia Commons, CC0 1.0. *http://commons.wikimedia.org/wiki/File:Biology_Illustration_Animals_Insects_Drosophila_melanogaster.svg*

LAB 22

p. 309: Peter Halasz, Wikimedia Commons, Public domain. *http://commons.wikimedia.org/wiki/File:Biological_classification_L_Pengo_vflip.svg*

LAB 23

p. 323: *http://ccl.northwestern.edu/netlogo/models/BugHuntSpeeds* via Victor Sampson

LAB 24

p. 333: Jerry Crimson Mann, Wikimedia Commons, CC BY-SA 3.0, GFDL 1.2. *http://commons.wikimedia.org/wiki/File:Evolution_pl.png.*

LAB 25

p. 346: Victor Sampson

p. 348: *http://ccl.northwestern.edu/netlogo/models/BugHuntCamouflage* via Victor Sampson

LAB 26

pp. 357, 362, and 363: Victor Sampson

p. 365: Modified by Victor Sampson from Patrick J. Lynch (medical illustrator), Wikimedia Commons, CC BY 2.5. *http://commons.wikimedia.org/wiki/File:Human_skull_lateral_view.jpg*; and User:Kaligula, Wikimedia Commons,CC BY-SA 3.0. *http://commons.wikimedia.org/wiki/File:Human_dental_arches.svg*

LAB 27

p. 371: User:DiBgd, Wikimedia Commons, CC BY 3.0, GFDL. *http://commons.wikimedia.org/wiki/File:Synoplotherium112DB.jpg*

p. 371 (top): Nobu Tamura, Wikimedia Commons, CC BY 3.0, GFDL. *http://commons.wikimedia.org/wiki/File:Pakicetus_BW.jpg;* (bottom): University of California Museum of Paleontology's Understanding Evolution. *http://evolution.berkeley.edu/evolibrary/article/phylogenetics_10*

p. 377: User:LadyofHats, Wikimedia Commons, Public domain. *http://commons.wikimedia.org/wiki/File%3AMain_protein_structure_levels_en.svg*

p. 376: University of California Museum of Paleontology's Understanding Evolution. *http://evolution.berkeley.edu/evolibrary/search/imagedetail.php?id=250&topic_id=&keywords=*

INDEX

*Page numbers printed in **boldface** type refer to figures or tables.*